West's Law School Advisory Board

A PRIMER FOR LAW & POLICY DESIGN:

UNDERSTANDING THE USE OF PRINCIPLE & ARGUMENT IN ENVIRONMENTAL & NATURAL RESOURCE LAW

By

Professor John Martin Gillroy

and

Professor Breena Holland

both

Environmental Law & Public Policy Studies
Lehigh University

with

Professor Celia Campbell-Mohn

Environmental Law Center
Vermont Law School

AMERICAN CASEBOOK SERIES®

THOMSON
———— ✶ ————™
WEST

Mat #40737175

American Casebook Series and West Group are trademarks registered in the U.S. Patent and Trademark Office.

© 2008 Thomson/West
      610 Opperman Drive
      St. Paul, MN 55123
      1–800–313–9378

Printed in the United States of America

ISBN: 978–0–314–19132–8

 *TEXT IS PRINTED ON 10% POST CONSUMER RECYCLED PAPER*

Preface

Harold Lasswell,[1] a patriarch of the discipline of policy studies, encourages the search for a "science" of policy analysis. Over the years, this task has grown in popularity and has been interpreted primarily as the search for quantitative and empirical economic methods that can be applied to public decision-making.[2] Twenty years ago, Richard Posner pioneered the application of this branch of "scientific" thought to the law by advocating the use of economic analysis in all corners of legal reasoning.[3] As the discipline of economics has grown to be considered the most "scientific" of the social sciences, law and policy studies have increasingly relied on mathematical models and quantitative methods as the foundation for analysis, evaluation, and recommendation of public law and policy. This trend continues to promote the market assumptions behind economic choice into the forefront of both theoretical and practical decision-making.[4]

Corresponding to the evolution of 'science' in both law and policy, is a widespread promotion of cost-benefit methodology as the representative of market assumptions in the assessment of law and public choice.[5] Cost-benefit method, in turn, has dominated both empirical and normative discussions of the theory and practice of law and policy. Those attempting to transcend dependence on market calculations as the basis for assessing environmental and natural resource law and policy have focused on critical arguments that point out flaws in specific applications of cost-benefit methodology, rather than constructive arguments that show alternative paradigms with which to approach environmental law in general.[6]

---

[1] DANIEL LERNER & HAROLD D. LASSWELL, THE POLICY SCIENCES (1951).

[2] See WILLIAM A. DUNN, PUBLIC POLICY ANALYSIS: AN INTRODUCTION (1981) or EDWARD BRYAN PORTIS & MICHAEL B. LEVEY, HANDBOOK OF POLITICAL THEORY AND POLICY SCIENCE (1988).

[3] RICHARD POSNER, ECONOMIC ANALYSIS OF LAW (2d ed. 1977) or A. MITCHELL POLINSKY, AN INTRODUCTION TO LAW AND ECONOMICS (1983).

[4] See ROBIN W. BOADWAY, PUBLIC SECTOR ECONOMICS (1979) ; ALLEN M. FELDMAN, WELFARE ECONOMICS AND SOCIAL CHOICE THEORY (1980); LESTER B. LAVE, THE STRATEGY OF SOCIAL REGULATION (1981) and A. C. PIGOU, THE ECONOMICS OF WELFARE (1932).

[5] For policy and philosophical applications see EDWARD G. GRAMLICH, BENEFIT-COST ANALYSIS OF GOVERNMENT PROGRAMS (1981); Aaron Director, *The Parity Of The Economic Market Place*, 7 J.L. & Econ. 1-10 (1964); E. J. MISHAN, INTRODUCTION TO NORMATIVE ECONOMICS (1981) and COST-BENEFIT ANALYSIS (1982); and RICHARD POSNER, THE ECONOMICS OF JUSTICE 60 (1983).

[6] See JOHN MARTIN GILLROY & MAURICE WADE, THE MORAL DIMENSIONS OF PUBLIC POLICY CHOICE: BEYOND THE MARKET PARADIGM, (1992) especially the contributions from Mark Sagoff, Steven Kelman and Laurence H. Tribe for excellent methodological criticisms of the market approach and Paul Churchill, Maurice Wade and J.M. Gillroy for first attempts at constructive arguments for alternative approaches to the philosophy of the market in the spirit of law and policy design. See also JOHN MARTIN GILLROY, JUSTICE & NATURE: KANTIAN PHILOSOPHY, ENVIRONMENTAL POLICY & THE LAW (2000) for an argument that attempts to treat alternatives to cost-benefit methods more comprehensively.

In this volume, we intend to fill this gap in the literature by demonstrating how the dominant economic approach to environmental and natural resource law and policy relies on a normatively questionable law and policy design paradigm as its essential foundation. In addition, we shall provide a map by which one can construct alternative normative paradigms with equally rigorous and reasonable foundations for the study of the environmental law.

Although the efficiency approach to law, policy design, and evaluation is now the conventional school of thought taught in policy programs, for those not yet familiar with it, we have included a review of its basic tenets as an *Appendix* to this book. The material covered in this Appendix will be especially helpful as a prelude to Chapter Three, which explains how this efficiency approach to law and policy manifests in the design and practice of environmental law and natural resource management. We think it is important to understand the logic and reasoning that guides current policy, however, the more essential goal of this book is to help the reader understand, develop, and apply methods that transcend the basic logic and reasoning of conventional law and policy analysis built on the Market Paradigm, from which the idea of efficiency as a policy goal has emerged. Toward this end, we provide a discussion of the philosophical roots of two alternative approaches to thinking and reasoning about policy decisions, as well as a more empirical discussion of how these approaches would transform environmental and natural resource law, policy design, and evaluation.

The basic argument of this book is that an adequate response to an increasingly degraded and threatened natural environment requires the development and application of new paradigms for environmental law, policy design, and evaluation. While we hope that our argument is applicable outside the American context, because of space and the need to communicate an unconventional way of thinking about environmental law, we felt it imperative to frame our argument for policy design within a single municipal legal system. Therefore, this small book undertakes its examination of environmental and natural resource practice in terms of American examples which we use to demonstrate the argument for the utility of *law and policy design* as a new methodology for approaching the governance relationship between humanity and nature. However, we do not want those interested in environmental and resource law from outside the United States, or those interested in regional or international law, to fail to see the utility of our approach to their legal and political contexts.

Overall, our argument is that the policy design approach is not limited to any specific legal context, and since most states, and even the international context, utilize the categories of constitutional or foundational law, administrative law, legislative, and judge-made law to one extent or another, we encourage those outside the United States to use legal sources and examples from their own environmental and natural resource law as a point of departure for the adaptation of law and policy design to their particular legal circumstances.

This is an argument about a generic, yet practical and theoretical approach to law. Within the reality of a global environment we are suggesting that a policy design method allows one to create alternatives to the dominance of Kaldor efficiency and the market approach. No matter in what jurisdiction the reader finds themselves, to use this primer all we ask is that you accept three ideas:

1. **That The State, As An Alternative To The Market, Represents a Distinct Institutional Structure For Environmental Decision-Making:** Policy Design will recognize the state as a separate and distinct governance structure that is capable of utilizing non-market assumptions in the evaluation of law and policy. In this role it can adopt different normative frameworks and theoretical paradigms to define its mission of responsibly solving collective action problems.[7]

2. **That The Individual Citizen Is More Than a Consumer:** The law and policy designer assumes that each person is a strategic actor with both a moral dimension to their individual and social life and the inherent capacity to combine values and principles with preferences in making public as opposed to private choices. For most areas of policy concern, it should be assumed that the individual is able to do more than simply order preferences for personal wealth and property. Citizens will be assumed to reason practically, to apply reason to choice, and to appreciate what is essential to their agency and the persistence of their society from what is elective to these ends. The lawyer and policy designer's point of departure should be that human beings function with a more sophisticated reasoning capacity than the market, Kaldor efficiency, or cost-benefit methods assume.

3. **That All Law And Public Policies Have a Normative Dimension That Cannot Be Avoided Or Subsumed In A Concentration On Empirical Practice:** Because the individual who creates and is affected by environmental law and public policy is a moral agent, those who propose to evaluate an existing policy or to suggest a new one must construct an adequate theory of the "good" or the "right" upon which to base their legal choice. Adequacy in this context means that public ends other than wealth must be part of the assumptions that justify the definition of the "public interest" lying at the base of collective choice. In addition, since humanity, and possibly nature, are of both instrumental and

---

[7] For policy as a collective action problem see MANCUR OLSON, THE LOGIC OF COLLECTIVE ACTION (1971); RUSSELL HARDIN, COLLECTIVE ACTION (1983) and two works by JON ELSTER, ULYSSES AND THE SIRENS: STUDIES IN RATIONALITY AND IRRATIONALITY (1979) and SOUR GRAPES (1983). Within game theory there are multiple formats in which public goods collective action problems can be studied, including the prisoner's dilemma [Hardin], the assurance game, AMARTYA SEN, *Isolation, Assurance and the Social rate of Discount,* 81 QUARTERLY JOURNAL OF ECONOMICS, 112-124 or MICHAEL TAYLOR, THE POSSIBILITY OF COOPERATION (1987) and the coordination game, DAVID LEWIS, CONVENTION: A PHILOSOPHICAL STUDY (1969).

intrinsic value, policy and law should incorporate more than merely instrumental economic values. If the evaluation of law cannot sustain, protect, and empower, both non-economic instrumental values and intrinsic value, then one must justify the exclusion of these standards from their analysis. In either case, law and policy argument cannot ignore the existence of such values without ignoring an important aspect of an inherently complex pursuit: the legal creation of a "better" environment in which human beings and nature can persist together.

Acknowledgements

What is now Chapter Two was built upon a skeletal structure provided by Jan Laitos; we thank him for his contribution. We also wish to thank our team at Thomson/West: Pamela Siege, Heidi Hellekson, Roxanne Birkel, and our editor, Jay Streitz, without whom this project would never have been possible. Lastly, we wish to thank Georgetown University Press[1] for permission to reprint selected words and figures for Chapters Three and Four and the University of Pittsburgh Press[2] for permission to reprint selected text for the Appendix of this volume.

*

[1] From JOHN MARTIN GILLROY, JUSTICE AND NATURE: KANTIAN PHILOSOPHY, ENVIRONMENTAL POLICY, AND THE LAW © 2001 by Georgetown University Press. Reprinted with Permission.

[2] From THE MORAL DIMENSIONS OF PUBLIC POLICY CHOICE: BEYOND THE MARKET PARADIGM, edited by JOHN MARTIN GILLROY & MAURICE WADE, © 1992 by the University of Pittsburgh Press. Reprinted with Permission.

Glossary

This is a list of concepts that are particular to the arguments of this book and the specific nomenclature of law and policy design. The reader will also benefit from having a pocket legal dictionary to help with the large number of legal terms that are used herein.

➤ **Blackletter Law:** Codified law that is decisive or dispositive in fact situations. The way the law appears in print, or in legal practice (e.g. Rules, Treaties, Statutes, Court Opinions).

➤ **Capabilities:** Refer to the conditions or states of enablement that make it possible for people to achieve things. Capabilities are people's real opportunities to achieve outcomes they value, such as being able to have bodily health and being able to have relations with plants, animals, and the world of nature.

➤ **Capabilities Paradigm:** A systematized and integrated line of argument for law, policy design, and evaluation that is developed from a particular set of principles, assumptions, and methods, and focuses on the economic and non-economic instrumental value of ecosystems to protecting a threshold level of centrally important human capabilities for each person.

➤ **Central Human Capabilities:** Also referred to as "central human functional capabilities" and "central capabilities," and are specifically defined by Martha Nussbaum's list of ten capabilities, as cited in Chapter Five.

➤ **Comprehensive Policy Argument:** Refers to detailed inductive and deductive process that synthesizes the theory and practice of law and policy design. CPA integrates the scientific basis and institutional context of law and the philosophical or metaphysical ideas that create the background conditions of the law within the policy design space.

➤ **Context Model:** At a theoretical level, refers to the worldview of a policy paradigm and therefore to the components, priorities, and general construction of a policy paradigm's core principle, conditions, maxims, and methods. For practical purposes, this worldview acts as an intermediary between a theoretical policy paradigm and that paradigm's implementation or policy instrument. Thus, in environmental law and policy, the context model operates as a managerial theme or reference point that can guide the application of a policy paradigm.

➤ **Core (of Meta-policy):** Part of Meta-policy that contains its fundamental principle. The core of meta-policy is resistant to change, but can change when there is a fundamental shift in the core normative principle, and consequently, in the basic character of meta-policy.

➤ **Core Principle:** Refers to the moral or legal principle that provides the normative foundation for legal arguments justifying a particular policy design. It is derived from the fundamental assumptions of a policy paradigm and therefore creates the reason for the law and its inherent policy design.

➤ **(CBA) Cost-Benefit Methodology:** The methodology of cost-benefit analysis (CBA), which is the Market Paradigm's method of application. In general, the method involves quantifying all of impacts of a policy in terms of its monetized costs and benefits in order to determine a policy's overall economic impact. CBA measures both the ends and means of a law or policy in terms of Kaldor Efficiency.

➤ **Dialectic:** A logical form of reasoning built on the idea that no philosophical concept has its essence in itself alone but in the tension between itself and its opposite. For example, the essence of 'good' is not just in this term but also in its opposite 'evil' so that to understand either good or evil you need to have a sense of good↔evil or how each influences and relates to the other.

➤ **Dispositive Law: See Blackletter Law**.

➤ **[E]cosystem:** As used in Chapter Four (with a capital "E"), includes the extensive interface between humanity and nature, and is not just a matter of a natural system considered independent of humanity or human society (as a scientist might use it—see next definition).

➤ **[e]cosystems:** Also referred to as "natural systems" or "ecological systems" and consists of the living organisms in an area and the living and non-living physical environment with which they interact.

➤ **Ecological Systems:** Refers to ecosystems as well as broader ecological cycles and processes of which particular ecosystems are part.

➤ **Ecosystem Health:** A measurement of the stability and sustainability of an ecological system, where "healthy" refers to an ecosystem that is active, maintains its organization over time and is resilient to stress, and "unhealthy" refers to an ecosystem in which characteristics such as primary productivity, biodiversity, and habitat suitability for endemic species, are reduced.

➤ **Ecosystem Health Context Model:** Context model for the Capabilities Paradigm that relates changes in the health of ecosystems to the economic and non-economic instrumental benefits of those systems to people's central human capabilities.

➤ **Ecosystem Integrity:** Ecosystems considered as ecological or functional wholes in dialectic relationship to the moral integrity of humanity within its built systems.

➤ **Ecosystem Law:** Law from policy design that takes an Ecosystem Paradigm seriously as a core concern within its meta-policy.

➤ **Ecosystem Paradigm:** A systematized and integrated line of argument for law, policy design, and evaluation that is developed from a particular set of principles, assumptions, and methods focused on the value of flourishing ecosystems.

➤ **Human Integrity:** When a person is enabled at the baseline and intact in terms of their capacity and ability to have and express agency in the world, then they are a moral agent with integrity and informed purpose. They are, in Kant's words, an end-in-themselves (See Categorical Imperative Insight Box, p. 237). Human Integrity contains the sub-principles of Freedom, Moral Equality and Civic Independence.

➤ **Market Paradigm:** A systematized and integrated line of argument for law, policy design, and evaluation that is developed from a particular principle, Kaldor Efficiency, and a particular method, CBA, seeking to maximize or optimize the economic resource benefits of the natural environment.

➤ **Materials Balance:** Based upon the second law of Thermodynamics, which contends that matter cannot be created or destroyed, the material balance maintains that all environmental matter is either inventory for the market, being processed in a market, or being disposed as waste by a market. In any case, these three conditions of environmental matter are equal in terms of the existence of nature.

➤ **Maximum Efficiency:** Defines a condition in which aggregate economic benefits (of a policy) are maximized. As a principle it defines maximization of aggregate benefits as a goal or standard for public policy. As the core principle in the Traditional Sector Approach-I to environmental management, it requires that government maximize wealth by supporting the disposal of public assets into private markets.

➤ **Meta-policy:** Originally defined by G. Majone, a meta-policy is a self-referential policy that contains its own standard of justification. Specifically, this refers to the *core* principle of the meta-policy that creates the character of the design argument and is resistant to change, surrounded by a *periphery* that contains the management institutions, codified law and implementation measures of the meta-policy and which is less resistant to change.

> **Moral Integrity:** An intact human capacity, ability, and purpose is defined here as a person's moral integrity. Without integrity one cannot have freedom.

> **Non-Economic Instrumental Value:** Refers to dimensions or aspects of the environment's instrumental value that economic valuation techniques cannot accurately or adequately account for in environmental law, policy design, and evaluation. People often experience the environment's non-economic instrumental outside of market interactions and cannot translate the value of these experiences into a quantified price that market exchange and valuation of environmental goods requires.

> **Optimal Efficiency:** Defines a condition in which aggregate economic benefits (of a policy) are optimal, as opposed to maximized (see Maximum Efficiency above). When a policy's aggregate economic benefits are optimal, or optimized, rates of natural resource extraction and pollution will maintain a sustainable "materials balance" (see Materials Balance above). As the core principle of the Traditional Sector Approach-II context model, optimal efficiency is an effort to save maximum efficiency within Traditional Sector Approach-I from its predisposition to overuse nature in an unregulated policy space.

> **Periphery:** Refers to the conceptual area of Meta-policy containing non-core principles and alternative arguments that are competing with the core principle and existing arguments for dominance. Also contains the institutional apparatus that implements the status quo core principle and argument; therefore, in the periphery, public debate shapes how policy is designed, legislated, applied, and evaluated.

> **Point of Departure:** Refers to starting point of an argument for policy design, which usually begins with an account of the existing understanding and definition of law that one plans to critique and/or improve.

> **Policy Design:** An approach to analyzing and recreating law for the purpose of moving it in a new direction. It assumes an inherent dialectic, and involves deconstructing a law into its component parts and exchanging specific of those components in order to synthesize a new and different definition of law.

> **Paradigm:** The theoretical core of policy design. A systemized and integrated set of assumptions, principles, material conditions, maxims and methods.

> **Policy Space:** Refers to the conceptual space that contains the various elements of meta-policy (e.g. the core principle and the periphery) as well as other related policies and meta-policies that concern a common issue and their interactions that

generate change and evolve over time. For example, the Environmental Policy Space would contain environmental meta-policy but also health meta-policy, agricultural meta-policy, economic meta-policy and safety meta-policy, among others.

➤ **Practical Reason:** Argument, Intelligence, Knowledge, Ideals and Human Insights, all directed to a 'practical' and especially to a 'moral' outcome. To be contrasted with Theoretical Reason which directs intellect toward non-material outcomes.

➤ **Preservation:** Preservation or reclamation of the functional integrity of any and all natural systems.

➤ **Resilience:** Characterizes the condition of ecosystems in which they are able to return to their original state after a human perturbation.

➤ **Resource to Recovery Context Model:** Context model for the Kantian Ecosystem Paradigm that integrates all resources and pollution law so that legal decisions consider the effects of human activities on functioning nature as a whole. It is advanced in Chapter Four as a replacement for the Market Paradigm's piecemeal and media-by-media Traditional Sector Approach to environmental management.

➤ **Rule of Law:** More than a law of rules, we define this idea as the dominance of legal argument and practice in the regulation of human individual and social life.

➤ **Snapshot:** Also referred to as a "current synthesis product," it defines the material or legal result of a dialectic at any particular point in time. In an ongoing policy design process where policy arguments compete to redefine the rule of law, the dialectics inherent in policy design must resolve themselves so that opposite concepts find common ground in the law. At any time a manifestation of this synthesis solution defines the valid blackletter law or the snapshot that characterizes the dominant or persuasive policy argument.

➤ **Willingness-to-Pay:** Refers to method of valuing environmental resources in which people express the amount they are willing to pay for access to, or for use and ownership of, environmental resources. Can also refer to a general approach to making political choices about policy in which decision-makers sum up the total amount of money people are willing to pay for a particular policy outcome (e.g. protection of a natural area in its pristine state, or attaining a particular standard of water quality) and design and promulgate policies for which the aggregate amount that people are willing to pay is the highest.

*

Summary of Contents

Table of Contents

Table of Cases

The principal cases are in bold type. Cases cited or discussed in the text are roman type. References are to pages. Cases cited in principal cases and within other quoted materials are not included.

List of Insight Boxes

*

A PRIMER FOR LAW & POLICY DESIGN:

UNDERSTANDING THE USE OF PRINCIPLE & ARGUMENT IN ENVIRONMENTAL & NATURAL RESOURCE LAW

*

Chapter 1

POLICY DESIGN FOR ENVIRONMENTAL LAW

This is a primer for the student, lawyer, or policy-maker who wants to be able to understand and analyze the current state of environmental and natural resource law and synthesize changes to it. Legal practice is the result of prerequisite policy argument. The process of taking apart a dispositive law to examine its inherent policy components and then exchanging specific of those components to affect change in that law, that is, infusing it with a new policy argument and consequent direction, we will call *policy design*.[1] Our book is a basic primer in policy design for those who wish to acknowledge the interrelationship between policy and law and understand environmental and natural resource law in terms of its inherent ideas and arguments as well as its empirical rules and conventional practice.

Policy Design, unlike traditional policy and legal analysis, assumes that an inherent *dialectic* or interdependent tension exists between any concept and its opposite, for example, the dialectic between the normative and empirical aspects of the way humans treat their environment. The presupposition of a dialectic requires lawyers and policy-makers to consider both aspects of any opposition as equally critical to understanding the law. If we consider values and facts, principles and institutions, theory and practice simultaneously, as dialectics, then the essential definition of the law changes. Law is no longer just a static rule, statute, or system

1. To our knowledge, the first use of this terminology came with DAVIS B. BOBROW & JOHN S. DRYZEK, POLICY ANALYSIS BY DESIGN (1987). Their approach musters multiple theoretical points of view in order to rework public policy. Although our use of the term—Policy Design—is indebted to this previous work, we give it a more specific definition, a more integrated and systematic method, a more dialectic philosophical foundation, and a more concerted focus on environmental and natural resource law and policy.

* consider dialectic or current synthesis product for policy design process

of conventional practice that can be empirically measured. It is a single synthesis product of dialectic relations for any one place and time. This *current synthesis product* or *snapshot* of an ongoing and evolving policy design process draws on the persuasiveness of competing policy arguments to distinguish that definition of black-letter law that defines current practice. This practice is a synthesis of the dialectic tension inherent in the policy design argument and represents that integrated product or snapshot that defines a currently valid rule of law. This primer is meant to be a self-study course on how to decipher such a snapshot of law and synthesize alternative policy arguments for the future of the dialectic design process.

Being dialectical, law and policy design does not treat the market and the state as two dichotomous, distinct, and independent governance systems. It starts with the idea that both are interdependent, in that each is necessary to the proper understanding of the role of the other. This premise presupposes that the public realm, with government as its allocation mechanism, has at minimum an equal part in the solution of public goods and collective action problems. The premise also requires us to contemplate that for any particular synthesis snapshot of legal practice the public/governmental dimensions of its policy design, rather than the market or its surrogate, may be the primary allocation mechanism for collective goods. In terms of environmental law and policy, it may frequently be the case that because of the characteristics of environmental collective action problems, the dialectic between market and government will be resolved in favor of government as the representative of a public interest in environmental quality.

Conventionally, the theory and practice of economic markets dominates the study of law and policy.[2] For a good deal of modern policy history the environment has been considered a warehouse of resources and a sink for waste, to be used at the pleasure of humanity, for our own purposes.[3] This makes conventional policy

---

2. This can be demonstrated in an examination of any Public Policy Analysis graduate program where micro-economics and quantitative methodology dominate the coursework of the program. For example, the Kennedy School at Harvard requires such courses as "Markets and Market Failure," "Economic Analysis of Public Policy," "Quantitative Analysis and Empirical Methods" and "Strategic & Financial Management of Public Organizations."

3. See RICHARD N. L. ANDREWS, MANAGING THE ENVIRONMENT, MANAGING OURSELVES: A HISTO-

RY OF AMERICAN ENVIRONMENTAL POLICY (1999) for an exposition of the history of environmental policy that depends on the market as the primary allocation system. See also JOHN MARTIN GILLROY, JUSTICE & NATURE: KANTIAN PHILOSOPHY, ENVIRONMENTAL POLICY AND THE LAW ch. 2 (2000) for an argument that the dominance of markets has been such that the only major shift in U.S. environmental law has been from government aided "maximum use markets" in the first 200 years of our history to government regulated "optimal use markets" with

[handwritten annotation: conventional policy/legal analysis = non-dialectic; focus on market]

and legal analysis non-dialectic and focused on the market dimensions of collective action problems as distinct, self-contained, and of primary importance.[4]

Our contention is that by approaching environment and resource questions primarily through economic assumptions, one is not taking proper notice of the characteristics of both public policy and the natural world that are inadequately analyzed by market assumptions alone. As at least an equal participant in the policy dialectic, government has an important role to play in how law defines the relationship between humanity and nature. In addition to markets and other allocation and distribution systems, government has particular abilities that make it, and the law it writes, a significant or even dominant agent in creating, implementing, and recognizing the public nature of environmental and natural resource issues.

Toward this end we begin by agreeing with Andrews[5] that government is necessary to environmental questions because it is the primary mechanism for assigning property rights within society. Rights to property grant people, institutions, and social groups power over nature, which gives them policy-making prerogatives that must be considered in the design process. Rights to nature are the essential starting point for environmental and resource issues. Property rights are also not a result of market choice but a prerequisite to it, as government provides the background legal structures (e.g. rights protection, contract, tort, criminal law), that make it possible for markets to persist. The dominion over property rights is part of a wider public responsibility of the state, as the primary agent for the public interest, protecting and empowering the general health, safety, and well-being of the society at large. Markets do not do more than allocate public goods through private wealth maximization. Political institutions are granted legal 'police power' for the primary purpose of promoting social coordination and preventing collective action problems (i.e. commons problems and externalities) that threaten the public peace and the survival of sound government[6] within any society.

[handwritten annotation: markets not as concerned w/ public interest as gov't is]

It is also the case that while both markets and government are allocation mechanisms that create goods for society, markets can achieve efficiency between production and consumption without a particular concern for the distributional affects of their allocations.

the advent of the environmental statute era in the 1970s.

4. For the importance of dialectic in politics and policy, see R. G. COLLINGWOOD, THE NEW LEVIATHAN OR MAN, SOCIETY, CIVILIZATION AND BARBARISM 181–183 (revised 1992).

5. See ANDREWS, *supra* note 3 at 2.

6. This is what is called POGG or Peace, Order and Good Government by Canadians.

Meanwhile, government's charge to address matters of justice and fairness, require it to be very conscious of the distributional affects of any public policy choice. This is true of environmental policy in particular, as pollution, risk, and the allocation of resources and environmental quality will empower some and harm others, and therefore make government responsible to justify the distributions that law creates.

In addition to these characteristics of government that make it invaluable to environmental law, nature itself exhibits qualities that make dialectical law and policy design even more necessary for solving resource-based collective action problems. To start with, the pressing nature of environmental dilemmas means that there are few areas of legal study that are more timely or important than those which set the relationship between humanity and nature in terms of the rule of law. With unique natural systems disappearing all around the globe, with climate change producing a permanent Northwest Passage through the Arctic, and since the manner in which the post-industrial world raised itself from poverty cannot be copied by developing nations without destroying the carrying capacity of the biosphere, a dynamic or dialectic vision of environmental law as policy design is necessary to study nature in a more comprehensive and serious way than market analysis allows.

In addition to the gravity of environmental problems, policy design is appropriate to environmental and resource law because the management of nature has a history of being dominated by ideas based upon isolated human market calculations and empirical analysis. It is only in the past thirty years that the environment has been recognized as giving rise to public collective action problems that a central government should play a role in solving. For most of our history with the natural world, humans have treated it as a part of the economic materials cycle; its value has been its use and instead of a dialectic between market and government solutions, economic efficiency determined the level of use in isolation from integrated moral or political considerations. Within the legal framework of social life the environment was not regulated nationally by statute and administrative law, but privately and locally through tort, contract, and civil law litigation (the background prerequisites for markets). The law of property, nuisance, or liability has set the terms of our relationship to nature and we have heavily discounted or totally ignored any concerns for the holistic integrity of nature, or the 'public' or philosophical–moral dimensions of natural resource and environmental decision-making.

Perhaps nature is not just an inventory of resources or a set of sinks for absorbing pollution and risk but a living system of interconnected ecosystems that have a functional integrity independent of humanity. If so, then the wholeness and flourishing, or

[handwritten margin note: In past, we have ianbred intrinsic value of nature]

[handwritten note at bottom: nature is living system independent of humanity]

integrity, of these systems needs to be a consideration of the law, especially if our regulation of human agency is to account for the critical characteristics of nature only properly evaluated within policy design. Environmental law calls on the lawyer as policy-maker to consider both the instrumental and intrinsic values involved in the interactions between humanity and the natural world. [Policy-makers should now consider two distinct, but dialectically-related, living communities, that of humanity and that of nature; they should consider both the instrumental and intrinsic value of each in their policy recommendations for tradeoffs between them.] The dialectic relationship between these values and communities will determine whether humanity and nature produce a legal synthesis snapshot representing mutual harmony or discord, fundamental harm or interdependent empowerment.

Therefore, because we have two distinct and living communities, each with a potential for integrity as well as use, one needs to consider not only the economic and instrumental value of nature as an elective good allocated by the preferences of individuals, but also the essential qualities of humanity and nature that grant each an inherent moral or functional-ecological value. In creating codified law, or a snapshot for any environmental issue, one needs to synthesize these two aspects of value. It is not enough for environmental law to isolate one from the other and make policy for that part. A policy-maker must consider the dynamic interdependence and tensions inherent in the meeting of the worlds of natural and human systems. The aim of the law should be legal synthesis as a harmony, or policy design, that recognizes dialectic and seeks an integrated solution that considers the two integrities at stake in the law so that a state of affairs may exist where each can flourish in the presence of the other.

Environmental matters are also not properly served by a primarily reactionary or retrospective policy analysis or legal system like that created by market values. Specifically, environmental concerns need to be addressed by the law before nature is altered by humanity, as these alterations may very well be irreversible and in any case may be harmful and continue being so while the law waits to react. Environmental and resource policy more than most issue areas, calls for planning and anticipatory law in addition to remedial policy. This reality requires a lawyer to understand the policy design alternatives inherent in the dialectic between theory and practice, and to adjust internal principle to fit the changing times and anticipate harm to humanity and the natural world, in the law they recommend.

Environmental dilemmas are both highly complex and uncertain, which requires more from the law and its policy foundation than merely superficial or one-dimensional analysis. In particular, nature is a complex system of physical and biological properties that will be difficult to protect in a legal system that requires definable causal chains as part of its common law. [If the law requires 'injury in fact' before public policy can act, or clear and isolated distinctions between guilty agents and innocent ones, then one-dimensional analysis may actually cause more harm than good.] The complexity of the natural world added to the complexity of human social life tends to overcome markets and their common or civil law background institutions.

This complexity also contributes to the uncertainty inherent in the connection between a particular policy, the law it renders, and the perceived environmental problem it is meant to solve. Even with a concern for the dialectic relationships involved in the policy design process, it will be difficult to take this level of complexity and uncertainty into account. Without a serious attempt to include nature's complexity and uncertainty, however, it is impossible to have a policy design process that is adequate to the environment it is trying to regulate. Since environmental and resource problems exhibit a level of complexity and uncertainty that makes their collective harms not only multi-faceted but able to produce synergistic effects with other elements in the biosphere, [the law must contemplate more, in its paradigm of policy design, than the instrumental economic value of nature to human wealth preferences.[7]]

Increased complexity and uncertainty is even further exacerbated by the distinction between traditional pollution problems and ***environmental risk dilemmas***.[8] The characteristics of environmental risk,[9] which include long latency periods between exposure and harm, an ignorance of scientific mechanism through which the risk affects us, and the stealth exhibited by risk agents which can harm us without our sensory awareness, make the design of law and policy even more difficult. With environmental risk problems, like radiation or global warming, the public is asked to give up

7. See JOHN O'NEILL, ECOLOGY, POLICY AND POLITICS: HUMAN WELL–BEING AND THE NATURAL WORLD (1993), for an argument that cost-benefit method is only able to properly account for the monetary value of nature given the preferences of individual humans. See GILLROY, *supra* note 3 at ch. 4 for a more complete argument that to adequately account for nature in human policy choice one must consider more than its mere economic value to mankind, and see the debate between Bob Pepperman Taylor and J. M. Gillroy in JOHN MARTIN GILLROY & JOE BOWERSOX, THE MORAL AUSTERITY OF ENVIRONMENTAL DECI-SION–MAKING: SUSTAINABILITY, DEMOCRACY, AND NORMATIVE ARGUMENT IN POLICY AND LAW 291–313 (2002) over the possibilities of considering the intrinsic as well as the instrumental value of nature in public policy decisions.

8. For a complete argument about the ramifications of risk see GILLROY, *supra* note 3.

9. For the distinctions between risk and traditional pollution problems see, Talbot R. Page, *A Generic View of Toxic Chemicals and Similar Risks* 7 ECOLOGY L.Q. 207 (1978).

tangible assets in the present for intangible and improbable results somewhere in the future. Because these situations exhibit a near zero probability of an infinitely catastrophic result (i.e. a *zero-infinity* problem), they cannot be ignored by lawyers and policy-makers but cannot be facilitated by democratic institutions that define responsible law through responsive policy. With a traditional pollution problem, like particulate in the air, one may be able to wait for the air to become obviously contaminated for the responsive organs of government to clean the air. But as we are finding out, for an environmental risk like global warming, by the time responsive institutions come around to addressing the problems, the damage of risk's stealth effects may already be causing very serious harm, or may even be irreversible. In a world where the only solution to an environmental problem is to prevent it in the first place and where the argument for this prevention is based on accepting low probabilities of intangible harms against the certain loss of tangible known benefits, law and policy design are made even more complicated.[10]

A legal solution to environmental collective action problems should, therefore, be sensitive to a series of dialectics that characterize the environmental policy design process. We have already discussed the dialectics (⇌) between normative⇌empirical, markets⇌government, theory⇌practice, allocation⇌distribution, pollution⇌risk, anticipatory⇌responsive, and instrumental⇌intrinsic as these are particularly applied to law and policy design for our relationship to nature. However, there are three more general political dialectics that influence all policy and legal decision-making and have a special place in the study of environmental law.

First, there is the more general dialectic between individual⇌collective. Policy decisions should address both the rights of individuals and the collective good. In terms of individuals, what interactive status do the rights and interests of humanity deserve in the calculation of environmental policy and law? In terms of collectives, should we be aware of both a human and a natural community that each have instrumental uses and intrinsic values as living, dynamic, and interdependently evolving entities? What does this mean for policy formulation in a democratic system? This

---

10. In this book we will concentrate on traditional pollution and resource problems as these present a more basic test of the policy design approach, but for an application of policy design to risk see, John Martin Gillroy, *Environmental Risk and the Traditional Sector Approach: Market Efficiency at the Core of Environmental Law* 10 RISK 139 (1999).

universal dialectic suggests a more complex menu of tradeoffs between those who are harmed and those who are empowered by a particular policy choice. Should law trade instrumental values for intrinsic ones? How about trades between human and nature's value? Does human agency require more responsibility to protect nature in these tradeoffs? How should these various values be calculated and included in the formulation, codification, and implementation of environmental and resource policy?

Second, there is the general dialectic between universal⇌local. What is the best and most effective way to provide for the conservation, preservation, or sustainability of the natural world? Should we leave it to law at its most local incarnation, or does fairness and responsible government demand that uniform national, or ever global, rules be the proper forum for the analysis and regulation of environmental and resource issues? Does the level of government involvement depend on the issue at hand, and if so, what dimensions of the issue should determine the institutional focus of the policy design project? The assignment of responsibility to government for the allocation and distribution of well-being begs the further questions of what level of law should be definitive in drawing the policy relationship between humanity and nature that creates these material conditions. With the growth of both regional and international environmental law the role of municipal systems and their sub-levels of law grow even more central to the disposition of policy design for the environment.

Finally, the entire area of environmental and resource law is one where science is intimately involved in the formulation of policy and law. Scientific evidence is critical to environmental policy argument, but also, because of its character, scientific evidence is never definitive, which creates a dialectic for the policy-maker between proof⇌prudence.

In public choice, doing nothing is not an option. Unlike many other areas of law where a stable status-quo is sought as a beneficial state-of-affairs, humanity's relationship to the environment is inherently dynamic and changing and goes unregulated without active and constant attention from law and policy design. To decide not to analyze or consider change in environmental or resource law is, in effect, to allow the unregulated status-quo to continue unabated, without consideration of the limits or capacity of nature that only the law can monitor and regulate. Delay, under these conditions, whether for political or research purposes, is a decision to allow pollution and market resource use to continue unsupervised. For example, a lack of global warming law at national and international levels, has allowed the continued production of greenhouse gases to proceed unabated and the collective global biosphere to progressively degenerate as we continue to study the issue.[11] Only with government action to regulate human markets can controls on any such perturbation be instituted and its dynamic qualities scrutinized.

The dialectic between proof⇌prudence is the essential legal and policy dilemma of whether governance institutions wait for definitive scientific evidence regarding the harm of an environmental or resource issue or whether managers move the law in prudent anticipation of worst-case assumptions. Considering the complexity and uncertainty of nature and the many dimensions of human social life involved, it is important that we make a sound judgment about whether the synthesis product (snapshot) requires waiting or making policy with what we have in hand.

Since not making policy is still making a decision in the sense that it allows market choice to continue to determine the uses of nature, and given the critical role of science as the evidence base for environmental law, a serious question arises: should science be determinative for legal action or treated as a part of a more comprehensive policy argument containing the values, principles, and fundamental assumptions of various policy design paradigms? Do we determine the law only when the scientific evidence is all in, or do we use the values and principles involved in our design argument, with the best science available at the time, to make a case for a prudent anticipatory legal solution.

Within international environmental law this dialectic has been resolved in favor of prudence through the use of two legal principles: prevention and precaution. Prevention is a principle for traditional pollution situations where we know what will result from a particular human perturbation and we work to allow as little harm to nature as possible. The precautionary principle is applied to environmental risk or situations where uncertainty reigns. Here this principle guides the policy-maker to anticipate risk and not allow it into the environment. But, to practice prevention, do we need to practice precaution? How do we use science properly and avoid both unnecessary regulation and 'paralysis by analysis'?

[handwritten margin note: lean towards prudence given legal: prevention + precaution]

---

11. For example, the George W. Bush Administration's approach to global warming has been to spend a great deal of money on research and none at all on the actual regulation of greenhouse gases.

Within the context of a democratic political system, a stream of policy design arguments will be made so that changes in values, facts, and legal practice, that define our relationship to nature, can be anticipated and addressed before the biosphere is pushed past its carrying capacity. But from the standpoint of law and policy design, a responsible government is not necessarily a responsive one. In many instances, by the time affected citizens realize that an environmental problem exists, and petition the government for redress, it may be too late to affectively alleviate the dilemma or produce regulation in line with principles such as conservation, preservation, or sustainability. In these instances, prudence requires that the government justify anticipatory law so that environmental quality can remain intact, even without definitive science. This will require expert analysis and moral justification in terms of both the instrumental and intrinsic values at stake.

All of these characteristics of government, policy and the natural world require us, as lawyers and policy-makers, to fully consider environmental and natural resource law as a philosophical subject. If one is to properly and effectively address the human relationship to nature one will need to take the philosophical dialectics and principles that are at the heart of the idea of policy design seriously. While not ignoring the legal practice, economic costs, or scientific facts involved with particular issues, lawyers and policy-makers will have to consider that the principles, presuppositions, and worldviews that ground these practical dimensions of the environment in comprehensive policy design argument are fundamental to a reasonable public solution.

§§

Given these practical qualities of environment and resource law, it is imperative that those charged with creating the law be able to understand its policy foundations and the design elements that can help to address these complexities and idiosyncrasies. With an understanding of the dialectic and policy design elements involved, and of the need for constant monitoring and change to keep up with the dynamic qualities of the environment, the lawyer or policy-maker can truly craft environmental law with a proper understanding of what is at stake.

We begin a detailed exposition of the policy design process with the presupposition that the legal reality in which one lives is a product of what various levels of law allow us to do or prohibit us from doing in our contact with the natural world. Further, we assume that these legal rules do not spring from the ground fully grown, but come out of a dialectic environment in which distinct principles and values involved in distinct paradigms of thought, create alternative public policy arguments which then must navigate governance structures in order to become blackletter law. This blackletter law will then set the terms of our relationship to nature and will represent specific values and principles that are persuasive within the circumstances of our democratic context at any particular time (a synthesis snapshot).

As stated, we presuppose that the role of values in the law is not independent from fact but dialectically related to it. It is the foundational presuppositions of one's policy argument, in support of change or the status-quo, which are the determinative factor not only in the persuasive power of a policy argument to become law, but also in setting those standards by which success or failure will be evaluated and judged. By presupposing a dialectic context for the law where values and facts are in tension with one another within a policy design space seeking to influence the current state of legal practice toward change, we also assume that legal analysis is more than the retrospective and technical study of empirical rules, cases, statutes and treaties. Alternatively, legal analysis includes the prospective study of possible future states of the law. From this perspective, change is a result of a shift in the persuasiveness of a law's background policy design argument that establishes a new relationship between humanity and the way we interact with the natural world. We assume that since the policy design argument frames and determines what are acceptable and unacceptable choices, a change in that argument, if more persuasive than the conventional argument, will legally realign the circumstances of our extraction of the earth's resources and the pollution of its air, water and land.

purpose → This primer is written so that the debate about changing the way we use the environment may be moved forward. Specifically, it is meant to give the reader the basic tools necessary to understand the established sources of environmental and natural resources law, how these relate to legal practice, the process of creating policy, and how these material conditions are dependent on the inherent norms that set any existing law's evaluative standards. More than this, we also provide a basic schema, through a logic of systematic examples, so that the reader can see how to combine law, philosophy and policy argument in order to analyze current law and synthesis a prospective and prescriptive legal picture of what humanity's relationship to nature ought to be.

Policy Design is not part of any other text or casebook in the subject area. Most approaches to environmental and natural resources law ignore the extent to which values underlie and are integrated into the law and, instead, consider these values unsystematic, contextual and non-rational. Conventionally, normative argument is considered separable from legal and policy practice and of lesser value, in that reason-based generalizations cannot be made about it. Legal practice is considered enough for the student to understand and non-empirical norms, if mentioned, are dismissed as either ideological or theistic.[12]

We, however, recognize moral or ethical principle as a secular and necessary part of the dialectic that creates the rule of law, approachable by human practical reason. Arguing herein that norms are dialectically connected to empirical practice, we also contend that they can be approached within a reasoned analysis without prosecuting any particular ideological or theistic perspective. We propose that law is a combination of empirical and normative components and this challenges the reader to move beyond a mere understanding of environmental 'laws' and their empirical practice, to an appreciation of the dialectic system in which law originates, evolves, and changes over time. The evolution of law is a narrative of practice but this narrative is the interaction of ideals, principles, and social concepts that combine within comprehensive policy design arguments to compete for persuasive power within our political system, eventually becoming dispositive law.

In order for students of law or policy to have a role in the evolutionary system of argument that is environmental law, they need to be equipped with a basic understanding of how facts and values, norms and rules, process and principle influence one another and form comprehensive logical arguments about what is at stake in environmental choices. Practitioners should be able to gauge who the winners and losers will be for any public outcome, and who they ought to be. This requires that the lawyer understand not only the practice of law but the prerequisite policy debate that provides the background conditions in which all law is codified.

---

12. Although the distinction between theism and moral argument has been well and truly demonstrated, see ALAN DONAGAN, THE THEORY OF MO- RALITY ch.1 (1977), casebooks still argue that the only intrinsic value arguments in natural resources law are those that involve theistic grounding.

Resource extraction, for example, is not just a matter of current law, science, and resource economics but has ideal- and want-regarding moral, social, and political components that are just as susceptible to reasoned analysis and argument as any piece of quantitative data. It is this broader comprehensive policy argument behind the law that gives it its teeth. One cannot understand the dynamics of change or the true nature of a statute, an administrative rule, or a court opinion without a sense of the content and role of its inherent comprehensive policy argument. The 21st Century lawyer or policy-maker should understand environmental law from this more comprehensive philosophical perspective. That is the purpose of this book.

Comprehensive Policy Argument (CPA) is the core of Policy Design. CPA is the detailed inductive and deductive process that integrates the theory and practice of law. CPA directs the course of law's evolution through an integration of both the scientific and institutional reality of the law's context and the philosophical or metaphysical ideas that create the background conditions of the law within the policy design space.[13] Policy Design as CPA is unlike traditional policy analysis because it addresses both empirical and normative dimensions of law. CPA not only poses the problem of how legal institutions, regulations, and public management *are* affecting the environment, but it also requires us to consider how these legal institutions, regulations, and management systems *should* be affecting nature.

The process of breaking down an existing environmental law within its institutional context and then synthesizing a new one is set out in our illustration of the CPA process.

13. See, R. G. COLLINGWOOD, AN ESSAY ON PHILOSOPHICAL METHOD (1933).

Look at existing law/policy in institutional env. and analyze using inductive reasoning to define a strategy for change (via paradigm + policy context model) in the theoretical env.

THEN use deductive reasoning to synthesize alternative law/policy into the institutional env.

The Strategy And Tactics Of Comprehensive Policy Argument

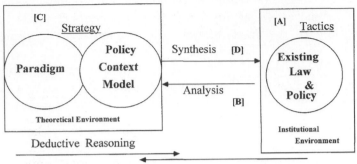

J.M. Gillroy 1995

A. The Current State Of Law & Policy. We Begin With The Existing Final
   Government Action Produced By Past Tactical Process Steps
   { e.g. Political Choice, Production, Final Government Action}

B. Inductive Reasoning Which Starts With The Specific Law & Policy
   And, Through Analysis, Derives Its More General Core Paradigm and
   Practical Context Model. Here, During The Critical Analysis Phase
   Of Comprehensive Policy Argument, One Makes The First Trip From
   The Institutional To The Theoretical Environment .

C. Analysis and Redefinition of Current Strategy To Change
   The Paradigm and Context Model That Is Into A New Strategy
   {Paradigm & Context Model} For What Ought To Be. Here The
   Binding Agent Of Moral Principle Is Added To Integrate An
   Overall Strategic Plan That Will Be Able To Prescribe The Proper
   Ground-Level Tactics To Apply Theory To Practice.

D. The Deduction of Alternative Policy From A New Paradigm & Context
   Model. Here During The Constructive Systhesis Pgase of Comprehensive
   Policy Argument, One Makes The Second, Return Trip, Moving Anew
   From The Theoretical To The Institutional Environment By Starting
   With The General Theory And Deriving Specific Recommendations
   For Policy Choice.

By preparing readers to integrate descriptive (scientific) and normative (philosophical) material, we hope this primer will help to (1) critically assess and analyze existing CPA; (2) connect existing law to its inherent normative principles, and (3) synthesize alternative CPAs with different core principles to affect persuasive change in the law.

Toward this end, Policy Design brings structure and systematic analysis to the way we sort the component parts of legal arguments, bringing them to bear on questions or dilemmas arising at the intersection of environmental degradation and the globalization of political, social, and economic institutions. It also allows many distinct philosophical and theoretical paradigms to be used, one at a time, to consider different principles and the distinct policy they prescribe. This approach is both more comprehensive and more flexible than traditional policy analysis that focuses on a single epistemology, that of positivism, a single theoretical paradigm, that of markets and Kaldor efficiency, a single valuation tool, that of cost-benefit analysis, and a single methodological predisposition, that of quantitative models and technical analysis.[14] In standard practice lawyers and policy-makers are trained to carry out retrospective analysis of existing policy and legal practice using empirical assumptions and quantitative tools, treating the law as a unitary actor, contained within a static or pre-determined context. In contradistinction, [Policy Design and CPA create a dynamic environment that integrates various values and principles, and creates new options for formulating and re-formulating environmental law.] *— not static*

In contrast to the one-size-fits-all approach of market analysis as policy and legal decision-making, Policy Design transcends, but does not ignore, market assumptions and economic/quantitative analysis. It uses scientific, economic, and technical data not as the sole basis for a legitimate analysis but as evidence for an integrated CPA that creates a synthesis policy design from the dialectic atmosphere of the legal process. It is *argument* rather than quantitative *data* that is the core of Policy Design, and *critical and systematic reason* rather than *efficiency* that sets the standards for a proper outcome in law.[15] Policy Design views a dialectic of 'value', both instrumental and intrinsic, as a critical component of environmental law. In this context, the environment's instrumental value may include economic use but also can mean that nature is instrumental to the health, well-being, or agency of the person(s). In this respect, Policy Design integrates both intrinsic and instrumental principles with scientific, economic, and socio-political factors to produce a CPA that offers reasonable choices to policy-makers and the public.[16] Overall, Policy Design is concerned not just with what 'is' but with what 'ought' to be. It integrates ideal-regarding concern for intrinsic values with want-regarding concern for instrumental norms[17] and examines the philosophical nature of the law without loosing sight of the material audience, constraints, and feasibility requirements of the decision-making environment.

14. See GIANDOMENICO MAJONE, EVIDENCE, ARGUMENT & PERSUASION IN THE POLICY PROCESS ch. 1 (1989), for a complete argument about the dominant presence of the Market Paradigm in policy discourse and its "decisionist" foundations.

15. Here the test of a dialectic argument is its ability to persuade all concerned that their point of view has been integrated into the synthesis solution.

16. The idea that the aim of public policy studies in a democracy is to present the people with reasonable alternatives was eloquently expressed in E. E. SCHATTSCHNEIDER, THE SEMI-SOVEREIGN PEOPLE (1960).

17. See BRIAN BARRY, POLITICAL ARGUMENT 38–40 (1965), for a definition and comparison of want—and ideal—regarding principles.

Law & Policy Design

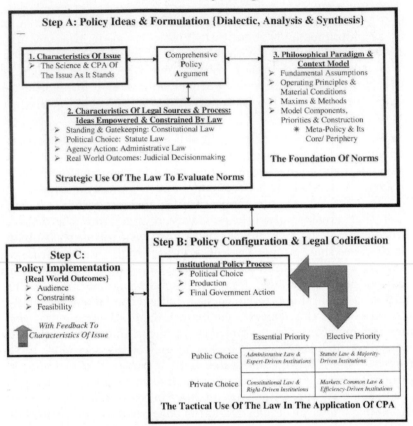

The policy design process can be divided into three steps. **Step A** is the use of CPA to first breakdown the existing law into its component parts and then re-design it in line with the course of change desired by a new strategy. **Step B** is the codification of the re-designed CPA through the political process, considering that different sources for law may be desirable given the public or private nature of the good and its essential or elective status as an intrinsic or instrumental value in the policy process. **Step C** is the implementation step which takes the codified law and makes it part of practice with the resulting limitations of audience, constraints and feasibility. Step C then is tied by a *feedback loop* to Step A, completing the policy design circuit.

Taking each step in turn, within Step A we have the analysis of an existing CPA and the synthesis of a re-designed policy, if necessary. This step has three component parts: the first (1) considers the characteristics of the existing environmental issue one wishes to analyze. What is the science? The facts on the ground? The status of the law on the question? How has the issue been argued? What core principle generates the policy? This element of the CPA is complemented by the sources of law and the political process considered as a strategic basis for legal analysis. Then, in the second component (2) the lawyer or policy-maker needs to consider what political process the old policy has gone through, what sources of law it has been drawn from and what specific pitfalls may await a re-designed CPA. The emphasis here is to understand the legal and political circumstances of the existing or re-designed policy which requires that the normative dimensions of the policy be fully considered. This is the role of the third component (3) of Step A.

In both the deconstruction of the existing CPA, and the reconstruction of a synthesis snapshot, the paradigm at the core of the policy must be deciphered. This paradigm[18] is that critical philosophical system behind the legal practice under scrutiny, and analysis of it is necessary for the design of any change in the law. Toward this end, the legal policy designer must take the existing CPA and identify, first, its fundamental assumptions or presuppositions about the characteristics of the *individual* person, the type of *collective action* problem(s) involved, and the *role of the state* or the definition of its responsibilities in terms of justice and the law. Second, based upon these presuppositions, one can decipher the *operating principle(s)* that provide the core normative foundation for the policy argument justifying the policy. This principle will be derived from the fundamental assumptions already defined, and by representing them, will be used to justify and evaluate the rest of the CPA.

Next, with the core principle in hand, one moves on to the *material conditions* of the paradigm, which define those things the policy-maker can manipulate to express the principle inherent in the paradigm. With an understanding of the material conditions of the normative principle, one can define an administrative *maxim* that provides a shorthand for the manager when making decisions representing the paradigm, and a *method* that can act to produce policy built upon the fundamental assumptions and core principle, without the need to retrace this paradigm deconstruction each time one wishes to use it.

The most important component of any argument is the core normative principle that creates the impetus for the policy and grants character to the law. This core principle is not always transparently clear but it will prejudice the rest of the argument so it needs to be understood and correctly deciphered from the funda-

---

18. See, GILLROY *supra* note 3 at 9–11, for a more complete definition of both the idea of a paradigm and the evolution of them within the social sciences and humanities.

mental assumptions. Is a law that allows clear-cutting based upon a concern for the health of the forest ecosystem, or a concern to efficiently maximize wealth? The answer to this question is critical, as a policy should be judged in terms of its core principle.

In order to answer this question, we first need to decipher the three fundamental assumptions or presuppositions of the CPA: the definition of the individual it assumes, the dynamics of any collective action problems it anticipates, and the role of the state or government in its allocation and distribution processes. As we will see in more detail in Chapter Three, the Market Paradigm can be recognized by its assumptions of individual self-interest, coordination of individual and collectively optimal outcomes through the operation of an "invisible hand" and a state that has only the obligation to mimic markets through the use of cost-benefit methods. The combination of these assumptions can then be synthesized into a principle, like Kaldor efficiency (see Appendix for details) for the market approach, which by itself stands for self-interested individuals maximizing wealth, and solving collective action problems with a state that does not interfere with market processes except to replicate them with cost-benefit methods when they fail to materialize.

The next component of policy argument connects the identified core principle with its material conditions, that is, with the actual material goods that can further the goals of the principle and be manipulated by the lawyer or policy-maker to the ends of that CPA. Money is the material condition of a market analysis. Biological flourishing is the material condition of an ecosystem approach based on the integrity of natural systems. With the fundamental assumptions, operating principle(s) and material conditions deciphered, the analyst moves on to define the maxim or imperative of the decision-maker which, again, is based upon the principle of the CPA and the creation of a method, like cost-benefit, to represent the principled CPA as a shorthand, producing results supporting the principle without having to go through the entire deconstruction of the CPA for every decision.

With the application of this logical schema, the CPA can be deconstructed and examined in detail. The principles and assumptions can be changed if this is necessary for improving a policy, and alternative CPAs can be created. The alternative policy is considered a meta-policy[19] containing a self-reflective core of principle and fundamental assumptions, and a periphery that contains the sources of law and the political process that codifies them. The

19. See, MAJONE, *supra* note 14 at 146–149, for his definition of "meta-policy."

deconstruction and then reconstruction of this CPA is the core of the meta-policy. It can be tracked in the dialectic of deductive and inductive reasoning illustrated in this logical model (see CPA Insight Box).

Once one identifies the paradigm, one needs to consider what the *context model* of the CPA looks like. A meta-policy or meta-law[20] should always be considered in terms of its context model, or the components, priorities, and construction of its overall world view determined by the core principle and its conditions, maxims, and methods. A market approach, for example, has a worldview that singles out nature's commercial goods and looks to the efficient use of them to maximize wealth. In contrast, a biocentric context model might value all living things as individuals and focus on preservation of life in all its forms with no priority for humanity.

With the construction of the context model one needs to bring consideration of the sources of law (A2), and their characteristics, back into the CPA. The sources play a strategic role at this juncture, creating both opportunities and constraints for the CPA. The task of the policy designer is to anticipate both of these types of eventualities and compensate for them in terms of argument and justification.

Overall, the interaction between the components of Step A render, in the end, a policy design that contains the strategic thinking about what values and facts are at stake in the policy and how these can best be handled to create dispositive law that represents them, given the constraints of political institutions and legal practice.

§§

Step A is the primary subject of this book. The focus on legal sources and practice in Chapter Two, and the alternative CPAs examined in Chapters Three, Four and Five, all concentrate on taking the characteristics of an area of environmental policy, examining the legal sources and practice in the area and, through deconstruction and then synthesis, take apart the argument for the existing meta-policy, change its inherent components and suggest an alternative CPA for codification (Step B) and implementation (Step C). Although these two latter steps are important, the key to policy design is the philosophical paradigm and context model for they make it possible to decipher and manipulate the components of existing law and then design alternative CPAs. Consequently, we will explain Steps B and C here only to the extent that we have created new elements for the decision process in each. Otherwise, when we talk of codification or implementation we are speaking of

20. Majone draws his definition of "meta-policy" from Berman's definition of "meta-law," HARLOD J. BERMAN, LAW AND REVOLUTION 8 (1983).

that phase of producing law and final government outcomes that are explained in almost every public law casebook or policy studies text.[21]

However, learning how to identify the philosophical foundation of a paradigm and context model that exists within a CPA is a crucial step in re-designing policy and affecting its progress through the governmental system toward becoming law. Thus, in providing a process for identifying this foundation and how it manifests in the paradigm and context model, we hope to give the reader a point of departure that will make the policy and legal process more enlightening and potentially creative.

With this understood, we can now move on to Step B of the design process. In the codification step, the strategically re-designed CPA is put into the tactical policy process. Within Step B the sources of law and the process of creating codified law that include political choice, the production of rules and the rendering of final government action must be considered tactically, as they are constrained by existing practice, institutions, and conventional social and personal values. The decision-maker here submits the CPA to the empirical reality of the political process and must navigate so that the new policy design has persuasive power to the audiences that matter in its adoption. What sources can be best utilized to make the CPA a dominant one? What parts of the real political and legal environment can be utilized to its best advantage?

In this step, we contend that the decision-maker should specifically take into account what source of law is the best conduit for the realization of the CPA's core principle. For this purpose, one needs to sort the sources of the rule of law by two critical dichotomies that reflect the complexity of making law for the environment. First, one should contemplate whether the choice under consideration involves primarily a *private* choice of the person or a *public* choice for the society at large.[22] The policy designer should consider both the characteristics of the goods to be delivered, and the optimal characteristics of the choice itself (i.e. whether the dialectic between a person's private and public roles weighs, in the particular case at hand, toward one's private rights or one's public agency as a citizen). For example, is the choice to protect environmental quality, primarily a choice affecting a single person as a private entity or the person as a citizen of the larger society?

In addition to the public or private nature of the choice, the analyst should also consider whether the good, such as environmen-

21. See, this book, Preface, n. 2.

22. For a definition of these terms see Duncan Snidal, *Public Goods, Property Rights, And Political Organizations* in THE MORAL DIMENSIONS OF PUBLIC POLICY CHOICE: BEYOND THE MARKET PARADIGM 285–312 (John Martin Gillroy & Maurice Wade eds., 1992).

tal quality, is an *essential* good or an *elective* good. Is the particular level of environmental quality under consideration here a core and basic level of essential quality that is a necessary ideal to the agency of the citizen (e.g. clean drinking water) or is it a non-essential want-regarding quality, say fluoridated water, that would be good for health but not necessary to life or conscious agency?

These two dichotomies create a four-cell box for Step B that prescribes an allocation mechanism and a particular source of law that is optimal for each cell. For example, in the northwest cell, we have **public choice and essential goods**, which administrative law and expert-driven institutions can best deliver. This combination of characteristics designates a law that is public and necessitates a general set of rules that place everyone in society on an equal field relative to what the law requires. As the law is also essential, that is, dealing with ideal public choices that allocate basic requirements of citizenship and human agency, the assessment of experts is necessary. This is because the law must be evaluated in detail and to an end that requires knowledge of what is required to accomplish any goal, which cannot be left to ignorance or the whim of democratic majorities.

In the southwest cell we have a **private choice over essential goods** which constitutional law and rights-driven institutions can best deliver. If a good is essential to the agency of a citizen but primarily concerns one's status as a private person making particular choices, then we are in the legal realm of rights as foundational elements that support the agency of the individual. It is the foundational or constitutional structure of a legal system that deals with these rights.

In the northeast cell we have **public and elective goods** which we argue are best allocated by statute law and the legislative majoritarian process. Because these goods are want-regarding and non-essential or elective in nature, their allocation can be subject to what emerges from the wants and desires of different segments of the population. However, since they are also public, that is, affecting the society at large, then the majoritarian institutions of the political process are best equipped to make decisions about these goods within the democratic context. The social dimension of one's citizenship requires a uniform set of rules and expectations but since this is being applied here to an elective good there is no reason to depend solely on experts. Statute law fits this situation. Here the democratic process is best equipped to decide if the elective good is to the advantage of enough citizens to protect it by law and whether or not it should be allocated, to whom and at what level.

In the final, southeast cell, we have ***private elective goods.*** *choice* This is the perfect choice situation for markets and their common law background institutions. Specifically, markets are best at processing and aggregating private choices over fungible private goods that are elective and therefore properly subject to pricing and trade. The common or civil law is the best means to adjudicate, at the margins, any difficulties with harm or injustice suffered in these private market transactions. While judge-made case law will decide conflict and distribute issues in and between all of the cells, its rules of civil law will be most at home and most effective here where specific altercations can be considered case-by-case and in terms of private injury.

Given the choices of primary sources of law[23] in this matrix, the decision-maker must understand that the choice of source takes place within the context of a pre-existing tactical political process where all the branches of the state are involved and the mutual interdependence of the sources of law with these process components needs to be a consideration in the codification process. The interaction of political and legal considerations in the codification process will change the CPA, but should not alter the core principal and assumptions as these create the character of the particular policy design, which would cease to be without them. Consequently, one must protect the core of the CPA's meta-policy without ignoring the practical requirements of the tactical world of law and politics. The goal here is to create a persuasive CPA that can convince those audiences involved in the codification process that the approach to the issue evident in the CPA under scrutiny is reasonable, that is, more reasonable and a fit replacement for the status-quo.

In addition to the tactical interaction of politics, policy, and law in the codification process, one must keep a simultaneous eye on the components of the third and final step in the policy design

---

23. Here, first, we understand that frequently the wrong source of law will end up with primary responsibility for public choices about a particular good, as when legislatures take the lead on rights issues that are properly the constitutional venue of the courts. We also understand that a particular environmental law will have elements from statute, administrative, and common law, but that the specific core of the regulation will need to focus upon the primary status of one of the sources. Perhaps it should be left to administrative experts, with vague framework legislation and judges that do not micro-manage; perhaps with very specific statutes with tight legislative oversight, narrowly subscribed administrative regulations and judges seeking the will of the legislative body; or as a third alternative, with judges taking the lead in synthesizing legal dialectics, with the legislature being, perhaps, constitutionally overruled and administrative discretion limited severely by the courts. The point is to decide, by the characteristics of the choice and the good involved, which source of law should take primary status in creating the design argument and promoting the policy design alternative itself, the others being relegated to secondary status.

process. This last step is the implementation of codified law through the constraints, audience requirements, and feasibility considerations of the world of practice that create the final outcome of the law. While this step will concern us the least in this exposition, the examples we use in future chapters should grant the reader insight into how implementation considerations influence Steps A and B of the design process and then provide *feedback* to the original characteristics of the issue in Step A.

§§

Concentrating on the content of Step A, this primer is written to supply its reader with the tools and examples necessary to change law through the Policy Design process, solving problems of their choosing. Before we can create law using Policy Design we must understand the current state of environmental and natural resources law. We will do this in Chapter Two by considering its sources and practices. Chapters Three, Four, and Five will be taken up with the process of analyzing the CPAs of existing paradigms that undergird current environmental law and with understanding the procedure by which alternative paradigms and context models might be deconstructed, evaluated and new CPAs synthesized.

In Chapter Three, we shall examine the Market Paradigm which underlies much of current environmental law. With the analysis of the Market Paradigm and context models and its illustration through examples, we will then offer two alternative policy design models for environmental law that approach the human relationship to nature from ideal-regarding rather than want-regarding foundations. These support, in Chapter Four, a meta-policy concerned for the intrinsic value of human and natural integrity and, in Chapter Five, a meta-policy concerned with the non-economic instrumental value of human capabilities dependent on flourishing ecosystems. Finally, in our conclusion, we will suggest a formal framework with which to write policy and legal argument and provide some exercises to hone one's skills with persuasive policy argument.

Chapter 2

SOURCES OF ENVIRONMENTAL & NATURAL RESOURCES LAW

The specific practice of environmental and natural resources law[1] is the point of departure for this chapter. As we have framed the idea of policy design and its connection to law in Chapter One, before we move ahead with the normative evaluation of the law, we need to have an understanding of where the law is now, and what sources we have to work with as instruments in the process of policy design and evaluation. The theoretical and practical dimensions of dialectic analysis involved in the theory and practice of the law will take up the rest of this small volume, but first we need to understand the legal circumstances in which environmental decisions are made. Toward this end, American environmental practice is primary focused on five "sources" of law:

▶ Constitutional Law: Foundational Law Providing Ultimate Standards;

▶ Statutory Law: Bills Written & Ratified By Legislative Bodies;

▶ Common Law: Case–Based Law Made By Judges;

---

1. The cases referenced and excerpted in this chapter are, by design, not always current or the most up-to-date cases. We have referenced what we consider to be important foundational cases that made classic statements in the formation of the current law and policy on the particular issue. These cases are chosen because they originally set the tone for the current definitions of the relationship between law and nature. Unlike a casebook which means to describe the most contemporary dilemmas, or a Nutshell, which has no footnotes or references at all, we took a third way. Our cases were chosen for their role or status when the policy argument was taking shape, for their utility in seeing the sources of law as instruments of policy design, and in order to set up the primary arguments for each legal⇌environmental dialectic so that the reader can use these older cases as a point of departure for a study of the more specific and complicated dilemmas that have since ensued, which, while important, do not have the timeless quality in setting argument that we were looking for.

▶ Administrative Law[2]: Regulations Written By Government Agencies.

We shall consider each of these in turn, setting out the background and the important precedence in these areas so that the reader can understand what each best evaluates and how each of these sets of institutions and ideas can be used to work with environmental problems. Although much of environmental law is dominated by statute and administrative regulation, it is important to understand the critical and traditional role still played by common law doctrines and constitutional limits.

How To Recognize & Cite The Sources Of United States Law

A) Constitution Law—References to the Constitution of the United States can be recognized in the following form: [U.S. Const. art III, §2] which read United States Constitution, Article 3, section 2.

B) Statute Law Federal Statutes are compiled in the United States Code. The format of this source is as follows: [Comprehensive Environmental Response, Compensation and Liability Act is at 42 U.S.C.A. §§ 9601-9675 (1988)] which reads the name of the statute followed by the Title (here number 42) of the United States Code Annotated (USCA), the section of the title where it appears (here sections 9601-9675) and finally the year of its codification in brackets. [See Also The Statute Pointers Insight Box]

C) Administrative Law— Federal Administrative Law & its Regulations can be found in the Code of Federal Regulations which is also arranged in Titles. For example, the regulations of Forest Service Timber Sales can be found at [36 C.F.R. §223 (1992)], which is read Title 36, Code of Federal regulations, section 223 from the 1992 edition of the Code.

D) Common Law: Cases From The Federal Courts—These are the 'article three' courts, because they are authorized by Article III , Section 2, of the U.S. Constitution: "The judicial power of the United States shall be vested in one Supreme Court and in such inferior courts as the Congress may from time to time ordain and establish" these are specified in *An Act To Establish The Judicial Courts of the U.S."* (1789), which established three levels of courts in the federal system: (1) trial courts of general jurisdiction, known as *District Courts*, (2) intermediate appellate courts, called *Courts of Appeals* or *Circuit Courts,* and (3) the *Supreme Court,* as provided for in the Constitution. There are also special jurisdiction courts which operate as District Courts.

1. **The District Courts** are divided into 91 judicial districts. Every state has at least one, including one for DC and Puerto Rico. Bigger states may have Eastern and Western Districts. Here it is usually a single judge who seeks the facts of the case in trial and then applies the relevant laws. District Court Cases can be recognized by their citations as in *Intermountain Forest v. Lyng* 683 F. Supp. 1330 (1988), which is read, as 'case name' volume 638 of the Federal Supplement, page 1330, of the case year.

2. **Court of Appeals** divided the United States into eleven Judicial Circuits, each with its own court of appeal. There are also the District of Columbia Circuit and the Federal Circuit for a total of 13. Here panels of three judges hear cases appealed from the District Courts within their geography on matters not of the facts in the case, but the application of law to the agreed facts. They hear, by right, all appeals from the district courts. A Circuit Court can also sit *en banc* or all together to hear a case of theirs where the three judge panel's decision is appealed. Circuit cases are cited like this, *American Mining Congress v. EPA* 824 F.2d. 1177 (D.C. Cir.1987) which reads 'case name,' volume 824 Federal Reporter second edition (could be third edition also) page 1177 reporting the District of Columbia Circuit in 1987.

3. **Supreme Court** is the highest Court of Appeal in the United States. With a *writ of certiorari*, about one in ten cases that have already been heard at the federal circuit level or by State Supreme Courts can be taken on by the Supreme Court. Supreme Court Cases have a couple of reporting media but the most cited are the United States Reports (U.S.) which are used as follows: *DuPont v. Train* 430 U.S. 112 (1977) which is read 'case name' in Volume 430 of the United States Reports, page 112 for a 1977 case.

---

2. We will use 'Administrative Law' in its meaning as 'Administrative Regulation.'

However, before we consider each of these "sources," we need to consider the most basic issue in the law, namely, establishing standing in court. The matter of standing combines elements of all of the "sources" and is the fundamental point of departure for the subject of environmental and natural resources law. In addition to the subject of standing, we shall also consider the allied concepts of ripeness and mootness before we proceed to Common, Statutory and Administrative Law (which will be treated together), and finally, to save the most definitive for last, Constitutional Law.

Standing: The Intersection of the Constitution, Statutory Law, Administrative Regulation & Common Law

In all legal systems, whether basically civil or common, there is a basic bar that must be crossed in order to utilize the legal system toward your ends. One must establish the issue of standing or who has the legal personality, or right, to bring suit in a judicial forum. Although standing may be related to civil, contract, tort, or any issue, which all need preliminary standing to be pursued, in environmental and resource law one of the central themes of our cases is standing for nature or its representatives in a challenge to an agency action affecting the use of environment and resources. A plaintiff who fails to establish standing cannot have the merits of the case reviewed by a court. So, persons attempting to sue must meet a series of prerequisites that, although arising from constitutional roots, have been well established in common law.[3] Specifically, standing has evolved so that at least three prerequisites are necessary for it to be granted:

▶ Establish An Imminent Injury–In–Fact;

▶ That Is Traceable To The Challenged Administrative Action;

▶ And Redressable By Judicial Intervention.

3. Duke Power Co. v. Carolina Environmental Study Group, Inc., 438 U.S. 59, 57 L.Ed.2d 595 (1978) and Environmental Defense et al. v. Duke Energy

The injury-in-fact element of standing often presents a difficult barrier to litigating issues concerning environmental and natural resource use. The non-monetary, precautionary, and often times speculative nature of environmental interests raised by the plaintiff requires reviewing courts to decide (1) whether the plaintiff has suffered injury-in-fact, or whether the plaintiff is asserting injury to others, and (2) whether there is a causal connection between the asserted injury and the challenged conduct. For example, assume a moratorium placed on federal timber sales is challenged by a logging company that obtains some of its timber from such sales. One may assume that the company's business is affected, but is this an injury to the person seeking standing? Does the agency have an obligation to conduct federal timber sales at all? Even if a sale were held, the company must be the low bidder to obtain the contract. How probable is the company's likelihood of successfully obtaining a contract, and then operating the contract profitably? If economic injury-in-fact to the company and probable causation are shown, may an employee of the company sue? In another example, suppose that an individual wanted to stop the timber sale. How could they show injury in fact to themselves when the major harm will be to the forest as an ecosystem? When the harm is potential rather than real? When one needs to anticipate and prevent rather than remedy an injury, can standing be justified? Especially on public lands, how can any particular individual person be injured by a decision of the USFS to conduct a timber sale? Obviously the standing issue can become quite complex.

These common law prerequisites to standing have been supplemented by specific legislative or *statutory standing*, which can be argued to enable standing in court through a statute controlling the resource activity rather than through the common law.

1) The Right to Sue Under an Enabling or Regulatory Statute

The best means of obtaining judicial review of agency actions is to establish that an enabling statutory or regulatory measure empowering an agency to act also confers a right to judicial review of such action. These statutory provisions are called "Citizen Suit"

Comp. et al. Supreme Court 05–848, Decided April 2, 2007. This case was superseded by statute in O'Conner v. Commonwealth Edison Co., 770 F.Supp. 448, 452. However, only for the proposition that the Price–Anderson Act is not cognizable in federal courts, which is not what this cite references.

provisions. For example, Section 89(b) of the Atomic Energy Act of 1954 (42 U.S.C.A. § 2239(b)), specifically provides for judicial review of final orders of the Nuclear Regulatory Commission suspending or granting operating licenses to operators of nuclear power plants. More often, however, the relevant statute is vague or 'silent' concerning judicial review. When faced with a silent statute, courts generally apply two rules. First, there is a presumption of judicial review that must be overcome by the agency.[4] Second, Congress must have precluded judicial review in unmistakable terms before access to a court will be forbidden.[5]

In *Peterson*, the Sierra Club alleged that the USFS must obtain a permit before spraying national forests with herbicides, and that failure to do so was reviewable under the regulating statute, the Federal Insecticide, Fungicide and Rodenticide Act (FIFRA, 7 U.S.C.A. § 135). The USFS asserted that since FIFRA was silent as to the Sierra Club's right to sue, and the legislative history of the act suggested a Congressional intent to disallow private lawsuits to prevent spraying, no right of standing existed under FIFRA. The circuit court held, however, that the USFS failed to demonstrate nonreviewability of its actions, and that neither the provisions of FIFRA nor its legislative history foreclosed judicial review of spraying schemes. Because a lawsuit was not forbidden under FIFRA, it was permissible under the APA, which is our next subject.

2) The Right to Sue Under the APA

In addition to specific Citizen Suit provisions within enabling statutes, plaintiffs may also rely on the federal Administrative Procedures Act (APA).[6] In fact, most cases involving challenges to administrative regulation are brought pursuant to Section 702 of the APA, which grants a right to sue federal agencies to any person "suffering legal wrong because of agency action, or to any person adversely affected or aggrieved by agency action within the meaning of a relevant statute . . ." 5 U.S.C.A. § 702. Despite the broad language of Section 702, and a favorable disposition of the courts toward judicial review generally, many cases have held that Section

---

4. Abbott Laboratories v. Gardner, 387 U.S. 136, 140 (1967) [Overruled on other grounds. Califano v. Sanders, 430 U.S. 99, 105, 51 L.Ed.2d 192, 192].

5. Sierra Club v. Peterson, 705 F.2d 1475 (9th Cir.1983).

6. Most states also have Administrative Procedures Acts which also allow for a right of standing.

702 does no more than codify the common law of standing.[7] Nevertheless, the APA is particularly useful in cases where a statute is silent or ambiguous concerning a plaintiff's right to judicial review of a specific administrative action. Overall, as long as the challenged agency action is (1) final, (2) imposes a legal obligation or right (5 U.S.C.A. § 704), or (3) involves the issuance of a permit or license from the agency, it will likely be reviewable.[8]

3) The Injury–In–Fact Requirement

However, as stated above, Section 702, as well as specific Citizen Suit provisions within environmental and natural resource statutes, may not be independent avenues to standing, but just codifications of the traditional prerequisites of constitutional/common law standing. The courts have a tendency to integrate common law and statutory standing to the benefit of the former. Specifically, the "Injury–In–Fact" requirement is limited to human harm and cannot be invoked for real or potential harm to ecosystems.

Section 702 of the APA requires that a plaintiff demonstrate personalized injury-in-fact brought about by the adverse administrative action, and that the asserted injury arguably be within the "zone of interests" protected or regulated by a statute claimed to have been violated by the agency. These requirements, derived from the Constitution of the United States and its "case or controversy" language in Article III, is there to ensure that plaintiffs will be sufficiently involved, and at risk to assured harm that will vigorously and adversely prejudice the issue. It is also the case that the standing requirement is designed to protect courts from dealing with hypothetical or non-concrete issues.[9] The courts have therefore created a "zone of interest" test which requires that even though injury-in-fact be present, the plaintiff's interest must be within the scope of the statute supposedly violated.[10]

---

7. See Kansas City Power & Light Co. v. McKay, 225 F.2d 924, 932–33 (D.C.Cir.1955).

8. This section is used in the National Environmental Policy Act (NEPA) cases where there is no other reviewability clause in the statute.

9. Association of Data Processing Service Organizations, Inc. v. Camp, 397 U.S. 150, 154 (1970); Barlow v. Collins, 397 U.S. 159 (1970). However, one should remember that only Article III courts have to follow the cases and controversy requirements.

10. Peoples Gas, Light and Coke Co. v. United States Postal Service, 658 F.2d 1182 (7th Cir.1981) (Postal Service conversion from steam heat to electric heat resulted in economic injury to the plaintiff (a utility company); suit disallowed because postal regulations only protected the public's interest in efficient and economic postal service).

One of the more frequently litigated standing issues under the APA is whether the injury asserted is sufficiently "personal."[11] Personalized injury is particularly difficult to establish when the asserted injury is aesthetic, or environmental in nature.[12] The injury element of standing is more easily demonstrated by plaintiffs who establish that their economic or environmental injury is due to the agency's failure to consider certain statutorily-mandated criteria when making the decision at issue.[13] However, if the personal injury barrier is overcome, standing will often be granted despite the tenuous subjective nature of the economic or environmental injury alleged.[14]

Plaintiffs must also demonstrate that the challenged conduct of the agency is not committed to the discretion of the agency by law. Section 701 of the APA forbids judicial review of an administrative action that is within the sole discretion of the agency (5 U.S.C.A. § 701(a)(2)) or precluded from review by statute (5 U.S.C.A. § 701(a)(1)). The consequence of this rule is that even if a plaintiff can show injury-in-fact resulting from the agency action, judicial relief will not be granted where the agency has sole discretion to act.[15]

4) Ripeness

If standing focuses on the plaintiff's injury, ripeness involves the agency decision itself and its timing. Because many environmental cases regarding ripeness concern review of past agency actions, the court has developed a three-part test for ripeness:

▸ The Agency's Decision Is Appropriate For Review Because It Presents A Legal Question Based On Well-developed Facts;

11. Environmental Defense Fund v. Marsh, 651 F.2d 983 (5th Cir.1981) (Several plaintiffs alleged environmental harm caused by an incorrect cost evaluation associated with a federal construction project. Only one plaintiff asserted specific economic injury sufficiently personal to that plaintiff to be granted standing; the other claims were found too speculative to constitute injury in fact).

12. Sierra Club v. Morton, 405 U.S. 727 (1972).

13. See Mahuiki v. Planning Commission, 65 Haw. 506, 654 P.2d 874 (1982) (standing granted landowners after planning commission failed to consider environmental impact of commission's decision as required by Federal Coastal Zone Management Act of 1972, 16 U.S.C.A. § 1451).

14. United States v. Students Challenging Regulatory Agency Procedures (SCRAP), 412 U.S. 669, 93 S.Ct. 2405, 37 L.Ed.2d 254 (1973) (standing allowed because plaintiffs alleged environmental injury to public areas which they frequented, hence plaintiffs were personally injured; aesthetic and environmental injury resulted from increased litter, caused by decreased recycling, linked to increased railroad rates for recycled materials).

15. Watt v. Energy Action Educational Foundation, 454 U.S. 151 (1981) (choice of bidding system for oil and gas leases within agency discretion and not subject to judicial review, despite acknowledged existence of injury-in-fact to plaintiff).

▶ The Agency Decision Will Cause Hardship To The Affected Party If The Court Does Not Review The Agency Action, And;

▶ The Agency Has Made Its Final Statement On The Matter.

If the issue concerns a legal interpretation of well developed facts, for instance, whether a federal agency action preempts a state statute, the issue is ripe for judicial review.[16]

If lack of review will put a plaintiff in a precarious position, then a court will more likely declare the case ripe and review the case.[17] But if review will not substantially alter the plaintiff's position, then the court will not be as inclined to review a case.[18] Determining the "finality" of an agency action also presents factual problems. For instance, an environmental impact study (EIS) may go through many revisions, none of which is final, over a period of years. Thus, if an agency may supplement a "final" EIS, a court will not interfere with the agency's on-going process.[19] On the other hand, review may be proper, even though the agency has only written an interim EIS, when the court finds that the agency has "spoken its last word on the environmental impact."[20]

Not all ripeness questions concern agency review. In water law cases involving interstate rivers, ripeness may be absent if a downstream state claims that an upstream state will in the future make excessive use of the water in the river. Ripeness is lacking because there is no present harm. In *Nuclear Engineering Co. v. Scott*, 660 F.2d 241 (7th Cir.1981), a state attorney general said he would prosecute a corporation for violating a state environmental protection law regarding radioactive waste facilities. The plaintiff believed it was not violating the statute and brought suit in a federal court asking for an interpretation of the statutory law. The case was not ripe because the prosecutor's threat only cost the plaintiff possible investors and because the plaintiff did not challenge the statute's validity. On the other hand, in *People of State of Illinois v. General Electric Co.*, 683 F.2d 206 (7th Cir.1982), the plaintiff challenged

---

16. Pacific Gas and Electric Co. v. State Energy Resources, 461 U.S. 190 (1983).

17. (See *Pacific Gas*, where millions of dollars of construction investments depended on court review).

18. See Kerr–McGee Chemical Corp. v. United States Department of Interior, 709 F.2d 597 (9th Cir.1983) (recommendation by Interior Department that state re-designate air quality designation of federal lands within state did not cause "injury" to corporation seeking to expand a chemical processing plant near the federal lands because states can act

independently of the recommendation; corporation's lawsuit thus not ripe); D'Imperio v. United States, 575 F.Supp. 248 (D.N.J.1983) (plaintiff's fear that in the future he might have to clean hazardous waste sites did not impose a present hardship on him).

19. National Wildlife Federation v. Goldschmidt, 677 F.2d 259 (2d Cir. 1982).

20. Friedman Brothers Investment Co. v. Lewis, 676 F.2d 1317 (9th Cir. 1982).

the validity of an Illinois statute which barred it from disposing nuclear waste from other states in an Illinois waste dump. The court declared the case ripe because prosecution was certain; the plaintiff had no other place to put the waste, and mere statutory interpretation, as opposed to statutory validity, was not at issue.

Therefore timing issues like ripeness address the matter of when suit may be brought. Timing restrictions prevent premature judicial intervention into an agency's fact-finding or adjudicatory functions and, conversely, avoid the litigation of issues where the plaintiff no longer has a legally cognizable interest at stake.

Overall, courts refrain from hearing administrative law cases presenting only abstract disagreements requiring advisory opinions. The ripeness doctrine ensures that the issue presented is sufficiently developed, concrete, and adverse for judicial review and overhaul. To avoid the pitfall of timing issues, a plaintiff must establish the presence of the following four factors:

▶ Agency Fact–finding Is Complete And The Issues Presented By The Case Are Purely Legal In Nature;

▶ The Challenged Agency Action Is Final Within The Meaning Of Section 704 Of The APA;

▶ The Challenged Administrative Conduct Has Or Will Have A Direct And Immediate Impact Upon The Plaintiff And;

▶ Judicial Intervention Will Promote, Rather Than Hinder, The Effective Regulatory Functions Of The Agency.[21]

Due to the often irreversible injuries involved in environmental and natural resources cases, plaintiffs often seek judicial review of agency action before a final administrative decision has been made or interagency appeals completed. Judicial review of non-final administrative action is permissible when the non-final action directly and substantially affects a party's ability to use a resource. Thus, plaintiffs often need only establish that the issues presented are legal in nature, and that they have suffered or will suffer substantial harm as a result of the non-final administrative act, but reversals have also shown that the courts are reluctant to judge standing or ripeness issues before actual injury is suffered.[22]

21. Abbott Laboratories v. Gardner, 387 U.S. 136 (1967).

22. Rocky Mountain Oil and Gas Association v. Andrus, 500 F.Supp. 1338 (D.Wyo.1980), reversed in, Rocky Mountain Oil and Gas Association v. Watt, 696 F.2d 734 (10th Cir.1982) (agency interpretation of Federal Land Policy Management Act (FLPMA) barred oil drilling in areas in which plaintiffs had incurred substantial exploration costs; the issue was considered by courts despite plaintiff's pending petition before the agency because of the substantial economic cost to plaintiffs, the loss of exploration costs already incurred, and the purely legal question of the interpretation of FLPMA); Alabama Power Co. v. Federal Energy Regulatory Commission, 685 F.2d 1311 (11th Cir.1983)

Despite an inclination by the courts to find that issues in environmental cases are ripe for review, a hearing will not be granted when a plaintiff fails to prove a personal injury resulting from a non-final administrative action. Thus, ripeness is missing in cases which challenge the facial validity of a regulation, rather than its application to a specific party.[23] Ripeness is also missing when an agency action has "no definitive impact on the rights of anyone."[24]

5) Mootness

The mootness doctrine is an element of the "case or controversy" requirement of Article III of the U.S. Constitution, which mandates that federal courts hear only cases presenting an ongoing controversy. The essence of mootness is that the parties to the litigation maintain a sufficient interest in the outcome to assure vigorous presentation of the issues. A case will be found moot, and excluded from judicial review, if subsequent developments have occurred to resolve the dispute or render it without consequence. For example, an environmental case may be moot if subsequent administrative action has provided adequate relief to an aggrieved party, or if a resolution is no longer necessary or possible.[25]

The doctrine of mootness differs from the doctrines of standing and ripeness because it concerns the court's ability to remedy an injury, not the position of the parties. In fact, the simplest test for mootness is whether a court can order relief that would cure an injury that would otherwise continue to exist. For example, in *Friends of the Earth v. Bergland*, 576 F.2d 1377 (9th Cir.1978), an environmental group protested the EIS for a mining operation. While the case was on appeal, the defendants halted work on the mine. Because the court could not undo the environmental damage, the case was moot.[26] On the other hand, in *Columbia Basin Land*

(agency determination of preference in processing competing licensing applications ripe for determination because substantial economic harm threatened and purely legal issue involved).

23. Pacific Legal Foundation v. California Coastal Commission, 33 Cal.3d 158, 188 Cal.Rptr. 104, 655 P.2d 306 (1982) (challenge to regulation not ripe because regulation had not been applied to plaintiffs and no harm or injury incurred).

24. Tennessee Gas Pipeline Co. v. FERC, 736 F.2d 747 (D.C.Cir.1984) (FERC interpretative statement on the meaning of a statutory text lacks the concrete quality and immediacy necessary to invoke judicial review).

25. See Natural Resources Defense Council v. United States Nuclear Regulatory Commission, 680 F.2d 810 (D.C.Cir.1982) (court challenge to an agency rulemaking procedure as being in violation of Section 553 of the APA found moot when rule reissued by agency in compliance with Section 553).

26. See also Luckie v. EPA, 752 F.2d 454 (9th Cir.1985) (residents of lots located near asbestos waste dump could not challenge an EPA emission standard for asbestos because their claims were mooted by an EPA decision to relocate residents).

Protection Association v. Schlesinger, 643 F.2d 585 (9th Cir.1981), the court said that it could require the EPA to reconsider an EIS even though, as a consequence, the defendant power company might have to remove 191 towers that had been in place three years. Because the court could fashion a remedy (however harsh), the case was not moot. Similarly, in *DeVilbiss v. Zoning Board*, 690 P.2d 260 (Colo.App.1984),[27] a complaint to enjoin construction of a coal load-out facility, although eventually judged moot, was adjudged not moot immediately after completion of the construction. Here the plaintiff was entitled to an injunction ordering restoration of the status quo before building was complete and operation began.

An exception to mootness exists if a dispute is capable of repetition yet evades review. For instance, in *Oregon Environmental Council v. Kunzman*, 714 F.2d 901 (9th Cir.1983), the plaintiff challenged the eradication spraying of moths. Although the spraying was completed and the court could not undo the alleged damage, the spraying represented a continuing policy; thus, the court would review the spraying policy.[28] *Res judicata* or the idea that an issue already decided by the court should not be reopened, may also make a case moot,[29] as would any subsequent legislative or judicial action.[30]

6) The "Case and Controversy" Language of the Constitution

In addition to the traditional common law prerequisites and the administrative and statutory law affecting standing, ripeness, and mootness, the ultimate voice on all of these issues is the Constitution of the United States. The doctrines of standing, ripeness, and mootness focus on whether a plaintiff may sue. All three doctrines are based on the Constitution, which limits a federal court to deciding "cases or controversies" (Art. III, 2). A case will be dismissed if the requirements are not maintained throughout the litigation even through an appeal.

---

27. [Overruled by Zoning Board of Adjustment of Garfield County v. DeVilbiss, 729 P.2d 353 (Colo. Dec. 08, 1986)]

28. See also California Energy Resources v. Bonneville Power, 754 F.2d 1470 (9th Cir.1985).

29. See Hall v. Federal Energy Regulatory Commission, 691 F.2d 1184 (5th Cir.1982) (parties continued long-standing litigation to determine if Supreme Court had in fact decided a key issue, making the case moot).

30. See Sea Ranch Association v. California Coastal Commission, 552 F.Supp. 241 (N.D.Cal.1982) (developer's challenge to a statute that allegedly took property without compensation became moot after legislature compensated developer for property); Bethell v. Florida, 741 F.2d 1341 (11th Cir.1984) (defendant who had been arrested for using fish traps beyond state boundaries alleged in lawsuit that the state statute as applied to activities outside state boundaries was unconstitutional; defendant's case mooted by state supreme court decision that statute did not apply outside state boundaries).

Standing focuses on the nature of the plaintiff's interest injured by a defendant. A federal "case or controversy" exists, for purposes of standing, if a plaintiff has a personal stake in a protectable interest that has been injured by conduct traceable to the defendant. To allege a personal stake, a plaintiff must show a personal injury, not an injury to others. "A mere 'interest in a problem,' no matter how longstanding the interest and no matter how qualified the organization is in evaluating the problem, is not sufficient by itself to render the organization [Sierra Club] 'adversely affected'."[31]

Protectable interests traditionally only included such legal rights as property rights, contracts rights, rights in tort, or rights protected by statute or the constitution. Since the 1960s, however, federal courts have replaced the requirement of "injury to a legal right" with the concept of "injury in fact." Financial injury usually guarantees standing.[32] But an "injury in fact" is also an injury that a court can cure. (See similar discussion regarding mootness). Therefore, a court can protect the environmental, recreational or aesthetic interests of a plaintiff. For instance, in *Duke Power Co. v. Carolina Environmental Study Group*, 438 U.S. 59, 98 S.Ct. 2620, 57 L.Ed.2d 595 (1978), the Court said that an individual's fear of daily radiation and aesthetic concern for thermal pollution to neighboring, but public, lakes, constituted injury to protectable interests. However, the Court specifically avoided saying that fear of a future nuclear melt-down would constitute an "injury in fact" because such a fear was not sufficiently concrete.[33]

In *Duke Power* the most controversial aspect regarding standing arose in "fairly tracing the injury to the defendant's challenged conduct." The plaintiffs could not challenge the fact of the nuclear plant; they could only challenge a statute [Price–Anderson] that limited the liability of the plant in the event of an accident. Under the plaintiff's theory, if a nuclear accident occurred, there would be an unconstitutional taking of plaintiff's property without full compensation. Therefore, the Court had to connect the injury alleged for purposes of standing (fear of radiation), with the injury alleged for purposes of subject-matter jurisdiction (unconstitutional taking). To solve this problem, the Court noted that "but for" the statute limiting liability the plant would not have been built. There was thus a connection, or "nexus," between the injury and the challenged conduct of the defendant (the conduct of Congress which

31. Sierra Club v. Morton, 405 U.S. 727, 739 (1972).

32. Portland General Elec. Co. v. Johnson, 754 F.2d 1475 (9th Cir.1985).

33. Also, this case has since been superceded by statute, as discussed in

O'Conner v. Commonwealth Edison Co., Nuclear Reg. Rep. P 20,544, 770 F.Supp. 448 (C.D.Ill. Jul. 10, 1991). In effect, the Price-Anderson Act gives sufficient remedy to constitutionally bar a common law right of action for nuclear incidents.

passed the statute). This nexus satisfies standing if a court has the power to cure the plaintiff's injury by changing the defendant's conduct, in this case by possibly ruling the statute unconstitutional.

The "cases and controversies" clause of the federal constitution does not restrict state courts. Nevertheless, state courts will "still carefully weigh the wisdom, efficacy, and timeliness of the exercise of their power before acting, especially where there may be an intrusion into areas committed to other branches of government."[34] A typical state standing rule requires a plaintiff's interests to be substantial, direct and immediate. States generally do not focus, for purposes of standing, on the nexus between the injury and the defendant's conduct. Instead, this consideration will arise in the requirement that a case not be moot.[35]

7) Cases

To demonstrate the role of standing in the courts of the United States, we have included excerpts from three seminal cases that have set the tone for the courts approach to standing. Take care to see how statutory, administrative, common and constitutional law all intertwine in this most critical subject of getting a dispute about humanity's use of nature into the judicial system.

§§

SIERRA CLUB v. ROGERS C. B. MORTON

Supreme Court of the United States, 1972.
405 U.S. 727.

Mr. Justice STEWART delivered the opinion of the Court.

I

The Mineral King Valley is an area of great natural beauty nestled in the Sierra Nevada Mountains in Tulare County, California, adjacent to Sequoia National Park. It has been part of the Sequoia National Forest since 1926, and is designated as a national game refuge by special Act of Congress. 16 U.S.C. § 688. Though once the site of extensive mining activity, Mineral King is now used almost exclusively for recreational purposes. Its relative inaccessibility and lack of development have limited the number of visitors each year, and at the same time have preserved the valley's quality

---

34. Life of the Land v. Land Use Commission, 63 Haw. 166, 623 P.2d 431, 438 (1981).

35. For typical state approaches to standing, see Franklin Township v. Commonwealth, 500 Pa. 1, 452 A.2d 718 (1982) (a township has sufficient interest in protecting itself from chemical seepage to challenge a state waste disposal permit); Matter of Various Water Rights in Lake DeSmet, 623 P.2d 764 (Wyo.1981) (mortgagee's interest in land too remote to challenge exercise of water rights by neighbor that affected the mortgaged land).

as a quasi-wilderness area largely uncluttered by the products of civilization.

The United States Forest Service, which is entrusted with the maintenance and administration of national forests, began in the late 1940's to give consideration to Mineral King as a potential site for recreational development. Prodded by a rapidly increasing demand for skiing facilities, the Forest Service published a prospectus in 1965, inviting bids from private developers for the construction and operation of a ski resort that would also serve as a summer recreation area. The proposal of Walt Disney Enterprises, Inc., was chosen from those of six bidders, and Disney received a three-year permit to conduct surveys and explorations in the valley in connection with its preparation of a complete master plan for the resort.

The final Disney plan, approved by the Forest Service in January 1969, outlines a $35 million complex of motels, restaurants, swimming pools, parking lots, and other structures designed to accommodate 14,000 visitors daily. This complex is to be constructed on 80 acres of the valley floor under a 30–year use permit from the Forest Service. Other facilities, including ski lifts, ski trails, a cog-assisted railway, and utility installations, are to be constructed on the mountain slopes and in other parts of the valley under a revocable special-use permit. To provide access to the resort, the State of California proposes to construct a highway 20 miles in length. A section of this road would traverse Sequoia National Park, as would a proposed high voltage power line needed to provide electricity for the resort. Both the highway and the power line require the approval of the Department of the Interior, which is entrusted with the preservation and maintenance of the national parks.

Representatives of the Sierra Club, . . . unsuccessfully sought a public hearing on the proposed development in 1965, and in subsequent correspondence with officials of the Forest Service and the Department of the Interior, they expressed the Club's objections to Disney's plan as a whole and to particular features included in it. In June 1969 the Club filed the present suit in the United States District Court for the Northern District of California, seeking a declaratory judgment that various aspects of the proposed development contravene federal laws and regulations governing the preservation of national parks, forests, and game refuges,[36] and also

---

36. As analyzed by the District Court, the complaint alleged violations of law falling into four categories. First, it claimed that the special-use permit for construction of the resort exceeded the maximum-acreage limitation placed upon such permits by 16 U.S.C. § 497 and that issuance of a 'revocable' use permit was beyond the authority of the Forest Service. Second, it challenged the proposed permit for the highway through Sequoia National Park on the grounds that the highway would not serve any of the purposes of the park, in

seeking preliminary and permanent injunctions restraining the federal officials involved from granting their approval or issuing permits in connection with the Mineral King project. The petitioner Sierra Club sued as a membership corporation with 'a special interest in the conservation and the sound maintenance of the national parks, game refuges and forests of the country,' and invoked the judicial-review provisions of the Administrative Procedure Act, 5 U.S.C.§ 701 et seq.

After two days of hearings, the District Court granted the requested preliminary injunction. It rejected the respondents' challenge to the Sierra Club's standing to sue, and determined that the hearing had raised questions 'concerning possible excess of statutory authority, sufficiently substantial and serious to justify a preliminary injunction. . . .' The respondents appealed, and the Court of Appeals for the Ninth Circuit reversed, 443 F.2d 24. With respect to the petitioner's standing, the court noted that there was 'no allegation in the complaint that members of the Sierra Club would be affected by the actions of (the respondents) other than the fact that the actions are personally displeasing or distasteful to them,' id., at 33, and concluded:

> We do not believe such club concern without a showing of more direct interest can constitute standing in the legal sense sufficient to challenge the exercise of responsibilities on behalf of all the citizens by two cabinet level officials of the government acting under Congressional and Constitutional authority. Id. at 30.

Alternatively, the Court of Appeals held that the Sierra Club had not made an adequate showing of irreparable injury and likelihood of success on the merits to justify issuance of a preliminary injunction. The court thus vacated the injunction. The Sierra Club filed a petition for a writ of certiorari which we granted, 401 U.S. 907, to review the questions of federal law presented.

II

The first question presented is whether the Sierra Club has alleged facts that entitle it to obtain judicial review of the challenged action. Whether a party has a sufficient stake in an otherwise justiciable controversy to obtain judicial resolution of that

alleged violation of 16 U.S.C. § 1, and that it would destroy timber and other natural resources protected by 16 U.S.C. §§ 41 and 43. Third, it claimed that the Forest Service and the Department of the Interior had violated their own regulations by failing to hold adequate public hearings on the proposed project. Finally, the complaint asserted that 16 U.S.C. § 45c requires specific congressional authorization of a permit for construction of a power transmission line within the limits of a national park. Overruled in part by Lujan I [Lujan v. National Wildlife Federation 110 S.Ct.3177 (1990)]. See Sierra Club v. Peterson, 185 F.3d 349, 361, 49 ERC 1204, 1204, 29 Envtl. L. Rep. 21,432, 21432 (5th Cir.(Tex.)).

controversy is what has traditionally been referred to as the question of standing to sue. Where the party does not rely on any specific statute authorizing invocation of the judicial process, the question of standing depends upon whether the party has alleged such a "personal stake in the outcome of the controversy" Baker v. Carr 369 U.S. 186, 204, as to ensure that "the dispute sought to be adjudicated will be presented in an adversary context and in a form historically viewed as capable of judicial resolution." Flast v. Cohen 392 U.S. 83, 101. Where, however, Congress has authorized public officials to perform certain functions according to law, and has provided by statute for judicial review of those actions under certain circumstances, the inquiry as to standing must begin with a determination of whether the statute in question authorizes review at the behest of the plaintiff.

The Sierra Club relies upon § 10 of the Administrative Procedure Act (APA), 5 U.S.C. § 702, which provides:

> A person suffering legal wrong because of agency action, or adversely affected or aggrieved by agency action within the meaning of a relevant statute, is entitled to judicial review thereof.

Early decisions under this statute interpreted the language as adopting the various formulations of 'legal interest' and 'legal wrong' then prevailing as constitutional requirements of standing. Kansas City Power and Light Co. v. McKay, 96 U.S. App. D.C. 273. But, in Association of Data Processing Service Organizations, Inc. v. Camp, 397 U.S. 150, and Barlow v. Collins, 397 U.S. 159, decided the same day, we held more broadly that persons had standing to obtain judicial review of federal agency action under § 10 of the APA where they had alleged that the challenged action had caused them 'injury in fact,' and where the alleged injury was to an interest 'arguably within the zone of interests to be protected or regulated' by the statutes that the agencies were claimed to have violated.

In Data Processing, the injury claimed by the petitioners consisted of harm to their competitive position in the computer-servicing market through a ruling by the Comptroller of the Currency that national banks might perform data processing services for their customers. In Barlow, the petitioners were tenant farmers who claimed that certain regulations of the Secretary of Agriculture adversely affected their economic position vis-a-vis their landlords. These palpable economic injuries have long been recognized as sufficient to lay the basis for standing, with or without a specific statutory provision for judicial review. Thus, neither Data Processing nor Barlow addressed itself to the question, which has arisen with increasing frequency in federal courts in recent years, as to what must be alleged by persons who claim injury of a non-economic nature to interests that are widely shared. That question is presented in this case.

III

The injury alleged by the Sierra Club will be incurred entirely by reason of the change in the uses to which Mineral King will be put, and the attendant change in the aesthetics and ecology of the area. Thus, in referring to the road to be built through Sequoia National Park, the complaint alleged that the development 'would destroy or otherwise adversely affect the scenery, natural and historic objects and wildlife of the park and would impair the enjoyment of the park for future generations.' We do not question that this type of harm may amount to an 'injury in fact' sufficient to lay the basis for standing under § 10 of the APA. Aesthetic and environmental well-being, like economic well-being, are important ingredients of the quality of life in our society, and the fact that particular environmental interests are shared by the many rather than the few does not make them less deserving of legal protection through the judicial process. But the 'injury in fact' test requires more than an injury to a cognizable interest. It requires that the party seeking review be himself among the injured.

The impact of the proposed changes in the environment of Mineral King will not fall indiscriminately upon every citizen. The alleged injury will be felt directly only by those who use Mineral King and Sequoia National Park, and for whom the aesthetic and recreational values of the area will be lessened by the highway and ski resort. The Sierra Club failed to allege that it or its members would be affected in any of their activities or pastimes by the Disney development. Nowhere in the pleadings or affidavits did the Club state that its members use Mineral King for any purpose, much less that they use it in any way that would be significantly affected by the proposed actions of the respondents.

* * *

The trend of cases arising under the APA and other statutes authorizing judicial review of federal agency action has been toward recognizing that injuries other than economic harm are sufficient to bring a person within the meaning of the statutory language, and toward discarding the notion that an injury that is widely shared is ipso facto not an injury sufficient to provide the basis for judicial review, Environmental Defense Fund, Inc. v. Hardin, 428 F.2d 1093. We noted this development with approval in Data Processing, 397 U.S. at 154, in saying that the interest alleged to have been injured "may reflect 'aesthetic, conservational, and recreational' as well as economic values." But broadening the categories of injury that may be alleged in support of standing is a different matter from abandoning the requirement that the party seeking review must himself have suffered an injury.

Some courts have indicated a willingness to take this latter step by conferring standing upon organizations that have demonstrated 'an organizational interest in the problem' of environmental or consumer protection. Environmental Defense Fund Inc. v. Hardin, 428 F.2d 1093, 1097. It is clear that an organization whose members are injured may represent those members in a proceeding for judicial review. See, e.g., NAACP v. Button, 371 U.S. 415, 428. But a mere 'interest in a problem,' no matter how longstanding the interest and no matter how qualified the organization is in evaluating the problem, is not sufficient by itself to render the organization 'adversely affected' or 'aggrieved' within the meaning of the APA. The Sierra Club is a large and long-established organization, with a historic commitment to the cause of protecting our Nation's natural heritage from man's depredations. But if a 'special interest' in this subject were enough to entitle the Sierra Club to commence this litigation, there would appear to be no objective basis upon which to disallow a suit by any other bona fide 'special interest' organization however small or short-lived. And if any group with a bona fide 'special interest' could initiate such litigation, it is difficult to perceive why any individual citizen with the same bona fide special interest would not also be entitled to do so.

The requirement that a party seeking review must allege facts showing that he is himself adversely affected does not insulate executive action from judicial review, nor does it prevent any public interests from being protected through the judicial process. It does serve as at least a rough attempt to put the decision as to whether review will be sought in the hands of those who have a direct stake in the outcome. That goal would be undermined were we to construe the APA to authorize judicial review at the behest of organizations or individuals who seek to do no more than vindicate their own value preferences through the judicial process. The principle that the Sierra Club would have us establish in this case would do just that.

As we conclude that the Court of Appeals was correct in its holding that the Sierra Club lacked standing to maintain this action, we do not reach any other questions presented in the petition, and we intimate no view on the merits of the complaint.

The judgment is Affirmed.

Mr. Justice DOUGLAS, dissenting.

I share the views of my Brother BLACKMUN and would reverse the judgment below.

The critical question of 'standing' would be simplified and also put neatly in focus if we fashioned a federal rule that allowed environmental issues to be litigated before federal agencies or federal courts in the name of the inanimate object about to be despoiled, defaced, or invaded by roads and bulldozers and where injury is the subject of public outrage. Contemporary public concern for protecting nature's ecological equilibrium should lead to the conferral of standing upon environmental objects to sue for their own preservation. See Stone, Should Trees Have Standing? Toward Legal Rights for Natural Objects, 45 S.Cal.L.Rev. 450 (1972). This suit would therefore be more properly labeled as Mineral King v. Morton.

Inanimate objects are sometimes parties in litigation. A ship has a legal personality, a fiction found useful for maritime purposes. The corporation sole—a creature of ecclesiastical law—is an acceptable adversary and large fortunes ride on its cases. The ordinary corporation is a 'person' for purposes of the adjudicatory processes, whether it represents proprietary, spiritual, aesthetic, or charitable causes.

So it should be as respects valleys, alpine meadows, rivers, lakes, estuaries, beaches, ridges, groves of trees, swampland, or even air that feels the destructive pressures of modern technology and modern life. The river, for example, is the living symbol of all the life it sustains or nourishes—fish, aquatic insects, water ouzels, otter, fisher, deer, elk, bear, and all other animals, including man, who are dependent on it or who enjoy it for its sight, its sound, or its life. The river as plaintiff speaks for the ecological unit of life that is part of it. Those people who have a meaningful relation to that body of water—whether it be a fisherman, a canoeist, a zoologist, or a logger—must be able to speak for the values which the river represents and which are threatened with destruction.

* * *

Mineral King is doubtless like other wonders of the Sierra Nevada such as Tuolumne Meadows and the John Muir Trail. Those who hike it, fish it, hunt it, camp in it, frequent it, or visit it merely to sit in solitude and wonderment are legitimate spokesmen for it, whether they may be few or many. Those who have that intimate relation with the inanimate object about to be injured, polluted, or otherwise despoiled are its legitimate spokesmen.

* * *

The voice of the inanimate object, therefore, should not be stilled. That does not mean that the judiciary takes over the managerial functions from the federal agency. It merely means that before these priceless bits of Americana (such as a valley, an alpine meadow, a river, or a lake) are forever lost or are so transformed as to be reduced to the eventual rubble of our urban environment, the voice of the existing beneficiaries of these environmental wonders should be heard.[8]

Perhaps they will not win. Perhaps the bulldozers of 'progress' will plow under all the aesthetic wonders of this beautiful land. That is not the present question. The sole question is, who has standing to be heard?

Those who hike the Appalachian Trail into Sunfish Pond, New Jersey, and camp or sleep there, or run the Allagash in Maine, or climb the Guadalupes in West Texas, or who canoe and portage the Quetico Superior in Minnesota, certainly should have standing to defend those natural wonders before courts or agencies, though they live 3,000 miles away. Those who merely are caught up in environmental news or propaganda and flock to defend these waters or areas may be treated differently. That is why these environmental issues should be tendered by the inanimate object itself. Then there will be assurances that all of the forms of life which it represents will stand before the court—the pileated woodpecker as well as the coyote and bear, the lemmings as well as the trout in the streams. Those inarticulate members of the ecological group cannot speak. But those people who have so frequented the place as to know its values and wonders will be able to speak for the entire ecological community.

Ecology reflects the land ethic; and Aldo Leopold wrote in A Sand County Almanac 204 (1949), "The land ethic simply enlarges the boundaries of the community to include soils, waters, plants, and animals, or collectively: the land."

That, as I see it, is the issue of 'standing' in the present case and controversy.

* * *

Mr. Justice BLACKMUN, dissenting.

The Court's opinion is a practical one espousing and adhering to traditional notions of standing ... and ... [i]f this were an ordinary case, I would join the opinion and the Court's judgment and be quite content.

But this is not ordinary, run-of-the-mill litigation. The case poses—if only we choose to acknowledge and reach them—significant aspects of a wide, growing, and disturbing problem, that is, the Nation's and the world's deteriorating environment with its resulting ecological disturbances. Must our law be so rigid and our

---

8. Permitting a court to appoint a representative of an inanimate object would not be significantly different from customary judicial appointments of guardians *ad litem*, executors, conservators, receivers, or counsel for indigents.

procedural concepts so inflexible that we render ourselves helpless when the existing methods and the traditional concepts do not quite fit and do not prove to be entirely adequate for new issues?

The ultimate result of the Court's decision today, I fear, and sadly so, is that the 35.3–million–dollar complex, over 10 times greater than the Forest Service's suggested minimum, will now hastily proceed to completion; that serious opposition to it will recede in discouragement; and that Mineral King, the "area of great natural beauty nestled in the Sierra Nevada Mountains," to use the Court's words, will become defaced, at least in part, and, like so many other areas, will cease to be "uncluttered by the products of civilization."

Rather than pursue the course the Court has chosen to take by its affirmance of the judgment of the Court of Appeals, I would . . . permit an imaginative expansion of our traditional concepts of standing in order to enable an organization such as the Sierra Club, possessed, as it is, of pertinent, *bona fide*, and well-recognized attributes and purposes in the area of environment, to litigate environmental issues. This incursion upon tradition need not be very extensive. Certainly, it should be no cause for alarm. It is no more progressive than was the decision in Data Processing itself. It need only recognize the interest of one who has a provable, sincere, dedicated, and established status. We need not fear that Pandora's box will be opened or that there will be no limit to the number of those who desire to participate in environmental litigation. The courts will exercise appropriate restraints just as they have exercised them in the past. Who would have suspected 20 years ago that the concepts of standing enunciated in Data Processing and Barlow would be the measure for today? And Mr. Justice Douglas, in his eloquent opinion, has imaginatively suggested another means and one, in its own way, with obvious, appropriate, and self-imposed limitations as to standing. As I read what he has written, he makes only one addition to the customary criteria (the existence of a genuine dispute; the assurance of adversariness; and a conviction that the party whose standing is challenged will adequately represent the interests he asserts), that is, that the litigant be one who speaks knowingly for the environmental values he asserts.

* * *

. . . Are we to be rendered helpless to consider and evaluate allegations and challenges of this kind because of procedural limitations rooted in traditional concepts of standing? I suspect that this may be the result of today's holding. As the Court points out, at 1367–1368, other federal tribunals have not felt themselves so confined. I would join those progressive holdings.

Notes & Questions

How does this case expand the concept of standing beyond the traditional constitutional—common law prerequisites?

What is the relationship between individual values and their vindication in the courts through standing? Whose values are presently represented in the common law prerequisites of standing? In statutory standing? Are there inherent conflicts here?

Is "injury in fact" the core of standing? If so, how is it now defined? Does this definition favor or oppose the use of natural systems for resource use? How might the definition be expanded or contracted to change this orientation?

What role does statutory standing play in this case? Does it trump common law standing or is it dominated by the common law requirements? If the latter, what good is statutory standing?

What are the timing and mootness issues connected with this case? Are they independent of the standing issue or coextensive with it?

How is the defense of natural systems enhanced by this case? How are they diminished?

Is the conventional definition of standing in this case based in assumptions from the Market Paradigm? Would interpreting constitutional—common law standing through the lens of the Ecosystem Paradigm change its interpretation or application? Come back to this question again after you have read the rest of the book ... how would an ecosystem design argument compensate for the constraints of the law of standing?

If dissents represent alternative policy arguments within the law, ones that have not yet been determinative of the law but which represent considerations that may be future law, what do the dissents in this case say about the future status of nature and its resources in the law? Could these dissents be argued as representative of an ecosystem design approach? How?

§§

MANUEL LUJAN, JR. v. NATIONAL WILDLIFE FEDERATION

Supreme Court of the United States, 1990.
497 U.S. 871.

Justice SCALIA delivered the opinion of the Court.

In this case we must decide whether respondent, the National Wildlife Federation (hereinafter respondent), is a proper party to challenge actions of the Federal Government relating to certain public lands.

I

Respondent filed this action in 1985 in the United States District Court for the District of Columbia against petitioners the United States Department of the Interior, the Secretary of the Interior, and the Director of the Bureau of Land Management (BLM), an agency within the Department. In its amended complaint, respondent alleged that petitioners had violated the Federal Land Policy and Management Act of 1976 (FLPMA), 90 Stat. 2744, 43 U.S.C.§ 1701 *et seq.* (1982 ed.), the National Environmental Policy Act of 1969 (NEPA), 42 U.S.C. § 4321 *et seq.,* and § 10 (e) of the Administrative Procedure Act (APA), 5 U.S.C. § 706, in the course of administering what the complaint called the "land withdrawal review program" of the BLM. Some background information concerning that program is necessary to an understanding of this dispute.

In various enactments, Congress empowered United States citizens to acquire title to, and rights in, vast portions of federally owned land. See, *e.g.,* 30 U.S.C. § 22 *et seq.* (Mining Law of 1872); 30 U.S.C. § 181 *et seq.* (Mineral Leasing Act of 1920). Congress also provided means, however, for the Executive to remove public lands from the operation of these statutes. The Pickett Act, 43 U.S.C. § 141 (1970) authorized the President "at any time in his discretion, temporarily [to] withdraw from settlement, location, sale, or entry any of the public lands of the United States . . . and reserve the same for water-power sites, irrigation, classification of lands, or other public purposes. . . ."

* * *

Management of the public lands under these various laws became chaotic. The Public Land Law Review Commission, established by Congress in 1964 to study the matter, 78 Stat. 982, determined in 1970 that "virtually all" of the country's public domain, see Public Land Law Review Commission, One Third of the Nation's Land 52 (1970)—about one-third of the land within the United States, see *id.,* at 19—had been withdrawn or classified for retention; that it was difficult to determine "the extent of existing Executive withdrawals and the degree to which withdrawals overlap each other," *id.,* at 52; and that there were inadequate records to show the purposes of withdrawals and the permissible public uses. *Ibid.* Accordingly, it recommended that "Congress should provide for a careful review of (1) all Executive withdrawals and reservations, and (2) BLM retention and disposal classifications under the Classification and Multiple Use Act of 1964." *Ibid.*

In 1976, Congress passed the FLPMA, which repealed many of the miscellaneous laws governing disposal of public land, 43 U.S.C. § 1701 *et seq.* (1982 ed.), and established a policy in favor of retaining public lands for multiple use management. It directed the Secretary to "prepare and maintain on a continuing basis an inventory of all public lands and their resource and other values," § 1711(a), required land use planning for public lands, and established criteria to be used for that purpose, § 1712. It provided that existing classifications of public lands were subject to review in the land use planning process, and that the Secretary could "modify or terminate any such classification consistent with such land use plans." § 1712(d). It also authorized the Secretary to "make, modify, extend or revoke" withdrawals. § 1714(a). Finally it directed the Secretary, within 15 years, to review withdrawals in existence in 1976 in 11 Western States, § 1714(*l*)(1), and to "determine whether, and for how long, the continuation of the existing withdrawal of the lands would be, in his judgment, consistent with the statutory objectives of the programs for which the lands were dedicated and of the other relevant programs," § 1714(*l*)(2). The activities undertaken by the BLM to comply with these various provisions constitute what respondent's amended complaint styles the BLM's "land withdrawal review program," which is the subject of the current litigation.

* * *

II

In its complaint, respondent averred generally that the reclassification of some withdrawn lands and the return of others to the public domain would open the lands up to mining activities, thereby destroying their natural beauty.... To support the point, the Court of Appeals pointed to the affidavits of two of respondent's members, Peggy Kay Peterson and Richard Erman, which claimed use of land "in the vicinity" of the land covered by two of the listed actions.

* * *

III

A

We first address respondent's claim that the Peterson and Erman affidavits alone suffice to establish respondent's right to judicial review of petitioners' actions. Respondent does not contend that either the FLPMA or NEPA provides a private right of action for violations of its provisions. Rather, respondent claims a right to judicial review under § 10(a) of the APA, which provides:

> A person suffering legal wrong because of agency action, or adversely affected or aggrieved by agency action within the meaning of a relevant statute, is entitled to judicial review thereof. 5 U.S.C.§ 702.

This provision contains two separate requirements. First, the person claiming a right to sue must identify some "agency action" that affects him in the specified fashion; it is judicial review "thereof" to which he is entitled.... When, as here, review is sought not pursuant to specific authorization in the substantive statute, but only under the general review provisions of the APA, the "agency action" in question must be "final agency action." See 5 U.S.C. § 704. "Agency action made reviewable by statute and *final* agency action for which there is no other adequate remedy in a court are subject to judicial review" (emphasis added).

Second, the party seeking review under § 702 must show that he has "suffer[ed] legal wrong" because of the challenged agency action, or is "adversely affected or aggrieved" by that action "within the meaning of a relevant statute." Respondent does not assert that it has suffered "legal wrong," so we need only discuss the meaning of "adversely affected or aggrieved ... within the meaning of a relevant statute." ... Rather, we have said that to be "adversely affected or aggrieved ... within the meaning" of a statute, the plaintiff must establish that the injury he complains of (*his* aggrievement, or the adverse effect *upon him*) falls within the "zone of interests" sought to be protected by the statutory provision whose violation forms the legal basis for his complaint. See Clarke v. Securities Industry Assn., 479 U.S. 388, 396–397 (1987). Thus, for example, the failure of an agency to comply with a statutory provision requiring "on the record" hearings would assuredly have an adverse effect upon the company that has the contract to record and transcribe the agency's proceedings; but since the provision was obviously enacted to protect the interests of the parties to the proceedings and not those of the reporters, that company would not be "adversely affected within the meaning" of the statute.

* * *

C

We turn, then, to whether the specific facts alleged in the two affidavits considered by the District Court raised a genuine issue of fact as to whether an "agency action" taken by petitioners caused respondent to be "adversely affected or aggrieved ... within the meaning of a relevant statute." We assume, since it has been uncontested, that the allegedly affected interests set forth in the affidavits—"recreational use and aesthetic enjoyment"—are sufficiently related to the purposes of respondent association that respondent meets the requirements of § 702 if any of its members do.

Hunt v. Washington State Apple Advertising Comm'n, 432 U.S. 333 (1997).

* * *

We ... think that whatever "adverse effect" or "aggrievement" is established by the affidavits was "within the meaning of the relevant statute"—*i.e.,* met the "zone of interests" test. The relevant statute, of course, is the statute whose violation is the gravamen of the complaint—both the FLPMA and NEPA. We have no doubt that "recreational use and aesthetic enjoyment" are among the *sorts* of interests those statutes were specifically designed to protect. The only issue, then, is whether the facts alleged in the affidavits showed that those interests *of Peterson and Erman* were actually affected.

The Peterson affidavit averred:

> My recreational use and aesthetic enjoyment of federal lands, particularly those in the vicinity of South Pass–Green Mountain, Wyoming have been and continue to be adversely affected in fact by the unlawful actions of the Bureau and the Department. In particular, the South Pass–Green Mountain area of Wyoming has been opened to the staking of mining claims and oil and gas leasing, an action which threatens the aesthetic beauty and wildlife habitat potential of these lands. App. to Pet. for Cert. 191a.

Erman's affidavit was substantially the same as Peterson's, with respect to all except the area involved; he claimed use of land "in the vicinity of Grand Canyon National Park, the Arizona Strip (Kanab Plateau), and the Kaibab National Forest." *Id.,* at 187a.

The District Court found the Peterson affidavit inadequate for the following reasons:

> Peterson ... claims that she uses federal lands in the vicinity of the South Pass–Green Mountain area of Wyoming for recreational purposes and for aesthetic enjoyment and that her recreational and aesthetic enjoyment has been and continues to be adversely affected as the result of the decision of BLM to open it to the staking of mining claims and oil and gas leasing.... This decision [W–6228] opened up to mining approximately 4500 acres within a two million acre area, the balance of which, with the exception of 2000 acres, has always been open to mineral leasing and mining.... There is no showing that Peterson's recreational use and enjoyment extends to the particular 4500 acres covered by the decision to terminate classification to the remainder of the two million acres affected by the termination. All she claims is that she

uses lands 'in the vicinity.' The affidavit on its face contains only a bare allegation of injury, and fails to show specific facts supporting the affiant's allegation. 699 T.Supp., at 331 (emphasis in original).

The District Court found the Erman affidavit "similarly flawed."

"The magnitude of Erman's claimed injury stretches the imagination...." Id. At 332.

* * *

The Court of Appeals disagreed with the District Court's assessment as to the Peterson affidavit (and thus found it unnecessary to consider the Erman affidavit) for the following reason:

If Peterson was not referring to lands in this 4500–acre affected area, her allegation of impairment to her use and enjoyment would be meaningless, or perjurious.... [T]he trial court overlooks the fact that unless Peterson's language is read to refer to the lands affected by the Program, the affidavit is, at best, a meaningless document.

At a minimum, Peterson's affidavit is ambiguous regarding whether the adversely affected lands are the ones she uses. When presented with ambiguity on a motion for summary judgment, a District Court must resolve any factual issues of controversy in favor of the non-moving party.... This means that the District Court was obliged to resolve any factual ambiguity in favor of NWF, and would have had to assume, for the purposes of summary judgment, that Peterson used the 4500 affected acres. 278 U.S. App. D.C., at 329, 878 F.2d, at 431.

That is not the law. In ruling upon a Rule 56 motion, "a District Court must resolve any factual issues of controversy in favor of the non-moving party" only in the sense that, where the facts specifically averred by that party contradict facts specifically averred by the movant, the motion must be denied. That is a world apart from "assuming" that general averments embrace the "specific facts" needed to sustain the complaint. As set forth above, Rule 56(e) provides that judgment "shall be entered" against the nonmoving party unless affidavits or other evidence "set forth specific facts showing that there is a genuine issue for trial."

* * *

At the margins there is some room for debate as to how "specific" must be the "specific facts" that Rule 56(e) requires in a particular case. But where the fact in question is the one put in issue by the § 702 challenge here—whether one of respondent's members has been, or is threatened to be, "adversely affected or aggrieved" by Government action—Rule 56(e) is assuredly not satisfied by averments which state only that one of respondent's members uses unspecified portions of an immense tract of territory, on some portions of which mining activity has occurred or probably will occur by virtue of the governmental action. It will not do to "presume" the missing facts because without them the affidavits would not establish the injury that they generally allege. That converts the operation of Rule 56 to a circular promenade: plaintiff's complaint makes general allegation of injury; defendant contests through Rule 56 existence of specific facts to support injury; plaintiff responds with affidavit containing general allegation of injury, which must be deemed to constitute averment of requisite specific facts since otherwise allegation of injury would be unsupported (which is precisely what defendant claims it is).

Respondent places great reliance, as did the Court of Appeals, upon our decision in United States v. Students Challenging Regulatory Agency Procedures (SCRAP), 412 U.S. 699 (1973). The SCRAP opinion, whose expansive expression of what would suffice for § 702 review under its particular facts has never since been emulated by this Court, is of no relevance here, since it involved not a Rule 56 motion for summary judgment but a Rule 12(b) motion to dismiss on the pleadings. The latter, unlike the former, presumes that general allegations embrace those specific facts that are necessary to support the claim. Conley v. Gibson, 355 U.S. 41, 45–46 (1957).

IV

We turn next to the Court of Appeals' alternative holding that the four additional member affidavits proffered by respondent in response to the District Court's briefing order established its right to § 702 review of agency action.

A

It is impossible that the affidavits would suffice, as the Court of Appeals held, to enable respondent to challenge the entirety of petitioners' so-called "land withdrawal review program." That is not an "agency action" within the meaning of § 702, much less a "final agency action" within the meaning of § 704. The term "land withdrawal review program" (which as far as we know is not derived from any authoritative text) does not refer to a single BLM order or regulation, or even to a completed universe of particular BLM orders and regulations. It is simply the name by which petitioners have occasionally referred to the continuing (and thus constantly changing) operations of the BLM in reviewing withdrawal revocation applications and the classifications of public lands and developing land use plans as required by the FLPMA. It is no more an identifiable "agency action"—much less a "final agency action"—than a "weapons procurement program" of the Department of Defense or a "drug interdiction program" of the Drug Enforcement Administration. As the District Court explained, the "land withdrawal review program" extends to, currently at least, "1250 or so individual classification terminations and withdrawal revocations." 699 F.Supp., at 332.[2]

Respondent alleges that violation of the law is rampant within this program—failure to revise land use plans in proper fashion, failure to submit certain recommendations to Congress, failure to consider multiple use, inordinate focus upon mineral exploitation, failure to provide required public notice, failure to provide adequate environmental impact statements. Perhaps so. But respondent cannot seek *wholesale* improvement of this program by court decree, rather than in the offices of the Department or the halls of Congress, where programmatic improvements are normally made. Under the terms of the APA, respondent must direct its attack against some particular "agency action" that causes it harm. Some statutes permit broad regulations to serve as the "agency action," and thus to be the object of judicial review directly, even before the concrete effects normally required for APA review are felt. Absent such a provision, however, a regulation is not ordinarily considered the type of agency action "ripe" for judicial review under the APA until the scope of the controversy has been reduced to more manageable proportions, and its factual components fleshed out, by some concrete action applying the regulation to the claimant's situation in a fashion that harms or threatens to harm him. (The major exception, of course, is a substantive rule which as a practical matter requires the plaintiff to adjust his conduct immediately. Such agency action is "ripe" for review at once, whether or not explicit statutory review apart from the APA is provided. See Abbott Laboratories v. Gardner, 387 U.S. 136, 152–154 (1967); Gardner v. Toilet Goods Assn., Inc., 387 U.S. 167, 171–173 (1967). Toilet Goods Assn., Inc. v. Gardner, 387 U.S. 158, 164–166, (1967)).

In the present case, the individual actions of the BLM identified in the six affidavits can be regarded as rules of general

2. Contrary to the apparent understanding of the dissent, we do not contend that no "land withdrawal review program" exists, ... We merely assert that it is not an identifiable "final agency action" for purposes of the APA. If there is in fact some specific order or regulation, applying some particular measure across the board to all individual classification terminations and withdrawal revocations, and if that order or regulation is final, and has become ripe for review in the manner we discuss subsequently in text, it can of course be challenged under the APA by a person adversely affected—and the entire "land withdrawal review program," insofar as the content of that particular action is concerned, would thereby be affected. But that is quite different from permitting a generic challenge to all aspects of the "land withdrawal review program," as though that itself constituted a final agency action.

applicability (a "rule" is defined in the APA as agency action of "general or particular applicability *and future effect*," 5 U.S.C. § 551(4) (emphasis added)) announcing, with respect to vast expanses of territory that they cover, the agency's intent to grant requisite permission for certain activities, to decline to interfere with other activities, and to take other particular action if requested. It may well be, then, that even those individual actions will not be ripe for challenge until some further agency action or inaction more immediately harming the plaintiff occurs.[3] But it is at least entirely certain that the flaws in the entire "program"—consisting principally of the many individual actions referenced in the complaint, and presumably actions yet to be taken as well—cannot be laid before the courts for wholesale correction under the APA, simply because one of them that is ripe for review adversely affects one of respondent's members.

The case-by-case approach that this requires is understandably frustrating to an organization such as respondent, which has as its objective across-the-board protection of our Nation's wildlife and the streams and forests that support it. But this is the traditional, and remains the normal, mode of operation of the courts. Except where Congress explicitly provides for our correction of the administrative process at a higher level of generality, we intervene in the administration of the laws only when, and to the extent that, a specific "final agency action" has an actual or immediately threatened effect. Toilet Goods Assn., 387 U.S., at 164–166. Such an intervention may ultimately have the effect of requiring a regulation, a series of regulations, or even a whole "program" to be revised by the agency in order to avoid the unlawful result that the court discerns. But it is assuredly not as swift or as immediately far-reaching a corrective process as those interested in systemic improvement would desire. Until confided to us, however, more sweeping actions are for the other branches.

* * *

---

3. Under the Secretary's regulations, any person seeking to conduct mining operations that will "cause a cumulative surface disturbance" of five acres or more must first obtain approval of a plan of operations. § 3809.1–4 (1988). Mining operations that cause surface disturbance of less than 5 acres do not require prior approval, but prior notice must be given to the district office of the BLM. § 3809,1–3. Neither approval nor notification is required only with respect to "casual use operations," 43 C.F.R. § 3089.1–2, defined as "activities ordinarily resulting in only negligible disturbance of the Federal lands and resources," § 3809.0–5. (Activities are considered "casual" if "they do not involve the use of mechanized earth moving equipment or explosives or do not involve the use of motorized vehicles in areas designated as closed to off-road vehicles. . . ." *Id.*) Thus, before any mining use ordinarily involving more than "negligible disturbance" can take place, there must occur either agency action in response to a submitted plan or agency inaction in response to a submitted notice.

For the foregoing reasons, the judgment of the Court of Appeals is reversed.

Justice BLACKMUN, with whom Justice BRENNAN, Justice MARSHALL, and Justice STEVENS join, dissenting.

In my view, the affidavits of Peggy Kay Peterson and Richard Loren Erman, in conjunction with other record evidence before the District Court on the motions for summary judgment, were sufficient to establish the standing of the National Wildlife Federation (Federation or NWF) to bring this suit. . . .

I

The Federation's asserted injury in this case rested upon its claim that the Government actions challenged here would lead to increased mining on public lands; that the mining would result in damage to the environment; and that the recreational opportunities of NWF's members would consequently be diminished. Abundant record evidence supported the Federation's assertion that on lands newly opened for mining, mining in fact would occur.[1] Similarly, the record furnishes ample support for NWF's contention that mining activities can be expected to cause severe environmental damage to the affected lands. The District Court held, however, that the Federation had not adequately identified particular members who were harmed by the consequences of the Government's actions. Although two of NWF's members expressly averred that their recreational activities had been impaired, the District Court concluded that these affiants had not identified with sufficient precision the particular sites on which their injuries occurred. The majority, like the District Court, holds that the averments of Peterson and Erman were insufficiently specific to withstand a motion for summary judgment. Although these affidavits were not models of precision, I believe that they were adequate at least to create a genuine issue of fact as to the organization's injury.

* * *

The requirement that evidence be submitted is satisfied here: The Federation has offered the sworn statements of two of its members. There remains the question whether the allegations in these affidavits were sufficiently precise to satisfy the requirements of Rule 56(e). The line of demarcation between "specific" and "conclusory" allegations is hardly a bright one. But, to my mind, the allegations contained in the Peterson and Erman affidavits, in

---

1. Prior to the District Court's entry of the preliminary injunction, 406 mining claims had been staked in the South Pass–Green Mountain area alone. App. 119. An exhibit filed by the federal parties indicated that over 7,200 claims had been filed in 12 Western States. Exh. 1 to Affidavit of Joseph Martyak (Apr. 11, 1986).

the context of the record as a whole, were adequate to defeat a motion for summary judgment. These affidavits, as the majority acknowledges, were at least sufficiently precise to enable Bureau of Land Management (BLM) officials to identify the particular termination orders to which the affiants referred. See *ante,* at 3187. And the affiants averred that their "recreational use and aesthetic enjoyment of federal lands ... have been and continue to be adversely affected in fact by the unlawful actions of the Bureau and the Department." App. to Pet. for Cert. 188a (Erman affidavit), 191a (Peterson affidavit). The question, it should be emphasized, is not whether the NWF has *proved* that it has standing to bring this action, but simply whether the materials before the District Court established "that there is a genuine issue for trial," see Rule 56(e), concerning the Federation's standing. In light of the principle that "[o]n summary judgment the inferences to be drawn from the underlying facts contained in [evidentiary] materials must be viewed in the light most favorable to the party opposing the motion," United States v. Diebold Inc., 369 U.S. 654, 655 (1962), I believe that the evidence before the District Court raised a genuine factual issue as to NWF's standing to sue.

No contrary conclusion is compelled by the fact that Peterson alleged that she uses federal lands "in the vicinity of South Pass–Green Mountain, Wyoming," App. to Pet. for Cert. 191a, rather than averring that she uses the precise tract that was recently opened to mining.

* * *

III

In Part IV–A, *ante,* at 3189, the majority sets forth a long and abstract discussion of the scope of relief that might have been awarded had the Federation made a sufficient showing of injury from environmental damage to a particular tract of land. Since the majority concludes in other portions of its opinion that the Federation lacks standing to challenge *any* of the land-use decisions at issue here, it is not clear to me why the Court engages in the hypothetical inquiry contained in Part IV–A.... Application of these principles to the instant case does not turn on whether, or how often, the Bureau's land-management policies have been described as a "program." In one sense, of course, there is no question that a "program" exists. Everyone associated with this lawsuit recognizes that the BLM, over the past decade, has attempted to develop and implement a comprehensive scheme for the termination of classifications and withdrawals. The real issue is whether the actions and omissions that NWF contends are illegal are themselves part of a plan or policy....

The majority, quoting the District Court, characterizes the Bureau's land management program as "1250 or so individual classification terminations and withdrawal revocations." The majority offers no argument in support of this conclusory assertion, and I am far from certain that the characterization is an accurate one. Since this issue bears on the scope of the relief ultimately to be awarded should the plaintiff prevail, rather than on the jurisdiction of the District Court to entertain the suit, I would allow the District Court to address the question on remand.[16]

IV

Since I conclude that the Peterson and Erman affidavits provided sufficient evidence of NWF's standing to withstand a motion for summary judgment, ... I would affirm the judgment of the Court of Appeals.

I respectfully dissent.

Notes & Questions

How do the roles of the individuals involved shape the case for standing? Only through injury? Does injury include how an agency action affects the individual? Nature?

What is the "in the vicinity" test? What is its role in this case?

Is there a "Program" here? A "Policy"? What is the difference to the court?

If one needs to wait for actual mining operations to begin to have standing does this not defeat the purpose of having standing in the first place? If so, how? If not, why?

How does this case build upon the Court's decision in *Morton*? Does it expand or restrict our ability as human beings to sue on behalf of nature?

Is the mix of common law and statute standing different here than in *Morton*? How?

What are the timing, ripeness and mootness issues here? Are they more decisive than in *Morton*?

How are the dissents representative of an alternative vision of natural resource policy? Do these dissents enhance those in *Morton*? Do they present a totally different argument?

---

16. The majority also suggests that the agency actions challenged in this suit may not be ripe for review. See *ante,* at 3190–3191. Since the issue of ripeness has not been briefed or argued in this Court, nor passed on by the courts below, I need not address it.

Does this decision represent the Market Paradigm or the Ecosystem Paradigm of resource law? You may want to address this question again, after you have read the rest of the book.

§§

MANUEL LUJAN, JR. v. DEFENDERS OF WILDLIFE

Supreme Court of the United States, 1992.
504 U.S. 555.

Justice SCALIA delivered the opinion of the Court with respect to Parts I, II, III–A, and IV, and an opinion with respect to Part III–B, in which THE CHIEF JUSTICE, Justice WHITE, and Justice THOMAS join.

This case involves a challenge to a rule promulgated by the Secretary of the Interior interpreting § 7 of the Endangered Species Act of 1973 (ESA), 87 Stat. 884, 892, as amended, 16 U.S.C. § 1536, in such fashion as to render it applicable only to actions within the United States or on the high seas. The preliminary issue, and the only one we reach, is whether respondents here, plaintiffs below, have standing to seek judicial review of the rule.

I

* * *

In 1978, the Fish and Wildlife Service (FWS) and the National Marine Fisheries Service (NMFS), on behalf of the Secretary of the Interior and the Secretary of Commerce respectively, promulgated a joint regulation stating that the obligations imposed by § 7(a)(2) of the Endangered Species Act extend to actions taken in foreign nations. 43 Fed.Reg. 874 (1978). The next year, however, the Interior Department began to reexamine its position. Letter from Leo Kuliz, Solicitor, Department of the Interior, to Assistant Secretary, Fish and Wildlife and Parks, Aug. 8, 1979. A revised joint regulation, reinterpreting § 7(a)(2) to require consultation only for actions taken in the United States or on the high seas, was proposed in 1983, 48 Fed.Reg. 29990, and promulgated in 1986, 51 Fed. Reg. 19926; 50 CFR 402.01 (1991).

Shortly thereafter, respondents, organizations dedicated to wildlife conservation and other environmental causes, filed this action against the Secretary of the Interior, seeking a declaratory judgment that the new regulation is in error as to the geographic scope of § 7(a)(2) and an injunction requiring the Secretary to promulgate a new regulation restoring the initial interpretation. The District Court granted the Secretary's motion to dismiss for lack of standing. *Defenders of Wildlife v. Hodel*, 658 F.Supp. 43, 47–48 (Minn. 1987). The Court of Appeals for the Eighth Circuit reversed by a divided vote. *Defenders of Wildlife v. Hodel*, 851 F.2d

1035 (1988). On remand, the Secretary moved for summary judgment on the standing issue, and respondents moved for summary judgment on the merits. The District Court denied the Secretary's motion, on the ground that the Eighth Circuit had already determined the standing question in this case; it granted respondents' merits motion, and ordered the Secretary to publish a revised regulation. *Defenders of Wildlife v. Hodel,* 707 F.Supp. 1082 (Minn. 1989). The Eighth Circuit affirmed. 911 F.2d 117. We granted certiorari, 500 U.S. 915 (1991).

* * *

III

We think the Court of Appeals failed to apply the foregoing principles in denying the Secretary's motion for summary judgment. Respondents had not made the requisite demonstration of (at least) injury and redressability.

A

Respondents' claim to injury is that the lack of consultation with respect to certain funded activities abroad "increas[es] the rate of extinction of endangered and threatened species." Complaint § 5, App. 13. Of course, the desire to use or observe an animal species, even for purely esthetic purposes, is undeniably a cognizable interest for purpose of standing. *See, e.g., Sierra Club v. Morton, 405 U.S. 743.* "But the 'injury in fact' test requires more than an injury to a cognizable interest. It requires that the party seeking review be himself among the injured." *Id.* at 734–735. To survive the Secretary's summary judgment motion, respondents had to submit affidavits or other evidence showing, through specific facts, not only that listed species were in fact being threatened by funded activities abroad, but also that one or more of respondents' members would thereby be "directly" affected apart from their " 'special interest' in th[e] subject." *Id.* at 735, 739. See generally *Hunt v. Washington State Apple Advertising Comm'n* 432 U.S. 333, 334 (1977).

With respect to this aspect of the case, the Court of Appeals focused on the affidavits of two Defenders' members—Joyce Kelly and Amy Skilbred. Ms. Kelly stated that she traveled to Egypt in 1986 and "observed the traditional habitat of the endangered nile crocodile there and intend[s] to do so again, and hope[s] to observe the crocodile directly," and that she "will suffer harm in fact as the result of [the] American . . . role . . . in overseeing the rehabilitation of the Aswan High Dam on the Nile . . . and [in] develop[ing] . . . Egypt's . . . Master Water Plan." App. 101. Ms. Skilbred averred that she traveled to Sri Lanka in 1981 and "observed th[e] habitat" of "endangered species such as the Asian elephant and the leopard" at what is now the site of the Mahaweli project funded by the Agency for International Development (AID), although she "was unable to see any of the endangered species," "this development project," she continued, "will seriously reduce endangered, threatened, and endemic species habitat including areas that I visited ... [which] may severely shorten the future of these species," that threat, she concluded, harmed her because she "intend[s] to return to Sri Lanka in the future and hope[s] to be more fortunate in spotting at least the endangered elephant and leopard." *Id.*, at 145–146. When Ms. Skilbred was asked at a subsequent deposition if and when she had any plans to return to Sri Lanka, she reiterated that "I intend to go back to Sri Lanka," but confessed that she had no current plans: "I don't know [when]. There is a civil war going on right now. I don't know. Not next year, I will say. In the future." *Id.*, at 318.

We shall assume for the sake of argument that these affidavits contain facts showing that certain agency-funded projects threaten listed species—though that is questionable. They plainly contain no facts, however, showing how damage to the species will produce "imminent" injury to Mses. Kelly and Skilbred. That the women "had visited" the areas of the projects before the projects commenced proves nothing. As we have said in a related context, "Past exposure to illegal conduct does not in itself show a present case or controversy regarding injunctive relief ... if unaccompanied by any continuing, present adverse effects." *Lyons*, 461 U.S. at 102 (quoting *O'shea v. Littleton* 414 U.S. 488, 495–496 (1974)). And the affiants' profession of an "inten[t]" to return to the places they had visited before—where they will presumably, this time, be deprived of the opportunity to observe animals of the endangered species—is simply not enough. Such "some day" intentions—without any description of concrete plans, or indeed even any specification of *when* the some day will be—do not support a finding of the "actual or imminent" injury that our cases require. See *supra*, at 2136.[2]

Besides relying upon the Kelly and Skilbred affidavits, respondents propose a series of novel standing theories. The first, inelegantly styled "ecosystem nexus," proposes that any person who uses *any part* of a "contiguous ecosystem" adversely affected by a funded activity has standing even if the activity is located a great

---

2.   ... Our insistence upon these established requirements of standing does not mean that we would, as the dissent contends, "demand ... detailed descriptions" of damages, such as a "nightly schedule of attempted activities" from plaintiffs alleging loss of consortium. *Post,* at 2153. That case and the others posited by the dissent all involve *actual* harm; the existence of standing is clear, though the precise extent of harm remains to be determined at trial. Where there is no actual harm, however, its imminence (though not its precise extent) must be established.

distance away. This approach, as the Court of Appeals correctly observed, is inconsistent with our opinion in *National Wildlife Federation* which held that a plaintiff claiming injury from environmental damage must use the area affected by the challenged activity and not an area roughly "in the vicinity" of it. 497 U.S., at 887–889; see also *Sierra Club*, 405 U.S., at 735. It makes no difference that the general-purpose section of the ESA states that the act was intended in part "to provide a means whereby the ecosystems upon which endangered species and threatened species depend may be conserved," 16 U.S.C. § 1531(b). To say that the act protects ecosystems is not to say that the act creates (if it were possible) rights of action in persons who have not been injured in fact, that is, persons who use portions of an ecosystem not perceptibly affected by the unlawful action in question.

Respondents' other theories are called, alas, the "animal nexus" approach, whereby anyone who has an interest in studying or seeing the endangered animals anywhere on the globe has standing; and the "vocational nexus" approach, under which anyone with a professional interest in such animals can sue. Under these theories, anyone who goes to see Asian elephants in the Bronx Zoo, and anyone who is a keeper of Asian elephants in the Bronx Zoo, has standing to sue because the Director of the Agency for International Development (AID) did not consult with the Secretary regarding the AID-funded project in Sri Lanka. This is beyond all reason. Standing is not "an ingenious academic exercise in the conceivable," *United States v. Students Challenging Regulatory Agency Procedures (SCRAP)*, 412 U.S. 669 (1973), but as we have said requires, at the summary judgment stage, a factual showing of perceptible harm. It is clear that the person who observes or works with a particular animal threatened by a federal decision is facing perceptible harm, since the very subject of his interest will no longer exist. It is even plausible—though it goes to the outermost limit of plausibility—to think that a person who observes or works with animals of a particular species in the very area of the world where that species is threatened by a federal decision is facing such harm, since some animals that might have been the subject of his interest will no longer exist, see *Japan Whaling Assn. v. American Cetacean Society*, 478 U.S. 221, 231, n. 4 (1986). It goes beyond the limit, however, and into pure speculation and fantasy, to say that anyone who observes or works with an endangered species, anywhere in the world, is appreciably harmed by a single project affecting some portion of that species with which he has no more specific connection.[3]

3. ... It cannot be that a person with an interest in an animal automatically has standing to enjoin federal threats to that species of animal, anywhere in the world. Were that the case, the plaintiff in *Sierra Club*, for example,

B

Besides failing to show injury, respondents failed to demonstrate redressability. Instead of attacking the separate decisions to fund particular projects allegedly causing them harm, respondents chose to challenge a more generalized level of Government action (rules regarding consultation), the invalidation of which would affect all overseas projects. . . .

The most obvious problem in the present case is redressability. Since the agencies funding the projects were not parties to the case, the District Court could accord relief only against the Secretary: He could be ordered to revise his regulation to require consultation for foreign projects. But this would not remedy respondents' alleged injury unless the funding agencies were bound by the Secretary's regulation, which is very much an open question. . . . with respect to consultation the initiative, and hence arguably the initial responsibility for determining statutory necessity, lies with the agencies, see § 1536(a)(2). . . .

Respondents assert that this legal uncertainty did not affect redressability (and hence standing) because the District Court itself could resolve the issue of the Secretary's authority as a necessary part of its standing inquiry. Assuming that it is appropriate to resolve an issue of law such as this in connection with a threshold standing inquiry, resolution by the District Court would not have remedied respondents' alleged injury anyway, because it would not have been binding upon the agencies. They were not parties to the suit, and there is no reason they should be obliged to honor an incidental legal determination the suit produced. The Court of Appeals tried to finesse this problem by simply proclaiming that "[w]e are satisfied that an injunction requiring the Secretary to publish [respondents' desired] regulatio[n] . . . would result in consultation." *Defenders of Wildlife*, 851 F.2d, at 1042, 1043–1044. We do not know what would justify that confidence, particularly when the Justice Department (presumably after consultation with the agencies) has taken the position that the regulation is not

could have avoided the necessity of establishing anyone's use of Mineral King by merely identifying one of its members interested in an endangered species of flora or fauna at that location. Justice BLACKMAN's accusation that a special rule is being crafted for "environmental claims," *post*, at 2154, is correct, but *he* is the craftsman. Justice STEVENS, by contrast, would allow standing on an apparent "animal nexus" theory to all plaintiffs whose interest in the animals is "genuine." Such plaintiffs, we are told, do not have to visit the animals because the animals are analogous to family members. *Post*, at 2148–2149, and n. 2. We decline to join Justice STEVENS in this Linnaean leap. It is unclear to us what constitutes a "genuine" interest; how it differs from a "nongenuine" interest (which nonetheless prompted a plaintiff to file suit); and why such an interest in animals should be different from such an interest in anything else that is the subject of a lawsuit.

binding.[5] The short of the matter is that redress of the only injury in fact respondents complain of requires action (termination of funding until consultation) by the individual funding agencies; and any relief the District Court could have provided in this suit against the Secretary was not likely to produce that action.

A further impediment to redressability is the fact that the agencies generally supply only a fraction of the funding for a foreign project. AID, for example, has provided less than 10% of the funding for the Mahaweli project. Respondents have produced nothing to indicate that the projects they have named will either be suspended, or do less harm to listed species, if that fraction is eliminated. As in *Simon*, 426 U.S., at 43–44, it is entirely conjectural whether the non-agency activity that affects respondents will be altered or affected by the agency activity they seek to achieve. There is no standing.

IV

The Court of Appeals found that respondents had standing for an additional reason: because they had suffered a "procedural injury." The so-called "citizen-suit" provision of the ESA provides, in pertinent part, that "any person may commence a civil suit on his own behalf (A) to enjoin any person, including the United States and any other governmental instrumentality or agency . . . who is alleged to be in violation of any provision of this chapter" 16 U.S.C. § 1540(g). The court held that, because § 7(a)(2) requires interagency consultation, the citizen-suit provision creates a "procedural righ[t]" to consultation in all "persons"—so that *anyone* can file suit in federal court to challenge the Secretary's (or presumably any other official's) failure to follow the assertedly correct consultative procedure, notwithstanding his or her inability to allege any discrete injury flowing from that failure. 911 F.2d, at 121–122. To understand the remarkable nature of this holding one must be clear about what it does *not* rest upon: This is not a case where plaintiffs are seeking to enforce a procedural requirement the disregard of which could impair a separate concrete interest of theirs (*e.g.,* the procedural requirement for a hearing prior to denial of their license application, or the procedural requirement for an environmental impact statement before a federal facility is constructed next door

---

5. Seizing on the fortuity that the case has made its way to *this* Court, Justice STEVENS protests that no agency would ignore "an authoritative construction of the [ESA] by this Court." *Post,* at 2149. In that he is probably correct; in concluding from it that plaintiffs have demonstrated redressability, he is not. Since, as we have pointed out above, standing is to be determined as of the commencement of suit; since at that point it could certainly not be known that the suit would reach this Court; and since it is not likely that an agency would feel compelled to accede to the legal view of a district court expressed in a case to which it was not a party; redressability clearly did not exist.

to them).[7] Nor is it simply a case where concrete injury has been suffered by many persons, as in mass fraud or mass tort situations. Nor, finally, is it the unusual case in which Congress has created a concrete private interest in the outcome of a suit against a private party for the government's benefit, by providing a cash bounty for the victorious plaintiff. Rather, the court held that the injury-in-fact requirement had been satisfied by congressional conferral upon *all* persons of an abstract, self-contained, noninstrumental "right" to have the Executive observe the procedures required by law. We reject this view.[8]

We have consistently held that a plaintiff raising only a generally available grievance about government—claiming only harm to his and every citizen's interest in proper application of the Constitution and laws, and seeking relief that no more directly and tangibly benefits him than it does the public at large—does not state an Article III case or controversy....

* * *

To be sure, our generalized-grievance cases have typically involved Government violation of procedures assertedly ordained by the Constitution rather than the Congress. But there is absolutely no basis for making the Article III inquiry turn on the source of the asserted right. Whether the courts were to act on their own, or at the invitation of Congress, in ignoring the concrete injury requirement described in our cases, they would be discarding a principle fundamental to the separate and distinct constitutional role of the Third Branch—one of the essential elements that identifies those "Cases" and "Controversies" that are the business of the courts rather than of the political branches. "The province of the court," as Chief Justice Marshall said in *Marbury v. Madison*, 5 U.S. (1 Cranch) 137, 170, 2 L. Ed. 60 (1803), "is, solely, to decide on the rights of individuals." Vindicating the *public* interest (including the public interest in Government observance of the Constitution and

---

7. There is this much truth to the assertion that "procedural rights" are special: The person who has been accorded a procedural right to protect his concrete interests can assert that right without meeting all the normal standards for redressability and immediacy. Thus, under our case law, one living adjacent to the site for proposed construction of a federally licensed dam has standing to challenge the licensing agency's failure to prepare an environmental impact statement, even though he cannot establish with any certainty that the statement will cause the license to be withheld or altered, and even though the dam will not be completed for many years.... What respondents' "procedural rights" argument seeks, however, is quite different from this: standing for persons who have no concrete interests affected—persons who live (and propose to live) at the other end of the country from the dam.

8. The dissent's discussion of this aspect of the case, *post*, at 2157–2160, distorts our opinion. We do *not* hold that an individual cannot enforce procedural rights; he assuredly can, so long as the procedures in question are designed to protect some threatened concrete interest of his that is the ultimate basis of his standing....

laws) is the function of Congress and the Chief Executive. The question presented here is whether the public interest in proper administration of the laws (specifically, in agencies' observance of a particular, statutorily prescribed procedure) can be converted into an individual right by a statute that denominates it as such, and that permits all citizens (or, for that matter, a subclass of citizens who suffer no distinctive concrete harm) to sue. If the concrete injury requirement has the separation-of-powers significance we have always said, the answer must be obvious: To permit Congress to convert the undifferentiated public interest in executive officers' compliance with the law into an "individual right" vindicable in the courts is to permit Congress to transfer from the President to the courts the Chief Executive's most important constitutional duty, to "take Care that the Laws be faithfully executed," Art. II, § 3. It would enable the courts, with the permission of Congress, "to assume a position of authority over the governmental acts of another and co-equal department," *Massachusetts v. Mellon*, 262 U.S., at 489, and to become " 'virtually continuing monitors of the wisdom and soundness of Executive action.' " *Allen supra*, 468 U.S., at 760 (quoting *Laird v. Tatum*, 408 U.S. 1, 15 (1972)). We have always rejected that vision of our role:

> When Congress passes an Act empowering administrative agencies to carry on governmental activities, the power of those agencies is circumscribed by the authority granted. This permits the courts to participate in law enforcement entrusted to administrative bodies only to the extent necessary to protect justiciable individual rights against administrative action fairly beyond the granted powers.... This is very far from assuming that the courts are charged more than administrators or legislators with the protection of the rights of the people. Congress and the Executive supervise the acts of administrative agents.... But under Article III, Congress established courts to adjudicate cases and controversies as to claims of infringement of individual rights whether by unlawful action of private persons or by the exertion of unauthorized administrative power. *Stark v. Wickard*, 321 U.S. 288, 309–310 (1944) (footnote omitted).

* * *

Nothing in this contradicts the principle that "[t]he ... injury required by Art. III may exist solely by virtue of 'statutes creating legal rights, the invasion of which creates standing.' " *Warth*, 422 U.S., at 500 (quoting *Linda R. S. v. Richard D.*, 410 U.S. 614, 617, n. 3 (1973)). Both of the cases used by *Linda R. S.* as an illustration of that principle involved Congress' elevating to the status of legally cognizable injuries concrete, *de facto* injuries that were previously inadequate in law (namely, injury to an individual's personal interest in living in a racially integrated community, see *Trafficante v. Metropolitan Life Ins. Co.*, 409 U.S. 205, 208–212 (1972), and injury to a company's interest in marketing its product free from competition, see *Hardin v. Kentucky Utilities Co.*, 390 U.S. 1, 6 (1968)). As we said in *Sierra Club* "[Statutory] broadening [of] the categories of injury that may be alleged in support of standing is a different matter from abandoning the requirement that the party seeking review must himself have suffered an injury." 405 U.S., at 738. Whether or not the principle set forth in *Warth* can be extended beyond that distinction, it is clear that in suits against the Government, at least, the concrete injury requirement must remain.

* * *

We hold that respondents lack standing to bring this action and that the Court of Appeals erred in denying the summary judgment motion filed by the United States. The opinion of the Court of Appeals is hereby reversed, and the cause is remanded for proceedings consistent with this opinion.

It is so ordered.

Justice KENNEDY, with whom Justice SOUTER joins, concurring in part and concurring in the judgment.

Although I agree with the essential parts of the Court's analysis, I write separately to make several observations.

I agree with the Court's conclusion in Part III–A that, on the record before us, respondents have failed to demonstrate that they themselves are "among the injured." *Sierra Club v. Morton*, 405 U.S. 727, 735 (1972).

While it may seem trivial to require that Mses. Kelly and Skilbred acquire airline tickets to the project sites or announce a date certain upon which they will return, see *ante*, at 2138, this is not a case where it is reasonable to assume that the affiants will be using the sites on a regular basis, see *Sierra Club v. Morton*, 405 U.S., at 735, n. 8, nor do the affiants claim to have visited the sites since the projects commenced. With respect to the Court's discussion of respondents' "ecosystem nexus," "animal nexus," and "vocational nexus" theories, *ante*, at 2139–2140, I agree that on this record respondents' showing is insufficient to establish standing on any of these bases. I am not willing to foreclose the possibility, however, that in different circumstances a nexus theory similar to those proffered here might support a claim to standing. See *Japan Whaling Assn. v. American Cetacean Society*, 478 U.S. 221, 231, n. 4 (1986) ("[R]espondents ... undoubtedly have alleged a sufficient 'injury in fact' in that the whale watching and studying of their members will be adversely affected by continued whale harvesting'').

* * *

I also join Part IV of the Court's opinion with the following observations. As Government programs and policies become more complex and far reaching, we must be sensitive to the articulation of new rights of action that do not have clear analogs in our common-law tradition. Modern litigation has progressed far from the paradigm of Marbury suing Madison to get his commission, *Marbury v. Madison*, 5 U.S. (1 Cranch) 137 (1803), or Ogden seeking an injunction to halt Gibbons' steamboat operations, *Gibbons v. Ogden*, 22 U.S. (9 Wheat.) 1, (1824). In my view, Congress has the power to define injuries and articulate chains of causation that will give rise to a case or controversy where none existed before, and I do not read the Court's opinion to suggest a contrary view. See *Warth v. Seldin*, 422 U.S. 490, 500 (1975); *ante,* at 2145–2146. In exercising this power, however, Congress must at the very least identify the injury it seeks to vindicate and relate the injury to the class of persons entitled to bring suit. The citizen-suit provision of the Endangered Species Act does not meet these minimal requirements, because while the statute purports to confer a right on "any person . . . to enjoin . . . the United States and any other governmental instrumentality or agency . . . who is alleged to be in violation of any provision of this chapter," it does not of its own force establish that there is an injury in "any person" by virtue of any "violation." 16 U.S.C. § 1540(g)(1)(A).

* * *

The Court's holding that there is an outer limit to the power of Congress to confer rights of action is a direct and necessary consequence of the case and controversy limitations found in Article III. I agree that it would exceed those limitations if, at the behest of Congress and in the absence of any showing of concrete injury, we were to entertain citizen suits to vindicate the public's nonconcrete interest in the proper administration of the laws. While it does not matter how many persons have been injured by the challenged action, the party bringing suit must show that the action injures him in a concrete and personal way . . . .

* * *

Justice STEVENS, concurring in the judgment.

Because I am not persuaded that Congress intended the consultation requirement in § 7(a)(2) of the Endangered Species Act of 1973 (ESA), 16 U.S.C. § 1536(a)(2), to apply to activities in foreign countries, I concur in the judgment of reversal. I do not, however, agree with the Court's conclusion that respondents lack standing because the threatened injury to their interest in protecting the environment and studying endangered species is not "imminent." Nor do I agree with the plurality's additional conclusion that respondents' injury is not "redressable" in this litigation.

I

In my opinion a person who has visited the critical habitat of an endangered species has a professional interest in preserving the species and its habitat, and intends to revisit them in the future has standing to challenge agency action that threatens their destruction. Congress has found that a wide variety of endangered species of fish, wildlife, and plants are of "aesthetic, ecological, educational, historical, recreational, and scientific value to the Nation and its people." 16 U.S.C. § 1531(a)(3). Given that finding, we have no license to demean the importance of the interest that particular individuals may have in observing any species or its habitat, whether those individuals are motivated by esthetic enjoyment, an interest in professional research, or an economic interest in preservation of the species. Indeed, this Court has often held that injuries to such interests are sufficient to confer standing...

The Court nevertheless concludes that respondents have not suffered "injury in fact" because they have not shown that the harm to the endangered species will produce "imminent" injury to them. See *ante,* at 2138. I disagree. An injury to an individual's interest in studying or enjoying a species and its natural habitat occurs when someone (whether it be the Government or a private party) takes action that harms that species and habitat. In my judgment, therefore, the "imminence" of such an injury should be measured by the timing and likelihood of the threatened environmental harm, rather than—as the Court seems to suggest, *ante,* at 2138–2139, and n. 2—by the time that might elapse between the present and the time when the individuals would visit the area if no such injury should occur.

* * *

... [W]e have denied standing to plaintiffs whose likelihood of suffering any concrete adverse effect from the challenged action was speculative. See, *e.g., Whitmore v. Arkansas,* 495 U.S. 149, 158–159 (1990); *Los Angeles v. Lyons,* 461 U.S. 95, 105 (1983); *O'Shea,* 414 U.S., at 497. In this case, however, the likelihood that respondents will be injured by the destruction of the endangered species is not speculative. If respondents are genuinely interested in the preservation of the endangered species and intend to study or observe these animals in the future, their injury will occur as soon as the animals are destroyed. Thus the only potential source of "speculation" in this case is whether respondents' intent to study or observe the animals is genuine.[2] In my view, Joyce Kelly and Amy Skilbred have introduced sufficient evidence to negate petitioner's contention that their claims of injury are "speculative" or "conjectural." As Justice BLACKMUN explains, *post,* at 2152–2153, a reasonable finder of fact could conclude, from their past visits, their professional backgrounds, and their affidavits and deposition testimony, that Ms. Kelly and Ms. Skilbred will return to the project sites and, consequently, will be injured by the destruction of the endangered species and critical habitat.

* * *

In short, a reading of the entire statute persuades me that Congress did not intend the consultation requirement in § 7(a)(2) to apply to activities in foreign countries. Accordingly, notwithstanding my disagreement with the Court's disposition of the standing question, I concur in its judgment.

Justice BLACKMUN, with whom Justice O'CONNOR joins, dissenting.

I part company with the Court in this case in two respects. First, I believe that respondents have raised genuine issues of fact—sufficient to survive summary judgment—both as to injury and as to redressability. Second, I question the Court's breadth of language in rejecting standing for "procedural" injuries. I fear the Court seeks to impose fresh limitations on the constitutional authority of Congress to allow citizen suits in the federal courts for injuries deemed "procedural" in nature. I dissent.

* * *

1

Were the Court to apply the proper standard for summary judgment, I believe it would conclude that the sworn affidavits and

---

2. As we recognized in *Sierra Club v. Morton*, 405 U.S., at 735, the impact of changes in the esthetics or ecology of a particular area does "not fall indiscriminately upon every citizen. The alleged injury will be felt directly only by those who use [the area,] and for whom the aesthetic and recreational values of the area will be lessened. . . ." Thus, respondents would not be injured by the challenged projects if they had not visited the sites or studied the threatened species and habitat. But, as discussed above, respondents did visit the sites; moreover, they have expressed an intent to do so again. This intent to revisit the area is significant evidence tending to confirm the genuine character of respondents' interest, but I am not at all sure that an intent to revisit would be indispensable in every case. The interest that confers standing in a case of this kind is comparable, though by no means equivalent, to the interest in a relationship among family members that can be immediately harmed by the death of an absent member, regardless of when, if ever, a family reunion is planned to occur. Thus, if the facts of this case had shown repeated and regular visits by the respondents, cf. *ante,* at 2146 (opinion of KENNEDY, J.), proof of an intent to revisit might well be superfluous.

deposition testimony of Joyce Kelly and Amy Skilbred advance sufficient facts to create a genuine issue for trial concerning whether one or both would be imminently harmed by the Aswan and Mahaweli projects. In the first instance, as the Court itself concedes, the affidavits contained facts making it at least "questionable" (and therefore within the province of the factfinder) that certain agency-funded projects threaten listed species. *Ante,* at 2138. The only remaining issue, then, is whether Kelly and Skilbred have shown that they personally would suffer imminent harm.

I think a reasonable finder of fact could conclude from the information in the affidavits and deposition testimony that either Kelly or Skilbred will soon return to the project sites, thereby satisfying the "actual or imminent" injury standard.... Contrary to the Court's contention that Kelly's and Skilbred's past visits "prov[e] nothing," *ibid.,* the fact of their past visits could demonstrate to a reasonable factfinder that Kelly and Skilbred have the requisite resources and personal interest in the preservation of the species endangered by the Aswan and Mahaweli projects to make good on their intention to return again. Cf. *Los Angeles v. Lyons,* 461 U.S. 95, 102 (1983) ("Past wrongs were evidence bearing on whether there is a real and immediate threat of repeated injury") (internal quotation marks omitted). Similarly, Kelly's and Skilbred's professional backgrounds in wildlife preservation, see App. 100, 144, 309–310, also make it likely—at least far more likely than for the average citizen—that they would choose to visit these areas of the world where species are vanishing.

By requiring a "description of concrete plans" or "specification of *when* the some day [for a return visit] will be," *ante,* at 8, the Court, in my view, demands what is likely an empty formality. No substantial barriers prevent Kelly or Skilbred from simply purchasing plane tickets to return to the Aswan and Mahaweli projects....

I fear the Court's demand for detailed descriptions of future conduct will do little to weed out those who are genuinely harmed from those who are not. More likely, it will resurrect a code-pleading formalism in federal court summary judgment practice, as federal courts, newly doubting their jurisdiction, will demand more and more particularized showings of future harm. Just to survive summary judgment, for example, a property owner claiming a decline in the value of his property from governmental action might have to specify the exact date he intends to sell his property and show that there is a market for the property, lest it be surmised he might not sell again. A nurse turned down for a job on grounds of her race had better be prepared to show on what date she was prepared to start work, that she had arranged daycare for her child, and that she would not have accepted work at another hospital instead....

2

The Court also concludes that injury is lacking, because respondents' allegations of "ecosystem nexus" failed to demonstrate sufficient proximity to the site of the environmental harm. *Ante,* at 2139. To support that conclusion, the Court mis-characterizes our decision in *Lujan v. National Wildlife Federation*, 497 U.S. 871 (1990), as establishing a general rule that "a plaintiff claiming injury from environmental damage must use the area affected by the challenged activity." *Ante,* at 2139. In *National Wildlife Federation* the Court required specific geographical proximity because of the particular type of harm alleged in that case: harm to the plaintiff's visual enjoyment of nature from mining activities. 497 U.S., at 888. One cannot suffer from the sight of a ruined landscape without being close enough to see the sites actually being mined. Many environmental injuries, however, cause harm distant from the area immediately affected by the challenged action. Environmental destruction may affect animals traveling over vast geographical ranges, see, *e.g., Japan Whaling Assn. v. American Cetacean Society*, 478 U.S. 221 (1986) (harm to American whale watchers from Japanese whaling activities), or rivers running long geographical courses, see, *e.g., Arkansas v. Oklahoma*, 503 U.S. 91 (1992) (harm to Oklahoma residents from wastewater treatment plant 39 miles from border). It cannot seriously be contended that a litigant's failure to use the precise or exact site where animals are slaughtered or where toxic waste is dumped into a river means he or she cannot show injury.

The Court also rejects respondents' claim of vocational or professional injury. The Court says that it is "beyond all reason" that a zoo "keeper" of Asian elephants would have standing to contest his Government's participation in the eradication of all the Asian elephants in another part of the world. *Ante,* at 2139. I am unable to see how the distant location of the destruction *necessarily* (for purposes of ruling at summary judgment) mitigates the harm to the elephant keeper. If there is no more access to a future supply of the animal that sustains a keeper's livelihood, surely there is harm.

I have difficulty imagining this Court applying its rigid principles of geographic formalism anywhere outside the context of environmental claims. As I understand it, environmental plaintiffs are under no special constitutional standing disabilities. Like other plaintiffs, they need show only that the action they challenge has injured them, without necessarily showing they happened to be physically near the location of the alleged wrong. The Court's decision today should not be interpreted "to foreclose the possibility ... that in different circumstances a nexus theory similar to those proffered here might support a claim to standing." *Ante,* at

2146 (KENNEDY, J., concurring in part and concurring in judgment).

B

A plurality of the Court suggests that respondents have not demonstrated redressability: a likelihood that a court ruling in their favor would remedy their injury. *Duke Power Co. v. Carolina Environmental Study Group, Inc.*, 438 U.S. 59, 74–75, and n. 20 (1978) (plaintiff must show "substantial likelihood" that relief requested will redress the injury). The plurality identifies two obstacles. The first is that the "action agencies" (*e.g.*, AID) cannot be required to undertake consultation with petitioner Secretary, because they are not directly bound as parties to the suit and are otherwise not indirectly bound by being subject to petitioner Secretary's regulation. Petitioner, however, officially and publicly has taken the position that his regulations regarding consultation under § 7 of the act are binding on action agencies. 50 CFR § 402.14(a)(1991). And he has previously taken the same position in this very litigation, ...

Emphasizing that none of the action agencies are parties to this suit (and having rejected the possibility of their being indirectly bound by petitioner's regulation), the plurality concludes that "there is no reason they should be obliged to honor an incidental legal determination the suit produced." *Ante*, at 2141. I am not as willing as the plurality is to assume that agencies at least will not try to follow the law. Moreover, I wonder if the plurality has not overlooked the extensive involvement from the inception of this litigation by the Department of State and AID. Under principles of collateral estoppel, these agencies are precluded from subsequently relitigating the issues decided in this suit.

* * *

As a result, I believe respondents' injury would likely be redressed by a favorable decision.

The second redressability obstacle relied on by the plurality is that "the [action] agencies generally supply only a fraction of the funding for a foreign project." *Ante*, at 2142. What this Court might "generally" take to be true does not eliminate the existence of a genuine issue of fact to withstand summary judgment. Even if the action agencies supply only a fraction of the funding for a particular foreign project, it remains at least a question for the finder of fact whether threatened withdrawal of that fraction would affect foreign government conduct sufficiently to avoid harm to listed species.

* * *

II

The Court concludes that any "procedural injury" suffered by respondents is insufficient to confer standing. It rejects the view that the "injury-in-fact requirement [is] satisfied by congressional conferral upon *all* persons of an abstract, self-contained, noninstrumental 'right' to have the Executive observe the procedures required by law." *Ante,* at 2143. Whatever the Court might mean with that very broad language, it cannot be saying that "procedural injuries" *as a class* are necessarily insufficient for purposes of Article III standing.

Most governmental conduct can be classified as "procedural." Many injuries caused by governmental conduct, therefore, are categorizable at some level of generality as "procedural" injuries. Yet, these injuries are not categorically beyond the pale of redress by the federal courts. When the Government, for example, "procedurally" issues a pollution permit, those affected by the permittee's pollutants are not without standing to sue. Only later cases will tell just what the Court means by its intimation that "procedural" injuries are not constitutionally cognizable injuries. In the meantime, I have the greatest of sympathy for the courts across the country that will struggle to understand the Court's standardless exposition of this concept today.

The Court expresses concern that allowing judicial enforcement of "agencies' observance of a particular, statutorily prescribed procedure" would "transfer from the President to the courts the Chief Executive's most important constitutional duty, to 'take Care that the Laws be faithfully executed,' Art. II, § 3." *Ante,* at 2145. In fact, the principal effect of foreclosing judicial enforcement of such procedures is to transfer power into the hands of the Executive at the expense—not of the courts—but of Congress, from which that power originates and emanates.

Under the Court's anachronistically formal view of the separation of powers, Congress legislates pure, substantive mandates and has no business structuring the procedural manner in which the Executive implements these mandates. To be sure, in the ordinary course, Congress does legislate in black-and-white terms of affirmative commands or negative prohibitions on the conduct of officers of the Executive Branch. In complex regulatory areas, however, Congress often legislates, as it were, in procedural shades of gray. That is, it sets forth substantive policy goals and provides for their attainment by requiring Executive Branch officials to follow certain procedures, for example, in the form of reporting, consultation, and certification requirements.

* * *

It is to be hoped that over time the Court will acknowledge that some classes of procedural duties are so enmeshed with the prevention of a substantive, concrete harm that an individual plaintiff may be able to demonstrate a sufficient likelihood of injury just through the breach of that procedural duty. For example, in the context of the NEPA requirement of environmental-impact statements, this Court has acknowledged "it is now well settled that NEPA itself does not mandate particular results [and] simply prescribes the necessary process," but *these procedures are almost certain to affect the agency's substantive decision." Robertson v. Methow Valley Citizens Council*, 490 U.S., at 350 (emphasis added). See also *Andrus v. Sierra Club*, 442 U.S. 347, 350–351 (1979) ("If environmental concerns are not interwoven into the fabric of agency planning, the 'action-forcing' characteristics of [the environmental-impact statement requirement] would be lost"). This acknowledgment of an inextricable link between procedural and substantive harm does not reflect improper appellate fact finding. It reflects nothing more than the proper deference owed to the judgment of a coordinate branch—Congress—that certain procedures are directly tied to protection against a substantive harm.

* * *

III

In conclusion, I cannot join the Court on what amounts to a slash-and-burn expedition through the law of environmental standing. In my view, "[t]he very essence of civil liberty certainly consists in the right of every individual to claim the protection of the laws, whenever he receives an injury." *Marbury v. Madison*, 1 Cranch 137 (1803).

I dissent.

Notes & Questions

How does Lujan II build upon Lujan I in terms of fixing the requirements for standing to represent environmental entities in court? How are the issues the same? Different?

Do the number of dissents and separate opinions mean that the court is less convinced of its narrowing of standing to the constitutional—common law rules?

Compare and contrast the standing with the redressibility issues. Which is the more powerful argument? Are there other common law rules of standing that could be applied here to make a case for standing? Explain.

What is the "airline ticket test"? How is it applied? Is it truly a point of the majority opinion, or something created in the dissent to make the majority argument seem less persuasive?

Is Justice Blackmun right to contend that environmentalists are held to a higher standard to establish standing than others seeking redress? When you read Chapter 4, create an argument for and against this point utilizing an Ecosystem Paradigm approach to the question of 'resources.'

Is statute standing a dead issue, being collapsed into the traditional requirements of common law standing? If so, what ramifications might this have for those who wish to defend natural systems in court? If not, what role is now played by statute standing?

What is the intent of Congress in creating citizen suit provisions? In this case the majority, lead by Justice Scalia, argues against the constitutionality of citizen suit provisions. Is this an argument against stature standing? Is it a persuasive one? Is statute standing necessary to the proper defense of natural systems from economic exploitation? If so, what would happen if, at a later date, the Supreme Court were to strike down the citizen suit provisions of environmental and natural resource statutes?

Given *Morton*, *Lujan I*, and *Lujan II*, what must one demonstrate to sue on behalf of nature? Is it the Constitution, Statute Standing (APA & Citizen Suits), or the traditional Common Law Prerequisites of standing that are the most critical to establishing one's right to take an environmental issue to court?

EXERCISE: LAW FROM SCRATCH

Anticipating its full exposition further along in the book, begin with the premise of the Ecosystem Paradigm for policy design in the law, that nature ought to have standing independent of human use of it. How might you establish this status for nature? Search the databases for cases where common law standing applied to non-humans was successful. If none can be found how else might you bring nature into the common law? What are the difficulties here? Next examine the legal history of statute standing under the APA and Citizen Suits to see if this is the best route to establish new law regarding the standing of nature. How might this work? What avenues of argument could be used to establish nature's status as more than mere resources? How would the statute route run into trouble with common and constitutional law? While you undertake this exercise remember what the Supreme Court has argued in the cases presented above. How do you make an argument for change that will work to reverse these trends?

The Common Law

The Common Law[37] is that law made by judges and the courts as they attempt to decide similar cases in similar ways creating a

---

37. This is distinct from common law as a system of law prevalent in   Britain and its former colonies.

set of conventions or rules that govern the interactions of private parties in matters of rights and responsibilities. This common law assumes that private matters between individuals are best settled on a case-by-case basis where each interaction over rights or responsibilities is taken and solved on its own terms. Each decision is expected to be calculated on the basis of the conventional pattern of how these cases have been treated in the past, that is, based on the principle of *stare decisis* or the idea that a court should follow its own previous decisions and those of courts of equal or greater seniority within their system of law. This principle has the utility that it sets expectation and establishes order and social cooperation.

A dependence on past decisions, and the necessary pre-existence of a dilemma before the law can intercede, predisposes the common law toward specific legal interactions for which after-the-fact remedy is reliable. This is law that looks to redress a particular failure of a particular human interaction; it is not created to prevent harm or cover classes of human interactions. Although more general rules evolve from multiple cases within the common law, these rules are not applied, as statutory law is, universally, to all before the fact, but only to specific 'like' parties after their transaction is complete. Therefore, common law principles can be said to govern private party transactions in the absence of statutory law.

Resources which are owned, used, and developed by private parties are subject to common law doctrines. Environmental disputes involving public land and joint natural media are more often resolved by application of administrative, statutory, or constitutional law principles, but common law has pride of place in that before there were any statutory or administrative regulations regarding the use of nature or extraction of resources from it, the rules and patterns of the common law existed to regulate human conflict over environmental and resource matters. But let us examine two examples where common law and environmental law interact. First the environmental law that bears on two specific doctrines of property and, second, on the law of nuisance.

1) Public Trust & Equitable Apportionment Doctrines

Property law protects state interests in the use of navigable waters by circumscribing private use of such waters. Two common law property doctrines have evolved to protect this interest: the public trust doctrine and the doctrine of equitable apportionment.

The essence of the ***public trust doctrine*** is that private rights to the use of navigable waters are subject to public rights to such waters for purposes of navigation, commerce, fishing, and recreation. The doctrine may arise when land owned by a private party completely surrounds a navigable lake or abuts a navigable stream. In such cases the issue is whether the private landowner can prevent public access to these waters on the grounds that they are privately owned. The general rule is that if the waters in question are found to be navigable, or suitable for commerce, navigation, fishing or recreation, and if access to such waters can be accomplished lawfully, a private landowner cannot exclude the public from the use of such water.[38] The public trust doctrine has also been imposed to limit the private use of non-navigable waters which are found to be suitable for public purposes, such as recreation, and which are lawfully accessible to the public by means of navigable streams or dedicated roadways.[39]

The public trust doctrine allows the state to assert superior rights in privately owned lands and waters on behalf of the public. Courts have also applied the public trust doctrine to prevent the exercise of rights to privately held timber and grass cutting, where such rights involved public lands.[40]

Equitable apportionment is a federal common law doctrine applied by the United States Supreme Court to govern disputes between states regarding the use of interstate waters flowing within their boundaries. In such cases, the state asserts the rights of all citizens of the state, not just the rights of separate individuals. Under the doctrine of equitable apportionment, the amount of non-navigable interstate waters allocated to a state is determined by three factors. First, the Court will assess the reasonableness and efficiency of current or proposed uses of water within a state. Second, the Court will determine whether the benefit caused by diversion of interstate water by one state substantially outweighs the harm to another state caused by that diversion. Third, the Court will decide whether a state that suffers loss because of another state's diversion of interstate waters can compensate for the loss by use of reasonable conservation measures.

In cases concerning the allocation of navigable waters between states, private rights to the use of such waters may be severely restricted because of the public nature of navigable waters and the

---

38. J.J.N.P. Co. v. Utah, 655 P.2d 1133 (Utah 1982) (despite the fact that a natural lake was completely surrounded by privately owned land, the private landowner could not exclude the public from using the lake for fishing since the lake was suitable for fishing).

39. See Bott v. Commission of Natural Resources, 415 Mich. 45, 327 N.W.2d 838 (1982).

40. Cushing v. Maine, 434 A.2d 486 (Me.1981) (successors to timber and grass cutting rights, originally granted by the state, could not cut timber and grass on publicly reserved township lots which were held by the state in trust for public usage).

superior state interest in the use of such waters for the benefit of the public. In Badgley v. City of New York, 606 F.2d 358 (2d Cir.1979), an impairment of private parties' water rights was caused by diversion of headwaters of the Delaware River by New York City for public water purposes. Since the injured parties were residents of a state which had been a party to four previous U.S. Supreme Court cases where equitable apportionment had been used to allocate the waters of the Delaware River and its tributaries, the water rights of the injured parties were held to be already adjudicated, and consequently, unable to be relitigated without consent of the parties' state.[41]

2) Nuisance

Private nuisance actions, trespass, and negligence are tort law[42] actions individuals use to protect their property and persons from unreasonable injury by persons conducting resource extraction or other activity that pollutes the natural environment. Although statutory relief through agency action predominates, these common law remedies were the original means of preventing harm to persons or the environment, and they still play a role in areas where no specific statute or administrative law has been written to regulate a use of the environment that causes pollution.[43]

Traditional tort law holds that a private business may constitute a nuisance if its operations significantly interfere with the use and enjoyment of adjoining private property. Modern tort law has expanded the scope of interference to include nuisances caused by the pollution of air and water. The property owner harmed by the operations of an air or water polluter must show substantial harm to property or health in order to bring a private nuisance action. If successful, the business against which a nuisance action is brought may be enjoined from further activities and may be required to pay damages to the property owner.[44]

Most environmental pollution is regulated by statutes that may allow private enforcement through injunction, or the application of penalties and fines if enforced by the government. However, private

---

41. We need to clarify that equitable apportionment is applied intrastate as well as inter-state. In addition, it is important to note that Western water allocation law differs from Eastern.

42. See, for example, ARTHUR BEST & DAVID W. BARNES, BASIC TORT LAW (2d ed. 2007) or RICHARD A. EPSTEIN, CASES AND MATERIALS ON TORTS (8th ed. 2004).

43. Missouri v. Illinois, 200 U.S. 496 (1906) and Georgia v. Tennessee Copper

Co. 206 U.S. 230 (1907), especially for Justice Holmes argument for a distinction between a private and a public nuisance.

44. See Jost v. Dairyland Power Co-op., 45 Wis.2d 164, 172 N.W.2d 647 (1969); Bie v. Ingersoll, 27 Wis.2d 490, 135 N.W.2d 250 (1965) (is an asphalt plant a private nuisance even though the plant was in an industrial zone which permitted it?).

damages are most often awarded under private tort actions. Consequently, courts increasingly allow private tort action to address injury despite the availability of statutory relief for environmental causes of action. This judicial receptiveness is in response to the growing scientific ability to link environmental nuisances to actual injury.[45] Specific property rights, such as access to sunlight for solar-energy purposes, may also be protected by private nuisance actions.[46] In addition to being subject to liability under nuisance law, businesses which conduct resource extraction operations near private lands may be liable in damages for the torts of trespass, conversion or negligence.[47]

In this section we shall examine the effectiveness of the common law, in terms of nuisance in regulating humanity's use of natural systems before there were specific statutes addressing these uses. Specifically, one should read these cases with the understanding that they are instances of treating pollution of the environment not as a collective goods problem[48] but as a private matter between specific parties where the market is the main allocation or institutional governance system. Here, redress after the fact through monetary compensation is usually considered adequate to solve the legal disputes over rights and responsibilities.

§§

STATE OF MISSOURI v. STATE OF ILLINOIS

Supreme Court of the United States, 1906.
200 U.S. 496.

Mr. Justice HOLMES delivered the opinion of the court:

45. See National Energy Corp. v. O'Quinn, 223 Va. 83, 286 S.E.2d 181 (1982) (despite state and federal laws regulating environmental issues, property owners were entitled to damages from coal preparation plant whose operations caused harm to health and property by emission of loud noises and excessive amounts of coal dust).

46. See Prah v. Maretti, 108 Wis.2d 223, 321 N.W.2d 182 (1982) (construction of a house created a private nuisance because it would obstruct an adjoining property owner's access to sunlight and significantly impair the use of that owner's solar-energy system).

47. See Sheppard v. Yara Engineering Corp., 248 Ga. 147, 281 S.E.2d 586 (1981) (mining company's unauthorized removal of topsoil and overburden from a landowner's property constituted the tort of conversion; the removal was a breach of a common law duty independent of any contractual duty owed by the mining company to the landowner).

48. In addition to the distinction between a public and a private good (where the former is distinguished from the latter by its jointness and nonexcludibility), one can also argue that any good, no matter its material characteristics, can be considered a "collective" good if it is allocated or distributed by the state. For the asymmetries of collective goods see RUSSELL HARDIN, COLLECTIVE ACTION ch.5 (1983) and for the definition of a public good see Duncan Snidal, *Public Goods, Property Rights, And Political Organizations* in THE MORAL DIMENSIONS OF PUBLIC POLICY CHOICE: BEYOND THE MARKET PARADIGM 285–312 (John Martin Gillroy & Maurice Wade eds., 1992).

This is a suit brought by the state of Missouri to restrain the discharge of the sewage of Chicago through an artificial channel into the Desplaines river, in the state of Illinois. That river empties into the Illinois river, and the latter empties into the Mississippi at a point about 43 miles above the city of St. Louis. It was alleged in the bill that the result of the threatened discharge would be to send 1,500 tons of poisonous filth daily into the Mississippi, to deposit great quantities of the same upon the part of the bed of the last named river belonging to the plaintiff, and so to poison the water of that river, upon which various of the plaintiff's cities, towns, and inhabitants depended, as to make it unfit for drinking, agricultural, or manufacturing purposes .... the nuisance must be made out upon determinate and satisfactory evidence, ... it must not be doubtful, and ... the danger must be shown to be real and immediate. The nuisance set forth in the bill was one which would be of international importance,—a visible change of a great river from a pure stream into a polluted and poisoned ditch. The only question presented was whether, as between the states of the Union, this court was competent to deal with a situation which, if it arose between independent sovereignties, might lead to war.

* * *

Before this court ought to intervene, the case should be of serious magnitude, clearly and fully proved, and the principle to be applied should be one which the court is prepared deliberately to maintain against all considerations on the other side. See *Kansas v. Colorado*, 185 U.S. 125.

As to the principle to be laid down, the caution necessary is manifest. It is a question of the first magnitude whether the destiny of the great rivers is to be the sewers of the cities along their banks or to be protected against everything which threatens their purity. To decide the whole matter at one blow by an irrevocable fiat would be at least premature. If we are to judge by what the plaintiff itself permits, the discharge of sewage into the Mississippi by cities and towns is to be expected. We believe that the practice of discharging into the river is general along its banks, except where the levees of Louisiana have led to a different course. The argument for the plaintiff asserts it to be proper within certain limits. These are facts to be considered. Even in cases between individuals, some consideration is given to the practical course of events. In the black country of England parties would not be expected to stand upon extreme rights. *St. Helen's Smelting Co. v. Tipping* 11 H.L. Cas. 642. See *Boston Ferrule Co. v. Hills,* 159 Mass, 147, 150, 20 L.R.A. 844, 34 N. E. 85. Where, as here, the plaintiff has sovereign powers, and deliberately permits discharges similar to those of which it complains, it not only offers a standard to which the defendant has the right to appeal, but, as some of those discharges are above the intake of St. Louis, it warrants the defendant in demanding the strictest proof that the plaintiff's own conduct does not produce the result, or at least so conduce to it, that courts should not be curious to apportion the blame.

We have studied the plaintiff's statement of the facts in detail, and have perused the evidence, but it is unnecessary for the purposes of decision to do more than give the general result in a very simple way. At the outset we cannot but be struck by the consideration that if this suit had been brought fifty years ago it almost necessarily would have failed. There is no pretense that there is a nuisance of the simple kind that was known to the older common law. There is nothing which can be detected by the unassisted senses,—no visible increase of filth, no new smell. On the contrary, it is proved that the great volume of pure water from Lake Michigan, which is mixed with the sewage at the start, has improved the Illinois river in these respects to a noticeable extent. Formerly it was sluggish and ill smelling. Now it is a comparatively clear stream to which edible fish have returned. Its water is drunk by the fishermen, [i]t is said without evil results. The plaintiff's case depends upon an inference of the unseen. It draws the inference from two propositions. First, that typhoid fever has increased considerably since the change, and that other explanations have been disproved; and second, that the bacillus of typhoid can and does survive the journey and reach the intake of St. Louis in the Mississippi.

We assume the now-prevailing scientific explanation of typhoid fever to be correct. But when we go beyond that assumption, everything is involved in doubt. The data upon which an increase in the deaths from typhoid fever in St. Louis is alleged are disputed. The elimination of other causes is denied. The experts differ as to the time and distance within which a stream would purify itself. No case of an epidemic caused by infection at so remote a source is brought forward and the cases which are produced are controverted. The plaintiff obviously must be cautious upon this point, for, if this suit should succeed, many others would follow, and it not improbably would find itself a defendant to a bill by one or more of the states lower down upon the Mississippi. The distance which the sewage has to travel (357 miles) is not open to debate, but the time of transit, to be inferred from experiments with floats, is estimated as varying from eight to eighteen and a half days, with forty-eight hours more from intake to distribution, and when corrected by observations of bacteria is greatly prolonged by the defendants. The experiments of the defendant's experts lead them to the opinion that a typhoid bacillus could not survive the journey, while those on the other side maintain that it might live and keep its power for twenty-five days or more, and arrive at St. Louis. Upon the question at issue, whether the new discharge from Chicago hurts St. Louis, there is a categorical contradiction between the experts on the two sides.

The Chicago drainage canal was opened on January 17, 1900. The deaths from typhoid fever in St. Louis, before and after that date, are stated somewhat differently in different places. We give them mainly from the plaintiff's brief: 1890, 140; 1891, 165; 1892, 441; 1893, 215; 1894, 171; 1895, 106; 1896, 106; 1897, 125; 1898, 95; 1899, 131; 1900, 154; 1901, 181; 1902, 216; 1903, 281. It is argued for the defendant that the numbers for the later years have been enlarged by carrying over cases which in earlier years would have been put into a miscellaneous column (intermittent, remittent, typho-malaria, etc., etc.), but we assume that the increase is real. Nevertheless, comparing the last four years with the earlier ones, it is obvious that the ground for a specific inference is very narrow, if we stopped at this point. The plaintiff argues that the increase must be due to Chicago, since there is nothing corresponding to it in the watersheds of the Missouri or Mississippi. On the other hand, the defendant points out that there has been no such enhanced rate of typhoid on the banks of the Illinois as would have been found if the opening of the drainage canal were the true cause.

Both sides agree that the detection of the typhoid bacillus in the water is not to be expected. But the plaintiff relies upon proof that such bacilli are discharged into the Chicago sewage in considerable quantities; that the number of bacilli in the water of the Illinois is much increased, including the *bacillus coli communis*, which is admitted to be an index of contamination, and that the chemical analyses lead to the same inference. To prove that the typhoid bacillus could make the journey an experiment was tried with the *bacillus prodigiosus*, which seems to have been unknown, or nearly unknown, in these waters. After preliminary trials, in which these bacilli emptied into the Mississippi near the mouth of the Illinois were found near the St. Louis intake and in St. Louis in times varying from three days to a month, one hundred and seven barrels of the same, said to contain one thousand million bacilli to the cubic centimeter, were put into the drainage canal near the starting point on November 6, and on December 4 an example was found at the St. Louis intake tower. Four others were found on the three following days, two at the tower and two at the mouth of the Illinois. As this bacillus is asserted to have about the same length of life in sunlight in living waters as the *bacillus typhosus*, although it is a little more hardy, the experiment is thought to prove one element of the plaintiff's case, although the very small number found in many samples of water is thought by the other side to indicate that practically no typhoid germs would get through. It seems to be conceded that the purification of the Illinois by the large dilution from Lake Michigan (nine parts or more in ten) would increase the danger, as it now generally is believed that the bacteria of decay, the saprophytes, which flourish in stagnant pools, destroy the pathogenic germs. Of course, the addition of so much water to the Illinois also increases its speed.

On the other hand, the defendant's evidence shows a reduction in the chemical and bacterial accompaniments of pollution in a given quantity of water, which would be natural in view of the mixture of nine parts to one from Lake Michigan. It affirms that the Illinois is better or no worse at its mouth than it was before, and makes it at least uncertain how much of the present pollution is due to Chicago and how much to sources further down, not complained of in the bill. It contends that if any bacilli should get through, they would be scattered and enfeebled and would do no harm. The defendant also sets against the experiment with the *bacillus prodigiosus* a no less striking experiment with typhoid germs suspended in the Illinois river in permeable sacs. According to this the duration of the life of these germs has been much exaggerated, and in that water would not be more than three or four days. It is suggested, by way of criticism that the germs may not have been of normal strength, that the conditions were less favorable than if they had floated down in a comparatively unchanging body of water, and that the germs may have escaped; but the experiment raises at least a serious doubt. Further, it hardly is denied that there is no parallelism in detail between the increase and decrease of typhoid fever in Chicago and St. Louis. The defendant's experts maintain that the water of the Missouri is worse than that of the Illinois, while it contributes a much larger portion to the intake. The evidence is very strong that it is necessary for St. Louis to take preventive measures, by filtration or otherwise, against the dangers of the plaintiff's own creation or from other sources than Illinois. What will protect against one will protect against another. The presence of causes of infection from the plaintiff's action makes the case weaker in principle as well as harder to prove than one in which all came from a single source.

* * *

What the future may develop, of course we cannot tell. But our conclusion upon the present evidence is that the case proved falls so far below the allegations of the bill that it is not brought within the principles heretofore established in the cause.

Bill dismissed without prejudice.

Notes & Questions

What role did science play in the case against Chicago? Was it decisive? Why? Why not?

What role does the establishment of a causal chain of events play in this case?

What evidence would St. Louis need in order to be successful in this suit?

What is the role of science in the common law of nuisance? How is it used to mitigate uncertainty?

Is the common law effective here? Why? Why not?

Does this case involve a question of private or public goods? Should it be settled by private or public law? How would it be handled by the legal system today? Which approach is most effective? Why?

Does the Supreme Court seem to be making assumptions more in line with the Market Paradigm or the Ecosystem Paradigm of resource use?

§§

OSCAR H. BOOMER v. ATLANTIC CEMENT COMPANY, INC.

Court of Appeals of New York, 1970.
26 N.Y.2d 219, 309 N.Y.S.2d 312, 257 N.E.2d 870.

BERGAN, Judge.

Defendant operates a large cement plant near Albany. These are actions for injunction and damages by neighboring land owners alleging injury to property from dirt, smoke and vibration emanating from the plant. A nuisance has been found after trial, temporary damages have been allowed; but an injunction has been denied.

The public concern with air pollution arising from many sources in industry and in transportation is currently accorded ever wider recognition accompanied by a growing sense of responsibility in State and Federal Governments to control it. Cement plants are obvious sources of air pollution in the neighborhoods where they operate.

But there is now before the court private litigation in which individual property owners have sought specific relief from a single plant operation. The threshold question raised by the division of view on this appeal is whether the court should resolve the litigation between the parties now before it as equitably as seems possible; or whether, seeking promotion of the general public welfare, it should channel private litigation into broad public objectives.

A court performs its essential function when it decides the rights of parties before it. Its decision of private controversies may sometimes greatly affect public issues. Large questions of law are often resolved by the manner in which private litigation is decided. But this is normally an incident to the court's main function to settle controversy. It is a rare exercise of judicial power to use a decision in private litigation as a purposeful mechanism to achieve direct public objectives greatly beyond the rights and interests before the court.

* * *

It seems apparent that the amelioration of air pollution will depend on technical research in great depth; on a carefully balanced consideration of the economic impact of close regulation; and of the actual effect on public health. It is likely to require massive public expenditure and to demand more than any local community can accomplish and to depend on regional and interstate controls.

A court should not try to do this on its own as a by-product of private litigation and it seems manifest that the judicial establishment is neither equipped in the limited nature of any judgment it can pronounce nor prepared to lay down and implement an effective policy for the elimination of air pollution. This is an area beyond the circumference of one private lawsuit. It is a direct responsibility for government and should not thus be undertaken as an incident to solving a dispute between property owners and a single cement plant—one of many—in the Hudson River valley.

The cement making operations of defendant have been found by the court of Special Term to have damaged the nearby properties of plaintiffs in these two actions. That court, as it has been noted, accordingly found defendant maintained a nuisance and this has been affirmed at the Appellate Division. The total damage to plaintiffs' properties is, however, relatively small in comparison with the value of defendant's operation and with the consequences of the injunction which plaintiffs seek.

The ground for the denial of injunction, notwithstanding the finding both that there is a nuisance and that plaintiffs have been damaged substantially, is the large disparity in economic consequences of the nuisance and of the injunction. This theory cannot, however, be sustained without overruling a doctrine which has been consistently reaffirmed in several leading cases in this court and which has never been disavowed here, namely that where a nuisance has been found and where there has been any substantial damage shown by the party complaining an injunction will be granted.

The rule in New York has been that such a nuisance will be enjoined although marked disparity be shown in economic consequence between the effect of the injunction and the effect of the nuisance.

The problem of disparity in economic consequence was sharply in focus in *Whalen v. Union Bag & Paper Co* 208 N.Y. 1, 101 N.E. 805. A pulp mill entailing an investment of more than a million dollars polluted a stream in which plaintiff, who owned a farm, was 'a lower riparian owner'. The economic loss to plaintiff from this pollution was small. This court, reversing the Appellate Division, reinstated the injunction granted by the Special Term against the argument of the mill owner that in view of 'the slight advantage to plaintiff and the great loss that will be inflicted on defendant' an injunction should not be granted (p. 2, 101 N.E. p. 805). "Such a balancing of injuries cannot be justified by the circumstances of this case", Judge Werner noted (p. 4, 101 N.E. p. 805). He continued: 'Although the damage to the plaintiff may be slight as compared with the defendant's expense of abating the condition, that is not a good reason for refusing an injunction' (p. 5, 101 N.E. p. 806).

Thus the unconditional injunction granted at Special Term was reinstated. The rule laid down in that case, then, is that whenever the damage resulting from a nuisance is found not 'unsubstantial', viz., $100 a year, injunction would follow. This states a rule that had been followed in this court with marked consistency (*McCarty v. Natural Carbonic Gas Co.*, 189 N.Y. 40, 81 N.E. 549; *Strobel v. Kerr Salt Co.*, 164 N.Y. 303, 58 N.E. 142; *Campbell v. Seaman*, 63 N.Y. 568).

* * *

Although the court at Special Term and the Appellate Division held that injunction should be denied, it was found that plaintiffs had been damaged in various specific amounts up to the time of the trial and damages to the respective plaintiffs were awarded for those amounts. The effect of this was, injunction having been denied, plaintiffs could maintain successive actions at law for damages thereafter as further damage was incurred.

* * *

This result at Special Term and at the Appellate Division is a departure from a rule that has become settled; but to follow the rule literally in these cases would be to close down the plant at once. This court is fully agreed to avoid that immediately drastic remedy; the difference in view is how best to avoid it.

One alternative is to grant the injunction but postpone its effect to a specified future date to give opportunity for technical advances to permit defendant to eliminate the nuisance; another is to grant the injunction conditioned on the payment of permanent damages to plaintiffs which would compensate them for the total economic loss to their property present and future caused by defendant's operations. For reasons which will be developed the court chooses the latter alternative.

If the injunction were to be granted unless within a short period—e.g., 18 months—the nuisance be abated by improved methods, there would be no assurance that any significant technical improvement would occur.

* * *

[The] techniques to eliminate dust and other annoying by-products of cement making are unlikely to be developed by any research the defendant can undertake within any short period, but will depend on the total resources of the cement industry nation-wide and throughout the world. The problem is universal wherever cement is made.

For obvious reasons the rate of the research is beyond control of defendant. If at the end of 18 months the whole industry has not found a technical solution a court would be hard put to close down this one cement plant if due regard be given to equitable principles.

On the other hand, to grant the injunction unless defendant pays plaintiffs such permanent damages as may be fixed by the court seems to do justice between the contending parties. All of the attributions of economic loss to the properties on which plaintiffs' complaints are based will have been redressed.

The nuisance complained of by these plaintiffs may have other public or private consequences, but these particular parties are the only ones who have sought remedies and the judgment proposed will fully redress them. The limitation of relief granted is a limitation only within the four corners of these actions and does not foreclose public health or other public agencies from seeking proper relief in a proper court.

It seems reasonable to think that the risk of being required to pay permanent damages to injured property owners by cement plant owners would itself be a reasonable effective spur to research for improved techniques to minimize nuisance.

The power of the court to condition on equitable grounds the continuance of an injunction on the payment of permanent damages seems undoubted. (See, e.g., the alternatives considered in McCarty v. Natural Carbonic Gas Co., Supra, as well as Strobel v. Kerr Salt Co., Supra.)

The damage base here suggested is consistent with the general rule in those nuisance cases where damages are allowed. "Where a nuisance is of such a permanent and unabatable character that a single recovery can be had, including the whole damage past and future resulting therefrom, there can be but one recovery" (66 C.J.S. Nuisances § 140, p. 947).

* * *

Thus it seems fair to both sides to grant permanent damages to plaintiffs which will terminate this private litigation.

* * *

The orders should be reversed, without costs, and the cases remitted to Supreme Court, Albany County to grant an injunction which shall be vacated upon payment by defendant of such amounts of permanent damage to the respective plaintiffs as shall for this purpose be determined by the court.

JASEN, Judge (dissenting).

I agree with the majority that a reversal is required here, but I do not subscribe to the newly enunciated doctrine of assessment of permanent damages, in lieu of an injunction, where substantial property rights have been impaired by the creation of a nuisance.

It has long been the rule in this State, as the majority acknowledges, that a nuisance which results in substantial continuing damage to neighbors must be enjoined. (*Whalen v. Union Bag & Paper Co.*, 208 N.Y. 1, 101 N.E. 805; *Campbell v. Seaman*, 63 N.Y. 586; see also, *Kennedy v. Moog Servocontrols*, 21 N.Y. 2d 966, 290 N.Y.S. 2d 193, 237 N.E. 2d 356.) To now change the rule to permit the cement company to continue polluting the air indefinitely upon the payment of permanent damages is, in my opinion, compounding the magnitude of a very serious problem in our State and Nation today.

In recognition of this problem, the Legislature of this State has enacted the Air Pollution Control Act (Public Health Law, Consol. Laws, c. 45, § 1264 to 1299) declaring that it is the State policy to require the use of all available and reasonable methods to prevent and control air pollution (Public Health Law § 1265).

The harmful nature and widespread occurrence of air pollution have been extensively documented. Congressional hearings have revealed that air pollution causes substantial property damage, as well as being a contributing factor to a rising incidence of lung cancer, emphysema, bronchitis and asthma.

* * *

I see grave dangers in overruling our long-established rule of granting an injunction where a nuisance results in substantial continuing damage. In permitting the injunction to become inoperative upon the payment of permanent damages, the majority is, in effect, licensing a continuing wrong. It is the same as saying to the cement company, you may continue to do harm to your neighbors so long as you pay a fee for it. Furthermore, once such permanent damages are assessed and paid, the incentive to alleviate the wrong would be eliminated, thereby continuing air pollution of an area without abatement.

It is true that some courts have sanctioned the remedy here proposed by the majority in a number of cases, but none of the authorities relied upon by the majority are analogous to the situation before us. In those cases, the courts, in denying an injunction and awarding money damages, grounded their decision on a showing that the use to which the property was intended to be put was primarily for the public benefit. Here, on the other hand, it is clearly established that the cement company is creating a continuing air pollution nuisance primarily for its own private interest with no public benefit.

This kind of inverse condemnation (*Ferguson v. Village of Hamburg*, 272 N.Y. 234, 5 N.E. 2d 801) may not be invoked by a private person or corporation for private gain or advantage. Inverse condemnation should only be permitted when the public is primarily served in the taking or impairment of property. (*Matter of New York City Housing Authority v. Muller*, 270 N.Y. 333, 343, 1 N.E. 2d 153, 156; *Pocantico Water Works Co. v. Bird*, 130 N.Y. 249, 258, 29 N.E. 246, 248.) The promotion of the interests of the polluting cement company has, in my opinion, no public use or benefit.

Nor is it constitutionally permissible to impose servitude on land, without consent of the owner, by payment of permanent damages where the continuing impairment of the land is for a private use. (*Fifth Ave. Coach lines v. City of New York*, 11 N.Y. 2d 342, 347, 229 N.Y.S. 2d 400, 403, 183 N.E. 2d 684, 686; *Walker v. City of Hutchinson*, 352 U.S. 112.) This is made clear by the State Constitution (art. I, s 7, subd. (a)) which provides that '(p)rivate property shall not be taken for Public use without just compensation' (emphasis added). It is, of course, significant that the section makes no mention of taking for a Private use.

In sum, then, by constitutional mandate as well as by judicial pronouncement, the permanent impairment of private property for private purposes is not authorized in the absence of clearly demonstrated public benefit and use.

I would enjoin the defendant cement company from continuing the discharge of dust particles upon its neighbors' properties unless, within 18 months, the cement company abated this nuisance.

* * *

I am aware that the trial court found that the most modern dust control devices available have been installed in defendant's plant, but, I submit, this does not mean that Better and more effective dust control devices could not be developed within the time allowed to abate the pollution.

Moreover, I believe it is incumbent upon the defendant to develop such devices, since the cement company, at the time the plant commenced production (1962), was well aware of the plaintiffs' presence in the area, as well as the probable consequences of its contemplated operation. Yet, it still chose to build and operate the plant at this site.

In a day when there is a growing concern for clean air, highly developed industry should not expect acquiescence by the courts, but should, instead, plan its operations to eliminate contamination of our air and damage to its neighbors.

Accordingly, the orders of the Appellate Division, insofar as they denied the injunction, should be reversed, and the actions remitted to Supreme Court, Albany County to grant an injunction to take effect 18 months hence, unless the nuisance is abated by improved techniques prior to said date.

FULD, C. J., and BURKE and SCILEPPI, J. J., concur with BERGAN, J.

In each action: Order reversed, without costs, and the case remitted to Supreme Court, Albany County, for further proceedings in accordance with the opinion herein.

Notes & Questions

As in the Missouri case, the common law was used here to try and rectify a use of ecosystems that caused harm to specific people. Do market concerns trump ecosystem protection? In these cases, how effective is the common law at protecting the ecosystems involved?

Is Judge Bergan correct to argue that this case presents issues that are "beyond the circumference of one private lawsuit"? What does he mean by this? What does this proposition mean for the use of common law in like cases? How does this proposition affect his decision?

What is the proper remedy here? What choices does the court have? What would be the ideal solution? Does the after-the-fact reality of common law narrow the choices for remedy?

What considerations need to be taken into account to properly represent what is at stake for both humanity and nature in this case?

Is Judge Jensen correct that the majority is, in effect, "licensing a continuing wrong"?

Today this problem would most likely be handled by a clean air statute. How would a statute approach the problem differently? Would it handle the problem more or less adequately?

EXERCISE: LAW FROM SCRATCH

Find other cases in which the law now treats an issue that was originally considered a private or common law issue as a public one regulated by statute and administrative law. Trace the evolution of public from private law in these cases and make a persuasive argument for this transition. Now find a resource issue that is still handled by common law. Can you make a persuasive argument for its transition into the public law? Is there a pattern here that allows you to create a set of characteristics of public law issues, which would allow you to make a more universal case for the transition from private law to public law in resource and environmental cases?

Try this exercise again, after you have read Chapters Three, Four and Five. How do the paradigms and context models in these arguments support distinct sources of environmental law?

Legislative Statutes & Administrative Regulation

Administrative regulation of natural resources arose in part as a result of the need for expertise in the implementation of resource conservation and development policies. While Congress or state legislatures may formulate general regulatory policies, only agencies with the necessary time and expertise can determine how these policies should be applied to individuals or categories of resource users.

Agencies are empowered to regulate resources through statutes enacted either by Congress or state legislatures. These regulatory statutes either create the agency (enabling statutes), or impose new resource regulatory duties upon an existing agency. Acting pursuant to rulemaking and adjudicatory powers conferred by these statutes, agencies carry out the regulatory policies of legislatures by promulgating rules, by issuing orders, permits or licenses, or by adjudicating disputes. Guidelines setting forth how federal agencies may act to regulate resources may be found in two places: enabling statutes, or the Administrative Procedures Act, codified in various parts of Title 5, United States Code.

The APA was enacted by Congress to designate the general procedures for federal agencies to use when exercising their rule-making and adjudicatory powers. The APA also specifies who may sue agencies and for what general types of administrative infringements of legal rights. The APA provides for judicial review of administrative actions that are in excess of statutory powers, discriminatory in application, or procedurally defective. State counterparts to the APA provide similar guidance as to the proper conduct of state agencies when controlling the use of resources.[49]

The core source of modern environmental and natural resource law is legislative and administrative. Statutory law, created and passed by local, state, or federal legislative bodies is executed through administrative agencies that create rules and adjudicate disputes in the name of these legislative bodies. On the federal level, the power of our Congress comes from Article I of the Constitution of the United States, while executive power flows from Article II, and judicial power from Article III. However, administrative agencies have no direct power through the Constitution, so the first question we must entertain is where the power of agencies like the USFS, EPA, National Park Service, or Bureau of Land Management comes from. In fact, as we will see, *Administrative Agencies* have three distinct powers, each of which is ceded or delegated to them by a Constitutionally empowered branch of government.

One power of an administrative agency is to write ***Interpretive*** and ***Procedural*** rules for the agencies themselves. These rules define how each agency will internally interpret the law and how it will organize itself. For example, the Department of the Interior may have an interpretive rule on how it will define a "valuable mineral" in order to clearly set the expectations of agency personnel in the face of existing case law.[50] In addition, agencies define everything from how they will be internally organized, to what color their uniforms and trucks will be by the passage of procedural rules. Agencies are delegated the power to write interpretive and procedural rules by the executive branch of government, which is granted this power in Article II of the Constitution.

A second power of agencies is to employ Administrative Law Judges (ALJ) to ***Adjudicate*** cases that deal with the internal jurisdiction of the agency. In this way the first person to hear an immigration case, for example, may not be an Article Three federal judge, but an ALJ from the Immigration & Customs Enforcement. The power to adjudicate is ceded to the agencies by the Courts, who have this power through Article III of the Constitution.

The last but most central power of administrative agencies is that of writing ***Legislative Rules***, which operationalize Congressional Statutes for ground level application, filling in the details and setting the expectations of those who must comply with Congressional intent. A legislative rule may define an acceptable level of benzene in the ambient air, or the price and quantity of timber

---

49. See Jefferson Landfill Committee v. Marion County, 297 Or. 280, 686 P.2d 310 (1984).

50. See Castle v. Womble 19 L.D. 455 1894.

sales, or the exact listing criteria for an endangered or threatened species, or what the responsibilities of a mining operation are on public lands, or the requirements that must be met before a forest can be clear-cut. All these legislative rules are written on the basis of statutes and must demonstrate the intent of Congress, as it is from Congress, and from Article I of the Constitution, that agencies receive the delegated power to write legislative rules.

To summarize, Administrative Agencies have no constitutional power of their own, but, from Congress they derive the power to quasi-legislate, from the Courts they derive the power to quasi-adjudicate and from the Executive they derive the power to create the internal organizational and interpretive rules necessary to implement the law.

This makes the most critical legal question one of reasonable or proper discretion on the part of agencies in using their delegated power. In writing its rule or in adjudicating a dispute has the agency acted within the law and the power delegated to it? To regulate these matters a separate set of *macro-rules* for agency action exists in the Administrative Procedures Act (APA).

Agency **adjudication** is regulated by the APA at 5 U.S.C. §§ 556, 557. Here administrative procedures require agencies to hold hearings, and keep a full record of proceedings. In effect the courts require that the full procedural due process is granted to those subject to these proceedings.

Application Of APA To Administrative Law

	Rule-Making	Adjudication
Informal	APA 553	Not Applicable
Formal	APA 556/557	APA 556/557

In terms of legislative rules, here the APA distinguishes between formal and informal legislative rulemaking. Informal rulemaking is the most common type and is defined in 5 U.S.C. 553. Here, in 553 (c), what is known as "notice and comment" rulemaking is prescribed. Informal rulemaking requires that a preliminary rule be written and submitted to the public for comment. The range of these comments then must be fully considered and reflected in the final rule. Formal rulemaking, which only holds when Congress specifically states that it applies to the rules written from a specific statute, combines notice and comment (§ 553) with the formal procedural and record-keeping requirements of adjudication and is regulated under § 556 & § 557 of the APA.

Judicial review of agency action is based upon the courts' judgment of how reasonable the agencies are in using the power delegated to them to fulfill their functions. As explained, since our political system evolved prior to our administrative state, the latter needed to receive its legitimacy from the three existing branches of government. From Congress (Art. 1) it received the power to legislate, from the judiciary (Art. 3) it received the power to adjudicate, from the executive (Art. 2) it received the power to regulate itself. Overseeing all of this delegation and discretion are the courts and their power of judicial review. Here one might argue that court review concentrates most heavily on agency adjudication as this is the power and legitimacy ceded by the courts themselves to the agencies. The courts are a little more liberal in examining agency writing of legislative rules, allowing Congress to supervise and set its agenda here, making the "intent of Congress" the ultimate test applied by the courts. The courts are most liberal where interpretive and procedural rules are concerned, allowing the President to supervise the use of power and legitimacy ceded to the agencies by his office and the federal executive.

THE CONSTITUTIONAL AUTHORITY OF ADMINISTRATIVE
AGENCIES

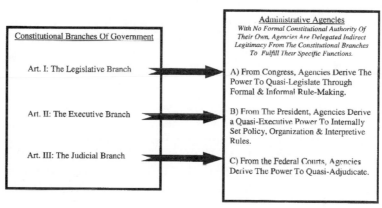

Constitutional Branches Of Government

Art. I: The Legislative Branch

Art. II: The Executive Branch

Art. III: The Judicial Branch

Administrative Agencies
With No Formal Constitutional Authority Of Their Own, Agencies Are Delegated Indirect Legitimacy From The Constitutional Branches To Fulfill Their Specific Functions.

A) From Congress, Agencies Derive The Power To Quasi-Legislate Through Formal & Informal Rule-Making.

B) From The President, Agencies Derive a Quasi-Executive Power To Internally Set Policy, Organization & Interpretive Rules.

C) From the Federal Courts, Agencies Derive The Power To Quasi-Adjudicate.

JUDICIAL REVIEW OF AGENCY ACTION: The legitimacy of administrative agencies is a mix of three specific powers delegated from three constitutional authorities within the federal government. The Federal Courts use their power of Judicial Review to respond to this second-hand constitutional legitimacy with distinct levels of scrutiny.

❖ *Greatest deference* is given to the internal exercise of executive power to set policy, organization and write interpretive rules, leaving detailed supervision to the President.
❖ *Less deference* is given to the exercise of legislative rule-making, with stricter attention to the balance between agency discretion and the intent of Congress.
❖ *Least deference* is given to the administrative use of adjudication, as this is the power the Art. III courts delegate to the agencies and are responsible to most closely supervise.

J.M. Gillroy 2007

Overall, when administrative rulemaking or adjudicatory proceedings provide inadequate relief to aggrieved parties, judicial review of environmental disputes may be sought based on the establishment of standing. Litigation involving challenges to administrative regulation often raise one or more of the following issues: standing to sue the agency (covered at the beginning of this chapter); the appropriate time and place for judicial review; the appropriate forum for review; the proper scope of judicial review of administrative actions; and the proper remedy for adverse agency action. Resolution of these five issues helps shape how agencies may act to regulate resource protection and exploitation of natural resources.

1) Ripeness, Finality, and Exhaustion

Judicial challenges to administrative regulation of the natural world frequently present a combination of issues that require resolution before a court may proceed to the merits: ripeness, finality, exhaustion, and primary jurisdiction are often intertwined.

In *Rocky Mountain Oil and Gas Association v. Watt*, 696 F.2d 734 (10th Cir.1982), the plaintiff association asserted that its members had suffered irreparable economic injury in the form of forfeited oil exploration costs, because of the Interior Department's decision to interpret the 1976 Federal Land Management Policy Act as barring mineral activities that threaten the preservation of public lands as wilderness areas. As a result of this Department decision, members of the trade association had abandoned plans to obtain permits to drill for oil on these lands; thus, permits had been neither sought nor denied.

First, the court found that the Department's interpretation of the act's wilderness provision was "ripe" for review because a legal question of statutory interpretation was involved. The ripeness standard was also met because there was evidence of actual and substantial economic harm to trade association members, who had given up development plans in the affected areas. Second, the court held that the Department's interpretation of the statute was a "final" one that denied plaintiffs the right to drill for oil on public lands. Third, the court concluded that the plaintiff members did not have to "exhaust" administrative remedies because the court did not need additional factual information from the agency to determine whether the wilderness provision of the act applied to the plaintiffs.

2) The Exhaustion Doctrine

The exhaustion doctrine requires that all available administrative remedies be pursued to completion before a plaintiff may seek judicial review of agency action. Courts use the finality rule (considered below) to determine whether an administrative action is final in nature and sufficiently affecting a party's substantive rights to be subject to judicial review. In contrast, the exhaustion doctrine determines whether an administrative act is barred from judicial review because it is initially cognizable by the agency alone. The rationale behind the exhaustion doctrine is that the agency should be given the opportunity to correct its own mistakes.

As with the final order rule, courts will apply the exhaustion doctrine to prevent premature judicial review of disputes more properly resolved by an agency, either because available administrative remedies are adequate to provide relief, or because the technical nature of the case requires the application of administrative expertise. The exhaustion doctrine is particularly important because of the prevalence of agency appellate procedures available for resolution of disputes concerning natural resource use.

The U.S. Supreme Court has listed several policy reasons for enforcing the exhaustion doctrine, aside from those noted above. First, application of the doctrine allows an agency to exercise its congressionally delegated discretionary powers, to employ its expertise to a situation, and to develop a full record of facts and conclusions. Second, the doctrine ensures that courts review only fully developed administrative records. Third, the doctrine promotes administrative efficiency by requiring that all administrative procedures be pursued to completion by a party before judicial review is sought.[51]

The exhaustion doctrine usually arises when a party prematurely seeks judicial review, or when a party fails to contest, in a timely fashion, its rights in an administrative forum. In both situations, plaintiffs usually argue either that they have suffered harm sufficient to warrant judicial review, or that exhaustion of administrative remedies will not provide adequate relief. Generally, however, judicial review is disallowed and the case remanded to the agency for resolution of the issue.[52] A contrary decision requires truly exceptional circumstances.[53]

51. McKart v. United States, 395 U.S. 185 (1969).

52. See Burlington Northern R. Co. v. United States, 752 F.2d 627 (Fed.Cir. 1985) (owner of coal reserves alleging a "taking" of property through application of a federal statute failed to exhaust administrative remedies by seeking a permit for coal mining from the Secretary of Interior).

53. See Hawthorne Oil and Gas Corp. v. Department of Energy, 647 F.2d 1107 (Em.App.1981) (judicial review regarding $600,000.00 fine denied because of pending agency appeal and availability of alternative administrative remedies); Energy Co-op., Inc. v. United States Department of Energy, 659 F.2d 146 (Em.App.1981) (judicial review of application of agency penalty denied because plaintiff failed to protest or comment during promulgation of the rule, or file for an administrative exception to the rule after its promulgation).

Although the *Hawthorne* and *Energy Co-op* cases indicate a strong judicial inclination to enforce the exhaustion doctrine despite evidence of substantial economic or other harm to a plaintiff's interest, there are five major exceptions to the doctrine: (1) the administrative action will, or has, resulted in irreparable harm to the plaintiff; (2) the agency has acted in excess of its statutory powers; (3) the available administrative remedies are inadequate to provide relief; (4) pursuit of administrative remedies would be futile to the plaintiff;[54] and (5) the agency has violated constitutional or statutory rights of an aggrieved party. Environmental cases more frequently fall within the first or fifth exceptions.[55]

3) The Proper Forum Issue and Primary Jurisdiction

The primary jurisdiction doctrine concerns whether a court or an agency should hear a claim concerning administrative regulation. It is similar to the exhaustion doctrine in that courts employ it to bar judicial review of cases more properly resolved by the agency. The difference between the two doctrines is that exhaustion mandates that a case which is initially cognizable by the agency alone should be remanded to the agency. By comparison, the primary jurisdiction doctrine governs whether a claim initially cognizable by either a court or an agency should be remanded to the agency for resolution of technical aspects of regulatory issues raised.[56] When the primary jurisdiction doctrine is imposed, judicial review of a case is suspended until the views of the agency can be obtained.

The policy reasons behind enforcement of the primary jurisdiction doctrine are similar to those of the exhaustion doctrine: the doctrine enforces the separation of powers by promoting proper governmental relationships between courts and agencies, and furthers the agency's right to exercise its discretionary powers and fact-finding functions. In addition, enforcement of the primary jurisdiction doctrine fosters uniformity and consistency in administrative regulation of natural resources. Based on these considerations, courts either suspend judicial review in order to obtain the

---

54. See Orion Corp. v. State, 103 Wash.2d 441, 693 P.2d 1369 (1985)

55. Southeast Alaska Conservation Council, Inc. v. Watson, 535 F.Supp. 653 (D.Alaska 1982), *affirmed,* 697 F.2d 1305 (9th Cir.1983) (agency approved mineral bulk sampling in public forest without preparing environmental impact statement as required by statute; since bulk sampling had begun and was causing ongoing irreparable harm, exhaustion of administrative remedies was not required prior to judicial review); Consumers Power Co. v. Michigan Public Service Commission, 415 Mich. 134, 327 N.W.2d 875 (1982) (rate increase to a public utility approved, then later denied pending the completion of public hearing on the rate increases; judicial review allowed because injury caused by the decision to postpone the increase during the hearings would not be alleviated by exhaustion of administrative remedies).

56. United States v. Western Pacific Railroad Co., 352 U.S. 59 (1956); United States v. Radio Corp., 358 U.S. 334, 346 n. 14 (1959).

views of the agency, or allow judicial review of issues exclusively within the jurisdiction of the court, such as issues of constitutional law.

The doctrine is commonly invoked in the following three instances to postpone judicial review: (1) when the technical expertise of the agency is needed to properly resolve complex issues; (2) when further facts are needed from the agency to complete the record before it; and (3) when Congress has specifically designated that the agency exercise its expertise over a regulatory matter. Most environmental cases fall within the first rationale, especially in energy and extraction cases where statutory provisions are in question concerning (1) rates of sale of domestic oil and gas resources, or (2) tariffs on exports or imports of these resources.[57] The primary jurisdiction doctrine is also invoked to prevent an agency from hearing a case presenting issues within the exclusive province of the courts, such as whether a plaintiff's constitutional rights have been violated by an agency.[58]

4) Exhaustion v. Primary Jurisdiction

The exhaustion doctrine is used by courts to ascertain the proper time for judicial review; the primary jurisdiction doctrine addresses the proper forum for judicial review. The issue of which doctrine applies often arises when a party challenges a non-final agency action as violating a regulatory statute. In this situation the exhaustion doctrine resolves whether the case requires the further pursuit of administrative remedies. The primary jurisdiction rule is next applied to determine whether administrative conduct that adversely affects substantive rights to the use of a resource allows judicial review.

Connecticut v. United States Environmental Protection Agency, 656 F.2d 902 (2d Cir.1981) illustrates the balancing of the two doctrines. The states of Connecticut and New Jersey had challenged the promulgation of a rule by the Environmental Protection Agency (EPA) approving a revision to an air pollution control plan of the state of New York. Although a public hearing was initiated by the EPA on the reasonableness of the plan, the lawsuit was brought before completion of the hearing. The court held that the exhaustion doctrine, not the doctrine of primary jurisdiction, governed the timing issue of the case because a non-final administrative action

57. See Distrigas of Massachusetts v. Boston Gas Co., 693 F.2d 1113 (1st Cir. 1982) (suit between private parties over calculation of federal tariffs remanded to agency for technical interpretation of tariff provisions because resolution not apparent by standard methods of statutory construction).

58. Mountain States Natural Gas Corp. v. Petroleum Corp. of Texas, 693 F.2d 1015 (10th Cir.1982) (this is a constitutional due process challenge to notice provisions of agency approval of oil pooling permit exclusively within judicial, not agency, jurisdiction).

was involved. However, the Clean Air Act (42 U.S.C.A. § 7401) under which the plaintiffs sought review, did not require the exhaustion of administrative remedies. Also, the court determined that the EPA rule constituted final agency action affecting substantive rights to the use of a resource and was thus, under primary jurisdiction, subject to judicial review.

5) The Final Order Rule & the Merits of the Case

Once plaintiffs challenging administrative action have surmounted the initial barriers of standing, ripeness, finality, exhaustion, mootness, and primary jurisdiction, the court may consider the merits. Courts may review all agency actions made reviewable by statute, and all final agency action "for which [otherwise] there is no other adequate remedy."[59] Review will be declined only when expressly precluded by statute, or when the action at issue has been committed to the discretion of the agency by law.[60]

Section 706 of the APA permits courts to decide "all relevant questions of law, interpret constitutional and statutory provisions, and determine the meaning or applicability of agency action." In all cases, agency action must be set aside and held unlawful by courts when found to be arbitrary, capricious, an abuse of discretion, or not in accordance with the law; courts may also overturn agency action that fails to meet statutory, procedural or constitutional requirements.[61]

Whereas the ripeness doctrine within standing is concerned with the presentation of sufficiently concrete and adverse issues to allow judicial resolution, the final order rule requires that the challenged administrative act be final. The final order rule bars judicial review when administrative procedures are available and adequate to provide relief to parties whose economic, environmental, or other interests in a resource have been harmed by administrative action. Basically, the theory behind the rule is that the agency should be allowed to complete its decision-making prior to judicial intervention.[62]

Section 704 of the APA states that only "[a]gency action made reviewable by statute and final agency action for which there is no

---

59. (5 U.S.C.A. § 704).

60. (5 U.S.C.A. § 701(a)(1) & (2)) See Thompson v. Clark, 741 F.2d 401 (D.C.Cir.1984) (express language of Regulatory Flexibility Act precludes judicial review of oil and gas developer's claim that there was insufficient evidence to support Interior Department rule).

61. Citizens to Preserve Overton Park v. Volpe, 401 U.S. 402 (1971). This

was modified in Califano v. Sanders, 430 U.S. 99, 97 S.Ct. 980, 51 L.Ed.2d 192 (U.S.Ind. Feb. 23, 1977) where the Supreme Court held that the APA is not an independent grant of subject matter jurisdiction, as could be inferred by *Citizens*.

62. See Pennzoil Co. v. FERC, 742 F.2d 242 (5th Cir.1984).

other adequate remedy in a court are subject to judicial review."[63] This provision has been construed to allow judicial review of administrative actions affecting environmental use which imposes obligation, or denies or grants legal rights "with consequences sufficient to warrant review."[64] Administrative rulings which are procedural in nature are generally not reviewable unless they affect the substantive rights of a party.[65]

Substantially, courts determine whether a particular administrative action is final and subject to judicial review according to a three-part test. First, the challenged administrative conduct must impose obligations or deny or grant legal rights. Second, courts determine whether withholding judicial review would cause irreparable injury to the plaintiff. Third, courts assess whether permitting judicial review would impair the agency's power to exercise its discretion regarding the issues presented by the dispute.[66]

Non-final agency actions are usually not reviewable by courts, even when the plaintiff suffers or may suffer serious harm due to such actions. Since most challenges to administrative regulation of the environment involve non-final actions, overcoming the finality rule of judicial review is a frequently adjudicated issue. Courts generally employ the three-part test just set forth, but are particularly careful not to undermine the agency's discretionary power to act, as conferred by statute.[67]

The most frequent types of final agency actions are those "[imposing] an obligation, [denying] a right, or [fixing] some legal relationship ... at the consummation of an administrative process."[68] Final agency actions reviewed by courts in natural resources cases are the promulgation of rules, the issuance of orders, permits or licenses, and the use of statutory procedures in rulemaking or adjudicatory proceedings. In reviewing these actions, courts apply one of the three standards of judicial review set forth in Section 706 of the APA.

---

63. 5 U.S.C. § 704.

64. Environmental Defense Fund v. Ruckelshaus, 439 F.2d 584 n. 8 (D.C.Cir. 1971).

65. Thermal Ecology Must Be Preserved v. Atomic Energy Commission, 433 F.2d 524, 526 (D.C.Cir.1970).

66. Papago Tribal Utility Authority v. FERC, 628 F.2d 235, 239 (D.C.Cir. 1980).

67. See Cities of Anaheim and Riverside, California v. Federal Energy Regulatory Commission, 692 F.2d 773 (D.C.Cir.1982) (since agency approval of a license application was procedural only, and did not constitute a final agency action conferring or denying a substantive right, agency action was non-final and judicial review not allowed); Natural Resources Defense Council v. United States Nuclear Regulatory Commission, 680 F.2d 810 (D.C.Cir.1982) (agency rule limited procedural rights of parties; since the rule affected procedural rather than substantive rights, it could not be challenged as a final agency action. Also, since the procedural rule had not been specifically applied against plaintiff, no irreparable injury had been suffered.).

68. Honicker v. NRC, 590 F.2d 1207, 1209 (D.C.Cir.1978).

The first standard, known as the ***ultra vires standard*** of judicial review, requires agencies to conform to applicable regulatory statutes when regulating resources.[69] The second standard is referred to as the ***arbitrary and capricious standard*** of judicial review, and mandates that agencies not abuse their discretionary powers when regulating the environment.[70] The third and final standard directs that agencies observe proper ***statutory procedures*** set forth in either the APA or other statutes when promulgating rules, or issuing orders, licenses, or permits.[71] Violation of any of these three standards may result in the issuance of either an injunction against the agency, or a declaratory judgment finding the challenged agency action unlawful.

a) Standard I: Ultra Vires Agency Actions

Judging an administrative action *ultra vires* involves a two-part analysis. First, the court ascertains whether the agency's conduct is within the scope of its delegated authority by examining the agency's enabling act and other statutory grants of authority; these statutes will set out the extent of the agency's authority or discretion to act in given circumstances. Second, the court determines whether, on the basis of the facts before it, an administrative official's decision can reasonably be said to fall within the scope of the agency's statutory authority.[72]

If an act or decision of an agency is found to be *ultra vires* that is outside its delegated authority, according to this two-part analysis, it is invalid and no further inquiry is necessary. The general presumption, however, is that the agency action is valid and that an action falls within the broad discretionary powers given the agency. The burden of proof is on those who challenge the action to demonstrate it is *ultra vires*.[73]

Despite judicial inclination to deny *ultra vires* challenges, such challenges will be sustained when agency action deviates from an express statutory mandate, or when the agency has acted in the absence of any statutory authority at all.[74]

---

69. 5 U.S.C.A. § 706(2)(c).

70. 5 U.S.C.A. § 706(2)(a).

71. 5 U.S.C.A. § 706(2)(d).

72. Citizens to Preserve Overton Park v. Volpe, 401 U.S. 402 (1971).

73. See Appeal of Concord Natural Gas Corp., 121 N.H. 685, 433 A.2d 1291 (1981) (challenge to state regulation denying advertising costs to utilities failed because: (1) federal statute granted states the option to create their own advertising regulations; and (2) the state

regulation fell within the scope of that option).

74. See Texas Oil and Gas Corp. v. Watt, 683 F.2d 427 (D.C.Cir.1982) (Secretary of the Interior denied mineral leases on military lands because of public dissatisfaction with agency leasing procedures; ultra vires challenge sustained because (1) such leasing was expressly allowed by statute; and (2) the Secretary's decision was based on factors outside the scope of his authority); City of Sherman v. Public Utilities Commission of Texas, 643 S.W.2d 681 (Tex.

b) *Standard II: Arbitrary and Capricious Agency Action*

An agency regulating use of natural resources is most likely to be challenged for being arbitrary and capricious, or for abusing its delegated power in a particular exercise of it. Such agency actions may be set aside under the APA, 5 U.S.C.A. § 706(2)(A). The arbitrary and capricious standard of judicial review focuses on an agency's actions which, although within the proper scope of its statutory power, are nevertheless invalid for one of three reasons: (1) failure to consider statutorily mandated criteria when making a decision; (2) failure to base decisions on rational consideration of all the facts; or (3) failure to articulate reasons for the decision.[75] This highly deferential standard of review contains a presumption that administrative action is lawful as long as there is some rational basis for the agency decision. If there is, the agency action should be upheld by the courts. The idea behind this deference is that it prevents the courts from substituting their own judgment for that of the agency, for example, when they disagree with the substantive content of the agency's decision.

Our courts have evolved a two-step inquiry process in determining whether an agency has acted in an arbitrary and capricious manner. A reviewing court first evaluates if the agency's decision has been based upon a consideration of all relevant factors; if the agency has not done so, courts then determine if the agency has made an obvious error of judgment by rejecting what seem to be relevant factors raised by an aggrieved party. The dominant trend in environmental law cases is to uphold agency action after subjecting it to this two-step inquiry. Parties may prevail, however, by showing that an administration official has either failed to consider factors mandated by statute or failed to state reasons for the decision.

The most common agency actions challenged on arbitrary and capricious grounds in environmental and natural resources law cases involve: (i) orders directing specific action or permits authorizing development activities; and (ii) agency rules and regulations governing economic and environmental aspects of the exploitation of nature.

(i) Agency Orders and Permits

Most orders and permits by agencies are upheld because of the presumption of the validity of administrative actions, particularly when an agency has been given broad discretionary power by

---

1983) (state PUC commission attempted to resolve dispute over ground water rights; ultra vires challenge sustained because PUC had no authority over ground water rights).

75. See Northern Spotted Owl v. Hodel, 716 F.Supp. 479 (1988).

statute. Despite frequent challenges, courts usually uphold agency issuance or denial of permits and orders when the agency action is consistent with prior administrative decisions and statutory requirements.[76]

For example, orders issued by state public utility commissions (PUC) denying rate increases to utilities are often challenged on arbitrary and capricious grounds for failure of the PUC to consider all relevant economic or other criteria when setting a utility's rate base. The challenges frequently fail because state law does not require that the PUC consider certain expense factors in its rate-base decisions.[77]

Agency action may be held unlawful by courts when the agency departs from statutory goals by failing to consider relevant factors and when the agency fails to articulate reasons for its decisions. These two exceptions to the usual presumption of agency validity protect aggrieved parties from an agency's refusal to consider factors mandated by statute, and provide the court with a means of securing a complete record for judicial review.

The requirement that an agency consider all relevant statutory criteria often arises in environmental law cases. Aggrieved parties, such as environmental protection groups, frequently assert that the agency has violated the National Environmental Policy Act (NEPA) of 1969 by issuing defective environmental impact statements on major federal actions that might effect the environment. If such allegations are proven, or if the agency has ignored NEPA's statutory mandate altogether (a surprisingly frequent occurrence), agency orders or construction permits will be set aside as arbitrary and capricious.[78]

The second exception to the presumption of validity of agency action is triggered when agencies fail to articulate understandable

---

76. See Superior Oil Co. v. Watt, 548 F.Supp. 70 (D.Del.1982) (challenge denied to Secretary's rejection of oil and gas lease bids because: (1) statute specifically granted broad discretionary power to accept or reject bids; (2) exercise of discretion consistent with statutory criteria; and (3) decision conformed to previous administrative orders); South Georgia Natural Gas Co. v. Federal Energy Regulatory Commission, 699 F.2d 1088 (11th Cir.1983) (challenge to agency interpretation of its own rules denied because the interpretation was reasonable and furthered the legislative goal of ensuring equitable gas prices for consumers).

77. Central Maine Power Co. v. Public Utilities Commission, 455 A.2d 34 (Me.1983) (since state law did not specifically require that the PUC take into account such factors as utility company's cost of equity, ongoing construction costs, and working capital requirements, the PUC's failure to do so was not unreasonable, arbitrary, or capricious).

78. See Sierra Club v. Sigler, 695 F.2d 957 (5th Cir.1983) (issuance of port improvements permits suspended because of failure of Corps of Engineers to consider "worst case" oil spill in its environmental impact statement; since improvements were specifically intended to increase oil tanker traffic, thus significantly increasing the risk of such spills, the omission was improper).

reasons for their actions. Vague administrative statements based upon an incomplete reading of the data gathered for the rule-making requires courts to guess at the reasons for an agency's decision, and are insufficient for presumed validity.[79]

(ii) Review of Agency Regulations

Whereas agency orders and permits set forth specific rights and duties with respect to the use of nature, agency rules are designed to implement broad statutory directives of resource regulation and have more general applicability. Most challenges to agency regulations in environmental law involve legislative rules which fulfill statutory goals and have the force and effect of law. The arbitrary and capricious standard of judicial review relevant to agency orders and permits is also applied in the review of agency rules and regulations. Courts use a two-step analysis: (1) Did the agency consider all factual or statutory factors relevant to the rulemaking process? (2) If so, was there a "clear error of judgment" by the agency?

Here again, however, the burden of proof falls upon the party challenging the legality of the rule. Most such challenges fail because courts typically find that the agency has complied with statutory goals, considered all relevant factual and statutory criteria, and articulated a rational connection between facts found and choices made. The position of the courts in reviewing agency rules is akin to that of an appellate court reviewing a lower court's decision; absent a compelling reason, the court does not re-adjudicate the factual issues behind an agency decision, especially in the presence of conflicting evidence.[80]

Despite the general trend of courts to sustain the validity of administrative rules affecting natural resources, these rules can be struck down on grounds that the agency has deviated from or failed

---

79. See Mitchell Energy Corp. v. Federal Energy Regulatory Commission, 651 F.2d 414 (5th Cir.1981) (agency order was arbitrary and capricious which stated only conclusions of law rather than substantiating factual reasons).

80. See American Paper Institute, Inc. v. American Electric Power Service Corp., 461 U.S. 402, 103 S.Ct. 1921, 76 L.Ed.2d 22 (1983) (the Federal Energy Regulatory Commission adopted two regulations requiring that utilities purchase power at full avoided cost, a premium rate, from small power producers and co-generators of power; the Court upheld the regulations on the grounds that the premium rate furthered the statutorily mandated goal of increasing the number of alternative energy sources, and promoted the statutory requirement that FERC establish and enforce equitable power rates); Baltimore Gas and Electric Co. v. Natural Resources Defense Council, 462 U.S. 87 (1983) (NRC licensing rule based on presumption of no leakage of nuclear waste into the environment, the "zero release assumption," was upheld because: (1) the use of the assumption was consistent with NEPA requirements; (2) the assumption reflected current scientific thought on the problem; and (3) the NRC's public disclosure of known facts on the problem of nuclear waste provided the Court with a rational explanation of the NRC's decision making process).

to comply with its own rules or regulations. Of course, the broad discretionary power granted most agencies will allow exceptions, but the agency must articulate acceptable reasons for neglecting the provisions of lawfully promulgated internal rules.[81]

c) Standard III: Judicial Review of Administrative Procedures

Agency action may be declared unlawful when procedures mandated by the APA or other relevant statute are not followed by the agency. Most environmental law cases holding administrative action invalid for procedural deficiencies involve improperly promulgated legislative or interpretative rules. Remember that interpretative rules set forth an agency's general statements of executive policy, such as how a statute will be applied to specific parties. These rules are exempt from the public notice, comment, and hearing procedures set forth in APA §§ 553, 556, and 557, unless otherwise required by the stated intent of Congress within a specific statute. Legislative rules implement statutory provisions and have the force and effect of law. These rules designate the legal rights and obligations of persons and are subject to the public notice and comment or hearing procedures of the APA. Therefore, the first inquiry in a challenge to the procedural validity of an administrative rule is whether the rule is interpretative or legislative in nature. Evidence that the agency used the word "interpretation" in the rule itself will support an "interpretative" classification.[82]

Legislative rules affecting legal rights to the use of nature may be exempt from the publication requirement of the APA if they "recognize an exception or relieve a restriction" (Section 553(d)(1)), or if the agency deems such procedures unnecessary for "good cause found and published with the rule."[83] But apart from the "relieve a restriction" and "good faith" exceptions, a showing by

---

81. See Shell Oil Co. v. Federal Energy Regulatory Commission, 664 F.2d 79 (5th Cir.1981) (the Federal Energy Regulatory Commission used a 7% interest rate in calculating a refund, rather than the 9% interest rate which was the authorized rate in use by the agency; the agency was required either to adjust the rate or state acceptable reasons for not doing so).

82. See Louisiana–Pacific Corp. v. Block, 694 F.2d 1205 (9th Cir.1982) (Forest Service memo regarding timber set-asides held to be interpretative and exempt from notice and comment requirements because the memo: (1) only added consistency to the set-aside program, rather than legal duties or rights; and (2) used the word "interpretation" and failed to reference any statutory rulemaking powers).

83. (Section 553(d)(3)). See Union Oil Co. of California v. United States Department of Energy, 688 F.2d 797 (Em.App.1982) (Department of Energy issued rule exempting tertiary recovery oil producers from price control without 30–day publication period; producers not included in the exemption, and who were placed at a competitive disadvantage, failed in their procedural challenge to the rule because it merely relieved a restriction).

the plaintiff that the agency failed to give any notice of a proposed legislative rule, or gave only insufficient notice, will often result in judicial invalidation of the rule. Section 706(2)(D) of the APA requires courts to invalidate agency actions found to be "without observance of procedure required by law."[84]

Sometimes an agency hearing is required by its enabling legislation before it may take affirmative action, as, for example, in granting a license. In such cases the issue is whether the enabling statute and the APA require formal procedures which would include a *trial-type* hearing.[85]

6) Remedies

In reviewing challenges to administrative regulation of natural resources, courts often must determine whether an injunction is a proper remedy. This issue is frequently raised in challenges to major construction projects which substantially affect the environment. Because essential environmental interests of public health, safety, and resource conservation or preservation may be at stake in these cases, courts will often issue permanent or temporary injunctions forcing agencies to halt the construction project despite the expenditure of great amounts of money or the near-completion of the project.[86]

Temporary injunctions are often used by courts in NEPA cases as alternatives to permanent injunctions; a temporary injunction is preferred because the remedy allows agencies to correct NEPA violations while permitting unaffected portions of the work to continue.[87]

---

84. On a state level, administrative failure to give adequate notice of a proposed rule is a common complaint of utility companies seeking rate increases from state public utility commissions. See Public Service Commission of Nevada v. Southwest Gas Corp., 99 Nev. 268, 662 P.2d 624 (1983) (a rate re-design order issued after a hearing but without prior public notice was found to be a substantive rule issued in violation of the Nevada APA (NRS B.060) because it affected the rates of utilities not parties to the hearing).

85. A trial-type hearing permits the calling of witnesses under oath, cross-examination, and compulsory process. See Pacific Gas and Electric Co. v. FERC, 746 F.2d 1383 (9th Cir.1984) (neither the APA nor the Federal Power Act require a hearing where no material facts are in dispute); Sierra Association for the Environment v. FERC, 744 F.2d

661 (9th Cir.1984) (a trial type hearing not warranted under the APA in FERC licensing of a hydroelectric project).

86. See TVA v. Hill, 437 U.S. 153 (1978) (a permanent injunction was issued against the impoundment of water behind the Tellico Dam as necessary to preserve an endangered species, the snail darter, from extinction, despite the fact that the $100 million project was nearly completed).

87. See Environmental Defense Fund v. Marsh, 651 F.2d 983 (5th Cir. 1981) (Corps of Engineers properly prepared environmental impact statement on waterway project, but failed to re-evaluate subsequent structural changes; a temporary injunction was issued against construction of the modified areas. A permanent injunction was denied because the temporary injunction: (1) permitted continuance of a major federal

7) Cases

In the cases for this section of the chapter, we will examine the evolving parameters within which agency action is considered and statutes are assessed by the courts. In both of these cases, in reviewing agency actions, the courts have refined and specified both the enabling statutes and the APA in order to specify the legal requirements that the agencies must meet in order to have valid legislative rules. Overall, the agencies seek to carry out their mission without excess interference by the courts. But when do the courts feel obliged by their charge to settle disputes?

STATUTE POINTERS BOX—SOME RULES OF THUMB: Legislatures set out their intent in terms of Environmental Law through the statutes they produce and these statutes are easier to understand with a few keys.

➤ The *intent of Congress* is always judged in *dialectic relationship* to the *discretion of the Agencies* that Congress charges with writing the legislative or regulatory rules that apply the statute. The statute is usually written in a general way leaving the details to the Agency and its discretion but frequently there are disagreements as to whether the agency rule or action is in line with the Legislature's intent. This is the stuff of court cases. Overall, the balance of this dialectic, when controversial, is in the hands of the court system and involves their interpretation of what the dialectic balance should be. The interpretation of the statute is usually done by the plain language of the statute or in terms of what is know as the *object and purpose* of the statute. When deciding on whether the intent of Congress is properly reflected in an act of an Agency, one usually considers whether the action is in line with the object and purpose of the statute or violates these variables. To accomplish this one must consider how the object and purpose are defined within the statute itself.

➤ For example, a statute usually has at least two distinct and parallel running arguments within it that both contribute to its object and purpose while maintaining a dialectic tension. For example, the Clean Air Act has an argument about *human welfare and markets* running dialectically with an argument for *human health and safety*. It is critical to decipher and understand these argument and their dialectic relations to assess how the court understands the object and purpose and to do this you need to find the important components of the statute.

➤ First, there is a section, usually near the beginning, that sets out the intent of the Legislature and the principles upon which the need for the statute and its objectives are justified. Here, one can decipher the policy arguments inherent in the statute and its object and purpose. For example, see the **Clean Air Act** at 42 U.S.C.A. §7401 (CAA §101).

➤ Second, one needs to look for a "definitions" section, for it is here that the Legislature distinguishes what it considered the important terminology connected to the object and purpose of the statute and the working legal definitions by which the law and policy design will be judged. For example, examine the critical definition of "take" within the **Endangered Species Act** at 16 U.S.C.A. §1532 (19) (ESA §3).

➤ Lastly, one needs to look for the action forcing section of the statute. This component indicates what the law requires in terms of the working out of the object and purpose in terms of legal practice. For example, the *National Environmental Policy Act* at 42 U.S.C.A. §4332 (NEPA 102) sets out the requirements of the **Environmental Impact Statement**, which is the core practice requirement of this statute that operationalizes its object and purpose.

➤ As you can see each of these citations has a USCA number, which refers to the United States Code (Annotated), and that sorts the statutes by type or title and then places them into order. However, there is also another number with the initials of the statute. This is the section of the original statute before it was integrated into the Code. Both numbers usually appear on any copy of the statute.

---

project over 55% complete; and (2) furthered the mandates of NEPA).

§§

UNITED STATES OF AMERICA v. NOVA SCOTIA FOOD PRODUCTS CORP.

United States Court of Appeals, Second Circuit, 1977.
568 F.2d 240.

[Action was brought here in order to stop regulations on the processing of whitefish, promulgated by the FDA under the statutory authority of Congress through the Food Drug and Cosmetic Act 21 U.S.C.A. § 342(a)(4). The question is whether the Agency had authority to write these regulations in protection of the public health, what the demands of APA § 553 rule-making are, and what role the scientific evidence gathered during § 553 rule-making should play in the creation of final regulations.]

* * *

GURFEIN, Circuit Judge.

The injunction was sought and granted on the ground that smoked whitefish which has been processed in violation of the T–T–S regulation [21 C.F.R. Part 128a (1976)] is "adulterated." Food, Drug and Cosmetics Act ("the act") §§ 302(a) and 301(k) 21 U.S.C. §§ 332(a), 331(k).

Appellant Nova Scotia receives frozen or iced whitefish in interstate commerce which it processes by brining, smoking and cooking. The fish are then sold as smoked whitefish.

The regulations cited above require that hot-process smoked fish be heated by a controlled heat process that provides a monitoring system positioned in as many strategic locations in the oven as necessary to assure a continuous temperature through each fish of not less than 180° F. for a minimum of 30 minutes for fish which have been brined to contain 3.5% Water phase salt or at 150° F. for a minimum of 30 minutes if the salinity was at 5% Water phase. Since each fish must meet these requirements, it is necessary to heat an entire batch of fish to even higher temperatures so that the lowest temperature for any fish will meet the minimum requirements.

* * *

The hazard which the FDA sought to minimize was the outgrowth and toxin formation of Clostridium botulism Type E spores of the bacteria which sometimes inhabit fish.

* * *

Congress decided to allow informal rulemaking to the FDA generally, § 371(a) but it also provided for formal rulemaking which, upon request, required "a public hearing for the purpose of receiving evidence relevant and material to the issues raised by such objections." § 371(e). It further provided that in such cases the "order shall be based only on substantial evidence of record at such hearing and shall set forth, as part of the order, detailed findings of fact on which the order is based."

* * *

.... [A] temporary suspension because of the presence of micro-organisms in food merits a formal procedure while permanent regulation of micro-organisms is achievable by informal "notice-and-comment" procedure. Even though we read the statute § 342(a)(4) broadly in terms of the authority delegated to the agency, we must, nevertheless, view with some strictness the minimal requirements for the informal "notice and comment" procedure that follows as of course....

We do not discount the logical arguments in support of a restrictive reading of § 342(a)(4), but we perceive a larger general purpose on the part of Congress in protecting the public health.

We come to this conclusion [because] ... until this enforcement proceeding was begun, no lawyer at the knowledgeable Food and Drug bar ever raised the question of lack of statutory delegation or even hinted at such a question. Second, [because] the body of data gathered by the experts, including those of the Technical Laboratory of the Bureau of Fisheries manifested a concern about the hazards of botulism....

* * *

The public interest will not permit invalidation simply on the basis of a lack of delegated statutory authority in this case. A gap in public health protection should not be created in the absence of a compelling reading based upon the utter absence of any statutory authority, even read expansively. Here we find no congressional history on the specific issue involved, and hence no impediment to the broader reading based on general purpose.[10]....

II

Appellants contend that there is an inadequate administrative record upon which to predicate judicial review, and that the failure to disclose to interested persons the factual material upon which the agency was relying vitiates the element of fairness which is essential to any kind of administrative action. Moreover, they argue

---

10. In December, 1972, Chief Counsel Hutt, speaking to the Annual Educational Conference of the Food and Drug Law Institute said, "(T)he Act must be regarded as a constitution." "(T)he fact that Congress simply has not considered or spoken on a particular issue certainly is no bar to the (FDA) exerting initiative and leadership in the public interest." 28 Food Drug Cosmetic Law Journal 177, 178–79 (March 1973). For a reply, see H. Thomas Austern, id. at 189 (March 1973). We do not take sides on the issue tendered, but we think Mr. Hutt's language to be conscious hyperbole. The test is not "initiative" but whether delegation may be fairly inferred from the general purpose.

that the "concise general statement of . . . basis and purpose" by the Commissioner was inadequate. 5 U.S.C. § 553.

[W]hat is an adequate "record"[11] [and] [t]he extent of the administrative record required for judicial review of informal rule-making is largely a function of the scope of judicial review. Even when the standard of review is whether the promulgation of the rule was "arbitrary, capricious, an abuse of discretion, or otherwise not in accordance with law," as specified in 5 U.S.C. § 706(2)(A), judicial review must nevertheless, be based on the "whole record" (id.). . . .

This raises several questions regarding the informal rulemaking procedure followed here: (1) What record does a reviewing court look to? (2) How much of what the agency relied on should have been disclosed to interested persons? (3) To what extent must the agency respond to criticism that is material?

A

With respect to the content of the administrative "record," the Supreme Court has told us that in informal rulemaking, "the focal point for judicial review should be the administrative record already in existence, not some new record made initially in the reviewing court." See *Camp v. Pitts*, 411 U.S. 138 (1973).

No contemporaneous record was made or certified. When, during the enforcement action, the basis for the regulation was sought through pretrial discovery, the record was created by searching the files of the FDA and the memories of those who participated in the process of rulemaking. This resulted in . . . the comments received from outside parties during the administrative "notice-and-comment" proceeding and . . . scientific data and the like upon which the Commissioner now says he relied but which were not made known to the interested parties.

* * *

B

The key issues were (1) whether, in the light of the rather scant history of botulism in whitefish, that species should have been considered separately rather than included in a general regulation which failed to distinguish species from species; (2) whether the application of the proposed T–T–S requirements to smoked whitefish made the whitefish commercially unsaleable; and (3)

---

11. Even under the standard of "arbitrary, capricious, an abuse of discretion or otherwise not in accordance with law," § 706(2)(A), generally used in informal rulemaking review, "the court shall review the whole record . . . and due account shall be taken of the rule of prejudicial error." § 706 (Emphasis added.) See Citizens to preserve Overton Park v. Volpe, 401 U.S. 402 (1971).

whether the agency recognized that prospect, but nevertheless decided that the public health needs should prevail even if that meant commercial death for the whitefish industry. The procedural issues were whether, in the light of these key questions, the agency procedure was inadequate because (i) it failed to disclose to interested parties the scientific data and the methodology upon which it relied; and (ii) because it failed utterly to address itself to the pertinent question of commercial feasibility.

* * *

2. The Scientific Data

Interested parties were not informed of the scientific data, or at least of a selection of such data deemed important by the agency, so that comments could be addressed to the data. Appellants argue that unless the scientific data relied upon by the agency are spread upon the public records, criticism of the methodology used or the meaning to be inferred from the data is rendered impossible.

We agree with appellants in this case, for although we recognize that an agency may resort to its own expertise outside the record in an informal rulemaking procedure, we do not believe that when the pertinent research material is readily available and the agency has no special expertise on the precise parameters involved, there is any reason to conceal the scientific data relied upon from the interested parties. As Judge Leventhal said in *Portland Cement Ass'n v. Ruckelshaus*, 486 F.2d 375, 393 (1973). "It is not consonant with the purpose of a rulemaking proceeding to promulgate rules on the basis of inadequate data, or on data that (in) critical degree, is known only to the agency." This is not a case where the agency methodology was based on material supplied by the interested parties themselves. Cf. *International Harvester Co. v. Ruckelshaus*, 478 F. 2d 615, 632 (1973). Here all the scientific research was collected by the agency, and none of it was disclosed to interested parties as the material upon which the proposed rule would be fashioned. Nor was an articulate effort made to connect the scientific requirements to available technology that would make commercial survival possible, though the burden of proof was on the agency. This required it to "bear a burden of adducing a reasoned presentation supporting the reliability of its methodology." *International Harvester*, supra, 643.

Though a reviewing court will not match submission against counter-submission to decide whether the agency was correct in its conclusion on scientific matters (unless that conclusion is arbitrary), it will consider whether the agency has taken account of all "relevant factors and whether there has been a clear error of judgment." *Overton Park* supra, 415–416.

If the failure to notify interested persons of the scientific research upon which the agency was relying actually prevented the presentation of relevant comment, the agency may be held not to have considered all "the relevant factors.".... Indeed, the FDA's own regulations now specifically require that every notice of proposed rulemaking contain "references to all data and information on which the Commissioner relies for the proposal (copies or a full list of which shall be a part of the administrative file on the matter ...)." 21 C.F.R. § 10.40(b) (1977).

.... When the basis for a proposed rule is a scientific decision, the scientific material which is believed to support the rule should be exposed to the view of interested parties for their comment ..... To suppress meaningful comment by failure to disclose the basic data relied upon is akin to rejecting comment altogether. For unless there is common ground, the comments are unlikely to be of a quality that might impress a careful agency. The inadequacy of comment in turn leads in the direction of arbitrary decision-making....

C

Appellants additionally attack the "concise general statement" required by APA, 5 U.S.C. § 553, as inadequate. We think that, in the circumstances, it was less than adequate. It is not in keeping with the rational process to leave vital questions, raised by comments which are of cogent materiality, completely unanswered. The agencies certainly have a good deal of discretion in expressing the basis of a rule, but the agencies do not have quite the prerogative of obscurantism reserved to legislatures. "Congress did not purport to transfer its legislative power to the unbounded discretion of the regulatory body." *F.C.C. v. RCA Communications, Inc.*, 346 U.S. 86, 90 (1953)....

The test of adequacy of the "concise general statement" was expressed by Judge McGowan in the following terms:

> We do not expect the agency to discuss every item of fact or opinion included in the submissions made to it in informal rulemaking. We do expect that, if the judicial review which Congress has thought it important to provide is to be meaningful, the 'concise general statement of ... basis and purpose' mandated by Section 4 will enable us to see what major issues of policy were ventilated by the informal proceedings and why the agency reacted to them as it did. *Automotive Parts & Accessories Ass'n v. Boyd*, 407 F.2d 330, 338, (1968).

* * *

The Secretary was squarely faced with the question whether it was necessary to formulate a rule with specific parameters that applied to all species of fish, and particularly whether lower temperatures with the addition of nitrite and salt would not be sufficient. Though this alternative was suggested by an agency of the federal government, its suggestion, though acknowledged, was never answered.

Moreover, the comment that to apply the proposed T–T–S requirements to whitefish would destroy the commercial product was neither discussed nor answered. We think that to sanction silence in the face of such vital questions would be to make the statutory requirement of a "concise general statement" less than an adequate safeguard against arbitrary decision-making.

* * *

One may recognize that even commercial infeasibility cannot stand in the way of an overwhelming public interest. Yet the administrative process should disclose, at least, whether the proposed regulation is considered to be commercially feasible, or whether other considerations prevail even if commercial infeasibility is acknowledged.... In the light of the history of smoked whitefish to which we have referred, we find no articulate balancing here sufficient to make the procedure followed less than arbitrary.

* * *

After seven years of relative inaction, the FDA has apparently not reviewed the T–T–S regulations in the light of present scientific knowledge and experience. In the absence of a new statutory directive by Congress regarding control of micro-organisms, which we hope will be worthy of its consideration, we think that the T–T–S standards should be reviewed again by the FDA.

We cannot, on this appeal, remand to the agency to allow further comments by interested parties, addressed to the scientific data now disclosed at the trial below. We hold in this enforcement proceeding, therefore, that the regulation, as it affects non-vacuum-packed hot-smoked whitefish, was promulgated in an arbitrary manner and is invalid.

When the District Court held the regulation to be valid, it properly exercised its discretion to grant the injunction. In view of our conclusion to the contrary, we must reverse the grant of the injunction and direct that the complaint be dismissed.

Notes & Questions

Apply the exhaustion doctrine and the final order rule to this case. Which is more pertinent to the case as decided? How might the other have been used by the court to produce another solution?

Find § 553, § 556 & § 557 of the APA and read them.

Does this case involve formal or informal legislative rulemaking? What sections of the APA are involved? How does this case refine the words of the APA?

After this case, how detailed an administrative record must be kept by an agency writing a legislative rule?

In a previous case the Court assumed that the facts of the issue could be assumed to support the rule. Does this case support or reverse this assumption?

As set in this case, what is the relationship between the administrative order and the record on which it is based?

What is the relationship between the intent of Congress and the Administrative rule? How restrictive are the courts in interpreting the latter in terms of the former?

What role does the legislative record play in this case?

What basis for judicial review is considered here? Upon which foundations for judicial review could you have made the best argument for overturning the agency's action?

What role does science play in this case? From this point forward would you argue that science will play a more or less important role in writing legislative rules.

If you were looking to establish a record of evidence to back-up a legislative rule, would you look to expertise within your agency, or from the outside? Explain.

How does this case further define "notice and comment" rulemaking from APA 553c?

§§

CHEVRON, U.S.A., INC. v. NATURAL RESOURCES DEFENSE COUNCIL, INC.

Supreme Court of the United States, 1984.
467 U.S. 837.

Justice STEVENS delivered the opinion of the Court.

In the Clean Air Act Amendments of 1977, Pub.L. 95–95 91 Stat. 685, Congress enacted certain requirements applicable to

States that had not achieved the national air quality standards established by the Environmental Protection Agency (EPA) pursuant to earlier legislation. The amended Clean Air Act required these "nonattainment" States to establish a permit program regulating "new or modified major stationary sources" of air pollution. Generally, a permit may not be issued for a new or modified major stationary source unless several stringent conditions are met. The EPA regulation promulgated to implement this permit requirement allows a State to adopt a plantwide definition of the term "stationary source."[2] Under this definition, an existing plant that contains several pollution-emitting devices may install or modify one piece of equipment without meeting the permit conditions if the alteration will not increase the total emissions from the plant. The question presented by these cases is whether EPA's decision to allow States to treat all of the pollution-emitting devices within the same industrial grouping as though they were encased within a single "bubble" is based on a reasonable construction of the statutory term "stationary source."

I

The EPA regulations containing the plantwide definition of the term stationary source were promulgated on October 14, 1981. 46 Fed. Reg. 50766. Respondents filed a timely petition for review in the United States Court of Appeals for the District of Columbia Circuit pursuant to 42 U.S.C. § 7607(b)(1). The Court of Appeals set aside the regulations. Natural Resources Defense Council, Inc. v. Gorsuch 685 F.2d 718 (1982).

The court observed that the relevant part of the amended Clean Air Act "does not explicitly define what Congress envisioned as a 'stationary source', to which the permit program ... should apply," and further stated that the precise issue was not "squarely addressed in the legislative history." Id., at 723. In light of its conclusion that the legislative history bearing on the question was "at best contradictory," it reasoned that "the purposes of the nonattainment program should guide our decision here." Id., at 726 n.39. Based on two of its precedents concerning the applicability of the bubble concept to certain Clean Air Act programs, the court stated that the bubble concept was "mandatory" in programs designed merely to maintain existing air quality, but held that it was "inappropriate" in programs enacted to improve air quality. Id., at 726. Since the purpose of the permit program—its "raison d'etre," in the court's view—was to improve air quality, the court held that the bubble concept was inapplicable in these cases under

---

2. "(i) 'Stationary source' means any building, structure, facility, or installation which emits or may emit any air pollutant subject to regulation under the Act." 40 CFR § 51.18(j)(1)(i)(1983).

its prior precedents. Ibid. It therefore set aside the regulations embodying the bubble concept as contrary to law. We granted certiorari to review that judgment, 461 U.S. 956 (1983), and we now reverse.

The basic legal error of the Court of Appeals was to adopt a static judicial definition of the term "stationary source" when it had decided that Congress itself had not commanded that definition. Respondents do not defend the legal reasoning of the Court of Appeals. Nevertheless, since this Court reviews judgments, not opinions, we must determine whether the Court of Appeals' legal error resulted in an erroneous judgment on the validity of the regulations.

II

When a court reviews an agency's construction of the statute which it administers, it is confronted with two questions. First, always, is the question whether Congress has directly spoken to the precise question at issue. If the intent of Congress is clear, that is the end of the matter; for the court, as well as the agency, must give effect to the unambiguously expressed intent of Congress.[9] If, however, the court determines Congress has not directly addressed the precise question at issue, the court does not simply impose its own construction on the statute,[10] as would be necessary in the absence of an administrative interpretation. Rather, if the statute is silent or ambiguous with respect to the specific issue, the question for the court is whether the agency's answer is based on a permissible construction of the statute.[11]

"The power of an administrative agency to administer a congressionally created ... program necessarily requires the formulation of policy and the making of rules to fill any gap left, implicitly or explicitly, by Congress." Morton v. Ruiz, 415 U.S. 199 (1974). If Congress has explicitly left a gap for the agency to fill, there is an express delegation of authority to the agency to elucidate a specific provision of the statute by regulation. Such legislative regulations are given controlling weight unless they are arbitrary, capricious, or manifestly contrary to the statute. Sometimes the legislative delegation to an agency on a particular question is implicit rather than

9. The judiciary is the final authority on issues of statutory construction and must reject administrative constructions which are contrary to clear congressional intent. If a court, employing traditional tools of statutory construction, ascertains that Congress had an intention on the precise question at issue, that intention is the law and must be given effect.

10. See generally, R. POUND, THE SPIRIT OF THE COMMON LAW 174–175 (1921).

11. The court need not conclude that the agency construction was the only one it permissibly could have adopted to uphold the construction, or even the reading the court would have reached if the question initially had arisen in a judicial proceeding.

explicit. In such a case, a court may not substitute its own construction of a statutory provision for a reasonable interpretation made by the administrator of an agency.

We have long recognized that considerable weight should be accorded to an executive department's construction of a statutory scheme it is entrusted to administer, and the principle of deference to administrative interpretations.

> ... has been consistently followed by this Court whenever decision as to the meaning or reach of a statute has involved reconciling conflicting policies, and a full understanding of the force of the statutory policy in the given situation has depended upon more than ordinary knowledge respecting the matters subjected to agency regulations.

> See, e.g., ... If this choice represents a reasonable accommodation of conflicting policies that were committed to the agency's care by the statute, we should not disturb it unless it appears from the statute or its legislative history that the accommodation is not one that Congress would have sanctioned. United States v. Shimer 367 U.S. 374, 382, 383 (1961).

In light of these well-settled principles it is clear that the Court of Appeals misconceived the nature of its role in reviewing the regulations at issue. Once it determined, after its own examination of the legislation, that Congress did not actually have an intent regarding the applicability of the bubble concept to the permit program, the question before it was not whether in its view the concept is "inappropriate" in the general context of a program designed to improve air quality, but whether the Administrator's view that it is appropriate in the context of this particular program is a reasonable one. Based on the examination of the legislation and its history which follows, we agree with the Court of Appeals that Congress did not have a specific intention on the applicability of the bubble concept in these cases, and conclude that the EPA's use of that concept here is a reasonable policy choice for the agency to make.

* * *

VII

In this Court respondents... contend that the text of the act requires the EPA to [say that] ... if either a component of a plant, or the plant as a whole, emits over 100 tons of pollutant, it is a major stationary source.

Statutory Language

The definition of the term "stationary source" in § 111(a)(3) refers to "any building, structure, facility, or installation" which emits air pollution. . . . [T]he text of the statute does not make this definition applicable to the permit program. Petitioners therefore maintain that there is no statutory language even relevant to ascertaining the meaning of stationary source in the permit program aside from § 302(j), which defines the term "major stationary source." . . . We disagree with petitioners on this point.

The definition in § 302(j) tells us what the word "major" means—a source must emit at least 100 tons of pollution to qualify—but it sheds virtually no light on the meaning of the term "stationary source." It does equate a source with a facility—a "major emitting facility" and a "major stationary source" are synonymous under § 302(j). The ordinary meaning of the term "facility" is some collection of integrated elements which has been designed and constructed to achieve some purpose. Moreover, it is certainly no affront to common English usage to take a reference to a major facility or a major source to connote an entire plant as opposed to its constituent parts. Basically, however, the language of § 302(j) simply does not compel any given interpretation of the term "source."

Respondents recognize that, and hence point to § 111(a)(3). Although the definition in that section is not literally applicable to the permit program, it sheds as much light on the meaning of the word "source" as anything in the statute. As respondents point out, use of the words "building, structure, facility, or installation," as the definition of source, could be read to impose the permit conditions on an individual building that is a part of a plant. . . . On the other hand, the. . . . language may reasonably be interpreted to impose the requirement on any discrete, but integrated, operation which pollutes. This gives meaning to all of the terms—a single building, not part of a larger operation, would be covered if it emits more than 100 tons of pollution, as would any facility, structure, or installation. Indeed, the language itself implies a "bubble concept" of sorts: each enumerated item would seem to be treated as if it were encased in a bubble. While respondents insist that each of these terms must be given a discrete meaning, they also argue that § 111(a)(3) defines "source" as that term is used in § 302(j). The latter section, however, equates a source with a facility, whereas the former defines "source" as a facility, among other items.

We are not persuaded that parsing of general terms in the text of the statute will reveal an actual intent of Congress. . . . . . To the extent any congressional "intent" can be discerned from this language, it would appear that the listing of overlapping, illustrative terms was intended to enlarge, rather than to confine, the scope of the agency's power to regulate particular sources in order to effectuate the policies of the act.

Legislative History

In addition, respondents argue that the legislative history and policies of the act foreclose the plantwide definition, and that the EPA's interpretation is not entitled to deference because it represents a sharp break with prior interpretations of the act.

Based on our examination of the legislative history, we agree with the Court of Appeals that it is unilluminating...... We find that the legislative history as a whole is silent on the precise issue before us. It is, however, consistent with the view that the EPA should have broad discretion in implementing the policies of the 1977 Amendments.

More importantly, that history plainly identifies the policy concerns that motivated the enactment; the plantwide definition is fully consistent with one of those concerns—the allowance of reasonable economic growth—and, whether or not we believe it most effectively implements the other, we must recognize that the EPA has advanced a reasonable explanation for its conclusion that the regulations serve the environmental objectives as well.

Our review of the EPA's varying interpretations of the word "source"—both before and after the 1977 Amendments—convinces us that the agency primarily responsible for administering this important legislation has consistently interpreted it flexibly—not in a sterile textual vacuum, but in the context of implementing policy decisions in a technical and complex arena. The fact that the agency has from time to time changed its interpretation of the term "source" does not, as respondents argue, lead us to conclude that no deference should be accorded the agency's interpretation of the statute. An initial agency interpretation is not instantly carved in stone. On the contrary, the agency, to engage in informed rulemaking, must consider varying interpretations.....

Significantly, it was not the agency in 1980, but rather the Court of Appeals that read the statute inflexibly to command a plantwide definition for programs designed to maintain clean air and to forbid such a definition for programs designed to improve air quality. The distinction the court drew may well be a sensible one, but our labored review of the problem has surely disclosed that it is not a distinction that Congress ever articulated itself, or one that the EPA found in the statute before the courts began to review the legislative work product. We conclude that it was the Court of Appeals, rather than Congress or any of the decisionmakers who are authorized by Congress to administer this legislation, that was primarily responsible for the 1980 position taken by the agency.

Policy

The arguments over policy that are advanced in the parties' briefs create the impression that respondents are now waging in a judicial forum a specific policy battle which they ultimately lost in the agency and in the 32 jurisdictions opting for the "bubble concept," but one which was never waged in the Congress. Such policy arguments are more properly addressed to legislators or administrators, not to judges.[38]

In these cases, the Administrator's interpretation represents a reasonable accommodation of manifestly competing interests and is entitled to deference: the regulatory scheme is technical and complex, the agency considered the matter in a detailed and reasoned fashion, and the decision involves reconciling conflicting policies. Congress intended to accommodate both interests, but did not do so itself on the level of specificity presented by these cases. Perhaps that body consciously desired the Administrator to strike the balance at this level, thinking that those with great expertise and charged with responsibility for administering the provision would be in a better position to do so; perhaps it simply did not consider the question at this level; and perhaps Congress was unable to forge a coalition on either side of the question, and those on each side decided to take their chances with the scheme devised by the agency. For judicial purposes, it matters not which of these things occurred.

Judges are not experts in the field, and are not part of either political branch of the Government. Courts must, in some cases, reconcile competing political interests, but not on the basis of the judges' personal policy preferences. In contrast, an agency to which Congress has delegated policy-making responsibilities may, within the limits of that delegation, properly rely upon the incumbent administration's views of wise policy to inform its judgments. While agencies are not directly accountable to the people, the Chief Executive is, and it is entirely appropriate for this political branch of the Government to make such policy choices—resolving the competing interests which Congress itself either inadvertently did

---

38. Respondents point out if a brand new factory that will emit over 100 tons of pollutants is constructed in a non-attainment area, that plant must obtain a permit pursuant to § 172(b)(6) and in order to do so, it must satisfy the § 173 conditions, including the LAER requirement. Respondents argue if an old plant containing several large emitting units is to be modernized by the replacement of one or more units emitting over 100 tons of pollutant with a new unit emitting less—but still more than 100 tons— the result should be no different simply because "it happens to be built not at a new site, but within a pre-existing plant." Brief for Respondents 4.

not resolve, or intentionally left to be resolved by the agency charged with the administration of the statute in light of everyday realities.

When a challenge to an agency construction of a statutory provision, fairly conceptualized, really centers on the wisdom of the agency's policy, rather than whether it is a reasonable choice within a gap left open by Congress, the challenge must fail. In such a case, federal judges—who have no constituency—have a duty to respect legitimate policy choices made by those who do. The responsibilities for assessing the wisdom of such policy choices and resolving the struggle between competing views of the public interest are not judicial ones: "Our Constitution vests such responsibilities in the political branches." TVA v. Hill, 437 U.S. 153, 195 (1978).

We hold that the EPA's definition of the term "source" is a permissible construction of the statute which seeks to accommodate progress in reducing air pollution with economic growth. "The Regulations which the Administrator has adopted provide what the agency could allowably view as . . . [an] effective reconciliation of these twofold ends. . . ." United States v. Shimer, 367 U.S. at 383.

The judgment of the Court of Appeals is reversed. It is so ordered.

Notes & Questions

What role is played in this case by concern for the "intent of Congress"? How is this consideration "constitutionally" important to agency action?

Does *Chevron* limit the discretion of the courts more than it limits the discretion of administrative agencies?

Why does the Supreme Court wish to limit the input of other Article III Courts into the legislative rulemaking process?

How does this case affect the definitions of *"ultra vires"* and "arbitrary and capricious" as grounds for judicial review? Are these definitions further developments of how *Nova Scotia* defined these terms, or changes of direction from where *Nova Scotia* was going with the concept of judicial review?

What role does the legislative history or record play in this case? Does its role here build upon or replace its role as defined in *Nova Scotia*?

Does this case make "new" policy? How? Why not?

Can you justify this decision on Constitutional grounds? [Think in terms of separation of powers and delegation of power.]

EXERCISE: LAW FROM SCRATCH

This case created the "Chevron" test which has been used in countless administrative law cases to judge the legitimacy of agency action during judicial review. The Chevron test has two parts. In **CHEVRON I**, the court asks if the statute is clear and unambiguous. If it is, then the court rules with the statute, as the agency must respect the obvious intent of Congress. However, if the statute is ambiguous, then the court applies **CHEVRON II**, which asks if the agency construction of the statute is "reasonable." If it is a reasonable construction of the statute, then it is a "permissible" construction and the court has no leeway to impose its interpretation of the statute over the agency's, even if the court does not agree with the agency. As you think about the codification and implementation of your policy design argument, remember to consider the CHEVRON test and what it means for a focus on administrative agencies within your legal argument. Also examine pre-Chevron cases and analyze them to see if the decisions would have been different had the Chevron test existed.

Constitutional Law

The ultimate source of legitimate legal authority in the United States is its Constitution. All Administrative, Statute, and Common Law must pass the constitutional test in order to be valid law. The role of this Constitutional "test" in the policy design process is marked by the decision-makers consciousness of how specific Articles and Amendments of our Constitution apply to environmental law. When creating a policy design argument, one needs to consider the opportunities and constraints presented by the Constitution. However, we are treating Constitutional Law last in this chapter as its role in the protection of nature has, to date, been minimal.

Specifically, as we will see, the environment, not being a stated component of the original freedoms and processes outlined in the Constitution, has not been able to depend on full consideration within this foundational document. However, the Constitution, by providing the ultimate standards of the rule of law itself, is necessary to environmental policy design for at least two reasons other than its foundational status. First, it provides pitfalls for those interested in conservation or preservation, by, for example, protecting private property rights against public efforts to use land sustainably. Second, in designing a policy one should always be conscious of the potential to argue that a particular environmental concern should be categorized as a public right, even if it was not in the past. The argument for the collective nature of resources may include a stronger argument for constitutional status that should always be considered a possibility.

The 1787 Constitution contains seven articles within the main body of its text. These create the main branches of the federal government (Art. I: Congress; Art. II: Executive; Art. III: Federal Courts) and invest them with specific powers and responsibilities, as well as a method by which the Constitution can, itself, be amended. These amendments, now numbering twenty-seven, create and define the rights and duties of citizens and are the bedrock of our republican form of government, which sets these rights and duties apart from majority rule as critical prerequisites to the basic freedom of the United States citizen.

This section of the chapter will examine some of these articles and amendments, identifying how they act as sources, constraints, or support for environmental and natural resource law.

THE SUPREMACY CLAUSE

"This Constitution, and the Laws of the United States which shall be made in Pursuance thereof; and all Treaties made, or which shall be made, under the Authority of the United States, shall be the supreme Law of the Land; and the Judges in every State shall be bound thereby, any Thing in the Constitution or laws of any State to the Contrary notwithstanding."

The Constitution's Supremacy Clause (Art. VI, § 2) mandates that federal laws (including ratified treaties) are superior to state and local law regarding issues of national concern. The federal government may legislate in fields traditionally reserved for the states. For instance, Congress gave the Nuclear Regulatory Commission exclusive power to regulate the safety of nuclear power plants, a police power normally left to the states. However, at the same time our Congress explicitly protected the states' traditional power to oversee the economic practicality of nuclear power plants.[88]

Congress may even preempt a policy space by implication, and if a federal scheme is "pervasive" a state may not do anything to impair the federal scheme.[89] However, although definitive law is elusive, it is normally considered that 'impair' means only actions by a state that do not meet the minimum standards set by the federal government. Usually, if a state wishes to regulate in excess of federal standards they are allowed to, the supremacy clause being considered a floor but not a ceiling. On the other hand, where

---

88. Pacific Gas & Electric v. State Energy Resources, 461 U.S. 190 (1983).

89. See Exxon Corp. v. Eagerton, 462 U.S. 176 (1983) (interstate natural gas rates are matters within FERC's authority and a state may not require that a state tax be absorbed by the producers; Congress may allow a state to regulate its intrastate gas rates).

Congress has not shown an intent to "occupy the field," or where local law does not present an obstacle to the accomplishment of the federal legislation, there is no preemption.[90]

Because most natural resource and environmental cases potentially involve national concerns, a state often may only regulate its natural resources in ways that Congress allows.[91] This has created our federal system and the basic theory of federalism that determined our modern environmental and resource law: ***cooperative federalism***. Specifically, cooperative federalism distributes the responsibilities of environmental protection and conservation so that the federal government is charged with setting national standards while the states have the duty to implement these standards, considering local conditions. For example, the Clean Air Act sets federal quality or performance standards know as National Ambient Air Quality Standards (NAAQS) but leaves implementation, through State Implementation Plans (SIPS), to the states.[92]

THE 10TH AMENDMENT

"The powers not delegated to the United States by the Constitution, nor prohibited by it to the States, are reserved to the States respectively, or to the people."

An exception at one time existed to the Supremacy Clause. Under the 10th Amendment, "state sovereignty shields the States from generally applicable federal regulations."[93] This "shield" was called into doubt by *State of Nev. v. Skinner*[94] and was overcome, especially in terms of international treaty as federal law, by the

---

90. See Gulf Oil Corp. v. Wyoming Oil and Gas Conservation Commission, 693 P.2d 227 (Wyo.1985) (Congress did not intend to exclude states from regulating mining activity on federal land so as to safeguard environmental values); Bass River Associates v. The Mayor, Township Commissioner, 743 F.2d 159 (3d Cir.1984) (township's prohibition of "floating homes" not preempted by regulation of vessel waste discharges in the Federal Water Pollution Control Act).

91. See North Dakota v. United States, 460 U.S. 300 (1983) (Congress allowed states to veto which lands Interior Department planned to set aside for waterfowl wetland areas, but if a state did not initially exercise a veto, it lacked the power to affect Interior's subsequent decisions); New Mexico v. Mescalero

Apache Tribe, 462 U.S. 324 (1983) (Indian tribe and federal agency developed tribe's hunting lands and therefore had exclusive power to license out-of-state hunters; because state did not help develop lands, state could not license hunters); Ventura County v. Gulf Oil Corp., 601 F.2d 1080 (9th Cir.1979), affirmed, 445 U.S. 947 (1980) (the Property Clause, Art. IV, § 3, allows Congress to restrict a state's traditional zoning power if the state tries to impose zoning regulations on federal lands).

92. See 42 U.S.C. §§ 7408–9 for NAAQS and 42 U.S.C. § 7410 for SIPS.

93. FERC v. Mississippi, 456 U.S. 742 (1982).

94. 884 F.2d 445, 58 USLW 2156 (9th Cir.(Nev.) Aug 31, 1989)

case of *Missouri v. Holland*.[95] Overall, a 10th Amendment violation is judged by a two-part test: (1) Congress must have exercised a legitimate federal power, (2) the federal statute or regulation must have affected the states as states and impaired their ability to structure integral operations of traditional state functions.

Tenth Amendment arguments found little success in natural resources litigation because a party had difficulty proving that the federal regulation affected the state as a state. In *Hodel v. Virginia Surface Mining*,[96] the Court found no 10th Amendment violation when Congress required states to establish minimum standards for land reclamation concerning surface coal mines. In *FERC v. Mississippi*,[97] the Court allowed Congress to require a state public utility commission to "consider" federal gas and electric rate-making standards. The Court reasoned that because Congress could preempt the field entirely through the Supremacy Clause and that the states have a defined role to play in cooperative federalism, it was not a violation of the 10th Amendment. This functional test was then called into doubt by *Alabama Elk River Development Agency v. Rogers*,[98] and with *Garcia v. San Antonio Metropolitan Transit Authority*,[99] a case concerned with the application of the Commerce Clause, the Supreme Court effectively eliminated the 10th Amendment as a limit on congressional power.

THE COMMERCE CLAUSE

"The Congress shall have the Power ... To regulate Commerce with foreign Nations, and among the several States, and with the Indian Tribes; ..."

The Commerce Clause (Art. 1, § 8, Cl. 3) grants exclusive federal jurisdiction to all activities that can reasonably be argued to be interstate commerce. The Clause also serves as a source of constitutional authority for federal legislation regulating natural resource matters within states.[100] In the natural resources field the exercise of this important constitutional power may also limit state regulatory authority. For example, in *New England Power Co. v. New Hampshire*,[101] an interstate power company regulated by the

95. Missouri v. Holland, 252 U.S. 416 (1920) (the 10th Amendment cannot trump an Article II Treaty transformed by Congress into municipal law).

96. 452 U.S. 264 (1981).

97. 456 U.S. 742 (1982).

98. 516 So.2d 637.

99. 469 U.S. 528 (1985).

100. See Utah v. Marsh, 740 F.2d 799 (10th Cir.1984) (Congress empowered under the Commerce Clause to regulate discharge of dredged material into lake located entirely within state).

101. 455 U.S. 331 (1982).

federal government produced cheap hydroelectric power in New Hampshire. The New Hampshire Utility Commission wanted to retain the cheap power within New Hampshire. Because the state commission believed that a federal power statute had granted the states authority to regulate their own hydroelectricity, it denied authority to the interstate power company to export out-of-state hydroelectricity. The U.S. Supreme Court reversed, holding that the Federal Power Act did not grant the state such power. In the absence of granted power, the Court said that "[o]ur cases consistently have held that the Commerce Clause ... precludes a state from mandating that its residents be given a preferred right of access, over out-of-state consumers, to natural resources located within its borders."[102]

New England Power partly relied on what commentators call the "dormant" Commerce Clause. "Even in the absence of congressional legislation, 'the Commerce Clause contains an implied limitation on the power of the States to interfere with or impose burdens on interstate commerce'."[103] This "implied limitation" precludes a state from regulating the interstate flow of its natural resources even if Congress has remained absolutely silent on the matter.

A classic dormant Commerce Clause case is *Sporhase v. Nebraska*.[104] The plaintiff owned land in both Nebraska and Colorado and irrigated both tracts from his well in Nebraska. The use of Nebraska water on Colorado land violated a Nebraska statute that allowed exportation of state water only if the importing state reciprocated. Colorado did not allow exportation of water. The Nebraska statute violated the Commerce Clause because it restricted the interstate flow of water.[105]

However, the Commerce Clause does not preclude a state from regulating its natural resources in a way that does not affect interstate commerce. For instance, in *Arkansas Electric* the state

---

102. 455 U.S. at 338.

103. Arkansas Electric Co-op. Corp. v. Arkansas Public Service Commission, 461 U.S. 375 (1983).

104. 458 U.S. 941 (1982)

105. See also United States v. Taylor, 752 F.2d 757 (1st Cir.1985) (a Maine statute prohibiting persons from importing live fish used for bait violates the Commerce Clause as facially discriminating against interstate commerce—this judgment has been subsequently reversed as being in line with the requirements of the Commerce Clause by Maine v. Taylor, 477 U.S. 131); South Central Timber Development v. Wun-

nicke, 467 U.S. 82 (1984) (state statute limiting sale of timber from state lands to those who would process the timber within state is unconstitutional as violating dormant Commerce Clause); Western Oil & Gas Association v. Cory, 726 F.2d 1340 (9th Cir.1984) (state regulations computing "rent" for leasing of state-owned tidelands based on volume of oil violates Commerce Clause since rent not directed to compensating state for use of land); People of State of Illinois v. General Electric Co., 683 F.2d 206 (7th Cir.1982) (Illinois statute that barred disposal in Illinois of nuclear wastes from other states, but allowed deposits from plants within Illinois, im-

utility commission wanted to regulate a co-op wholesaler of electricity that sold only to in-state retailers. Because the applicable federal agency, FERC, had previously ruled that it had no jurisdiction over such co-ops, no federal agency regulated the rates of the wholesaler. However, the Court did not find an implied intention from Congress to regulate such in-state wholesalers of electricity. Because the burden on interstate commerce caused by the state regulation was slight in comparison to the local benefits, the state regulations did not "affect" interstate commerce and did not violate the Commerce Clause.[106]

Overall, there are *judicially enforceable outer limits* to the Commerce Clause in terms of the subject of the case being connected to interstate commerce and therefore accessible from this constitutional provision.[107] In 1997 the D.C. Circuit[108] judged that the Delhi Sand Fly, an insect only found in one particular part of California, was nonetheless a part of Interstate Commerce and a subject of federal jurisdiction under the Commerce Clause. The court argued that it was interstate commerce because it was both connected to the "use of the channels of interstate commerce" and had a "substantial relation to interstate commerce." In the first instance it is necessary for Congress to control the interstate transport of species and so the fly falls under Congress' power to "keep the channels of interstate commerce free from immoral and injurious uses." In the second case the fly was a necessity to biodiversity which was interstate commerce while its regulation as an endangered species would aid in the control of adverse effects to interstate commerce. The court, in effect associated ecosystems with commerce.[109]

This expansion of the Commerce Clause was then curtailed by the Supreme Court in the *Lopez* case.[110] Here the Court set down a test that allowed the Commerce Clause to be used only if at least one of three conditions applied: (1) if the channels of interstate commerce were affected by the thing in question, (2) if the subject's instrumentalities related to interstate commerce, or (3) if the facts

permissibly burdened interstate commerce).

106. See also Rochester Gas & Elec. Corp. v. Public Service Com'n, 754 F.2d 99 (2d Cir.1985) (state public service commission's policy of including estimate of electric company's wholesale electric sales in company's revenue base did not violate dormant Commerce Clause); City of Centralia, Washington v. FERC, 661 F.2d 787 (9th Cir.1981) (if a hydro-electric plant which served local needs failed, out-of-state power would not necessarily enter state and therefore

the plant did not affect interstate commerce; consequently, the plant did not need a federal license).

107. These limits are first confronted in United States v. Lopez, 514 U.S. 549 (1995) and set into detail in United States v. Morrison, 529 U.S. 598 (2000).

108. National Association Of Home Builders v. Babbitt 130 F.3d 1041 (D.C. Cir. 1997)

109. *id.* Sentelle, Circuit Judge, dissenting, "An ecosystem is an ecosystem and commerce is commerce."

110. Lopez *supra* note 110.

related to activities had a substantial relation to interstate commerce.[111]

This test was used to support the Fish and Wildlife Service and their effort to create an experimental wolf population. In *Gibbs v. Babbitt*[112] the majority identified the taking of wolves as covering a number of economic markets and as an integral dimension to the preservation of species important to the welfare of the country. They contended that invalidating this effort would call into question the ability of the federal government to preserve local scarce resources for the future benefit of all Americans and to protect economic activity for which the wolves were taken in the first place. Without the wolf there would be less tourism, scientific research, and no commercial trade in pelts, all of which are interstate activities. Although the establishment of this wolf population both protects and inhibits interstate commerce, the Court said that this balance was for the Congress to decide.

THE 5TH AMENDMENT: TAKING AND DUE PROCESS

"No person shall be . . . . deprived of life, liberty, or property, without due process of law; nor shall private property be taken for public use without just compensation."

A very important area of environmental law is land use. The government has the power of eminent domain to take private property for public use after paying "just compensation" to the owner for the "taking" of the property. Just compensation in most cases means fair market value of property on the date it is appropriated.[110]

The government has police power so that it can act in support of the public health and safety, to regulate matters that have a public purpose. Diminution in private property values caused by occasions of this police power are not always subject to compensation because "[t]o require compensation in all such circumstances would effectively compel the government to regulate by pur-

---

111. See Gibbs v. Babbitt 214 F.3d 483 (4th Cir. 2000).

112. 214 F.3d 483 (4th Cir. 2000).

113. See Kirby Forest Industries, Inc. v. United States, 467 U.S. 1, 104; S.Ct. 1887 (1984), (where there is a substantial delay between the date of valuation of the timberland taken for a national preserve, and the date judgment is paid, the condemnation award may be modified if the value of the land changes due to the delay); City of Shawnee v. Webb, 236 Kan. 504, 694 P.2d 896 (1985) (fair market value ascertained by evidence of sales of comparable properties); St. Genevieve Gas Co. v. TVA, 747 F.2d 1411 (11th Cir.1984) (where TVA flooded an area where condemnee held mineral leases, condemnee was entitled to nominal damages of $1 if the leases had no commercial value at the time of the taking).

chase."[114] The standard here is that the state should only use private property if it *substantially advances* the public purposes as a type of *rough proportionality* between private and public benefit.[115]

So, if the government can justify land use, as within its police power, it can always take the property as long as it compensates the owner. However, under certain circumstances, police power can be used without the demands of compensating the owners. In general, therefore, eminent domain disputes focus on what constitutes "public use" or "property" under the Fifth Amendment.[116] The argument is usually over whether the exercise of police power is in fact a "taking," requiring compensation or a legitimate use of police power which does not. This involves a judgment as to whether a property owner has received procedural and substantive due process protection regarding the regulation of the property.

The argument over eminent domain is further complicated by government's regulation of one's use of property, short of condemnation, to protect the public health and safety. Specifically, the question regards the public regulation of private uses of property. The contention is that public interest should be able to regulate the use of private property for public ends. For example, to protect wetlands, to stop beach erosion, to maintain the character of a community, should the government be able to prevent a landowner's use of his property?

In these cases, where the government does not condemn, or take over ownership of the property using eminent domain, but leaves it in the hands of the private landowner, restricting their use of it through public regulation, significant constitutional controversies arise. Specifically, in the last fifteen years, the Supreme Court has adjudicated a number of "inverse condemnation" cases and judged whether they were or were not "takings" or proper uses of police power, under the 5th Amendment.[117] These cases have significantly restricted the government's power to regulate private property in the public interest as anything other than an outright taking requiring compensation to the landowner. Recently, however, two members of the Court, Justices Kennedy and O'Connor,

114. Andrus v. Allard, 444 U.S. 51, 65, 100 S.Ct. 318, 326, 62 L.Ed.2d 210 (1979).

115. The Supreme Court has denied the advances test for a combination of due process and proportionality. See Justice O'Conner's majority opinion in Lingle v. Chevron, U.S.A., Inc., 544 U.S. 528 (2005).

116. United States v. 50 Acres of Land, 469 U.S. 24, 105 S.Ct. 451, 83 L.Ed.2d 376 (1984) ("private property" in the Fifth Amendment encompasses property of state and local governments, and just compensation applies to public condemnees).

117. Nollan v. California Coastal Commission 483 U.S. 825 (1987); Lucas v. South Carolina Coastal Council 505 U.S. 1003 (1992); Dolan v. City of Tigard 114 S.Ct. 2309 (1994).

indicated that the strictest reading of these cases may be incorrect and that the legitimate use of police power to regulate private use of property short of outright taking may be stronger than heretofore assumed.[118] Overall, the courts have stated that while a police action that "denies all economically beneficial or productive use of land" is a taking, so are some inverse condemnations, depending on character, 'investment-backed expectations' and effect on landowners. The Supreme Court has also stated that post-regulation acquisition of property does not necessarily ban a takings claim.[119]

The "taking" does not always have to be for a public purpose. The government may exercise its eminent domain power to take private land from "A" to benefit private party "B", for instance when a local government takes property to allow a private development of it.[120] The government does not have to use the property to legitimate the "taking." If the government transfers property by its eminent domain power to private beneficiaries, the "taking" may be valid if it is for a public purpose.[121] This happened in the Hawaii Housing case which concerned the peculiar situation where a few owners controlled vast amounts of private land. The Hawaiian legislature adopted a plan whereby tenants could ask for a condemnation and a subsequent opportunity to purchase the land. Because the plan attacked the evils of concentrated ownership, it was imbued with a public purpose. Likewise, the exercise of eminent domain over a reservoir does not have to benefit the "entire community, nor even a considerable portion," for it to be for a public purpose.[122] If the government's objectives in condemning private property are "public in nature," such as the development of a water port, the incidental financial benefits to private parties are immaterial.[123]

If only a portion of a property owner's rights have been "taken" by government exercise of its police power, the owner need not be compensated. *Andrus v. Allard*,[124] involved the Eagle Protection Act which outlawed selling artifacts made of bald eagle feathers. A defendant, prosecuted under the act, argued that the regulation unconstitutionally "took" property owned by the defendant containing eagle feathers because the defendant lost all financial interest in the artifact. "The Eagle Protection Act did not require

---

118. Tahoe–Sierra Preservation Council, Inc. v. Tahoe Regional Planning Agency, 535 U.S. 302 (2002); Palazzolo v. Rhode Island, 533 U.S. 606 (2001).

119. Palazzolo v. Rhode Island 533 U.S. 606 (2001)

120. See Amen v. Dearborn, 718 F.2d 789, 798 (6th Cir.1983) and Kelo v. City of New London 545 U.S. 469 (2005).

121. Hawaii Housing Authority v. Midkiff, 467 U.S. 229 (1984).

122. Associated Enterprises v. Toltec Watershed, 656 P.2d 1144, 1148 (Wyo. 1983).

123. Griffin v. Bendick, R.I. 463 A.2d 1340 (1983).

124. 444 U.S. 51 (1979).

compensation because a full "taking" had not occurred." However, the Court reasoned that because ... "an owner possesses a full 'bundle' or property rights [such as possession and private owner- ship of the artifact], the destruction of one 'strand' of the bundle [the right to sell] is not a taking, because the aggregate must be viewed in its entirety.... [L]oss of future profits unaccompanied by any physical property restriction provides a slender reed upon which to rest a takings claim."[125] The taking of future interests also does not require compensation.[126]

However, if the regulation causes a substantial financial hard- ship to a private owner for the sake of minimal public interest, the regulation will either be an invalid exercise of the police power, or a "taking" subject to constitutional compensation.[127] For example, in *Kaiser Aetna v. United States*,[128] Kaiser Aetna spent millions of dollars to open a landlocked pond to the sea and to develop property around the pond. The government asserted that the pond's water was navigable and thus public property. The Court held that the government could not, without compensation, make the waters public because the government's interest in making a public right of access was small compared to Kaiser Aetna's interest in preserving its substantial private investment.[129]

A contrary result occurred in *Texaco, Inc. v. Short*.[130] Here the Supreme Court considered an Indiana statute which voided mineral interests that had been severed from the surface owner's estate if the mineral owner had not used the mineral interest for 20 years or registered it within two years after the passage of the act. To

---

125. 444 U.S. at 65, 66.

126. See PVM Redwood Co., Inc. v. United States, 686 F.2d 1327 (9th Cir. 1982) (lumber mill has no ownership interest in source of unowned timber supply and therefore a regulation con- verting supply lands into national park only frustrated plaintiff's expectations and did not constitute a "taking"); Sev- en Islands Land Co. v. Maine Land Use Regulation Commission, 450 A.2d 475 (Me.1982) (plaintiff owned 25,000 tim- bered acres of which the state set aside 2,700 acres for temporary deer refuge; "in 'taking' cases there is no place for expectations of future profits except to the extent those expectations are re- flected in present market value"); Luf v. Town of Southbury, 188 Conn. 336, 449 A.2d 1001 (1982) (diminution in proper- ty value as a result of city not complet- ing road to owners' land was not yet a "taking" because plaintiffs could still develop private access). Cf. Foster v. United States, 221 Ct.Cl. 412, 607 F.2d

943 (1979) (government refusal to per- mit holders of mineral interest on gov- ernment land access to the minerals constituted a permanent taking requir- ing compensation).

127. See Agins v. Tiburon, 447 U.S. 255 (1980); Skaw v. United States, 740 F.2d 932 (Fed.Cir.1984); Yuba Goldfields v. United States, 723 F.2d 884 (Fed.Cir. 1983).

128. 444 U.S. 164 (1979).

129. See also Whitney Benefits v. United States, 752 F.2d 1554 (Fed.Cir. 1985) (Federal prohibition of surface coal mining may so totally defeat coal owner's investment-backed expectations as to be a taking requiring compensa- tion); Noranda Exploration v. Ostrom, 113 Wis.2d 612, 335 N.W.2d 596 (1983) (statute providing for public disclosure of confidential mining exploration data found to be an unconstitutional taking).

130. 454 U.S. 516, 102 S.Ct. 781, 70 L.Ed.2d 738 (1982).

determine if there had been a "taking," the Court balanced the public benefit against the private burden. In the end, the statute was judged not to constitute a "taking" because it benefited the state by encouraging development of mineral interests and payment of taxes, while placing only minor burdens on the mineral interest owner to register or use the mineral interest.

The mineral interest owners in *Texaco, Inc.* also argued that the statute violated procedural due process because the owners received no actual notice of the new law. On this issue the Court split 5–to–4 against the owners; the majority held that the owners were charged with knowledge of all new statutes affecting property. *Texaco, Inc.* points out that a person has few procedural due process rights in relation to a legislative body. But if an administrative body performs an adjudicatory function, procedural due process rights grow.[131] These rights primarily include the right to notice and a hearing. This is both a tactical and strategic consideration when deciding which source of law is best for a particular law and policy design argument.

As with the Takings Clause, the right to procedural due process protection exists only if state action affects a plaintiff's recognized property rights.[132] Furthermore, procedural due process protections arise only if the government, not individuals, affect the property. Thus, in *Walker v. Cleary Petroleum Co.*[133] a government adjudication to force a pooling of natural gas violated procedural due process protections because newspaper publication was not reasonably calculated to reach an overseas owner. However, in another "forced pooling" case,[134] because the state merely provided a neutral forum for the dispute, it did not regulate the parties, and notice was not a constitutional necessity.

Statutes may provide exceptions to procedural protections. For instance, swift action may require the government to deprive an owner of certain property rights before affording a hearing. Even

---

131. Remember that the adjudicatory function is one delegated to administrative agencies by the courts.

132. See City of West Chicago v. NRC, 701 F.2d 632 (7th Cir.1983) (in a suit by a city to enjoin a company from demolishing its buildings contaminated with radioactivity, the city's generalized health, safety, and environmental concerns did not constitute "property" subject to procedural due process protection); Utah International Inc. v. Department of Interior, 553 F.Supp. 872 (D.Utah 1982), reversed on other grounds, Drummond Coal Co. v. Watt, 735 F.2d 469 (11th Cir.1984) (potential, as opposed to actual, coal lessees have no mineral property that may be afforded due process protection); Public Service Co. of Colorado v. PUC, 653 P.2d 1117 (Colo.1982) (under the 5th Amendment, consumers have a sufficient "property interest" in the expectation of utility service to receive a hearing before termination of the service, but have an insufficient "property interest" to receive a hearing before rate changes).

133. 421 So.2d 85 (Ala.1982).

134. Mountain States Natural Gas v. Petroleum Corp., 693 F.2d 1015 (10th Cir.1982).

considering that the functional test has been called into doubt,[135] an agency may halt a mine project prior to a hearing,[136] in order to protect the public health. A utility company which is considered a quasi-governmental body, may assess a $10,000–per-day emergency rate hike on a plaintiff, without any hearing, if at year end the plaintiff receives a full hearing with refunds available.[137] A regulation requiring a mining company to pay a fine before a hearing on the offense did not offend procedural due process because the fine was subject to later reimbursement with interest.

A party may also challenge government action on substantive due process-police power grounds.[138] A substantive due process challenge may differ little from a Takings Clause test, as both commonly balance the public's interest against the private owner's hardship.[139] Moreover, the remedy for a regulation found unconstitutional either as being a "taking" or for violating substantive due process is usually invalidation of the regulation.[140]

A substantive due process—police power analysis usually considers three factors: (1) the plaintiff's interest and the hardship imposed on them by the government action, (2) the nature of the public interest, and (3) whether the means chosen by the regulation are reasonable in light of the alternatives. Under the first factor, as the governmental burden on the owner's property becomes greater, a court will more likely declare the burden violative of substantive due process. For instance, a regulation making a tenant pay the landlord's water utility bills, or suffer termination of the service, violates substantive due process because the tenant cannot easily bear the burden; but making a landlord pay the tenant's bills does not cause the landlord a corresponding hardship because the landlord is in a better position to pay.[141] The second factor, the nature of the public interest, arises in cases like *Kaiser Aetna*, where the public interest in a pond's navigable waters was found to be insubstantial. The third factor, the reasonableness of the regulation in light of alternatives, is evidenced in a case like *Cougar Business Owners Association v. State*,[142] where the court found that the

135. By Alabama Elk River Development Agency v. Rogers, 516 So.2d 637.

136. As in Hodel v. Virginia Surface Mining Reclamation Association, 452 U.S. 264, 300 (1981).

137. Allegheny Ludlum Steel Corp. v. Pennsylvania PUC, 501 Pa. 71, 459 A.2d 1218 (1983). In B & M Coal v. Office of Surface Mining Reclamation, 699 F.2d 381 (7th Cir.1983).

138. Seven Islands Land Co. v. Maine Land Use Regulation Com'n, 450 A.2d 475 (Me.1982).

139. Luf v. Town of Southbury, 188 Conn. 336, 449 A.2d 1001 (1982) (the difference between there being a taking or a valid exercise of the police power is one of degree).

140. See Fred F. French Investing Co. v. City of New York, 39 N.Y.2d 587, 385 N.Y.S.2d 5, 350 N.E.2d 381 (1976).

141. Chatham v. Jackson, 613 F.2d 73 (5th Cir.1980).

142. 97 Wash.2d 466, 647 P.2d 481 (1982).

Governor of Washington had exercised reasonable police power, with no other alternatives available, when she closed a town near to Mt. St. Helens prior to and after that volcano's eruption.

THE 14TH AMENDMENT: EQUAL PROTECTION

". . . No State shall make or enforce any law which shall abridge the privileges or immunities of citizens of the United States, nor shall any State deprive any person of life, liberty, or property, without due process of law; nor deny to any person within its jurisdiction the equal protection of the laws."

Equal protection analysis under the 14th Amendment, in effect, resembles substantive due process protections.[143] While both require analyses that focus on the "fairness" accorded a private party by government regulation, substantive due process specifically involves the balance between public and private interests, while equal protection analysis involves the fairness of classifications. Both afford great deference to legislative decisions. However, if the state action discriminates against a fundamental right of the plaintiff (e.g., the right to practice religion or the right to vote), or contains a suspect classification (e.g., race), the state action will be subject to "strict scrutiny" and likely be found unconstitutional. The next level of scrutiny, "intermediate scrutiny," is applied to rights that are less than fundamental, such as the right to receive water service,[144] or to classifications that are not suspect, such as a zoning ordinance that has a separate classification for mentally disabled persons.[145] All other rights or classifications are subject to the lenient standard of minimum rationality, which allows the government to "discriminate" between similar classifications if the government has any rational reason for doing so.[146] Under minimum rationality, it "is up to the legislature, not courts, to decide on the wisdom and utility of legislation."[147]

In *Clover Leaf Creamery*, the minimum rationality test was used in considering whether an environmental statute banning the sale of milk in plastic containers, but not non-returnable paperboard cartons, violated the Equal Protection Clause. Because non-

---

143. Minnesota v. Clover Leaf Creamery Co., 449 U.S. 456, 470 (1981).

144. Chatham v. Jackson, 613 F.2d 73 (5th Cir.1980).

145. Cleburne Living Center v. Cleburne, Texas, 726 F.2d 191 (5th Cir. 1984). This last case has since been affirmed in part and reversed in part by City of Cleburne, Tex. v. Cleburne Living Center, 473 U.S. 432, 105 S.Ct. 3249, 87 L.Ed.2d 313, 53 USLW 5022 (U.S.

Tex. Jul 01, 1985). Also, it has been superceded by state law, as recognized in Innovative Health Systems, Inc. v. City of White Plains, 931 F.Supp. 222, 7 A.D. Cases 1268, 17 A.D.D. 1212, 8 NDLR P 210 (S.D.N.Y. Jun. 12, 1996).

146. Exxon Corp. v. Eagerton, 462 U.S. 176 (1983).

147. Clover Leaf Creamery, 449 U.S. at 469.

returnable cartons were environmentally undesirable, the state had a rational reason to halt the entry of a new form of non-returnable cartons, the plastic carton. But equal protection did not require elimination of the already established paperboard carton because to do so would completely dislocate the milk industry. Thus a rational basis existed upon which to distinguish between the old and new cartons.

Similarly, a tax increase on gas producers, which did not increase the tax of royalty owners, passed the rational basis test because it promoted investment by royalty owners.[148] An interstate water compact board may discriminate against new entries into the compact by making them pay for a heretofore free public service because the new entries had not put forth the effort to formulate the compact as the original members had done.[149] Natural gas utility rates for which residential users paid on the basis of system-wide costs, while industrial users paid on the basis of more expensive replacement costs, had a rational basis because industrial users also received tax credits.[150]

THE CONTRACT CLAUSE

"No State shall ... pass any Law impairing the Obligation of Contracts."

The Contract Clause of the Constitution (Art. I, § 10, cl. 1) "must be accommodated to the inherent police power of the State to safeguard the vital interests of its people.... If the law were otherwise, 'one would be able to obtain immunity from state regulation by making private contractual arrangements.' "[151] The Supreme Court has limited Contract Clause violations to circumstances where the state substantially impairs private contracts in order to provide benefits to special private interests or to the State itself.[152]

In *Energy Reserves Group, Inc. v. Kansas Power & Light Co.*,[153] a Kansas act limited newly deregulated intrastate gas prices, thus altering the escalation clauses of the producers' contracts. Kansas enacted the legislation to eliminate windfall profits. Even though the statute substantially impaired the contracts, the statute did not

148. Exxon Corp. v. Eagerton, 462 U.S. 176 (1983).

149. Delaware River Basin Commission v. Bucks County, 545 F.Supp. 138 (E.D.Pa.1982).

150. Great Western Sugar v. Johnson, 624 P.2d 1184 (Wyo.1981).

151. Exxon Corp. v. Eagerton, 462 U.S. 176 (1983).

152. See Continental Illinois National Bank and Trust Company of Chicago v. Washington, 696 F.2d 692 (9th Cir. 1983) (Contracts Clause violated by citizen's initiative requiring voter approval for municipal bonds for major energy projects).

153. 459 U.S. 400 (1983).

violate the Contract Clause because (1) the public interest was legitimate, (2) the producers who stood to reap the windfall profits did not expect such profits at the time of making the contracts, and (3) the parties operated in a highly regulated industry in which government regulations were expected.[154]

The Contract Clause applies only to contractual obligations where the plaintiffs are beneficiaries. In *Exxon Corp.*, a Kansas statute exempted royalty owners from paying the state tax increase, thus apparently impairing the contractual relationship between royalty owners and producers in which both parties shared all tax increases. However, because the producers were free under the statute to shift a fair burden of the tax increase to the royalty owners, the contractual obligation between owners and producers was preserved. In *Texaco, Inc. v. Short*,[155] an Indiana statute voided severed mineral rights. This statute impaired property rights (the right to extract minerals) but not contractual rights (the right to lease with the owner to extract the minerals), and consequently did not violate the Contract Clause.

The Delegation of Power Clause

"All legislative Powers herein granted shall be vested in a Congress of the United States, which shall consist of a Senate and House of Representatives."

The Constitution (Art. 1, § 1) seems to direct that Congress may breach its constitutional duty if it delegates its legislative power to another body. However, federal case law allows delegations of legislative power to executive officials so long as there are *de minimus* standards to guide executive discretion.[156] Thus, the executive branch may violate Art. 1, § 1 only if it assumes power that Congress did not properly grant to it. For example, Congress may allow the executive branch to regulate oil imports if Congress "lays down by legislative act an intelligible principle to which the [President] is directed to conform."[157] In this case, the Supreme Court found that legislation authorizing the President to take such action "as he deems necessary to adjust the imports" of oil was an

---

154. See also *Exxon Corp.*, 103 S.Ct. at 2296, 76 L.Ed.2d at 511 (the statute prohibited producers from passing tax increases on to consumers, which the producers' contracts had allowed; the Court held that this contract restriction "was incidental to [the statute's] main effect of shielding consumers from the burden of the tax increase").

155. 454 U.S. 516 (1982).

156. See, e.g., Industrial Union v. American Petroleum Institute, 448 U.S. 607 (1980).

157. FEA v. Algonquin SNG, Inc., 426 U.S. 548, 559 (1976).

acceptable delegation granting the President "a measure of discretion in determining the method to be used to adjust imports."[158]

While it is now virtually impossible to strike down federal legislation for improperly delegating legislative authority to executive agencies, at the state level courts require stricter legislative standards to guide executive discretion. Thus, if a state legislature gives the executive body the power to create criteria for its policy judgments, the delegation of authority is improper.[159] However, in *Matter of Egg Harbor*,[160] the state legislature could delegate authority to the State Department of Environmental Protection because the agency's guidelines were specific enough to guide the agency's discretion and permit judicial review. Whereas the rule in Illinois is that the legislature may delegate authority to a state agency if the statute identifies "the persons and activities subject to regulation, the harm sought to be prevented, and the general means intended to be made available to prevent the harm."[161]

A delegation of power issue may closely resemble a separation of powers issue. For example, a legislature may not authorize an agency to adjudicate water rights if the determination of rights rests within the sole power of a court; but if a court, not an agency, makes only the final determination of rights, then the delegation of authority is proper.[162]

The Treaty Clause

"The President ... shall have Power, by and with the advice and consent of the Senate to make Treaties, provided two thirds of the senators present concur...."

Under the Treaty Clause of the Constitution (Art. 2, § 2), the President and the Senate can commit the United States to the provisions of any international treaty. If you combine this Treaty Clause with the Supremacy Clause in Art. VI, you create a circumstance where the ratification of a treaty incorporates it as the supreme law of the United States, equal to any federal law and superior to any state law.

158. 426 U.S. at 561.

159. Matlack v. Board of Chosen Freeholders of Burlington County, 191 N.J.Super. 236, 466 A.2d 83 (1982) (a legislative body could not create an Exchange which purchased conservation easements without providing guidelines for the Exchange's decisions).

160. (Bayshore Center), 94 N.J. 358, 464 A.2d 1115 (1983).

161. Rockford Drop Forge v. Pollution Control Board, 79 Ill.2d 271, 37 Ill.Dec. 600, 402 N.E.2d 602 (1980) (statute authorized pollution control agency to control noise emissions).

162. In re Adjudication of the Water Rights, 642 S.W.2d 438 (Tex.1982).

The issue of the supremacy of international treaties is a very important issue for environmental and natural resource law as it is through the use of international treaty that the domestic law of the United States has been changed to preserve natural resources, like migratory birds.

The seminal case that decided the supremacy of treaties was *Missouri v. Holland*.[163] In this case, the Congress had passed a law to regulate the killing of migratory birds in order to preserve their numbers. As a consequence, the statute regulated hunting which the state of Missouri claimed violated its rights. This put the migratory bird law under immediate attack by states-rights advocates who cited the 10th Amendment and its capacity to designate all regulation, including environmental, not strictly given to the federal government, as the prerogative of the states. The 10th Amendment argument was convincingly made to the lower courts and the act was found to be unconstitutional.

Subsequently, the United States government concluded a treaty with the Government of Canada, which created identical protections for migrating ducks and geese. The Senate, having ratified this treaty, and with the Congress passing legislation to transform these treaty obligations into U.S. law, the protection of the birds was again challenged by 10th Amendment advocates. The states-rights advocates again countered that the federal government had limited powers in cases of rights granted to the states (i.e. hunting) under the 10th Amendment and took the treaty/statute combination to court. In *Missouri v. Holland*, Justice Holmes, speaking for the Supreme Court, now rejected this argument:

§§

... It is said that a treaty cannot be valid if it infringes the Constitution, that there are limits, therefore, to the treaty-making power, and that one such limit is that what an act of Congress could not do unaided, in derogation of the powers reserved to the States, a treaty cannot do. An earlier act of Congress that attempted by itself and not in pursuance of a treaty to regulate the killing of migratory birds within the States had been held bad in the District Court. United States v. Shauver, 214 Fed. 154. Those decisions were supported by arguments that migratory birds were owned by the States in their sovereign capacity for the benefit of their people, and that under cases like Geer v. Connecticut (161 U.S. 519), this control was one that Congress had no power to displace. The same argument is supposed to apply now with equal force....

* * *

---

163.   252 U.S. 416 (1920).

Whether the two cases cited were decided rightly or not they cannot be accepted as a test of the treaty power. Acts of Congress are the supreme law of the land only when made in pursuance of the Constitution, while treaties are declared to be so when made under the authority of the United States...

* * *

We do not mean to imply that there are no qualifications to the treaty-making power; but they must be ascertained in a different way. It is obvious that there may be matters of the sharpest exigency for the national well being that an act of Congress could not deal with but that a treaty followed by such an act could, and it is not lightly to be assumed that, in matters requiring national action, 'a power which must belong to and somewhere reside in every civilized government' is not to be found ... What was said in that case with regard to the powers of the States applies with equal force to the powers of the nation in cases where the States individually are incompetent to act. We are not yet discussing the particular case before us but only are considering the validity of the test proposed. With regard to that we may add that when we are dealing with words that also are a constituent act, like the Constitution of the United States, we must realize that they have called into life a being the development of which could not have been foreseen completely by the most gifted of its begetters. It was enough for them to realize or to hope that they had created an organism; it has taken a century and has cost their successors much sweat and blood to prove that they created a nation. The case before us must be considered in the light of our whole experience and not merely in that of what was said a hundred years ago. The treaty in question does not contravene any prohibitory words to be found in the Constitution. The only question is whether it is forbidden by some invisible radiation from the general terms of the Tenth Amendment. We must consider what this country has become in deciding what that amendment has reserved.

The State as we have intimated founds its claim of exclusive authority upon an assertion of title to migratory birds, an assertion that is embodied in statute. No doubt it is true that as between a State and its inhabitants the State may regulate the killing and sale of such birds, but it does not follow that its authority is exclusive of paramount powers. To put the claim of the State upon title is to lean upon a slender reed. Wild birds are not in the possession of anyone; and possession is the beginning of ownership. The whole foundation of the State's rights is the presence within their jurisdiction of birds that yesterday had not arrived, tomorrow may be in another State and in a week a thousand miles away. If we are to be accurate we cannot put the case of the State upon higher ground than that the treaty deals with creatures that for the moment are within the state borders, that it must be carried out by officers of the United States within the same territory, and that but for the treaty the State would be free to regulate this subject itself.

As most of the laws of the United States are carried out within the States and as many of them deal with matters which in the silence of such laws the State might regulate, such general grounds are not enough to support Missouri's claim. Valid treaties of course are as binding within the territorial limits of the States as they are elsewhere throughout the dominion of the United States. No doubt the great body of private relations usually fall within the control of the State, but a treaty may override its power. . . .

In addition to the controversy over the constitutional supremacy of treaty-law over all domestic sources of law, there is the question of whether the treaty is "self-executing," or whether further domestic legislation is necessary, beyond the treaty itself, to make its provisions United States law. The relationship between municipal and international law is generally divided in terms of customary international law which is considered to incorporate itself into domestic law without any legislative transformation, and treaty law, which normally must be transformed by domestic legislation. The courts have adopted the practice that this must be decided on a case-by-case basis where the intentions of the parties are paramount,[164] but a conventional rule of thumb is that commercial treaties are self-executing while human rights and other types of treaties are not, unless Congress specifies otherwise.[165]

Cases

Pollution and natural resource extraction creates damage to ecosystems. To address this pollution problem and to protect the

---

164. Asakura v. City of Seattle 265 U.S. 332 (1924); The People of Saipan v. United States Department of Interior 502 F.2d 90 (9th Cir. 1974); United States v. Postal 589 F.2d 862 (5th Cir. 1979).

165. Congress, in 1953, tried in one action to make all treaties non-self-exe-

cuting. In the infamous *Bricker Amendment*, S.J. Res. 1, 83rd Cong. 1st Sess. § 2 it stated, "A treaty shall become effective as internal law in the United States only through legislation which would be valid in the absence of a treaty." However this amendment failed to pass.

natural systems that resources are extracted from, many argue that a fundamental right to a clean environment for all Americans must be established. This argument is built on the idea that only by making environmental quality part of the system of constitutional rights will it be possible to fully protect nature in its conflicts with humanity. While this constitutional right cannot be held by nature, by tying human rights to a clean environment, the argument is that a high enough level of protection can be justified that will empower both humanity and nature. These cases address this issue on two levels: first on the federal level where statute law, administrative law, and constitutional law are used in an effort to establish such a right where none explicitly exists. The second case tries to operationalize the right on the state level, in Pennsylvania, where the state constitution does prescribe such a right. The latter case also contains as issue about the self-executing nature of state constitutional provisions.

§§

GEORGE N. TANNER v. ARMCO STEEL CORPORATION

United States District Court, S. D. Texas, Galveston Division.
340 F.Supp. 532.

NOEL, District Judge.

Plaintiffs, residents of Harris County, Texas, bring this action to recover for injuries allegedly sustained as a result of the exposure of their persons and their residence to air pollutants emitted by defendants' petroleum refineries and plants located along the Houston Ship Channel. It is asserted that plaintiff George W. Tanner, as a proximate result of these emissions, has suffered pulmonary damage with consequent medical expenses and loss of income to himself and his family. By way of remedy, it appears from the rather prolix complaint that plaintiffs pray "to recover their damages from the Defendants, jointly and severally, for their personal injuries, past and future medical expenses, pain and suffering, loss of services, mental anguish, loss of support, damages to the homestead and lands of the Tanners, general damages, puntative (sic) damages and all other damages allowed by law, in the combined amount of FIVE MILLION DOLLARS."

* * *

In their jurisdictional statement, citing a potpourri of federal constitutional and statutory provisions, plaintiffs purport to construct a claim upon the following foundations: (1) the Constitution of the United States "in its entirety"; (2) the Due Process Clause of the Fifth Amendment; (3) the Ninth Amendment; (4) the Fourteenth Amendment in conjunction with the Civil Rights Act of

1871, 42 U.S.C. § 1983, and its jurisdictional counterpart, 28 U.S.C. § 1343; (5) the National Environmental Policy Act of 1969, 42 U.S.C. §§ 4321 et seq.; (6) and, finally, the general federal question jurisdictional statute, 28 U.S.C. § 1331(a). All of the foregoing shall now be considered seriatim.

I.   The allusion in the complaint to the Federal Constitution "in its entirety" is not a plain statement of the ground upon which the Court's jurisdiction depends, and is therefore insufficient pleading. . . .

II.   Plaintiffs next assert that their claim arises under the Due Process Clause of the Fifth Amendment to the Federal Constitution, and is therefore cognizable in this Court. The contention is without merit. It is well settled that the Fifth Amendment operates only as a restraint upon the National Government and upon the States through the Fourteenth Amendment, but is not directed against the actions of private individuals such as defendants. . . . It is not alleged in the instant complaint that the Federal Government is involved in the activity complained of. In their responsive brief, plaintiffs do assert that the Federal Government has advanced funds to the State of Texas and City of Houston for the purpose of antipollution efforts. The relevance of this is not immediately apparent; however, taken as true, it clearly does not amount to federal complicity or participation in the alleged transgressions of the defendant private corporations, and it just as clearly will not support a Fifth Amendment claim.

III.   Plaintiffs next seek solace in the Ninth Amendment, and concede on brief that this is a pioneering enterprise:

> This case is believed to be unique in that counsel for the Tanners is not aware of any other cases that have sought damages for personal injuries caused by the air pollution in the United States District Courts based upon the premise that the right to a healthy and clean environment is at the very foundation of this nation and guaranteed by the laws and Constitution of the United States. Plaintiffs maintain that their right not to be personally injured by the actions of the Defendants and their right to non-interference with their privacy and the air that they breathe are protected by the Ninth Amendment. Responsive Brief of Plaintiffs, at p. 1.

Since its promulgation, the Ninth Amendment has lain largely quiescent, its most ambitious sortie being in the form of a concurrence in Griswold v. Connecticut, 381 U.S. 479, 486 (1965). . . . The parties have cited and the Court has found no reported case in which the Ninth Amendment has been construed to embrace the rights here asserted. Such a construction would be a historical and

would represent essentially a policy decision. In effect, plaintiffs invite this Court to enact a law. Since our system reserves to the legislative branch the task of legislating, this Court must decline the invitation. The Ninth Amendment, through its "penumbra" or otherwise, embodies no legally assertable right to a healthful environment. Environmental Defense Fund, Inc. v. Corps of Engineers, 325 F. Supp. 728, 739 (E.D.Ark. 1971) . . .

IV.   Plaintiffs also contend that this action is entertainable by reason of the Fourteenth Amendment in conjunction with the Civil Rights Act of 1871, 42 U.S.C. § 1983, and its jurisdictional counterpart, 28 U.S.C. § 1343. The Supreme Court of the United States, in Adickes v. S.H. Kress & Co. 398 U.S. 144 (1970), has recently defined plaintiffs' task:

> The terms of § 1983 make plain two elements that are necessary for recovery. First, the plaintiff must prove that the defendant has deprived him of a right secured by the "Constitution and laws" of the United States. Second, the plaintiff must show that the defendant deprived him of this constitutional right "under color of any statute, ordinance, regulation, custom, or usage, of any State or Territory." This second element requires that the plaintiff show that the defendant acted "under color of law".

Therefore, it is clear that a sufficiently stated claim under § 1983 must embrace two elements properly alleged: (1) a constitutional deprivation, and (2) state action. On brief, all parties have devoted considerable attention to state action, the second requisite.

This Court is persuaded that plaintiffs have not alleged the quantum of state or municipal regulatory involvement necessary to clothe defendants with the mantle of the State for the purposes of § 1983. See T. W. Guthrie v. Alabama By–Products Company, 328 F.Supp. 1140 (N.D. Ala.1971), and cases cited therein at 1143, n.7. However, it is unnecessary to dwell upon the point at length. For, assuming arguendo that state action were present, the fact remains that the first requisite of a § 1983 suit-constitutional deprivation-has not been satisfied.

Taking as true all factual allegations in the complaint, plaintiffs have failed to allege a violation by defendants of any judicially cognizable federal constitutional right which would entitle them to the relief sought. Once again, the parties have cited and the Court has found no reported case which persuasively suggests that the Fourteenth Amendment is susceptible to the interpretation urged. Although there has been something of a boom recently in what Judge Seals of this Court has described as "grandiose claims of the right of the general populace to enjoy a decent environment". . . . such claims "have been more successful in theory than in operation.".... In view of the dearth of supportive authority, this Court must decline "to embrace the exhilarating opportunity of anticipating a doctrine which may be in the womb of time, but whose birth is distant." Spector Mortor Service v. Walsh, 139 F.2d 809, 823 (2nd Cir. 1943).

First, there is not a scintilla of persuasive content in the words, origin, or historical setting of the Fourteenth Amendment to support the assertion that environmental rights were to be accorded its protection. To perceive such content in the Amendment would be to turn somersaults with history. For, as the Congressional sponsor of a proposed federal environmental amendment recently observed:

> We are frank to say that such a provision to the Constitution would have been meaningless to those attending the Constitutional Convention in Philadelphia almost 200 years ago. Indeed, this amendment would have been altogether unpersuasive twenty years ago, although the handwriting was then visible on the wall, if one cared to look for it. Remarks of Representative Richard L. Ottinger of New York, Cong. Rec. 17116 (1968)...

Second, it is apparent that nowhere in the Fourteenth Amendment—or its "incorporated" amendments—can be found the decisional standards to guide a court in determining whether the plaintiffs' hypothetical environmental rights have been infringed, and, if so, what remedies are to be fashioned. Such a task would be difficult enough with the guidance of a statute, but to undertake it in the complete absence of statutory standards would be simply to ignore the limitations of judicial decisionmaking.

Third, from an institutional viewpoint, the judicial process, through constitutional litigation, is peculiarly ill-suited to solving problems of environmental control. Because such problems frequently call for the delicate balancing of competing social interests, as well as the application of specialized expertise, it would appear that their resolution is best consigned initially to the legislative and administrative processes. Furthermore, the inevitable trade-off between economic and ecological values presents a subject matter which is inherently political, and which is far too serious to relegate to the ad hoc process of "government by lawsuit" in the midst of a statutory vacuum.

Finally, to the extent that an environmental controversy such as this is presently justiciable, it is within the province of the law of torts, to wit: nuisance ... There would seem little good reason in law or policy to conjure with the Fourteenth Amendment and § 1983 for the purpose of producing the wholesale transformation of state tort suits into federal cases. In any event, if such a result is deemed desirable in order to cope with pollution on a nationwide scale, then it should be accomplished by Congress through legislation, and not by the courts through jurisdictional alchemy. Therefore, this Court must follow Guthrie v. Alabama By–Products Co., supra, where the Court, in dismissing a similar pollution suit, observed that several bills have been introduced to challenge conduct alleged to result in environmental pollution. From this, Chief Judge Lynne of the Northern District of Alabama quite reasonably concluded that:

> Though this circumstance may be only faintly persuasive, it does indicate that the sponsors of these bills believe that the right to maintain such suits in federal court is not provided by existing legislation. This Court is firmly of the opinion that if plaintiffs are to be allowed to bring private damage suits for injuries traditionally local in nature and already covered by local statutory and common law, additional federal legislation is imperative. Such authority cannot be found in the existing law. 328 F.Supp. at 1149.

For the foregoing reasons, this Court holds that no legally enforceable right to a healthful environment, giving rise to an action for damages, is guaranteed by the Fourteenth Amendment or any other provision of the Federal Constitution. As the United States Supreme Court recently observed in rejecting a similarly imaginative constitutional claim, "the Constitution does not provide judicial remedies for every social and economic ill." Lindsey v. Normet, 405 U.S. 56 (1972). It follows, of course, that a claim under § 1983 has not been stated and subject matter jurisdiction under 28 U.S.C. § 1343 has not been invoked.

V.   Next, plaintiffs urge this Court to find an implied civil damage remedy in certain provisions of the National Environmental Policy Act of 1969, 42 U.S.C. § 4321 et seq. In this, the Court is again apparently invited to break new ground, for no case has been cited in which such a remedy was inferred. The absence of such authority is understandable. By its terms, the statute is directed only to the agencies and instrumentalities of the Federal Government, with a primary purpose being full disclosure of the environmental consequences of federal governmental activities. It follows that plaintiffs may derive from the statute no private cause of action against these private defendants. For the sake of thoroughness, however, each section of the act cited by plaintiffs shall be separately considered.

(a)   As to 42 U.S.C. § 4321, this is merely a preamble to the act, in which Congress declares its purpose to encourage harmony between man and his environment, to promote efforts for the prevention of environmental damage, to enrich man's understanding of his environment, and to establish a Council on Environmental Quality. In so doing, Congress said nothing of rights or reme-dies. As it embodies no prescriptive command and creates no duties or liabilities, this section of the statute clearly cannot be made to embrace a private cause of action. . . .

(b) In their jurisdictional statement, plaintiffs also cite 42 U.S.C. § 4331(a) and (b) as supportive of this action. There is contrary authority on the point, and we need look no further than Environmental Defense Fund, Inc. v. Corps of Engineers, supra, in which the Court held that these sections of the statute create no substantive private rights.

> Plaintiffs contend that NEPA creates some "substantive" rights in addition to its procedural requirements. They base this contention on the language contained in § 101 of the act. Although the Court may be oversimplifying their position in this respect, essentially they claim that the act creates rights in the plaintiffs and others to "safe, health-ful, productive, and esthetically and culturally pleasing surroundings;" and to "an environment which supports diversity and variety of individual choice," and "the widest range of beneficial values." See § 101(b). The Court dis-agrees. Section 101(a) takes note of the environmental problems facing the nation and then declares it to be the policy of the federal government to use all practical means "to create and maintain conditions under which man and nature can exist in productive harmony, and fulfill the social, economic, and other requirements of present and future generations of Americans." In order to carry out this policy § 101(b) declares it to be the "continuing responsibility of the Federal Government to use all practi-cable means. . . . to improve and coordinate Federal plans, functions, programs, and resources to the end that the Nation may—"attain certain stated objectives, including those, quoted above, which plaintiff contend create sub-stantive rights. The Act appears to reflect a compromise which, in the opinion of the Court, falls short of creating the type of "substantive rights" claimed by the plain-tiffs. . . . If the Congress had intended to leave it to the courts to determine such matters; if, indeed, it had intend-ed to give up its own prerogatives and those of the execu-tive agencies in this respect, it certainly would have used explicit language to accomplish such a far-reaching objec-tive. 325 F.Supp. at 755 (emphasis added).

(c) Plaintiffs' reliance upon 42 U.S.C. § 4331(c) is similarly misplaced. This section provides only that "(t)he Congress recog-nizes that each person should enjoy a healthful environment and that each person has a responsibility to contribute to the preservation and enhancement of the environment." Like the language of § 4321, these words are almost predatory in nature. Had the Congress intended to create a positive and enforceable legal right or duty, it would have said so, and would not have limited itself to words of entreaty. In the absence of any clear statement, this Court must assume that no such intention existed. Although such a reading stands by itself as the only plausible construction, it is interesting to note that it is supported by the legislative history of the provision in question. Originally, the Senate version, Senate Bill 1075, provided that "(t)he Congress recognizes that each person has a *fundamental and inalienable right to a healthful environment....*" (emphasis added). However, these strong words did not survive the conference committee, where they were deleted lest they be interpreted to create legal consequences which the Congress did not intend. In the words of the Conference Report:

> Section 101(c) of the conference substitute states that "Congress recognizes that each person should enjoy a healthful environment and that each person has a responsibility to contribute to the preservation and enhancement of the environment." The language of the conference substitute reflects a compromise by the conferees with respect to a provision in the Senate bill (but which was not in the House amendment) which stated that Congress recognizes that "each person has a fundamental and inalienable right to a healthful environment ..." The compromise language was adopted because of doubt on the part of the House conferees with respect to the legal scope of the original Senate provision. See Conference Report No. 91–765, 1969 U.S.Code Cong. & Admin. News pp. 2767, 2768.

This "doubt" was resolved by stripping the Senate bill of the language which might arguably have been construed as creating a legally enforceable right to a "healthful environment." As the Congress took assiduous care to foreclose the possibility of such an interpretation, this Court is obviously powerless to adopt it. From this it follows that no claim upon which relief can be granted has been stated under 42 U.S.C. § 4331(c).

VI. Finally, in their jurisdictional statement, plaintiffs cite 28 U.S.C. § 1331, conferring upon federal district courts original jurisdiction of suits arising under the Constitution, laws, and treaties of the United States. It is well settled that this provision is operative only when "a right of immunity created by the Constitution or laws of the United States [is] an element, and an essential one, of the plaintiff's cause of action."... Jurisdiction exists in this Court for the purpose of determining whether a cause of action has been stated.... For the reasons expressed previously, plaintiffs have not stated a federal claim upon which relief can be granted. Therefore, the action must be dismissed.

Accordingly, for the foregoing reasons, this action must be dismissed because of plaintiffs' failure to state a claim upon which relief can be granted. Rule 12(b)(6), Fed.R.Civ.P.

Judgment shall enter for the defendants.

Notes & Questions

This seems to be a private complaint, brought by a private citizen against a private corporation seeking damages for injury in fact. Is this not simply a case in common law? Why? Why not? How would this case change if it were a common law case?

How would this case, and its inherent policy design argument, change if it were a statute/administrative law case instead of a Constitutional case? Why is it not exclusively a matter of statute/administrative law?

How many of the articles and clauses of the Constitution were used by Tanner to try and establish his right? Of the ones covered in this chapter but not used in the case, are there any that might provide a better, more persuasive, argument?

How many different "sources" of law did Tanner use?

Is there one argument, among the many here that is the most persuasive? Do the others add or detract from it? How?

What is the relationship between constitutional and statute law in this case? How is it important to the outcome? How could the environment be considered a "civil" right?

§§

TRUSTEE FOR THE PEOPLE OF THE COMMONWEALTH v. NATIONAL GETTYSBURG BATTLEFIELD TOWER, INC.

Supreme Court of Pennsylvania, 1973.
454 Pa. 193, 311 A.2d 588.

O'BRIEN, Justice.

On July 3, 1971, National Gettysburg Battlefield Tower, Inc. (the Tower Corporation) and Thomas R. Ottenstein, two of the appellees, negotiated an agreement with the United States Government, acting through the Director of the National Park Service, in which the Tower Corporation conveyed certain land to the government and agreed to abandon construction of an observation tower near the Gettysburg Battlefield, at an area found objectionable to the Park Service, in exchange for the government's cooperation and permission to build the tower in another area near the battlefield. The Tower Corporation also agreed to establish a charitable foundation to support the Park Service's activities at Gettysburg and at the Eisenhower Farm Historical Site and to construct the tower in accordance with certain specifications, with the height of the tower to be limited to 307 feet. The Park Service also conveyed a right of way for limited access to the proposed observation tower site.

What the National Park Service was originally willing to permit, the Commonwealth of Pennsylvania, appellant herein, sought to enjoin. On July 20, 1971, the Commonwealth brought an action in the Court of Common Pleas of Adams County, to enjoin construction of the proposed 307–feet tower, alleging that the proposed construction was 'a despoilation of the natural and historic environment'. . . .

* * *

The chancellor, after making detailed findings concerning the location and characteristics of the tower and the neighborhood of the park, concluded that the Commonwealth had failed to show by clear and convincing proof that the natural, scenic, historic or aesthetic values of the Gettysburg environment would be injured by the erection of the tower. . .

* * *

[T]here is no statute of the Pennsylvania Legislature, which would authorize the Governor and the Attorney General to initiate actions like the law suit in the instant case. Rather, authority for the Commonwealth's suit is allegedly based entirely upon Art. 1, § 27 of the State Constitution, ratified by the voters of Pennsylvania on May 18, 1971, which reads as follows:

> The people have a right to clean air, pure water, and to the preservation of the natural, scenic, historic and esthetic values of the environment. Pennsylvania's public natural resources are the common property of all the people, including generations yet to come. As trustee of these resources, the Commonwealth shall conserve and maintain them for the benefit of all the people.

It is the Commonwealth's position that this amendment is self-executing; that the people have been given a right 'to the preservation of the natural, scenic, historic and esthetic values of the environment,' and 'that no further legislation is necessary to vest these rights in the people.'

The general principles of law involved in determining whether a particular provision of a constitution is self-executing were discussed at length in O'Neill v. White, 343 Pa. 96 (1941). In that case, we explained at pages 99–100:

> The constitutional provision invoked by appellees is unavailing in this case, for this provision is not self-executing and its mandate cannot be carried out because the legislature has not provided the means for doing so. 'A Constitution is primarily a declaration of principles of the fundamental law. Its provisions are usually only commands to the legislature to enact laws to carry out the purposes of the framers of the Constitution, or mere restrictions upon the power of the legislature to pass laws, yet it is entirely within the power of those who establish and adopt the Constitution to make any of its provisions self-executing.' 6 R.C.L. section 52, p. 57.... [B]efore the constitutional provision can be made effectual, supplemental legislation must be had; and the provision may be in its nature mandatory to the legislature to enact the needful legislation, though back of it there lies no authority to enforce the command. Sometimes the constitution in terms requires the legislature to enact laws on a particular subject; and here it is obvious that the requirement has only a moral force; the legislature ought to obey it; but the right intended to be given is only assured when the legislation is voluntarily enacted.

In Davis v. Burke, 179 U.S. 399, 403, the United States Supreme Court said:

> Where a constitutional provision is complete in itself it needs no further legislation to put it in force. When it lays down certain general principles, as to enact laws upon a certain subject, or for the incorporation of cities of certain population, or for uniform laws upon the subject of taxation, it may need more specific legislation to make it operative. In other words, it is self-executing only so far as it is susceptible of execution.

The Commonwealth makes two arguments in support of its contention that § 27 of Art.1 is self-executing. We find neither of them persuasive.

First, the Commonwealth emphasizes that the provision in question is part of Art.1 and that no provision of Art.1 has ever been judicially declared to be non-self-executing. The Commonwealth places particular emphasis on the wording of § 25 of Art.1. § 25 of Art.1 reads as follows:

> To guard against transgressions of the high powers which we have delegated, we declare that everything in this

article is excepted out of the general powers of government and shall forever remain inviolate.

However, it should be noted that Art.1 is entitled 'Declaration of Rights' and all of the first twenty-six sections of Art.1 which state those specific rights, must be read as limiting the powers of government to interfere with the rights provided therein.

§ 25 of Art.1 should be read as summarizing the philosophy of the first twenty-four sections of Art.1, particularly when it declares that:

> . . . everything in this article is Excepted out of the general powers of government and shall forever remain inviolate . . .

Unlike the first twenty-six sections of Art.1, § 27, the one which concerns us in the instant case, does not merely contain a limitation on the powers of government. True, the first sentence of § 27, which states:

> The people have a right to clean air, pure water, and to the preservation of the natural, scenic, historic and esthetic values of the environment . . .

can be read as limiting the right of government to interfere with the people's right to 'clean air, pure water, and to the preservation of the natural, scenic, historic and aesthetic values of the environment.' As such, the first part of § 27, if read alone, could be read to be self-executing.

But the remaining provisions of § 27, rather than limiting the powers of government, expand these powers. These provisions declare that the Commonwealth is the 'trustee' of Pennsylvania's 'public natural resources' and they give the Commonwealth the power to act to 'conserve and maintain them for the benefit of all the people.' Insofar as the Commonwealth always had a recognized police power to regulate the use of land, and thus could establish standards for clean air and clean water consistent with the requirements of public health, § 27 is merely a general reaffirmation of past law.[3] It must be recognized, however, that up until now, aesthetic or historical considerations, by themselves, have not been considered sufficient to constitute a basis for the Commonwealth's exercise of its police power . . .

Now, for the first time, at least insofar as the state constitution is concerned, the Commonwealth has been given power to act in areas of purely aesthetic or historic concern.

---

3. No one has ever contended that the exercise of such police powers does not require specific legislation.

The Commonwealth has cited no example of a situation where a constitutional provision which expanded the powers of government to act against individuals was held to be self-executing.

* * *

If we were to sustain the Commonwealth's position that the amendment was self-executing, a property owner would not know and would have no way, short of expensive litigation, of finding out what he could do with his property. The fact that the owner contemplated a use similar to others that had not been enjoined would be no guarantee that the Commonwealth would not seek to enjoin his use. Since no executive department has been given authority to determine when to move to protect the environment, there would be no way of obtaining, with respect to a particular use contemplated, an indication of what action the Commonwealth might take before the owner expended what could be significant sums of money for the purchase or the development of the property.

We do not believe that the framers of the environmental protection amendment could have intended such an unjust result, one which raises such serious questions under both the equal protection clause and the due process clause of the United States Constitution. In our opinion, to insure that these clauses are not violated, the Legislature should set standards and procedures for proposed executive action.

[2]   The Commonwealth also argues that the Pennsylvania environmental protection amendment is self-executing by comparing it with similar constitutional amendments enacted in Massachusetts, Illinois, New York, and Virginia, all of which are obviously not self-executing. The Commonwealth seeks to put great store in the fact that Pennsylvania's amendment, alone, does not specifically provide for legislative implementation. However, we find it more significant that all of these other states, which expanded the powers of their governments over the natural environment in the same way as Art.1 § 27 expanded the powers of the Commonwealth, recognized that legislative implementation was necessary before such new power could be exercised.

To summarize, we believe that, the provisions of § 27 of Art.1 of the Constitution merely state the general principle of law that the Commonwealth is trustee of Pennsylvania's public natural resources with power to protect the 'natural, scenic, historic, and esthetic values' of its environment. If the amendment was self-executing, action taken under it would pose serious problems of constitutionality, under both the equal protection clause and the due process clause of the Fourteenth Amendment. Accordingly, before the environmental protection amendment can be made effective, supplemental legislation will be required to define the values which the amendment seeks to protect and to establish procedures by which the use of private property can be fairly regulated to protect those values.

By reason of our disposition of this appeal, it is unnecessary to decide the other issues raised by the Commonwealth. Order of the Commonwealth Court, affirming the Decree of the Court of Common Pleas of Adams County, is affirmed. Costs on appellant.

JONES, C.J., filed a dissenting opinion in which EAGEN, J., joins.

ROBERTS, J., filed a concurring opinion in which MANDERINO, J., joins.

NIX, J., concurs in the result.

ROBERTS, Justice (concurring).

I agree that the order of the Commonwealth Court should be affirmed; however, my reasons for affirmance are entirely different from those expressed in the opinion by Mr. Justice O'Brien (joined by Mr. Justice Pomeroy).

I believe that the Commonwealth, even prior to the recent adoption of Art.1 § 27 possessed the inherent sovereign power to protect and preserve for its citizens the natural and historic resources now enumerated in § 27. The express language of the constitutional amendment merely recites the 'inherent and independent rights' of mankind relative to the environment which are 'recognized and unalterably established' by Art.1 § 1 of the Pennsylvania Constitution.

Prior to the adoption of Art.1 § 27, it was clear that as sovereign 'the state has an interest independent of and behind the titles of its citizens, in all the earth and air within its domain....' Georgia v. Tennessee Copper Co., 206 U.S. 230 (1907). The proposition has long been firmly established that:

> [i]t is a fair and reasonable demand on the part of a sovereign that the air over its territory should not be polluted ... that the forests on its mountains, be they better or worse, and whatever domestic destruction they have suffered, should not be further destroyed or threatened ... that the crops and orchards on its hills should not be endangered... Id. at 238.

Parklands and historical sites, as 'natural resources' are subject to the same considerations.

Moreover, 'it must surely be conceded that, if the health and comfort of the inhabitants of a state are threatened, the state is the proper party to represent and defend them....' Missouri v. Illinois,

180 U.S. 208, 241 (1901). Since natural and historic resources are the common property of the citizens of a state, see McCready v. Virginia, 94 U.S. 391 (1876), the Commonwealth can—and always could—proceed as parens patriae acting on behalf of the citizens and in the interests of the community, or as trustee of the state's public resources.

However, in my view, the Commonwealth, on this record, has failed to establish its entitlement to the equitable relief it seeks, either on common-law or constitutional (prior or subsequent to § 27) theories. The chancellor determined that

> [t]he Commonwealth has failed to show by clear and convincing proof that the natural, historic, scenic, and aesthetic values of the Gettysburg area will be irreparably harmed by the erection of the proposed tower at the proposed site.

I believe that the chancellor correctly denied equitable relief. The Commonwealth Court concluded that the chancellor's findings should not be disturbed and that the Commonwealth was not entitled to relief.

MANDERINO, J., joins in this opinion.

JONES, Chief Justice (dissenting).

This Court has been given the opportunity to affirm the mandate of the public empowering the Commonwealth to prevent environmental abuses; instead, the Court has chosen to emasculate a constitutional amendment by declaring it not to be self-executing. I am compelled to dissent.

Art.1, § 27 of the Commonwealth's Constitution was passed by the General Assembly and ratified by the voters on May 18, 1971 Its provisions are clear and uncomplicated. . . .

If the amendment was intended only to espouse a policy undisposed to enforcement without supplementing legislation, it would surely have taken a different form. But the amendment is not addressed to the General Assembly . . . It does not require the legislative creation of remedial measures. Instead, the amendment creates a public trust. The 'natural, scenic, historic and aesthetic values of the environment' are the trust Res; the Commonwealth, through its executive branch, is the trustee; the People of this Commonwealth are the trust beneficiaries. The amendment thus installs the common law public trust doctrine as a constitutional right to environmental protection susceptible to enforcement by an action in equity.

The majority relies on constitutional amendments of Massachusetts, Illinois, New York and Virginia to support its holding that § 27 is not self-executing. The Court finds it 'significant that all of these other states, which expanded the powers of their governments over the natural environment in the same way as Art.1 § 27 expanded the powers of the Commonwealth, recognized that legislative implementation was necessary before such new power could be exercised.' I find no significance in the fact that the constitutional provisions of these several jurisdictions are not self-executing for it is evident to me that each of the cited amendments is materially distinguishable from Art.1 § 27. Each of these amendments purports to establish a policy of environmental protection, but either omits the mode of enforcement or explicitly delegates the responsibility for implementation to the legislative branch. The Pennsylvania amendment defines enumerated rights within the scope of existing remedies. It imposes a fiduciary duty upon the Commonwealth to protect the people's 'right to clean air, pure water, and to the preservation of the natural, scenic, historic and esthetic values of the environment.' That the language of the amendment is subject to judicial interpretation does not mean that the enactment must remain an ineffectual constitutional platitude until such time as the legislature acts.

Because I believe Art.1 § 27 is self-executing, I believe that our inquiry should have focused upon the ultimate issue of fact: does the proposed tower violate the rights of the people of the Commonwealth as secured by this amendment?

* * *

The facts presented, even as construed in a light most favorable to the appellees, permit me only one conclusion: the proposed structure will do violence to the 'natural, scenic, historic and aesthetic values' of Gettysburg. This Court's decision today imposes unhappy consequences on the people of this Commonwealth. In one swift stroke the Court has disemboweled a constitutional provision which seems, by unequivocal language, to establish environmental control by public trust and, in so doing consequently sanctions the desecration of a unique national monument. I would enjoin the construction of this tower by the authority of Art.1 § 27 of the Pennsylvania Constitution.

I dissent!!

EAGEN, J., joins in this dissent.

Notes & Questions

How is this case distinct from Tanner? Similar?

Does this "right" within the Pennsylvania Constitution infringe on the 5th amendment rights of the landowners who wish to put up the tower? What other constitutional issues are involved? Is what we have here a clash of constitutional provisions? How should the Court arbitrate these conflicts? By what standard?

Three months later the same Court decided that when used by a citizen against the state, the clause in question was self-executing. Why would the opinion shift in light of the public obligations of the state?

How do the dissenters in this case suggest alternative policy?

If this right were "self-executing" would it expand or contract the power of government? Explain. How does the question of "limiting" the power of government become a central part of this argument?

EXERCISE: LAW FROM SCRATCH

(1) Let us assume that it is not possible, within American jurisprudence, to establish a "right" to a clean environment. First, list the reasons for which one might want to establish such a right. Second, take each component of this list and find at least two distinct ways in which the "sources" of law outlined in this chapter might be used to establish this reason in law. Third, re-write the Tanner argument listing the specific constitutional, statute, administrative and common law standards that you would use to regulate humanity's use of natural systems. (2) Research the international law of self-executing treaties. How might international law be used to argue for the dissent's position in the Gettysburg case?

Conclusion: Legal Sources as Instruments of Policy Design

The means by which the ends of policy and law are realized can be defined in terms of the 'policy instrument' that is chosen to implement one's legal objectives.[166] Within the arguments that define law and policy design, a major source of instruments is the law itself. The purpose of this chapter has been to familiarize the reader with these sources so that they can be assessed in terms of the operationalization of a specific set of legal norms.

Within the policy design model (see Chapter One), the sources appear twice. In Step A, they are part of the strategic evaluation of the policy design argument. Here they play a role in the consideration of what each source is best at evaluating, what its advantages and disadvantages are in terms of making the argument more or less persuasive and whether, given the paradigm and context model created within this step, which is the most ideal in terms of best representing what is at stake in the legal decision.

For Step B, the sources as instruments play a tactical role in the actual creation of law. Each of the sources must be considered

166. GIANDOMENICO MAJONE, EVIDENCE, ARGUMENT, & PERSUA- SION IN THE POLICY PROCESS 116– 118 (1989).

in terms of what it brings to the creation of codified law from policy argument. At this stage one must take into consideration the public or private nature of the choice and the essential or elective character of the environmental good, testing the sources and institutions of law in order to give the policy design argument the most persuasive power possible, considering the ends made critical by the paradigm and context model.

Overall, the sources are instruments of the policy design process that allow the ideas in the paradigm and context model to find material relevance in both the general strategic argument for a legal course of action as well as its specific tactical codification. Here, the sources of environmental and resource law play the role of means to the codification of ends. But what of these ends? The next three chapters will deal with the evaluation of alternative paradigms and context models that provide the ends of the law and policy design process. Specifically, we shall examine the Market Paradigm and its context model as the conventional approach to environmental law and then two alternative 'ecosystem' paradigms that consider the value of nature intrinsically and in terms of its instrumental value to individual capabilities.

While you read these arguments for alternative paradigms and their context models, as well as the application of these strategic arguments through examples of contemporary environmental and resource law, remember that the sources of law used in each example are not written in stone but could be different, if that difference better enables the norms from which the comprehensive argument is made.

Chapter 3

THE MARKET APPROACH
TO THE NATURAL WORLD:
A TEMPLATE FOR
LEGAL ARGUMENT

In previous chapters we have examined both the elements of policy design as they relate to the evolution of the rule of law and the positive law sources themselves that shape the creation of humanity's relationship to the natural world. However, this formal and empirical raw material is of little use to the lawyer or policy-maker unless we can organize it logically as persuasive argument. Comprehensive Policy Argument (CPA) provides for logical reasoning and argument inside and outside of the legal system. It can infuse public discourse with an analysis of existing law and it can synthesize change in the law toward a redefinition of our relationship to the environment around us.

The argument in this book is that the logical form of legal argument takes the elements of policy design and creates a paradigm of assumptions, presuppositions, and dialectic relations that enable the lawyer as policy-maker to work with alternative sets of normative principles and positive circumstances so that various legal ideals can be rendered into rules and processes that further them in the world. These arguments combine the normative and positive aspects of any policy issue, place them in a policy design framework so that we can understand the demands of logic and dialectic, and then produce distinct alternative ideas about what source of law is most relevant to the issue and what specific rules reflect the principle at stake.

In this chapter we will present the reader with a template of categories and logical connections that they can use to create a "paradigm," or systemized and integrated line of argument for policy design from any set of principles, assumptions, and methods.

purpose →

Our example will be the market approach to the law, which is generally acknowledged as the conventional approach to decision-making in the area of environmental and natural resource law.

A Template for Policy Design Paradigms

In order to have an affective set of legal institutions that create rules for, and prosecute the idea of, a paradigm of policy design, the policy design paradigm that is foundational to that legal structure must be able to represent the importance of ecosystems and their various values. We suggest that a specific map of the normative and logical sub-structure of legal argument can help one understand the central place of normative concerns in creating positive legal practice.

1) Template—Stage I: Fundamental Assumptions

The first step in creating a legal argument paradigm is recognizing one's intuitions about a legal issue and the fundamental theoretical assumptions one makes across the three levels of interests that bear on public decision-making (the individual, the collective, and the state). The characterization of these interests must justify practical action by the decision-maker, who perceives a distinction between what is and what ought to be, and, seeks to bring about the latter through "public" or "collective" action.[1]

This normative intuition that what **is**, is not what **ought** to be, is the point of departure for constructing rational legal argument. Next, definition and substance must be added to the intuitions by specifying or characterizing the actors and interests that the legal result must satisfy. One should understand these actors and interests if one wants to detect where law is inadequate and where government policy can correct the situation. But, to admit that government policy should act as a corrective for inadequate law rejects the contention that law is necessarily working within and to support the status-quo.[2] Rather it assumes that codified law is both assessed and adjusted by policy design arguments.

a) The Individual

The basic component of all foundational assumptions in legal argument is the characterization of the individual. Here the analyst must define how the individual is assumed to act and why? What

---

1. We will define a collective good as any public or private good (by definition of jointness and non-exclusion) that is distributed or allocated by the state through policy. See JOHN MARTIN GILLROY, JUSTICE & NATURE: KANTIAN PHILOSOPHY, ENVIRON- MENTAL POLICY AND THE LAW ch. 2 (2000), for a fuller explanation.

2. EDITH STOKEY & RICHARD ZECKHAUSER, A PRIMER FOR POLICY ANALYSIS 4 (1978).

motivates the individual and how is the characterization of the individual critical to the solution of the problem? Who is the person? What concerns them? By what standards will they judge legal problems and solutions? Will preference, interests, rights, or other variables close the gap between is and ought, solving the decision problem?

The Market Paradigm,[3] with its foundations in classical economics, assumes the individual is a rational consumer. The individual's preferences for material goods, and the provision of these products by the market is inhibited by central regulation, which should not have precedence over it. Classical economics assumes that the individual is a self-interested welfare maximizer concerned with little but personal satisfaction.[4] The individual's wants as a consumer and their overall welfare will matter most in any policy choice. Further, no one can judge the wants of the individual better than that individual.[5] Self-interested motivation is both a want-regarding description of individual behavior and an ideal-regarding assumption that individuals are the best judge of such preference-based considerations.[6] The policy analyst, working from a normative base in classical economics, must render policy prescriptions that respond to the consumer's "willingness-to-pay" for a benefit that reflects his or her self-defined welfare preferences.

b) Community and Collective Action

In addition to the isolated consideration of the individual, the dynamics of inter-personal choice and interaction should be considered in making legal choices. The decision-maker should specify what dynamic role the community plays in defining a "good" policy. Does the collective action of the political community and its interests represent more than the sum or aggregate of individual interests? What is the goal of collective action? What problems do individuals face in establishing cooperation? Is society a necessary level of analysis or concern? How does the community and the way

3. Some economists will argue that markets are only one mechanism through which economics works, that economics also allocates through the state and other institutions. However, what they don't tell you is that all economic allocations, no matter the institutional context, are made on the basis of fundamental market assumptions about self-interest, efficiency, wealth maximization, and a limited role for the state to mimic what markets would do if they were functioning. If the same principles apply, then it is these market norms that are decisive not the institutional governance structures that are being used. It is the fundamental assumptions of the Market Paradigm that this chapter will set out.

4. Amartya K. Sen, *Rational Fools* in PHILOSOPHY AND ECONOMIC THEORY BOOK 87–109 (Frank Hahn and Martin Hollis eds., 1979).

5. AMARTYA K. SEN, COLLECTIVE CHOICE AND SOCIAL WELFARE (1970); E. J. MISHAN, WHAT IS POLITICAL ECONOMY ALL ABOUT? (1982).

6. BRIAN BARRY, POLITICAL ARGUMENT 38–40 (1992).

it coordinates the actions of individuals give rise to the problem necessitating public action? How can attention to the collective action problems of the society help to provide answers to these logical process questions?

Any legal argument embodies a set of presuppositions about the problems inherent in convincing individuals to cooperate toward a common end: socio-political community. These assumptions build on the formal definition of the person that precedes it, and they inform the parameters of the "legitimate" state (that will be subsequently defined). The political community and the terms of collective action, operate as transition points between assumptions about the individual and the state. Specifically, the importance of the community and the dilemmas of collective action help the decision-maker to locate and clarify her intuitions about what a "socially-better" policy is and how she might achieve it.

The Market Paradigm builds a collective level of organization with no distinct character independent of the individuals of which it is an aggregate. The whole of the political community is no more than the aggregate sum of individual wants and preferences. The purpose of collective action is primarily to establish just enough cooperation to satisfy the material interests of the most people possible without force or fraud connected to trade.[7] This represents a collective action problem akin to a prisoner's dilemma,[8] which is iterated in order to find an aggregation rule that can avoid either continuous exploitation or complete cessation of trade.

The solution to the prisoner's dilemma assumed by the Market Paradigm begins with a functioning "invisible hand"[9] that coordinates the self-interested acts of each person toward the collective well-being of all. The effectiveness of the invisible hand, however, wanes when we move from a pure market context to the public sector. The collective action problems involving over or under-supply of common goods, free-riders, and pollution effects external to markets, causes the market to fail. This is where the market paradigm comes in. If we cannot have markets because of externality and commons[10] problems, then we can have administrators

*"invisible hand" solution to prisoner's dilemma fails b/c of common goods, free-riders + pollution effects

---

7. In terms of force or fraud, this is primarily focused upon that which is external to the market. Force and fraud are part of market operations in that unequal economic power and ability, as well as false claims and information, are prevalent within basic market operations. What the Market Paradigm does require is a state sufficient to limit fraud without its action forcing or restricting personal preference and its satisfaction in market trade or willingness-to-pay. See ALLAN FELDMAN, WELFARE ECONOMICS AND SOCIAL CHOICE THEORY (1980).

8. ROBERT E. GOODIN, THE POLITICS OF RATIONAL MAN (1976); ROBERT AXELROD, THE EVOLUTION OF COOPERATION (1984); and RUSSELL HARDIN, COLLECTIVE ACTION (1982).

9. ADAM SMITH, THE WEALTH OF NATIONS bk. 4, ch. 2 (1776 [1937]).

10. The original description of a "commons" problem is attributed to

utilizing market assumptions to make collective decisions for us. In other words, the Market Paradigm solves collective goods problems by having policy argument mimic the solutions markets would produce, were they able to function.

Whatever the solution, community must be formed out of consumers through the terms of market exchange and, where markets fail, through the aggregation of individual preference into a social ordering that reflects individual wants in collective choices.[11] The state may act as an aggregation mechanism, but no specific definition of a distinct political community exists to concern the analyst.

The Prisoner's or Polluter's Dilemma

We assume two actors, in isolation, weighing the subjective costs and benefits of a decision to pollute. Further, we assume that each has the expectation that the other will act rationally, in that, she will try to achieve the highest utility payoff by satisfying her highest preference. The actors are assumed to have the following preference order:

	(utility to i)	(preference)
(best)	1	unilateral polluting *best to pollute while competitor doesn't*
	2	universal restraint → *better to both keep clean than*
	3	universal polluting → *both pollute*
(worst)	4	unilateral restraint *worst to keep clean while competitor pollutes*

For all (i): $u_i(1) > u_i(2) > u_i(3) > u_i(4)$ and $1\ P_i\ 2\ P_i\ 3\ P_i\ 4$.

These rational (complete, transitive) preference orders or individual payoffs are contained in the following strategic matrix:

Garrett Hardin, *The Tragedy of the Commons* 162 SCIENCE 1243–45 (1968), who connects the tendency to overgraze a collective or public commons to the self-interest of the individuals and the free nature of the collective or public good. The problems confronted by private welfare calculations confronting collective goods, and the propensity for consumers to free-ride, under supplying the good, has been examined as the generic problem of "common pool resources" (See ELINOR OSTROM, GOVERNING THE COMMONS: THE EVALUATION OF INSTITUTIONS FOR COLLECTIVE ACTION and SUSAN BUCK, THE GLOBAL COMMONS: AN INTRODUCTION (1998)).

11. DENNIS C. MUELLER, PUBLIC CHOICE (1979).

Is universal restraint better than universal polluting b/c when both pollute, neither can continue to free-ride on environment?

best (1)
↓
worst (4)

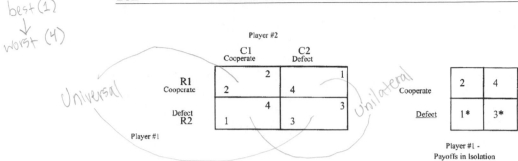

Universal

Unilateral

In this matrix, row (R) and Column (C) have two strategy choices (S): to cooperate in the provision of the collective good of environmental quality by not polluting (R1 and C1), or to continue to pollute and free-ride on the quality of the environment (R2 and C2). The contention is that individuals, considering their self-interested preferences in isolation, will have a tendency to pollute based on the assumption that comparing the personal costs and benefits of unilateral restraint v. pollution, the latter will win out as waste management will always be a cost, while polluting will always be a benefit. From within this strategic context, as we can see looking at Player #1 payoffs in isolation, it is the <u>dominant strategy*</u> for each player to defect, whatever choice the other makes (1 is preferred 2 and 3 is preferred to 4). With both agents playing their dominant strategy the resulting payoffs will be (3,3). This is a dilemma for the polluters as long as they independently prefer Universal Cooperation to Universal Defection but collectively end up with the latter (Goodin 1976, 166–168).

Dominant strategy is to pollute.

J.M. Gillroy—1997

c) *The Legitimate/Just State*

The requirements of solving the collective action problems faced by public decision-makers, and the normative attributes of the individual citizen as described above, help to define the last level of fundamental assumptions, concerning the role of the just state. Paradigm design is concerned with the basic assumptions that define what makes a government legitimate.[12] When considering legitimacy, one is concerned with what standards define social justice. What is the form, role, and objective of a just state achiev-

---

12. Here we shall follow the lead of JAMES S. FISHKIN, TYRANNY AND LEGITIMACY: A CRITIQUE OF POLITICAL THEORIES (1979), who uses both justice and legitimacy to describe the state because in constructing a paradigm, one needs to consider what role legitimizes the state within the paradigm as well as how this role reflects the operational principle of the paradigm and, in this way, defines justice within the logic of the argument.

ing the overall goals of policy? What are the legitimate ends and moral limits of state action?

For the Market Paradigm, the state has only two functions: to police and adjudicate contracts and to provide a surrogate decision process that can substitute when markets fail and allocations cannot be made without the involvement of government.[13] The normative system underlying the market therefore defines the legitimate state as the "minimal" state,[14] maintaining the background legal institutions of common law that protect market exchange and substituting economic preference calculations when markets fail. The state is therefore active only to the extent it mimics market allocations.[15] The paramount moral role of the legitimate state is to maintain existing markets, the property of the individual and her right to trade it.

The institutions of the "minimal state" function to facilitate individual want-satisfaction and regulate behavior only to further this end. For the Market Paradigm, as a framework for policy analysis, the purpose of political institutions is produced by a confrontation between the individual consumer and the need for government to facilitate cooperation, solve any prisoner's dilemma and provide collective goods as the market would itself.

The Market Paradigm defines all three of its fundamental assumptions in terms of intuitions about how the conditions and results of private choice can be translated into public choice. It searches for an answer to the "Why?" question by transferring the assumptions of a competitive market into the public sphere. With this as a base, the analyst clarifies normative priorities and sets up a foundation for CPA that will influence the rest of the process and the resulting policy recommendations.

2) Template—Stage II: Operating Principles and Material Conditions

In creating a paradigm for policy design argument, operating principles are derived from the fundamental assumptions and the material conditions of these principles are then defined. We need to understand what principle(s) set the best standard of choice, given the fundamental assumptions, and then what material conditions, accessible to the decision-maker, make the imperatives of the principle(s) physically real within the political community.

13. E. J. MISHAN, COST–BENEFIT ANALYSIS (3rd ed. 1982); and FELDMAN, *supra* note 7.

14. ROBERT NOZICK, ANARCHY, STATE, AND UTOPIA (1974); RICHARD POSNER, THE ECONOMICS OF JUSTICE (1983).

15. JOHN MARTIN GILLROY & MAURICE WADE, THE MORAL DIMENSIONS OF PUBLIC POLICY CHOICE: BEYOND THE MARKET PARADIGM 8 (1992).

a) *Operating Principles*

To inform the developing policy argument and produce actual alternative public choices, it is critical to simplify the theoretical assumptions into principle(s) that can provide a shorthand for what is essential in whatever law is eventually produced. The operating principle sets the standard that will define what is right or good as well as what is and is not a "reasonable" policy or a "persuasive" legal argument. Defining a "rational" policy requires operating principles that can form the basis of the policy imperative for the decision-maker and then help to create techniques or methods that the policy-maker can easily use for applying these principles to practical decisions.

For the Market Paradigm, the protection and facilitation of each person's voluntary economic trade is the essential concern. Policy should not focus on community or state except to the degree to which they aid the individual in protecting his property and satisfying his wants. The levels of interests we have previously characterized (individual, collective, state) do not each render a distinct principle, but all are represented in a single one. The normative operating principle of the market is economic <u>efficiency</u> as it aggregates and satisfies individual preferences for wealth. Within the market, efficiency is defined by the Pareto condition, which asserts that a new state of affairs is more efficient than the status quo only if everyone is as well off or better off. This strong condition, that there exist no welfare losers in efficient trade, is not practical in legal or public policy choice.[16] In public decisions there are likely to be both winners and losers and therefore efficiency is redefined as the Potential Pareto Improvement. Otherwise known as Kaldor efficiency, a new state of affairs is now efficient if the winners gain enough that they could "hypothetically" compensate the losers and make everyone as well off or better off. Using Kaldor efficiency, one aggregates personal costs and benefits in order to maximize collective wealth, but one is basically indifferent to wealth distribution within the society.[17] [See Appendix.]

Although some may argue that profit maximization or other principles trump efficiency in the Market Paradigm, we contend that Kaldor efficiency is not only basic to profit, production, and consumption, but also that the classical economists who apply it assume it protects the freedom of the individual and maximization of his utility. "Freedom as consent" is realized in one's liberty to

---

16. RICHARD N. L. ANDREWS, MANAGING THE ENVIRONMENT, MANAGING OURSELVES 8–9 (1999).

17. GILLROY AND WADE, *supra* note 15; FELDMAN, *supra* note 7; STOKEY AND ZECKHAUSER, *supra* note 2 at 24.

consume while consumer choice defines the material 'good' of the person.[18]

Kaldor efficiency is derived from characterization of the individual as a self-interested welfare maximizer, the definition of collective action as a preference aggregation problem, and the concern for a minimal state which charges the policy-maker to protect property and voluntary trade. The policy imperative is to satisfy as many individuals as possible and provide a growing economy that is as productive as possible so that the maximum number of individuals can find preference satisfaction in maximizing wealth. Using Kaldor efficiency as the operating principle of the Market Paradigm makes it possible to achieve the policy objective of maximizing aggregate social welfare.

b) Material Conditions

Merely defining the operating principles of a law is insufficient. One should also define what material conditions the policy-maker can manipulate to make these principles manifest in the day-to-day lives of constituents.

For the market, the primary material condition is **wealth**. This can be defined in many ways including resources, property, and possessions, but within markets all such concerns must be defined using the common metric of money. Price is the preeminent sensor of the market and money is the currency of the price system. The signals of price are the only ones recognized and responded to by markets; it becomes critical for an entity or "thing" to have a proper price, reflecting its economic or instrumental value to the individual, so that it is properly counted in trade and evaluated as part of wealth maximization.

The generation of profit in markets through Pareto efficiency is transferred into the public sector as wealth maximization through Kaldor efficiency. The material conditions of interest from the market point of view, therefore, are those that maximize economic production and produce the most goods for consumption, thus maximizing wealth, trade, and preference satisfaction as public policy.

At this point the boundaries of acceptable policy alternatives have been set by establishing the operating principles and material conditions of these principles. The only hurdle that remains is to have a shorthand that can provide a practical decision-maker with the immediate tools in terms of maxims for day-to-day decision-

---

18. John Martin Gillroy, *The Ethical Poverty of Cost–Benefit Methods: Autonomy, Efficiency and Public Policy Choice* 25 POLICY SCIENCES 83–102 (1992). Reprinted in GILLROY AND WADE, *supra* note 15 at 195–216 and GILLROY *supra* note 1 at ch. 2.

making and a methodology that citizens and administrators can use to apply the paradigm without having to directly reflect on its core principle or fundamental assumptions.

3) Template—Stage III: Maxims and Methods of Application

Stage III deals with those imperatives and rules of thumb, or methods of application, that each environmental or resource decision-maker uses in order to make the moral force of the underlying normative system "real" for citizens and other policy-makers wishing to apply the same normative standards without detailed considerations of their foundations. The central concern of the decision-maker at this crucial point in the generation of an argument paradigm, is to create a maxim, or imperative, that combines the operating principle and its material conditions. From this maxim one then derives a method of application that can eventually select tactical legal instruments (e.g. taxes, standards, liability law) reflecting the fundamental assumptions of the paradigm.

We understand, from Majone,[19] that a policy instrument is a means to achieve the ends of the policy. Even though choosing specific instruments is a tactical choice determined by the context model of the paradigm (examined below), the proper choice of means requires, first, that the ends of the policy be represented by the moral imperatives of decision maxims as these have been defined by the fundamental assumptions and principles of action. Then, second, the methods of application, built upon these maxims, can render the complex framework of moral theory underlying a choice into simple and accessible methodological tools for decision-making. In this way, the maxims define the choice and the methods implement them through the selection of proper policy instruments (e.g. taxes, standards).[20]

a) Maxims

By combining operating principle and the material conditions it defines, one can produce an imperative or maxim for legal argument that helps the decision-maker distinguish which alternative policy choices are compatible with the argument (those which promote the principle) and which are not compatible (those which reject the principle).

The Market Paradigm has but one maxim for the decision-maker: **_Maximize Wealth!_** Kaldor efficiency is represented by maximization and the material conditions by wealth. The maxim implores the policy-maker, in every choice she makes, to satisfy

19. GIANDOMENICO MAJONE, EVIDENCE, ARGUMENT & PERSUASION IN THE POLICY PROCESS 116 (1989).

20. _Id._ at ch. 6.

individual welfare preferences (one's willingness-to-pay) by maximizing net social welfare across the population. Under certain conditions, treated further on in this chapter, the imperative may be to optimize instead of maximize wealth. In either case, the maxim seeks a state of affairs in which individual willingness-to-pay is properly aggregated and maximized with as little government interference and cost to the economy as possible. However, how wealth is distributed by the policy is not critical.

distribution not important, only maximization

b) *Methods*

The purpose of creating an argument paradigm from our template is to provide a framework or schema of categories that allow an individual decision-maker either to recognize what underlies a method that he conventionally applies to his collective choices or to utilize an existing moral theory for the purposes of redirecting a public choice. We have argued that the key to doing both analysis and synthesis is to have a schema that combines the normative strength of philosophical theory with the practical strength of a simple method.

After one has constructed the paradigm from underlying normative and empirical conditions and identified the operating principle, this paradigm is readily accessible to anyone, without reconsideration of its details. This easy access comes from a methodology that is derived from the maxims, which are derived from material conditions and principles, which are ultimately derived from fundamental assumptions of the paradigm. Ideally, with only an application of the method, a decision-maker represents the entire paradigm in his policy choice.

In order to realize the condition of efficiency, the Market Paradigm relies on the methodology of cost-benefit[21] analysis (CBA).[22] Through CBA, the ends and means of public issues are submitted to the Kaldor efficiency test, and if passed, these ends and means can be recommended as reasonable public policy. ***Cost-Benefit Methodology*** acts as practical shorthand for the decision-maker and allows him to apply the principle of efficiency and protect the foundational assumptions, from which the principle is derived, with a minimum of intellectual effort. Without having to answer any questions or retrace one's steps through the logical schema, concern for the definition and balance of cost and benefits has set the standard for policy choice and a decision can be made among policy alternatives. [See Appendix.]

---

21. MISHAN, *supra* note 13.

22. It must be kept in mind here that cost-benefit methods are not cost-effectiveness methods, as the former places both means and ends under the principle of efficiency while the latter limits efficiency to the means and allows other principles to determine ends. See GILLROY AND WADE *supra* note 15 at 5–15.

Cost-Benefit As Present Value

PV < 0 → reject project
PV > 0 → undertake project

$$PV = \sum_{t=0}^{T} B_t - C_t / (1+r)^t$$

The present value of a project {where $(1+r)^t$ is the discount rate, that is, \$1 in year zero is worth \$(1+r) in year one}, is an appropriate yardstick with which to judge its desirability assuming, that all benefits and costs are captured in B_t and C_t. If PV<0 the project ought to be rejected since it would reduce economic welfare. …if PV>0 the project would increase society's welfare and so might profitably be undertaken.

[ROBIN W. BOADWAY, PUBLIC SECTOR ECONOMICS 175 (1979)]

Once the analyst has identified the Market Paradigm's maxim and its method of application he can use the paradigm to select, design, or evaluate a policy that fits within the normative and empirical constraints of arguments rendered by the paradigm and context model. Each principle is then connected to a policy instrument through the maxims and methods rendered by those principles.[23]

For application of the Market Paradigm to environmental law, the choice between alternative policies must be based on the principle of Kaldor efficiency as it applies to the extraction of resources and the regulation of the economy. The analyst's maxim to *Maximize Wealth* causes him to make connections between choice and welfare on the one hand, and preference and welfare maximization on the other hand.[24] These connections are realized in the effort to maximize social benefit through the use of cost-benefit methods. In this kind of efficiency analysis, alternatives will be acceptable to the degree they involve cost incentives and protect voluntary trade. Of primary concern is the allocation of goods that satisfy individual preferences and how the state might curtail them by *third-party* regulation of the economy that limits production of goods and externalities in favor of a cleaner environment. The burden of proof is on those who regulate the market, and in this way, interfere with its capacity to satisfy preferences. The use of economic incentives to affect consumer behavior informs the choice of alternative policy. The standard of evaluation demands policy that minimizes government regulation while maximizing benefits

23. This matching process can be seen as a test of the argument's feasibility. If a principle requires cheap and effective solar energy to be operational, then this policy must be created before the current argument is sound. In addition, if a policy design argument requires institutions or governance structures that are not legal, this too should divorce it from adequate policy instruments and make it less persuasive (e.g. if it requires the unconstitutional use of power).

24. AMARTYA K. SEN, CHOICE WELFARE AND MEASUREMENT 66–67 (1982).

over costs, and therefore efficiently satisfies more individual wealth preferences than it disappoints.

Overall, for the Market Paradigm, the self-interest of the individual consumer, as made manifest in expressed preferences, forms the touchstone for all resource policy decisions. Supplying policies that satisfy people's willingness-to-pay preferences is assumed to be of central importance. Government policy should be limited so it does not interfere with material production that maximizes satisfaction across the population.

Thus, from the perspective of the Market Paradigm, nature is adequately valued as 'Natural Resources,' which, in this context, can only be regulated subject to an individual's wealth preference and choices. Establishing markets for resources is the solution to problems of resource extraction and pollution, and the state's mimicing of private resource markets will suffice as sound policy when private markets fail.[25] A market setting requires that individual choices for instrumental wealth accumulation be respected regardless of the risks or damage involved.[26] Assuming that individuals will recognize and weigh resource choices within the strategic framework, where individual self-interest is the rational motivation, the collective action problem allows only maximum development and trade of resources between actors with minimal third-party interference. An environmental resource, like all things in the market, is a commodity, the disposition of which is left up to each trader who is assumed to have sovereignty over his choices. The policy designer's concern to maximize wealth is therefore weighed against leaving the natural system alone, which will not generate wealth, and thus pose a potential cost to the individual and society. The minimal state is only minimal if it uses as few non-market forces as possible.[27]

Overall, the Market Paradigm finds a means to the ends of efficient preference aggregation in the policy instrument of a surrogate market price system that would allow individual as well as collective resource generators to develop and/or trade resources on the basis of their willingness-to-pay for them. This internalizes the cost of any resource, supports an expanding economy, and places one's preferences for wealth on an identical level with all other preferences, so that environmental quality is established at the

---

25. YAIR AHARONI, THE NO RISK SOCIETY (1981); W. KIP VISCUSI, RISK BY CHOICE (1983).

26. Mark Sagoff, *On Markets for Risk*, 41 Md. L. Rev. 755–773 (1982).

27. The problem with a minimal state is if the market creates a prisoner's dilemma and there is a 'failure' of the "invisible hand" (a piece of market metaphysics) which causes less than collectively optimal outcomes, then authoritarianism is not far away. This would support the argument that true markets best survive in totalitarian environments, and would be supported by some interpretations of market theory. See NOZICK *supra* note 14.

point where the overall aggregate costs exceed the benefits. People will get the "balance" between environment and resource development for which they are willing-to-pay.

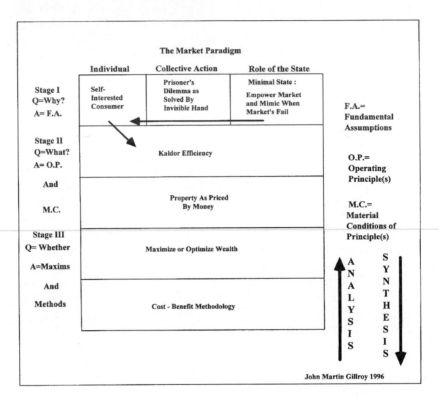

The details of choosing appropriate tactical policy instruments for the full application of the Market Paradigm, given the characteristics of environmental issues in particular, require that we next consider the second component of a complete argument evolving from the paradigm. This component involves constructing a practical context model from the principles and methods that the theoretical paradigm produces. Only with both components in hand—the paradigm and the context-model—can the policy-maker enter the tactical phase of the policy design process assured that inappropriately chosen means will not compromise primary ends.

A Context Model for the Market Paradigm

Law is a combination of theory and practice or strategy and tactics. The tactical enactment of the policy is in administrative institutions, implementation instruments and "real world outcomes."[28] Law is also the strategic conceptualization of ends, standards, ideals, and plans that justify choices and the means of evaluation and accountability. In describing the strategy of a legal policy, one is not only considering the theoretical argument paradigm that forms the foundation of the idea, but also the context model which mediates between the paradigm and the policy instruments chosen for codification and implementation. The context model is formed by defining what material components shape the particular policy space,[29] and by defining how these components are to be evaluated and ordered relative to one-another. In contemplating the implementation of a paradigm, one is considering the feasibility of the strategy, its possible constraints, audiences, and implementation instruments, which will themselves be defined in terms of the context model or worldview of the person employing the paradigm.

Both the strategy and tactics of a law can be described as involving argument.[30] In the strategic phase of legal design one constructs one's paradigm from the foundation of the fundamental assumptions, while in the tactical phase of argument design one

28. STEVEN KELMAN, MAKING PUBLIC POLICY: A HOPEFUL VIEW OF AMERICAN GOVERNMENT 7 (1987).

uses the context model to judge feasibility and adjust one's argument to empirical political, economic, and social contingencies. The importance of a theoretical paradigm and its designation of methods from fundamental assumptions is that it forms the foundation for a worldview. In terms of natural science, the Newtonian paradigm created a mechanical worldview that affected how the human being and his environment were pictured outside the realm of science. When Einstein's vision replaced Newton's as the pertinent argument paradigm, the worldview it spawned changed the way in which the world around us was perceived.

While legal argument emerging from a new paradigm may not be as influential as argument emanating from an older and more established paradigm, it is reasonable to suggest that one of the critical entailments of a paradigm for environmental regulation is the model of the social and natural environment it produces. We will call this worldview configuration the ***practical context model***, and define it as what is rendered from the paradigm's conceptualization of how it interrelates to, and arranges, both other paradigms within a designated policy space and the components of the world around it (i.e. humanity, nature, government, economy).

Thus the context model defines the worldview of the paradigm and is the practical intermediary between the theoretical paradigm and the material operation of the policy process in political choice, production, final action, and real-world outcome. The practical context of choice defines what components make up the world and which one has priority in collective decisions.

29. MAJONE, *supra* note 19 at 158–159.   **30.** *Id.* ch. 5.

1) Model Components, Priorities, and Construction of the Traditional Sector Approach

The first premise of our argument about the conceptual core of environmental law and policy is that it was preceded into the policy space by the meta-policy[31] of economic growth and prosperity, where market assumptions and principles held pride of place.[32] The dominant ethic of the first hundred years of our nation's history concerned growth, expansion, and private wealth maximization; this caused us to conceptualize the environment as a source of resources and a receptacle for waste as the American economy expanded.[33] This conceptualization also created the institutions and administrative apparatus of environmental and resource regulation and our present uncoordinated and ineffective policy map.[34]

According to Posner,[35] what motivates economic efficiency as a principle is its focus on the welfare preferences of the individual consumer and their maximization of wealth. He argues that this definition of efficiency is compatible with the Kaldor criteria, and the basic assumptions of cost-benefit methodology.[36] Posner contends that through this criteria and methodology, the principle of economic efficiency can serve as an ethical imperative in the search for maximizing private and social prosperity through law.

Applied to the context of nature, we can see the goal of creating a national economy and expanding westward as motivated and justified by this principle. Within the market context all goods and services can be substituted for one another. Trade is based on the individual's preferences and proceeds until no further trade is profitable to any person. Efficiency, when transferred into the public realm from the market, gives government the imperative to mimic what the market would do were it able to function and seeks the efficient level of collective (or in this case environmental) goods.

This brings us to the first Traditional Sector Approach model: TSA–I. In this model the market dominates the policy space and the natural environment is simply one of its sub-systems. The core of economic policy, which is set-up to expand the market and produce prosperity, values everything instrumentally as it contributes to growth and the production of 'wanted' things. From the market standpoint, the earth is merely a source of raw material that gives no utility to the consumer in its 'raw' state. Therefore,

→ natural resources are raw materials to be turned into goods/services to maximize wealth

---

31. *Id.* at 146–149.

32. GILLROY, *supra* note 1 at ch. 3.

33. ANDREWS, *supra* note 16 at 104–106.

34. CELIA CAMPBELL-MOHN ET AL., ENVIRONMENTAL LAW: FROM RESOURCE TO RECOVERY vii at note

3 (1993). See also JOHN S. DRYZEK, RATIONAL ECOLOGY: ENVIRONMENT AND POLITICAL ECONOMY (1987).

35. POSNER, *supra* note 14.

36. GILLROY & WADE, *supra* note 15 at 6–13.

the imperative is to transform as much of this raw material as possible into products and services that can improve the economy and maximize the collective wealth.

TRADITIONAL SECTOR APPROACH TSA-1

Efficiency Means The Maximum Use Of The Environment, By Market Forces, With Government Assistance, For Both Resource Extraction & Waste Disposal

J.M. Gillroy 1998

One fact was especially relevant to the imperative to maximize social benefit over cost amidst the expanding economy in the Nineteenth and early Twentieth Centuries: the perceived zero cost of environmental media as sinks, and of virgin materials as resources. This free access to raw materials, and the government's concern to get as much land and resources into private hands as possible (i.e. the Land Disposal Policy), encouraged the market system to absorb as many raw materials into the economic process as its technology could consume and transform.

In order to facilitate an expanding economy we divided nature into its separate species, minerals, and media and sought an economic use for each. We found immediate tangible market value in some (e.g. timber and fur), and potential in others (e.g. ore and oil), but ultimately we sought only to maximize their use for economic purposes. The effort to maximize nature's use value created the foundation for present environmental law, policy and management institutions.

In addition to categorizing species and minerals as 'natural resources' the expanding economy also used air, water, and land as 'efficient' receptacles for the disposal of wastes. The near-zero price of resources was matched by the perceived zero cost of disposal into water, air, and onto land. In these ways, nature presented a bottomless capacity as both inventory of raw materials for the generation of wealth and sinks for the free disposal of waste. The imperative to seek maximum benefit was therefore aided by the zero price at both ends of the economic process: extraction and disposal.

TSA–I can be described as a market-driven model where the perception of a boundless and unprotected nature, combined with the driving force of the normative standard of Kaldor efficiency,[37] encourages the maximum use of nature to fuel economic progress. In this drama, the government's role is to make nature available to economic forces, facilitating private commerce and its technological innovations.

However, by the late Nineteenth Century, perceptions about the free use of the environment were changing. As technology allowed for greater and faster use of resources, concerns arose about long-term sustainability of their supply. Although many assumed science and technology would be able to replace any raw materials that ran out, for the first time in our history we began to consider the long-term use of nature's species and minerals. Meanwhile, the growing density of urban areas, where most of the production was going on, changed perceptions about the free disposal of waste. Smoke, dirty water, disease, and the odors of industrialization led some to question whether maximizing production would, in the long run, lead to an optimal use of environmental media as sinks.

From the market point of view, the near zero price of species, minerals, and media in TSA–I, combined with the unregulated advancement of technology, would lead to market failure. Specifically, without the economic calculation of efficiency reflecting the "true" price of resources and pollution, and with the growing sophistication of technology, the market failed to account for all the contingencies that might interfere with the long-term persistence of both the natural and the social world. As a result, efficiency might extract too much from nature and put too much back into the environment as pollution.[38] When the *collective goods* nature of public policy problems causes market failures and the true price of an item is not reflected in its market value, then the role of the government in an efficiency-based regime is to mimic the market and allocate accordingly, maximizing social benefit over cost.

Instead of allowing the market to set the maximum rate of extraction from, and disposal into, the environment (as in TSA–I), it becomes the job of government to compensate for market failure

---

37. Normative in the sense that it set the standards by which public choice and action are judged, justified, and evaluated.

38. Larry E. Ruff, *The Economic Common Sense of Pollution* in ECONOMICS OF THE ENVIRONMENT (Robert Dorfman and Nancy S. Dorfman eds. 1977).

[handwritten: gov. must set]

and set *optimal* rates of extraction and disposal, given the technology available and the natural contingencies of species, minerals, and media. This brings us to the second variant of the traditional sector approach.

Traditional Sector Approach - TSA-II

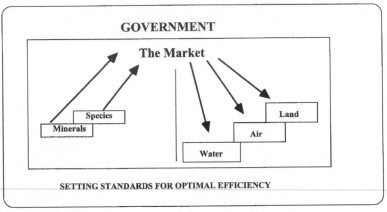

J.M. Gillroy 1997

Examining the model of TSA–II, one can see that instead of the many arrows of extraction and disposal that appear in TSA–I, we now have single controlled rates of extraction and disposal, regulated by government, based upon the demands of a materials balance. This represents the idea that for each species and mineral a single optimal rate of extraction has been deciphered and for each media a corresponding rate of disposal has been set. In effect, efficiency is now defined not in terms of **maximization** but in terms of the **optimal** long-term relationship between economy and nature. Efficiency is now defined by policy maxims to establish the optimal level of extraction and the optimal level of pollution and risk, which implies a government centered search for what economists call the "materials balance."[39]

[handwritten margin note: Under TSA II, efficiency is →]

The materials balance describes all of nature as an inventory of natural resources. Based on the second law of thermodynamics (i.e. that matter cannot be created or destroyed), the economy is assumed to neither create nor destroy nature, but "merely" to transform it.[40] All natural material is of value to the extent that it can be used to support human life, "fulfill human values,"[41] and

39. EDWIN S. MILLS AND PHILIP E. GRAVES, THE ECONOMICS OF ENVIRONMENTAL QUALITY 8–18 (2nd ed. 1986)

40. *Id.* at 8.

41. DAVID W. PEARCE AND R. KERRY TURNER, ECONOMICS OF NATURAL RESOURCES AND THE ENVIRONMENT 140 (1990).

create economic wealth. The materials balance, as an expression of the principle of efficiency applied to human use of nature, contains the assumption that all of nature can be considered as either inventory, product, or waste. All material that is extracted from the environment equals that within the capital stock of products plus that returned to the environment as waste. This equivalence is the "balance." All natural material is therefore a constant quantity in fungible symmetric states of being that change form for the sake of optimizing human economic wealth. The importance of the idea of a materials balance, as an expression of efficiency, is the continued presumption of *use*.[42] The use of nature for human wealth maximization provides a way of accounting for each resource in terms of its form and place in the overall consumption process (i.e. take, use, dispose).

For example, the concept of the optimal level of pollution requires one to assume that pollution is a natural by-product of the economic process, which does not require that all pollution be controlled. To define pollution as "damage to the environment that impairs its usefulness to people,"[43] is to treat environmental media (e.g. air, water, land, groundwater) as having definable tolerance levels in terms of continued human use, which, if stressed, will breakdown that media's ability to hold and process pollution.[44]

Tolerance however has a more pertinent meaning to the individual consumer's perception of environmental quality. It is not just that the airshed, for example, can only absorb X amount of pollution before it is organically incapable of absorbing any more, but also that it can only absorb so much before consumers perceive a change in quality that causes them to lose utility. Both of these definitions of tolerance have a place in the discussion and definition of 'optimal' levels of pollution.

In any case, for a market-based policy analysis, the environment is valuable as a natural cleaning and storage media and the goal of the efficient system, as described by TSA–II, is to use this

[handwritten margin note: by environment to hold pollution]

[handwritten margin note: by individuals of pollution in envi. as it affects them]

---

42. Even economic approaches like Ecological Economics, which are oriented toward sustainable conservation still assume *use* as the primary instrumental value of all natural attributes and Kaldor efficiency as the core principle of their analysis of environmental and resource law, see ROBERT COSTANZA, ET AL. ECOSYSTEM HEALTH: NEW GOALS FOR ENVIRONMENTAL MANAGEMENT (1992). For an argument that Ecological Economics does not significantly affect the search for wealth maximization in Kaldor efficiency and that therefore to make room for natural systems with intrinsic value, we must replace the Market Paradigm, see John Martin Gillroy, *A Practical Concept of Nature's Intrinsic Value* in THE MORAL AUSTERITY OF ENVIRONMENTAL DECISION MAKING: SUSTAINABILITY, DEMOCRACY, AND NORMATIVE ARGUMENT IN POLICY AND LAW (John Martin Gillroy & Joe Bowersox eds. 2002).

43. MILLS AND GRAVES, supra note 39 at 18.

44. ROBERT E. GOODIN, THE POLITICS OF RATIONAL MAN 175–6 (1976).

'facility' to its optimum without violating tolerance levels. "Discharge of limited amounts of wastes is a legitimate use of the absorption capacity of each environmental medium."[45]

Here the capacity of the environment to hold and purify pollution is examined against the backdrop of the demands of individual wealth maximization, which require as many individuals as possible to avoid the costs of pollution control. If each effort to avoid polluting costs the individual, and all efforts to control pollution are not necessary to preserve the minimal functioning of environmental media, then the trick is to minimize the costs of pollution control to the economy by allowing the maximum amount of pollution possible, while abating just enough so as not to exceed the tolerances of these media as storage and purification devices.[46]

The idea that optimal levels of extraction and pollution can be used to maintain a materials balance, implies, again, the instrumental value of the environment to humanity. Use of species, mineral, and media is the imperative and efficiency is the driving principle. The qualitative state of a natural entity or system does not matter, as long as that state serves long-term wealth accumulation. Here the economy neither destroys nor creates but merely transforms: trees into lumber, tigers into coats.

Within both TSA–I & II, efficiency remains the core principle guiding government's regulation of the market and is still the basis for the justification of resource law. First, efficiency is the foundation for a law and policy of natural resource extraction that achieves optimal efficiency in the use of nature's raw materials. Second, efficiency produces a law and policy of pollution and risk abatement that seeks the optimal level of contamination. Both models of the traditional sector approach promote the dissection of nature into tangible economic values (i.e. raw materials and absorbent media). The models only differ in the connotation of the principle of Kaldor efficiency.

In TSA–I, resources are zero-priced and Kaldor efficiency requires that government maximize wealth by encouraging and facilitating the maximum use of nature. Toward this end, government must keep prices low or non-existent and provide or protect technological innovation and infrastructure that empower use (e.g. trails, canals, timber roads, legal patents etc.). Within TSA–II, Kaldor efficiency requires government to seek optimal, not maximum, rates of extraction and pollution; the government's role is to compensate for market failure and utilize CBA to determine the

[handwritten margin note: TSA-I = maximum use of resources, gov. keeps prices low & promotes price of nature use (facilitation)]

[handwritten margin note: TSA-II = optimal use of resources, gov. compensate for market failure by helping keep materials balance (regulation)]

45. MILLS AND GRAVES, supra note 39, at 19.

46. See both ANTHONY C. FISHER, RESOURCES AND ENVIRONMENTAL ECONOMICS (1981) and

KENNETH M. STOKES, MAN AND THE BIOSPHERE: TOWARD A COEVOLUTIONARY POLITICAL ECONOMY (1994).

'optimal' rates of use and disposal—rates that maintain a regulated 'materials balance' over time.[47]

Both context models have three basic components with priority among them determined by the Market Paradigm's worldview. The first component is the ***market*** itself. Here efficiency holds the moral highground in both model variants and the continued persistence of the market is the ultimate standard for all policy and administrative decisions. The second component, also second in priority, is the ***government*** existing to facilitate market decision-making and to mimic market allocations through cost-benefit methods when the market itself fails. The third component, and last in priority for both the **Maximum Use** and **Optimal Use** models, is the ***natural environment***, which exists for use and can be divided into a set of raw materials or an eco-inventory for input into the market, and a series of environmental media as sinks for disposal of waste that the market generates.

Both TSA's prioritize;
1. market
2. gov.
3. natural env.

From the perspective of the **Traditional Sector Approach** (TSA–I & TSA–II), the market worldview perceives the economy as a whole system while it divides the natural environment into **sectors** for use. It is also the case that the Market Paradigm is **traditional** in that it has become the conventional approach to environmental law and policy design since before it was recognized as a public choice problem and a collective action issue at the beginning of the Twentieth Century.

The critical difference between TSA–I and TSA–II is one of emphasis: it reflects a definition of efficiency that has evolved in order to maintain market persistence. The evolution from maximum use to optimal use necessitates that the government shift its role from one of facilitation of market processes with public resources to one of regulating use of resources and media in an effort to prolong their effective life and provide for a persisting economy over a longer period of time. The priority of the market and the regulation of nature for use does not change. What changes is the role of government, which must intercede in different ways in order to respond to the evolving definition of efficiency, and guarantee those resources for which individuals are willing-to-pay.

TSA-I
(gov. facilitation)
↓ evolved
TSA-II
(gov. regulation)

---

47. The TSA models both create a world were resource and pollution issues are separate concerns rather than dialectical or interdependent concepts. It is not surprising that when this worldview created environmental law, that it created two distinct areas of legal rules, one devoted to natural resources (with then distinct laws for each component of this area, species, minerals etc.) and another to pollution and risk abatement (with distinct statutes for each media, air, water, land etc.).

Applications of TSA: Moving
from Strategy to Tactics

Using both the paradigm and context model, the lawyer or policy-maker can map the strategic dimensions of legal paradigm design and create a fully integrated and logically grounded argument. What remains is to take this analytic model of theory and practice and apply it to the subject of environmental law decision-making. The choice here is value dependent. Is the use value of a natural resource more important than the integrity of the natural system it is part of? Does nature have instrumental or intrinsic value? How defined?

Answering these questions requires that one assign values to humans, and to nature, and decide, or make a tradeoff between them. The lawyer or policy-maker selects a moral standard that defines what is most fundamentally at stake in the decision. This core principle will determine what is valued and how.[48] But before one decides what principle *ought* to define resource use, one must first understand what principle *does* define resource use, for this creates a point of departure for further deliberations.

According to Celia Campbell–Mohn,[49] there are many problems with the current application of principle to policy.

> Despite ever-growing public and private expenditures to implement environmental law, surprisingly few actual improvements occur. Often, spending large sums of money has only kept problems from worsening. Meanwhile, the gap between environmental quality and the objectives of environmental law widens. Congress responds to environmental problems by adding more administrative law fixes, creating an acropolis of administrative structures. Still, the administrative capacity to resolve environmental problems diminishes. Eventually administrative institutions become overwhelmed by the piecemeal approach.[50]

48. We use the word 'principle' in the singular because we contend that in making collective decisions about policy and law, one is faced with a situation where one must be fair and consistent to all constituents over time. Without this consistency, expectations could not be created and no one could define or anticipate the requirements of administrative law. Therefore, while one may consider a number of values in making a collective choice, one must, in the end, consistently allow one synthesis value to represent the dialectics involved in the decision and to be the trump standard in the argument. This trump standard becomes the core principle of the dominant policy argument for any area of policy or legal choice. Unless one either sacrifices consistency, or assumes that one value will never conflict with another, then a dominate core principle or synthesis principle will emerge, over time, to define 'conventional' environmental law. While it is possible for a competing argument to replace a conventional one, this takes great effort and political capital against convention.

49. CELIA CAMPBELL–MOHN ET AL., *supra* note 34.

50. *Id.* at vii.

If the current law defining our relationship with nature is not achieving the level of environmental quality that we think best (e.g. if it extracts resources without regard to the environmental damage left behind), then the fundamental principle upon which our law is built may need reconsideration and reform. Most critically, the fundamental principle that sets the standards for 'persuasive' policy argument and 'reasonable' law may need to be changed.

Recently, the answer to improving the general state of environmental affairs involves blaming government regulation, arguing for abandonment of command and control, and supporting the introduction of more market mechanisms to make resource extraction and environmental law efficient.[51] If indeed efficiency has not determined our policy to date, this might be a reasonable course of action. But efficiency is, and has always been, the core principle that brought us to this point.[52] So to introduce more market mechanisms would only add fuel to fire.

Before we make judgments about the future, before we can move ahead to new models and solutions,[53] before we can envision the requirements of any alternative principle for environmental law and policy or construct competing arguments for what is 'truly' at stake in extraction decisions,[54] we need to understand how the principle of efficiency has shaped the way we view the environment

---

51. See TERRY L. ANDERSON AND DONALD R. LEAL, FREE MARKET ENVIRONMENTALISM (1991) and STEPHEN BREYER, BREAKING THE VICIOUS CIRCLE, (1993).

52. One might counter-argue that a statute like the Endangered Species Act (16 U.S.C.A. §§ 1531–1544) provides an exception to the claim that market assumptions and the principle of efficiency are the foundations of environmental law. However, we would argue that although this statute comes the closest to representing different core values in the law, the instrumental value of nature for economic purposes remains a core and superseding value to any intrinsic value nature might have. Market efficiency considerations appear throughout the ESA. For example, in the determination of "critical habitat" (§ 1533 (b2)); in the establishment of the Endangered Species Committee (§ 1536 (e)–(p)), and in the allowances for economic hardship exemptions (§ 1539 (b)), to name only a few. Even within the Congressional Findings section of the statute that outlines the reasons for the act, only one of six values ("ecological" (§ 1531 (a3))

can be said to have a completely non-market definition.

53. Another solution requires a conceptual reorientation away from a concentration on individual media or sectors of the environment (land, water, air etc.) to a consideration of the economic process as a series of interfaces between human action and nature, beginning with the extraction of resources from the environment and ending with their reintegration into nature. See CAMPBELL–MOHN ET AL. *supra* note 34 at ch. 10. She claims that "[u]nlike traditional approaches to environmental law that either explain each statute or group the statutes by media, this [argument] reflects the fact that laws govern activities, not the environment. It develops a new approach, called resource to recovery, that explains all the laws that apply to an activity, from the time resources are allocated for extraction, through their manufacture into products, and on to their disposal." *Id.* at vii, note 3.

54. See GILLROY, *supra* note 1, for a complete argument that it is the intrinsic value of humanity and nature that ought to set the standards for environmental law and policy.

and conceptualize our place within it. [Specifically, we need to understand how a concern for economic efficiency has created the natural resources law we now have.]

Efficient Natural Resource Law & Policy

The first clue to the ethical core of natural resources law and policy is the word used to describe this area of study: 'resources.' The language is not ecological, nor is it a philosophical description of the components of the natural world. Rather, it is the language of human use: economics. Why would our primary concern be for nature as a resource if we do not consider it primarily of economic, and therefore instrumental, value? Is it possible to include a concern for the *intrinsic value* of nature if we begin with this vocabulary? Does the word not symbolize the core of the meta-policy?

The term resources is descriptive of an age, of a time when it was the zero-cost, abundance, and utility of nature to economic growth and human wealth that defined it, and our relationship to it. The pertinent policy inquiry is whether we are still within this age, or have moved on to another.

For the first century of our existence as a nation, we had no governmental control over the use of nature. What we now know as environmental law is actually a two-part evolution of regulations shaping nature's components and systems that began with a concern for the exhaustion of raw materials at the turn of the Twentieth Century. The first economic controls on the maximization of wealth were controls on our natural resources argue that these controls were an effort to find the optimum level of resource extraction (TSA–II) as a definition of efficiency to replace maximization within the market (TSA–I).

The practical evolution of the law in this area, is and has always been, based upon the shifting connotation of efficiency. The statutes, court cases and legal arguments represent a search for a *reasonable* definition of Kaldor efficiency that evolves from sole control by a maximizing market to government aid in the deciphering of the optimal level of resource use. Throughout this evolution of law, the inherent value of nature and its internal systems has been of secondary concern as the aim remains that of amending our definition of efficiency and not replacing it with a new core principle for environmental meta-policy.

The maximization model (TSA–I) characterizes the meta-policy of our nation's growth through its first one-hundred years. The realization that the market was over-using un-priced resources, and that technology was increasing use faster than nature could regenerate those resources, brought the operational connotation of the core principle of maximum efficiency into question. The principle of efficiency was then redefined to include government's establishment of a long-term, optimally efficient, level of extraction. Now TSA–II becomes the context model for the Market Paradigm as government attempts to mimic market allocations while maintaining a materials balance. An examination of some public land issues may help us to consider the persistent role efficiency plays in resource law.[55]

1) Mining

Much of the United States was or still is owned by the federal government[56] and it has been the policy of the federal Government to transfer as much of the public lands as possible into private hands. With the Homestead Act of 1862 (43 U.S.C.A, §§ 161–284) and other statutes,[57] the state sought to maximize the use and economic value of land under its control.

The General Mining Act of 1872 (30 U.S.C.A. §§ 21–42) is one of the best examples of government legislation designed to maximize the use of public lands within TSA–I. This law, which originally applied to all mining[58] now applies to over three million acres of the Bureau of Land Management's property. A response to the 1849 gold rush, it established districts and administrative procedures to facilitate exploration and filing mining claims. In facilitating private extraction of public resources, this law expresses the idea of efficiency as maximization of wealth. It assumes that minerals in the ground are not of utility to anyone and ought to be transformed by the economy at as fast a rate as technologically possible.

The law requires that an individual do the assessment work, stake a claim, and discover minerals on this claim. Once an individual discovers the minerals they are protected by the law which grants exclusive ownership rights in the minerals to the miner. The courts have supported the *free enterprise* dimensions of the act by finding, first, that as long as the individual continues to work a claim they maintain their rights (*Union Oil Co. v. Smith*, 249 U.S. 337 (1919)) and, second, that he who produces the wealth has title

---

55. In order to find adequate case studies for the application of the Market Paradigm we decided to go back to the last time there was significant political activity surrounding these resource issues. Because environmental law has suffered extreme neglect in the two terms of George W. Bush and limited effort in Clinton's second term, we have chosen to focus on the first term of the Clinton Administration, that is, 1993–1996. At this time there was a clear effort to refocus on resource and environmental issues and to make reforms in all areas of this law that should shed light on the power of the Market Paradigm.

56. GEORGE CAMERON COGGINS ET AL., FEDERAL PUBLIC LAND AND RESOURCE LAW 11–25 (1993).

57. *Id.* at 55–105.

58. In 1920 oil and gas came under different legislation.

to the minerals (*Geomet Exploration, Limited v. Lucky Mc Uranium Corp.*, 124 Ariz. 55, 601 P.2d 1339, cert. dismissed, 448 U.S. 917 (1980)).

The act aims to extract "valuable minerals" (30 U.S.C.A. § 22) which it defines according to a reasonableness test,[59] which is determined by whether a market exists for the mineral. The statute, although continually under review by Congress, currently sets no environmental standards for the natural system surrounding the exploration and mining of the minerals, or for the use of public lands for mining. Furthermore, it extracts no royalties for mineral finds and provides incentives for exploration and extraction of minerals through its efforts to place claims in private hands. Nor is there any requirement for reclamation of the land after mining.

Some of the reforms perpetually considered by Congress include leasing the land rather than granting rights to it, setting a price on extraction by requiring that royalties be paid to the government, and mandating that all mining be followed by complete reclamation of the land. At this writing, no environmentally-centered amendments are close to becoming law.[60]

As far as mining on public lands is concerned, the government continues to encourage maximum use of public lands and has not even set a price on exploration or extraction of economically valuable minerals. Mining still exhibits the characteristics of TSA–I, as the government allows the market to dictate extraction policy.

2) Grazing

Another area of resource use on public land involves the private grazing of sheep and cattle. Here an active debate over what price creates the optimal use of rangeland illustrates the conceptual shift from TSA–I to TSA–II.

The law and policy of grazing fees[61] encourages the use of public lands for optimal efficiency, and shows that government intercession into the market is not intended to protect nature for its own sake, but to ensure that a low-cost resource is supplied for

---

59. See both Castle v. Womble Opinion of the Secretary of the Interior, 1894. 19 L.D. 455 and United States v. Coleman 390 U.S. 599 (1968).

60. This has been especially true during the Republican controlled Congress that was elected with George W. Bush and stayed in power until the 2006 elections. Legislators in both the House and Senate worked to restore the Market Paradigm to all phases of environmental and natural resources law, much like the Taft Administration worked to

reverse all of the advances for the reservation of public lands and environment established during the administration of Theodore Roosevelt at the onset of the Progressive Era.

61. Although grazing is allowed on land under the authority of the Forest Service as well as the Bureau of Land Management (BLM), we will concentrate on the BLM and its fee policy, as this is where the main Congressional debate has focused itself.

the agricultural economy. An interesting dimension of the price debate is that it is still influenced by the logic and rationality of TSA–I, as prices are kept low in order to stay as close as possible to a zero-price for the resource. That the state is assigning a price to mimic the market means we have moved from TSA–I to TSA–II, but the fact that it remains so low betrays the prejudice for the conventional definition of efficiency within TSA–I. The redefinition of the core principle of efficiency, from maximization to optimality, is a gradual process of argument, that is still incomplete.

The origin of grazing fees, and their political environment, exhibit at least two noteworthy considerations: first, the incapacity of the market to regulate itself, and second, the use of policy arguments that justify governmental efforts to mimic market allocations and preserve the principle of efficiency in law and policy. Public grazing lands are a type of common resource that individuals expect to be able to extract and use without cost. However, the collective goods nature of these public lands leaves them open to overgrazing, which motivates the current debate over grazing prices.

When the market cannot establish the proper rate of resource use government action is necessary to set a price and, in so doing, establish an *optimal* rate of use for rangeland. Whether or not the current price sets the proper or optimal rate of use, the core imperative in grazing policy was, and continues to be, the maintenance of rangeland as a tangible economic commodity.

Currently the Bureau of Land Management (BLM) is responsible for more than 260 million acres of public rangeland which represents approximately ten percent of all the land in the lower forty-eight states.[62] On this land the BLM grants permits to graze livestock to more than 28,000 individuals and corporations. Most of the permits issued are not owned by private ranchers but by large corporate entities.[63] The difference between the fee BLM charges the permit holders to graze their livestock and the administrative cost to the BLM resulted in a loss of $52 million to the treasury in 1993,[64] and has gotten worse since.

Grazing on public lands is regulated, principally, through three statutes, which are, in chronological order: The Taylor Grazing Act

---

62. These figures are from JACQUELINE VAUGHN SWITZER, ENVIRONMENTAL POLITICS 76 (1994). However, COGGINS ET AL., *supra* note 56, report that grazing takes place on 159 million acres and involves 19,000 ranchers.

63. For example, as far back as 1993 the Rock Springs Grazing Association of

Wyoming owns 1,000,000 acres; the Metropolitan Life Insurance Company owns 800,000 acres and the Zenchiku Corporation of Japan owns 40,000 acres of BLM land. See William Kitteredge, *Free Range: The War Over Grazing Fees,* THE NEW REPUBLIC, Dec. 1993.

64. *Id.*

of 1934 (43 U.S.C.A. §§ 315–315r); The Federal Land Policy and Management Act of 1976 (43 U.S.C.A. §§ 1701–84) and the Public Rangelands Improvement Act of 1978 (43 U.S.C.A. §§ 1901–08).[65]

The fees for use of the public lands are handled by specific parts of these statutes and a study of these provisions exhibit an evolution of method and authority that has resulted in a marked failure over the past twenty years to effectively raise fees to, or near market value.

Originally, the public lands were open to sheep, cattle, and goats without fee (TSA–I). In this era the market was the sole regulator of this natural resource. It was not until the Taylor Grazing Act (43 U.S.C.A. §§ 315–315r) [hereafter TGA] that grazing districts were defined and a permit and fee system was adopted for public lands under § 315 of the act. Here the Secretary of the Interior was authorized to issue permits to contiguous landowners to graze livestock on the public lands and further, "from time to time," to set "reasonable fees" for such use of the public lands (TSA–II).

The general authority of the Secretary of the Interior began to decline in the Federal Land Policy and Management Act of 1976 (43 U.S.C.A. §§ 1701–84) [hereafter FLPMA]. In SUBCHAPTER IV of this legislation, specifically in § 1751a, the responsibility for grazing fees becomes more complex, as Congress mandates that both the Secretary of the Interior and the Secretary of Agriculture should take joint responsibility to study and report to Congress on the "value of grazing on the lands under their jurisdiction," and to submit this report "together with recommendations to implement a reasonable grazing fee schedule based upon such study." This section of FLPMA also prohibits raising fees until the report is submitted to Congress. From TGA to FLPMA, we move from fee-free rangeland to a policy where the Secretary of the Interior sets reasonable fees at his/her own discretion, to the imposition of a fee formula that is mandated by, and for all intents and purposes, ratified by Congress.

Ratification of the fee formula, with additional strictures on the administrative setting of grazing fees, came in the third recasting of rangeland policy in Congress: the Public Rangelands Improvement Act of 1978 (43 U.S.C.A. §§ 1901–08) [hereafter PRIA]. Based on the report mandated by FLPMA (§ 1751a), this legisla-

---

65. The National Environmental Policy Act also regulates public lands and grazing to the degree that Environmental Impact Statements must be written for government action to allow grazing on public lands (Natural Resources Defense Council, Inc. v. Morton 388 F.Supp. 829, aff'd per curiam, 527 F.2d 1386 (D.C. Cir. 1976), cert. denied, 427 U.S. 913 (1976)). This case caused the BLM to write 212 site specific Environmental Impact Statements for its grazing program between 1977 and 1994.

tion established a fee formula in law that was to govern grazing fees from 1979–1985. The formula is as follows:

> ... the $1.23 base established by the 1966 Western Livestock Grazing Survey multiplied by the result of the Forage Value Index (computed annually from data supplied by the Economic Research Service) added to the Combined Index (Beef Cattle Price Index minus the Price Paid Index) and divided by 100...[66]

Aside from the quantitative parameters,[67] an interesting feature of this formula is that it is preceded by specific language that establishes its authority to set grazing fees. Instead of language that affirms the administrative authority of the Secretary of the Interior (as in TGA) or the Secretaries of Interior and Agriculture (as in FLPMA) we find text stating that:

> ... the Secretaries of Agriculture and Interior shall charge the fee for domestic livestock grazing on public rangelands which Congress finds represents the economic value of the use of the land to the user, and under which Congress finds fair market value for public grazing equals... (formula in quote above follows).[68]

The only discretion in this application of the Congressionally-defined formula is a sentence added to this section which allows a fee change of plus or minus 25% for any given year based on the previous year's fee, without Congressional approval.

In 1985, the Reagan Administration extended this formula by restating it, verbatim (Executive Order No. #12548). This Executive Order set the Congressional Formula into law from 1985 onward with the additional provision that the minimal grazing fee be set at $1.35 per animal unit month[69] (Executive Order No. 12548, Section 1). The practical effect of this string of legislation has been to raise grazing fees from near zero[70] before the Taylor Grazing Act to five cents per AUM with its passage. The formula adopted in FLPMA again raised the fees to $2.36 per AUM in 1980 but then back down (due to fluctuations in the formulas indexes) to

---

66. (PRIA § 1905)

67. This fee is set up so that grazing on the public land is costed considerably below the private market rate (See CONGRESSIONAL QUARTERLY WEEKLY REPORTS 2151 (1993)).

68. (PRIA § 1905—emphasis added)

69. The fees themselves are determined on the basis of what is called an *Animal Unit per Month* or AUM. An

AUM is defined as the "the amount of forage required to feed a cow and her calf, a horse, or five goats or sheep for a month," SWITZER, *supra* note 62 at 77.

70. In fact the Forest Service charged a minimal fee that was upheld in court as early as 1906 and began regular fees in 1931 before the TGA. However, the legislative authority to charge fees was formally granted by the TGA in 1934.

$1.86 per AUM which is the 1993 price.[71] Even today the price floats around this point. In 2006 the fee was $1.56 AUM, in 2007, it fell to $1.35 AUM and expectations are that it will be lowered again to $1.23 AUM in 2008. Overall, grazing continues to be regulated by the establishment of grazing districts and a permit fee system set by formula that fails to achieve fair market value for use of the rangeland.

The policy debate surrounding grazing on public land centers, not on any harm it may do to natural systems, or the capacities of these systems to maintain their functional integrity, but on the damage grazing may do to the long-term resource potential of the land itself. Using an efficiency-based argument, overgrazing is bad because it makes the land economically useless.[72]

Before the TGA, the policy of the government was to allocate as much private grazing on public lands as possible (TSA–I). As in all public land policy, the idea/ideal was to maximize the yield of resources from the public domain.[73] This policy of maximum use has yielded, over time, two common problems, overgrazing and a growing concern that a proper "price" for grazing cannot be set in the market and requires government intervention to find the optimal level of use for a long-term and efficient materials balance. In addition, FLMPA and PRIA cite damage to rangeland as a reason for their existence; PRIA echoes FLPMA in arguing that government ought to regulate the public lands to the economic advantage of the many and not the few, that is, keep the public lands a public resource (FLMPA § 1701 a(1)).[74] Throughout this discussion, however, even as non-economic concerns are acknowledged, the focus continues to be on the efficient use of rangeland, where the definition of efficiency is filtered through the idea of maintaining a long-term materials balance so that the resource can be productive for the foreseeable future.

The growing emphasis on maintaining a long-term materials balance is in reaction to a concern that maximum use has caused overgrazing which is a type of market failure. Because of this failure, government should raise the price exacted for grazing on rangeland (past zero) if the land is to be available for long-term,

71. SWITZER,*supra* note 62 at 77.

72. See KITTEREDGE, *supra* note 63; James Conway, *Babbitt in the Woods: The Clinton Environmental Revolution that Wasn't*, HARPER'S, Dec. 1993 and *Grazing*, WICHITA EAGLE, October 25, 1993.

73. See COGGINS ET AL., *supra* note 56 at ch. 1.

74. FLPMA § 1701 (a1) states that public lands should be "retained in Federal ownership" with concern to "serve the national interest." In § 1751 (b1) FLPMA states that "Congress finds a substantial amount of the Federal range land is deteriorating in quality?"; PRIA § 1901 (a1) states that the rangeland is in "unsatisfactory condition"; while § 1901 (a3) speaks to soil loss and desertification.

optimal use. In recent times, this concern is reflected in criticism of 'welfare cowboys' who benefit from public grazing fees that are much lower than private grazing fees and, in effect, are a subsidy to Western livestock ranchers.[75] The fact is that while a rancher with a permit to graze on public lands may pay as much as $1.86 per AUM, he would pay more than $12.00 per AUM to graze his livestock on comparable private lands.[76] Therefore, some argue that instead of setting an optimal use level at market prices, government has been subsidizing grazing and actually encouraging the maximizing behavior that government intervention was supposed to curtail. One could contend that the pressure for low price rangeland comes from those who are accustomed to a policy based upon a TSA–I definition of Kaldor efficiency. The convention of zero-price is hard to replace when you have come to expect it.

However it is framed, the argument, especially since the advent of the second Bush administration in 2001, is about 'efficient' price. What price will result in the optimal use of public rangeland for economic growth? Although this efficiency argument would be a surprise to anyone who thinks resource law exists to protect the environment for its own sake, it is no surprise if we begin with the premise that grazing policy is motivated by the core principle of efficiency, and the pride of place it has in the evolution of environmental law and meta-policy. From this viewpoint, the evolution of fees and the concern for overgrazing are attempts to correct for market shortcomings and to establish a balanced use of an instrumentally valuable resource. The public law on the issue supports the efficiency argument.

FLPMA § 1701(a7) states that public land management should be founded on the "basis of multiple use and sustained yield," and further, in § 1701(a9), that the law mandates "the United States [to] receive fair market value of the use of the public lands." This call for the reasonable and fair use of public lands has generated a fierce debate about the terms of efficiency, and whether the fees charged for grazing on public lands reflect "fair market value" and allow "multiple use and sustained yield" of public resources.

On one side of the issue are ranchers and Western Congressional Representatives, especially in the Senate. These parties maintain that although a rancher pays less to graze their livestock on public lands than they would on comparable private ranges, the additional costs of range improvements (fences, water holes, etc.)

---

75. See SWITZER, *supra* note 62 at 80; Fred Gregg, *Public Land Policy: Controversial Beginnings for the Third Century in Michael Lacey*, GOVERNMENT AND ENVIRONMENTAL POLITICS, 141–181 (1991).

76. The consensus is that public fees are, at best 1/5 of private rates. See *Id.* at 154–55; KITTEREDGE *supra* note 63 at 16.

which they must construct on public land to make it comparable to private land, means that they do, in effect, pay fair market value. These parties also maintain that while some overgrazing does occur, the permit holders represent mostly family ranchers who have both traditional and business ties to the land that require them to be conservationists, respecting the ideal of sustainable yield.[77]

The opposite side of this issue is represented by environmental groups and parties not grazing on public lands who argue that a "tragedy of the commons" continues to exist on public lands, caused by wide-scale overgrazing.[78] They contend that the fees paid by permit holders are significantly below what permit holders would have to pay on private land and in no way represent fair market value. In addition, these parties maintain that overgrazing occurs on a wide scale and inhibits multiple use and sustainable yield of resources.[79]

A fascinating aspect of this debate is that both ranchers and environmentalists are arguing over different interpretations of the same principle: efficiency. It would not be too unusual to expect that environmental interest groups might want to argue against overgrazing on the basis of non-instrumental environmental values. For example, we might expect the environmental debate to center on whether rangeland in the public domain ought to be considered a resource at all, or whether the natural systems of the western range should be expected to accommodate grazing. But the argument persists over efficiency and sustainable yield, around different definitions of use value. (not non-use)

In the 1992 Presidential Campaign, those who supported higher fees and more sustainable rangeland policy, found a champion in candidate Bill Clinton. Clinton promised "a new day in public lands policy" and pledged he would raise grazing fees and regulate use of the rangelands toward more environmentally responsible ends.[80]

Upon winning the 1992 Presidential Election, Clinton appointed Bruce Babbitt of Arizona as Secretary of the Interior and thus the move toward a new rangeland policy was set into motion.[81] On

---

77. A particular manifestation of the Western Cause was the so called "Sagebrush Rebellion" which was an effort, championed by Western Senators, to transfer responsibility for public lands from the federal to state governments. Specifically on this issue see GREGG *supra* note 75 at 154–56 and COGGINS ET AL., *supra* note 56 at 194–5.

78. COGGINS ET AL., *supra* note 56 at 592 and GREGG *supra* note 75 at 150–53.

79. GREGG *supra* note 75 at 169.

80. Daniel Glick, *Barbarians Inside the Gate*, NEWSWEEK, November 1, 1993 at 32.

81. On many occasions before the advent of the George W. Bush administration, House Democrats and even some Republicans have tried to raise grazing fees. For example, on June 15, 1993 the House Interior Appropriations Subcommittee included a proposal by its ranking Republican Ralph Regula to in-

August 9, 1993, Bruce Babbitt announced a sweeping new federal rangelands policy that referenced natural systems values and a substantial hike in grazing fees. Specifically,[82] the highlights of the "Babbitt Plan" include an effort to (1) increase fees from $1.86 per AUM to $4.28 over a three year period; (2) deny water and other improvement rights to those who hold permits; (3) abolish grazing advisory boards and establish "resource advisory boards" that include environmentalists and wildlife managers as well as ranchers; (4) protect natural systems though a national rangeland standard; and (5) link the duration of a grazing permit to a holder's land stewardship record. In addition to announcing the plan, Babbitt stated that he had administrative authority to establish it without Congressional approval, but never did.[83]

For the first time in this debate, environmental values were suggested as a basis for meta-policy. Babbitt's suggestion that policy ought to include the "protection of ecosystems" and the establishment of "stewardship" requirements for permit holders works directly against the core efficiency values of natural resources meta-policy and represents a fairly drastic departure from the conventional terms of debate in this issue area. If Majone is correct, changing the core of a meta-policy is a serious affair, because it requires forsaking the status-quo core principle for a new one, resulting in a new identity for the meta-policy. Babbitt's experience demonstrates this.

The "Babbitt Plan" gained support in the House, but instant negative reaction from the Senate that sidetracked the proposal with an amendment to their Interior Appropriations Bill that, by a vote of 59–40 on September 14, 1993, acted "to bar for one year the expenditure of funds to implement any fee increase and any rangeland reforms."[84] After a fight back and forth between the House, who wanted fee increases, and the Senate, who did not, the Senate won and the final bill had no language at all on "ecosystem values" or fee increases.[85]

---

crease grazing fees by 33%. This fee raise, included in the draft appropriations bills for fiscal 1994 would have raised fees from $1.86 to $2.48. However, this attempt, like all similar measures over the years either failed in the House or by the work of a small group of Western Senators.

82. CONGRESSIONAL QUARTERLY WEEKLY REPORTS, *supra* note 67 at 2223.

83. For example, in our case year of 1993 there are twelve references in Congressional Quarterly to the "fact" that the administration did not need Con-

gress to establish its new policy. CONGRESSIONAL QUARTERLY WEEKLY REPORTS, *supra* note 67 at 833, 834, 2150, 2316, 2389, 2449, 2546, 2723, 2803, 2875, 2876 and 2957.

84. *Id.* 2723.

85. On September 29, 1993 the House instructed its conferees on Interior Appropriations to reject the Senate moratorium. This stalemate remained until a deal was worked out between Secretary Babbitt and Senator Reid of Nevada which was to increase the fee to $3.45. This allowed the House and Senate conferees to move the bill out and

Suffering the defeat of fee hikes in Congress, Babbitt said he would revisit the issue with new grazing rules in April 1994, but never did.[86] Senator Domenici of Arizona maintains that any such rules would be "too drastic" a change to become law without Congressional approval.[87] It is unclear what is meant by "drastic," but in addition to the drastic effect on the agricultural economy that Domenici's comment may indicate, it is also a drastic reordering of the ethical core of natural resources policy. Specifically, the new rules would replace a trump concern for efficiency with a concern for the intrinsic value of ecosystems. New environmental values would define grazing and the institutions and administrative rules that govern it.[88]

At the heart of this debate is not just the tension between Executive and Congressional politics but a dispute over what core principle ought to provide the imperative for BLM policy. The introduction of concern for environmental values by the Clinton Administration created a confrontation between the core principle of efficiency and the core principle of natural system integrity. An active debate continues to exist between the status-quo core, which has created the current law, policy, and institutions, and a competitor for core status. Those concerned with efficiency see higher fees as inefficient, and as one step down a slippery slope that would forsake wealth maximization for environmental values.[89] Those wanting a change of policy and the inclusion of environmental values however, have reverted to arguing their case in terms of efficiency and are trying to achieve ends characterized by intrinsic values using a contradictory principle as the core of their policy design.

[handwritten: Arguing for intrinsic value as efficiency to avoid change in core principle.]

back to both Houses of Congress for final passage. However, Senator Domenici of New Mexico filibustered the bill. Although the House passed the new Interior Appropriations bill with the Reid compromise on October 20, the Senate failed, on October 21, 26 and 28 to muster the 60 votes needed to end the filibuster. Senator Domenici and the anti-fee forces finally won, the Reid compromise was taken out of the bill, and it is finally passed and sent to the President on the 9th of November.

86. CONGRESSIONAL QUARTERLY WEEKLY REPORTS, *supra* note 67 at 3380.

87. *Id.* at 2389.

88. With the defeat of higher fees in 1993, the administrator of the BLM, who can be said to support the ecosystem over the efficiency arguments, was fired because he failed to be a "consen-sus" builder needed to form the necessary alliances between Congress and the Agency. See, John H. Cushman Jr. *Top Land Bureau Official Resigns*, NEW YORK TIMES, February 4, 1994 at A18.

89. This was a part of the 'Babbitt Plan' but one overlooked in the focus on grazing fees. In subchapter IV of FLMPA § 1752, one might argue that the Secretaries of Interior and Agriculture are given wider discretion, than they appear to have in setting fees, to "cancel, suspend, or modify a grazing permit" currently held. This includes suspension for "violation of a grazing regulation" which is also set by executive policy. The Secretaries also have the power to set permit conditions, and, here again, one might be able to restrict permits and accomplish the same ends as higher fees without the same problems.

In the case of mining law, we found the domination of TSA–1 and an entrenched and unchallenged core principle of efficiency as maximization. Examining grazing policy we find that there is an active debate not only over the proper definition of efficiency (as maximization under TSA–I or optimality under TSA–II), but also over whether environmental values ought to replace efficiency at the core.

In the current debate about price we see that, although TSA–II is firmly established and the government is regulating use, the vestiges of efficiency as maximization still struggle to maintain as close to a zero-price as possible. Meanwhile, with the 1992 election, a competitive argument for core status, centered on the non-economic value of natural systems, took shape and attempted to influence the definition of the meta-policy. It still acts as a competitive argument today.

In the areas of both mining and grazing we have seen the role efficiency plays as a core principle within the Market Paradigm. It is the conceptual core of current policy and renders statute law that defines the terms of the political debate to discourage deviation from the demands of market assumptions and expectations. Next we will examine the importance of this core principle in the creation of an administrative or institutional setting for political decision-making. We shall see how an agency's 'mission' reinforces and maintains the dominance of economic values even when the law allows alternative interpretations of case precedence, statutes, and regulations.

3) Timber

In describing the evolution of timber policy, we will examine a more mature policy debate than that which exists for mining or grazing. We will describe a case where there are two well-developed arguments competing for core status in the application of environmental law to a specific resource.

The law concerning timber sales recognizes two ethical motivations: one is to preserve the forest and maintain its quality as a natural system, while the other is to assure its long-term economic resource value. We shall argue that, while the statutory law on this issue has both an *environmental* and an *economic* dimension to it, the status-quo core principle of natural resources policy is efficiency. This has created an institutional atmosphere that has defined the mission of the United States Forest Service (USFS) so that it favors the economic interpretation of the law over any environmental competitor. Specifically, we shall contend that the agency 'mission' of the USFS, as situated within the Department of Agriculture, has had the effect of designating trees as an agricultural crop for harvest, and therefore has elevated the economic policy orientation over the environmental orientation as the trump card in Forest Service decision-making.

The law governing timber sales is principally contained within three laws and two sets of written regulations.[90] The statutes are (in chronological order): The Forest Service Organic Act of 1897 (16 U.S.C.A. § 467)[91]; The Multiple–Use, Sustained–Yield Act of 1960 (16 U.S.C.A. §§ 528–31); and the Forest and Rangeland Renewable Resources Planning Act of 1974, which was amended by The National Forest Management Act of 1976 (16 U.S.C.A. §§ 1600–14).

1897

The Organic Act originally limited timber sales to "dead, matured, or large growth trees" and stipulated that these trees could not be sold for "less than their appraised value" (16 U.S.C.A. § 476).[92] This act began the practice of selling timber by advertisement and bidding. It required that timber not be sold until it was individually marked and that all cutting was to be supervised by an official of the Forest Service.

With the advent of the Multiple Use and Sustained Yield Act of 1960 (hereafter MUSY), Congress gave the USFS the task of administering the forests for multiple use and sustained yield (16 U.S.C.A. §§ 528 & 531). This mandate required the USFS to take six specific uses into consideration: "outdoor recreation, range, timber, watershed, and wildlife and fish purposes" (16 U.S.C.A. § 528).[93] It defined "multiple use" as "[T]he management of all the various renewable surface resources of the national forests so that they are utilized in the combination that will best meet the needs of the American people; ..." (16 U.S.C.A. § 531a) and "sustainable yield" as "... the achievement and maintenance in perpetuity of a high level annual or regular periodic output of the various renewa-

90. Timber sales are affected by the National Environmental Policy Act (42 U.S.C.A. §§ 4321–4370) which requires that an environmental impact statement be prepared for each one, the Endangered Species Act (16 U.S.C.A. §§ 1531 to 1544) which requires that listed species be considered in designating possible cutting areas and by other minor statutes like the Federal Roads and Trails Act of 1964 (16 U.S.C.A. 532–38) which regulates road construction in national forests and the Timber Contract Modification Act of 1964 (16 U.S.C.A. § 618) which designates the terms of returning a timber contract to the government.

91. This act was repealed in 1976.

92. Even though this law seemed to severely limit timber sales, it was liberally interpreted by the Forest Service which established the practice of widespread clear cutting of forests for timber harvest. This practice was finally halted by the decision in the *Monongahela Case*—West Virginia Div. of the Izaak Walton League of America, Inc. v. Butz, 522 F.2d 945 (4th Cir.1975) which affirmed the limited nature of cutting but which then resulted in the repeal of the Organic Act and its replacement, eventually, by the National Forest Management Act.

93. Even though "multiple use" is the mandate, one can interpret this list as an attempt to add to the traditional use of the forest as exclusively a timber resource. Read this way, the multiple uses are to limit timber harvesting and promote recreation, watershed and wildlife purposes.

ble resources of the national forest without impairment of the productivity of the land" (16 U.S.C.A. § 531b).

The most comprehensive document, and the one that requires writing the most specific regulations for timber sales, is the National Forest Management Act of 1976 (NFMA). In this document, the Secretary of Agriculture, through local Forest Service managers, is made responsible for comprehensive forest assessment and planning (16 U.S.C.A. § 1601 & § 1602), and for the production of Land and Resource Management Plans (LRMP)[94] for each and every forest unit (16 U.S.C.A. § 1604). These planning requirements reinforce the mandate for multiple use and sustained yield, require the service to use an interdisciplinary approach (16 U.S.C.A. § 1604b) to defining the specific application of these objectives, and establish provisions for public participation in the "development, review, and revision of land management plans" (16 U.S.C.A. § 1604d).

Timber sales are specifically defined under (16 U.S.C.A. § 1604g(E) & (F)). These sections of NFMA limit timber harvesting or increases in the levels of harvest to those that fit within the application of the Multiple-Use and Sustained Yield Act of 1960 and to specific context conditions that protect "soil, slope and watershed" (Ei) as well as streams and lakes (Eiii), which make sure that the lands can be "restocked within five years" (Eii), and that economic concerns will not dominate the selection of a "harvesting system" (Eiv).

In addition, this section of the act limits harvesting by clear cutting to only those situations where it is determined to be the "optimum" method to carry out the forest plan (Fi) and only after both multiple use as well as "the environmental, biological, esthetic, engineering, and economic impacts ... have been assessed" (Fii).

Overall the amount of timber to be cut is decided by the local forest manager and approved by the Secretary of Agriculture through the preparation and submission of an LRMP. This plan will designate both the areas to be cut and the acceptable way in which the harvesting will be done as well as what reforestation plans must be instituted. Legally, timber is only to be harvested according to the objectives of multiple use and sustained yield and it is to be sold at fair market value.

---

94. NFMA planning, symbolized by the LRMP requires the service to decide what land is suitable for cutting, the amount of timber to be harvested (including volume and rotation period), what method will be used to harvest, how the forest will be regenerated. In order to implement this planning the Forest Service has written computer software called FORPLAN. The existence of a common algorithm is evidence of an attempt by the Forest Service to coordinate their overall planning efforts.

Actual timber sales are controlled by the local forest service manager as authorized by the Secretary of Agriculture. These sales are governed by specific regulations that establish the requirements for both general forest planning (36 C.F.R. § 219) and specific timber sales (36 C.F.R. § 223). All timber sales are regulated by the forest plan and require presale preparation, which includes a multiple-use survey and timber report (36 C.F.R. § 219.12). The "fair market value"[95] of the timber must then be appraised (36 C.F.R. § 223.60). This appraised value is then advertised for sale (36 C.F.R. § 223.63) and the thirty days advertisement is followed by either an auction or the receipt of sealed bidding (36 C.F.R. §§ 223.80–223.89). The winner of the bidding is given a timber contract (36 C.F.R. § 223 Subpart B) which is the means by which the sale is made. The price of the timber, determined by the assessment and bidding process, is required to be at fair market value.

[handwritten: Timber is sold then harvested]

Once the sale is completed, the harvest is authorized and the USFS specifies what roads and services must be constructed to facilitate the timber harvest.[96] The service supervises the cut and the preparation of the land for reforestation.

The present cutting and pricing policy has evolved within a dialectic argument over whether a forest should be seen as a crop or a natural system.[97] The history of the USFS, especially since the

---

95. There is great controversy about the sale price of timber. A General Accounting Office report in 1983 found that in 3,244 timber sales between 1981 and 1982 the government did not cover its costs in 42% of these sales. Between 1973 and 1983 timber sales produced a deficit of $1.6 billion. See ZACHARY A. SMITH. THE ENVIRONMENTAL POLICY PARADOX 200–202 (1992). In the 1990s' while the average price per 1000 board feet on the open market was $590.00, the average government sale was $390.00. *Lynn Graebner Wetsel v. Forest Service,* 10 THE BUSINESS JOURNAL 4 (1994).

96. Road building by the Forest Service is a major expense which, in most cases, is not compensated for in the sale of the timber. The Forest Service even gives credits in appraisals for already existing roads (36 C.F.R. § 233.62) and has been accused of constructing roads in order to establish an area as susceptible for cutting. Mike Weiss *Federal Timber Policy* 18 MOTHER JONES 50 (March 1993). The designation of "roadless areas" for future development, which includes cutting roads even when

no sales are designated, caused two reports on Roadless Area Review and Evaluation (RARE I & II) to be written by the Service, the first in 1976 and the second in 1978. These lead to more potential wilderness being designated for cutting during the Carter and Reagan Administrations but also to the intervention of Congress on behalf of environmentalists to limit designation of more wildlife refuges in Oregon and California. WALTER A. ROSENBAUM, ENVIRONMENTAL POLITICS AND POLICY 295–97 (1991).

97. For some analysis of the "crop" paradigm see Bryan G. Norton *Forest Service Policy* in THE ENVIRONMENTAL ETHICS AND POLICY BOOK 545–48 (Donald VanDeVeer and Christine Pierce eds., 1994). For the "ecosystem" paradigm see Perri Knize, *The Mismanagement of the National Forests* 268 THE ATLANTIC MONTHLY (October 1991); Madelyn Kempf and Michael Hoops, *A New Way To Oversee the Public Forests? Ecosystem Management.* 99 AMERICAN FORESTS 28 (1993); WEISS, *supra* note 96.

Second World War, has been marked with a maximum effort to facilitate lumber companies in the harvesting of trees as a crop.[98] Although many voices, including those in the former Clinton Administration, struggled to integrate environmental values into Forest Service practice, and even though the law and the courts can be interpreted as pushing the Service away from a maximum yield philosophy and toward a reappraisal of public forests as worthy of consideration as functioning natural systems, the USFS has consistently seen its role as facilitating timber harvesting.[99] This orientation has since been supported by the Administration of George W. Bush and has resulted in below-cost timber sales, clear-cutting, and the continued sale of "old-growth" forests in the face of serious environmental and resource ramifications. Why this dedication to economic values and timber sales?

Steven Kelman[100] has argued that the single most important characteristic of an executive department or agency is its "mission." By this he means that the personnel and the agency come to have an "ethic" including a point of view which frames everything they do and which determines their interpretation of law and their writing of regulations. The USFS, originally placed within the Department of the Interior was transferred in 1905 to the Department of Agriculture.[101] The "mission" of the Department of Agriculture is to facilitate the growing and harvesting of crops for the

---

98. Lumber is measured in 'board feet'. A board foot is a unit of measurement that is equal to the cubic contents of a piece of lumber 1 foot square by 1 inch thick. An average American house contains 10,000 board feet of lumber. Cutting on national forest land reached 1 billion board feet for the first time in 1923. By 1950 it had reached 9 billion and reached its peak in 1989 when more than 12.7 billion feet were harvested. Even these large harvests represent less than 20% of the nation's lumber production. See Eric Pryne and Bill Dietrich, *Neither Side Elated With Latest Clinton Forest plan—But Environmentalists Say Revisions in Right Direction*, THE SEATTLE TIMES, February 24, 1994 at B1; Frank Gregg *Public Land Policy: Controversial Beginnings For a Third Century* in GOVERNMENT AND ENVIRONMENTAL POLITICS 156–159 (Michael J. Lacey ed. 1991); COGGINS ET AL., *supra* note 56 at 642.

99. Our argument here is that the evolution of statute law in this area could have produced a regime of fewer, higher cost timber sales. The Courts in the Monongahela case (*supra* note 92),

and in the Seattle Audubon case (*supra* note 103) have supported a modified "ecosystem" reading of the law, but has also allowed the Forest Service to continue an aggressive timber sales policy (especially under Reagan and Bush I & II).

100. STEVEN KELMAN, MAKING PUBLIC POLICY: A HOPEFUL VIEW OF AMERICAN GOVERNMENT 154–56 (1987); For administrative mission see also CORNELIUS M. KERWIN, RULEMAKING: HOW GOVERNMENT AGENCIES WRITE LAW AND MAKE POLICY (1994) and CLARKE E. COCHRAN, LAWRENCE C. MAYER, T.R. CARR & N. JOSEPH CAYER, AMERICAN PUBLIC POLICY (1993).

101. The original Forest Service Organic Act, which was protective of forest as natural systems, came about before inclusion of the Forest Service in the Department of Agriculture. See, CHRISTOPHER BOSSO, PESTICIDES & POLITICS: THE LIFE CYCLE OF A PUBLIC ISSUE (1987) and Michael Kraft & Norman Vig, ENVIRONMENTAL POLICY IN THE 90'S 1–31 (1994).

public interest. Therefore, it should be no surprise that the policy of the USFS is to maximize the yield of trees and to subsidize lumber companies (just as its parent Department of Agriculture would subsidize farmers) to produce wood for the national economy.

Treating trees as a crop allowed clear-cutting to become an established USFS practice until 1975 when the *Monongahela Case*[102] ushered in a new era of multiple use and forest planning. Even with planning, defined as multiple use and sustainable yield, the USFS continued to encourage the low cost sale of old growth forests at an increasing rate, especially under the Presidency of Ronald Reagan. This did not change until the designation of the Spotted Owl as an endangered species and the consequent 1991 injunction against logging the Northwest by Judge Dwyer which indicted the USFS for not following its own multiple use planning guidelines intended to prevent excessive timber sales in environmentally sensitive forest systems.[103]

The Reagan policy encouraged logging by keeping prices low and maximizing the forest area subject to cutting. The Clinton Administration and its new forest plan attempted to be more faithful to multiple use while introducing environmental values into the debate.[104] This environmental values approach aimed to set

102. WEST VIRGINIA DIV. OF THE IZAAK WALTON LEAGUE OF AMERICA, INC. v. BUTZ, 522 F.2d 945 (1975).

103. The district court decision by Judge Dwyer in Seattle Audubon Society v. Evans 771 F.Supp. 1081 (W.D. Wash. 1991), affd., 952 F.2d 297 (9th Cir. 1991), resulted in the general suspension of all timber sales over millions of acres of Northwest, old-growth forest. Although tested in Congress, this injunction held and became the center of attention in the evolution of forest policy in the 1990's. Because of the suspension of timber contracts the war between 'jobs and owls' began and the Clinton Forest Summit in April 1993 had, as its central concern, helping the log-dependent communities and coming up with a new plan that would satisfy Judge Dwyer, the loggers and environmentalists. See *President Clinton's policy on Northwest Lumber Cutting* 40 BUILDER (September 1993).

104. The original Clinton Plan was set out in July 1993, (see 1726–28 CONGRESSIONAL QUARTERLY, July 3, 1993) in response to the forest summit held the previous April. This plan, called 'option 9', was the subject of an environmental impact statement and public participation which generated thousands of comments. In response to these comments the final plan, sent to Judge Dwyer for an April 1, 1994 decision, had the following attributes: (1) increased estimates of job losses in the Pacific Northwest, (2) the establishment of "no-logging zones" around streams and watersheds, doubling the distance between cuts and water from the 50–foot strip called for under Option 9 to 100 feet, (3) More logging would be allowed in Northern California but less in the old-growth forests of Washington and Oregon. Overall, about 4 million acres of forest would be open to logging, 7.4 million acres would be protected reserves where only some thinning and salvage logging could take place, 1.5 million acres would be used for the application of experimental selective logging techniques and 2.6 million acres of land adjacent to watersheds would be off-limits to any logging. See Tom Kenworthy, *Revised Clinton Plan Saves More Forest; Administration Concedes It Underestimated Logging's Job Losses*, THE WASHINGTON POST, February 24, 1994 at A4; Timothy Egan, *Tight Logging Limit Set in Northwest*, THE NEW YORK TIMES, February 24, 1994 at A18; Clive Capps, *Under Siege; Bill Clinton's Option Plan*, 218 INFOR-

aside more old-growth forest from cutting, limit timber sales else-where, and promote a vision of the forests as natural systems and not crops, replacing multiple-use management with ecosystem management. However, we contend that within a law and policy design paradigm built on the principle of Kaldor efficiency, it will be difficult, if not impossible, to replace both the market-based mission of the USFS and its underlying Market Paradigm with a more environmentally-sensitive alternative.

The long-term resource implications of this debate are very important. In addition to the intrinsic value of old-growth forests,[105] spotted owls, and the other species that are on the brink of becoming endangered, the stress to nature caused by human use places the future availability of resources at the mercy of the functioning of the greater natural systems of which they are a component part.[106] Concerns about the stress placed upon greater ecosystems by timber sales and harvests, particularly as occurs with damage to watersheds, caused the Clinton Administration to focus its forest plan on "watershed" management and on "ecosystem" approach to forest planning that emphasizes the preservation of old growth forests as integrated natural systems.[107] But even this limited change met with considerable opposition.

In January 1994 the Clinton Administration promoted Jack Ward to be chief of the U.S. Forest Service replacing Dale Robertson. Ward, a biologist, has long been in favor of the ecosystem approach to the forests, in which timber sales are set at market value, limited, and used only to enhance the forest for wildlife and human recreation. He was a major actor in the Clinton Forest Summit of April 1993 and has been hailed as ushering in a new era in USFS practice,[108] one that would eventually be ended by Secretary Norton and the second Bush administration.

MATION ACCESS 41 (October 1993) and Melissa Healy, *U.S. Proposes Cutting Timber Sales 10% More To Save Owls; Environment: Administration Doubles Estimate of Job Losses In The Northwest In A Revision of Compromise Reached Last Summer. Plan Goes To Judge Next Month*, LOS ANGELES TIMES, February 24, 1994 at A3.

105. Old–Growth includes not only the forests of the Pacific Northwest but also the Tongass rain forest in Alaska, and much of the tree cover in Northern British Columbia. See John H. Cushman Jr., *U.S. To Cancel A Timber Deal In Alaska* NEW YORK TIMES, January 15, 1994 at A8.

106. With the spotted Owl already listed as an endangered species, biologists became additionally concerned about two species of salmon, the pacific fisher, the American marten, the Sierra Nevada red fox and the wolverine that also inhabit the ecosystem. See Chris Bowman, *New Effort to Save Old–Growth Forest* SACRAMENTO BEE, February 11, 1994 at A1.

107. *Id.*

108. See *Forests and Logging: Imitating Nature* 26 THE ECONOMIST (November 1993) and especially, *Getting A Better Deal For The Forests* CHICAGO TRIBUNE, January 17, 1994 at A16.

Mr. Ward's first act as chief was to implement the Clinton Forest Plan which had gone through extensive revision since it was formally proposed in July of 1993, and which had originally been described as more of a compromise with industry than a clear victory for environmentalism.[109] Although the final version of this plan was adjusted toward lower timber sales and the preservation of old growth forests, and although Judge Dwyer had accepted it as more sensitive to the law and therefore removed his injunction against logging, the question remained as to whether Ward could accomplish the transformation of the meta-policy, and replace the status-quo principle of efficiency, without either changing the institutional setting of timber issues or reorienting the mission of his agency after 90 years of tradition.[110]

In all of the resource cases we have examined in this chapter, the Clinton Administration, whether knowingly or not, tried to change the core principle of environmental meta-policy. Within the Meta–Policy Model, this effort describes the deliberative zone where alternative arguments compete for position with the core argument (see Chapter Four). Here the debate is between the status-quo core principle of efficiency, which has pride of place in the policy space, and a competitive argument based on the integrity of natural systems. This parallel argument is most evident in ecosystem-based timber policy, but it also exists, as a less powerful variant, in the discussion of overgrazing and in the reconsideration of the 1872 Mining Act.

In this situation, we have either a case of unconstrained market forces being replaced by an imperative for government to establish the optimal rate of extraction, modifying the status-quo principle of efficiency, or the effort to re-characterize the legal argument paradigm with a replacement of efficiency at the core. The shift to ecosystem management will take a lot more than simply a move from TSA–I to TSA–II, or a new institutional setting. If the policy design approach is correct, it will require a new meta-policy with an integrity-based paradigm and a consequently redefined context model (see Chapter Four). In fact, all of the attempts of the Clinton Administration to move away from Kaldor efficiency in public lands policy were unsuccessful. It was easy for George W. Bush to reverse what few successes there were.

109. Stephen M. Meyer, *Dead Wood: Clinton's Timber Loser; Old Growth Logging Compromise,* 209 NEW RE-PUBLIC 12 (August 1993).

110. For an examination of the history and pitfalls associated with administrative policy in the Forest Service see Nancy J. Manring *Reconciling Science and Politics in Forest Service Decision–Making: New Tools For Public Administration.* 23 AMERICAN REVIEW OF PUBLIC ADMINISTRATION (1993).

Conclusion

Overall, the conventional legal paradigm regulating humanity's relationship to the natural world is one dominated by the Market Paradigm that classifies nature as a *material resource* and supports the dominance of the principle of efficiency in public land use decisions. In addition, we can also argue that pollution law illustrates our attempt to use the principle of efficiency to come to terms with the opposite end of the materials balance, that is, with the use of media as sinks for pollution and waste. In terms of the sources of law, and their strategic and tactical relevance, public resource issues are treated by conventional market assumptions as if they are private choices over elective goods. This confirms a dominant role for markets as an allocation mechanism, the common law as an authoritative instrument of policy, and efficiency-driven institutions as the basis of conventional environmental law.

As we move from TSA–I to TSA–II, environmental and public land law can be said to have evolved from a legal framework that allowed the dominance of the Market Paradigm to justify land disposal policy for all natural resources and media, to a framework that gently amended the dominance of the Market Paradigm to justify government involvement in defining *optimal* rather than *maximum* extraction levels within the materials balance. Abatement policy can also be described as the effort to maintain the dominance of market assumptions within a policy space where efficiency was prior to, and dominant over, environmental values. In other words, abatement policy, like its resource cousin, depends on market axioms to define efficiency and aid government regulators in defining and achieving the optimal level of pollution.

Now that we have a sense of how a paradigm can be analyzed according to its component parts, and of what the dominant Market Paradigm looks like as applied to environmental law, we can move on to argue that this one paradigm for policy design is not the only one available to legal practitioners trying to affect change in environmental law. In the next two chapters we will demonstrate that the categories and logic of law and policy design can be used to define and redirect the law regulating human—nature relations, so that protecting the value of functional ecosystems becomes central to the creation of effective legal practice and institutions within a new meta-policy.

Chapter 4

AN ECOSYSTEM APPROACH TO ENVIRONMENTAL & RESOURCE LAW: ALTERNATIVE I

In this chapter we will present a second template of categories and logical connections that the reader can use to create an ***Ecosystem Paradigm***. By Ecosystem Paradigm, we mean a systemized and integrated line of argument for policy design developed from a particular set of principles, assumptions, and methods that focus on the value of flourishing ecosystems to environmental law.

In order to provide critical argument for the analytic component of Comprehensive Policy Argument (CPA) in terms of how the market approach to Environmental Law is inadequate, and then move to a synthetic and constructive argument on how Ecosystem Law is necessary, we shall begin this chapter with an in-depth case study involving the United States Forest Service (USFS) and its efforts to replace ***multiple use management*** with ***ecosystem management***.

We will argue, as we have in the previous chapter, that this effort has been largely unsuccessful and that the reason for this is because the substructure of the move toward ecosystem management is built on a normative foundation and empirical agency mission that still relies on the Market Paradigm and its components. We know from the last chapter that this paradigm cannot evaluate more than the instrumental value of the environment. As long as ecosystem management requires more than concern for economic wealth generation, the distinct demands of multiple-use management and ecosystem management in the law can only be resolved through the creation of a distinct paradigm that places ecosystem integrity, or the non-use value of nature, as a core component of resource law. This move will be accomplished by the development of an Ecosystem Paradigm for policy design using the formal template from step A2 of the policy design process (see Chapter One). In this way we can organize new principles, assumptions, and maxims more applicable to the demands of this distinctive approach to law and the environment.

Specifically, we will examine the case of ecosystem management in the USFS, the ideas of meta-policy, core, and periphery as these affect the policy design process, and we will analyze the apparent failure of ecosystem management to take hold and change the law. We will then, being interested in the intrinsic values involved, argue for a shift from conservation to preservation and proscribe the requirements for a model of legal practice that takes the characteristics of ecosystems seriously. We will finally build a new theoretical paradigm that we will designate as *Ecosystem Model I*, and connect the logic and content of this model of legal practice to the understanding of our duties to nature argued by the Enlightenment philosopher Immanuel Kant.

Sustainability v. Ecosystem Integrity: The Case of the United States Forest Service

In response to increasing calls for greater consideration of ecosystems, and their functional or ecological requirements, in the formulation and implementation of public environmental and land-use policy, the Federal Government responded with what is known as the *Ecosystem Approach to Management*.[1] This methodology was to be adopted by all of the major resource and land-management agencies[2] and is characterized as a drastic "paradigm shift" away from traditional use-based approaches to the natural world.[3]

For our purpose, we will concentrate on the use of this concept within the USFS.[4] Since it entered official circles in 1990, the

---

1. There are excellent bibliographies of the vast literature of Ecosystem Management in both MARK S. BOYCE, & ALAN HANEY, ECOSYSTEM MANAGEMENT: APPLICATIONS FOR SUSTAINABLE FOREST AND WILDLIFE RESOURCES (1997) and YAFFEE ET AL., ECOSYSTEM MANAGEMENT IN THE UNITED STATES: AN ASSESSMENT OF CURRENT EXPERIENCE (1996).

2. Richard Hauber, *Setting The Environmental Policy Agenda: The Case of Ecosystem Management*, 36 NATURAL RESOURCES JOURNAL 1 and George

Coggins, *Legal Problems and Powers Inherent in Ecosystem Management*, 5 NATURAL RESOURCES JOURNAL 36.

3. Jerry F. Franklin, *Ecosystem Management: An Overview* in ECOSYSTEM MANAGEMENT: APPLICATIONS FOR SUSTAINABLE FOREST AND WILDLIFE RESOURCES 21–53 (Mark S. Boyce and Alan Haney eds. 1997).

4. See UNITED STATES FOREST SERVICE, *The Forest Service Program For Forest And Rangeland Resources: A Long-term Strategic Plan* (1990); *Char-*

ecosystem approach, instead of considering environmental media strictly as resources for human use, focuses upon the health or functional integrity of natural systems as wholes, which is now considered to be the proper guide for law, policy design and evaluation.[5]

Over the past 17 years, however, the ecosystem approach to the management of our National Forests has not actually provided a paradigm shift in the management of resources, nor has it lead to the degree of restoration or preservation of forest ecosystems that might be expected. A substantial part of this failure, in our estimation, comes from an inherent logical and moral pitfall in the policy argument for the ecosystem approach to management, which is merely superficial change in the periphery of the meta-policy and not connected to an essential change of core principle.[6] Specifically, the problem is that those who are defining and promoting a shift to the ecosystem approach are also committed to the acceptance of *sustainability* as an appropriate core norm or standard through which to achieve the implementation of this *new* administrative orientation toward nature.[7] But before our analysis of ecosystem management we must define the concept of meta-policy and the role of its core principles in the determination of the law (also see Chapter One).

Meta-policy contains the elements of continuity and change. In order to conceptualize the components that provide for both, it is useful to make the distinction, as Majone does, between core and periphery.[8] Majone defines these two elements of a meta-policy to distinguish between "... the relatively stable and rigid part of a policy and its more changing and flexible components."[9] For our purposes, we can understand the core as that part of the meta-policy which contains its fundamental assumptions and operating principle. Specifically, the core principle gives a policy its character, and sets the standard for judging its ends, means, accountability, and success. Therefore, a meta-policy's core is the essential element in defining its dominant paradigm. The core principle with its

ter for New Perspectives for Managing The National Forest System (1991); *New Perspectives Project Notebook.* (1992). The Forest Service has been chosen because it was the lead agency in the early 1990's in terms of the implementation of ecosystem management. We have also chosen this era of the Forest Service because it was the most concerted effort, before or since, to shift the paradigm upon which resource agencies approached nature.

5. Oliver Houck, *On the Law of Biodiversity and Ecosystem Management,* 81 Minn. L. Rev. 869 (1997); Robert B. Keiter, *Beyond The Boundary Line: Con-*

structing a Law of Ecosystem Management, 65 U. Colo. L. Rev. 293 (1994); UNITED STATES FOREST SERVICE, *supra* note 4.

6. GIANDOMENICO MAJONE, EVIDENCE, ARGUMENT & PERSUASION IN THE POLICY PROCESS 55–57 (1989).

7. GREGORY H. APLET ET AL., DEFINING SUSTAINABLE FORESTRY (1993); BOYCE AND HANEY, *supra* note 1.

8. MAJONE, *supra* note 6 at 150–54.

9. *Id.* at 150.

dominant argument gives the meta-policy its identity. Although not unchanging, the core resists change, and successful change represents a fundamental shift in the standard, and therefore the basic character, of the meta-policy.

By our working definition of meta-policy, change takes place when a parallel argument and its essential principle, which exist within the meta-policy (although not in its core), replace the dominant or status-quo principle of the meta-policy in the core. Here we agree with the spirit, if not the letter, of Majone's definition.

> To say that the core represents the rigid part of the policy is not to suggest that it is immutable, but only that it changes more gradually and continuously than the elements of the periphery that are its transitory end-products. A radical transformation or abandonment of the core signifies a major change in policy—revolution rather than evolution, so to speak.[10]

In contrast to the core principles that create the essential standards and the identity of the dominant legal argument, the periphery contains the other elements of the meta-policy that are less directly critical to the integrity of the dominant argument but which contribute to the operationalization of the core principle.

> If the core provides continuity, the periphery—largely composed of programs and other concrete administrative activities that are intended to give effect to the core principles—provides flexibility. The need to adapt the particular programs through which the policy operates to ever-changing economic, social, and political conditions keeps the periphery in constant flux, but peripheral changes do not usually affect the core, except perhaps through their cumulative impact.[11]

The periphery also can be described as containing those parallel lines of argument that compete for dominance within any meta-policy. So, in addition to the institutions and processes that implement the core principles, the periphery also contains alternative paradigms and principles that can be a part of the deliberation over means and ends within the meta-policy. But they do not give the current policy its justification, identity, or immutable standards. The idea of alternative principles in the periphery supports the dynamic quality of our definition of meta-policy and also creates the possibility within the policy design process of a persistent dialectic about proper ends and the standards by which these should be judged.

10. *Id.*   **11.** *Id.* at 151.

Majone's image actually consists of a core surrounded by "concentric circles" or levels of periphery,[12] but it will suffice, for our purposes, to make the distinction between what principle supports the dominant or persuasive paradigm within the meta-policy (the core) and those principles which present alternative arguments but have less persuasive power and are, therefore, for the present, consigned to the periphery. In effect, what we are describing is a three-tiered pyramid-shaped conception of a meta-policy.

Meta- Policy Model

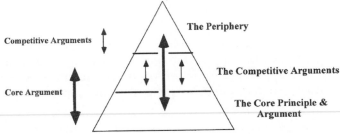

J.M. Gillroy 1996

As part of our framework, the top tier, the *periphery*, contains the codified law, institutional, and administrative apparatus, with its rules and regulations, which define the status-quo meta-policy and which operationalize the dominant or persuasive policy paradigm. At this level we find the public rhetoric associated with a debate over how a meta-policy is legislated, executed, and evaluated by experience. Here, law is codified and tested by the dominate meta-policy argument and its core principle.

The middle tier, which we shall call *deliberative*, is broader than the first, and is the reservoir of alternative principles and arguments for the policies that do not define it as a status-quo meta-policy, but which represent opportunities for future change and redefinition. Given the effects of the status-quo meta-policy, here is where a debate about the *reasonable* or *proper* ends of policy takes place. Here judgments are made about the difference between what *is* and what *ought* to be. This deliberative zone contains the competitors for the core paradigm and the backup lines of argument that can be called upon when the core no longer persuasively serves the meta-policy or its constituents.[13]

---

12. *Id.*

13. For example, if we decide that efficiency is not producing an adequate resource policy, as it ought to be, we may find an alternative argument, based upon the principle of integrity, within the deliberative zone, to act as a replace-

The third tier, containing the *core* principle and its policy paradigm, is essential and defines the character of the meta-policy, providing the stable standard for the pyramid. The core principle determines the context and constraints for the deliberation in the second tier and the proper tools and legal arguments for the public processes, debate, and institutional framework of the first tier.

Because the core principle creates the standards of choice for the decision-maker, it will determine how the law defines the human-environment relationship, and what characteristics of humanity and nature count in the deliberation and choice process. Since, we will argue, sustainability can only support an instrumentalist view of nature, if sustainability as a new manifestation of Kaldor efficiency remains a key article of faith and the core principle of ecosystem policy choice, then the ground-level changes, away from a market or resources-based policy and toward ecosystem management, will never fully materialize.[14]

First, we shall describe the ecosystem approach and its history with the principle of sustainability at its core and critically argue that the principle of sustainability is inadequate to the task of supporting and producing a comprehensive ecosystem approach to environmental policy. Second, we will review the underlying relationship between principle and policy, as that is a relationship between standards for reasonable argument and the collectively persuasive policy alternatives rendered by these normative standards. Third, we will constructively argue that only a principle of preservation as functional integrity, replacing the conservation-based principle of sustainability, will result in the transcendence of multiple use with ecosystem management. Functional Integrity will be shown to be both as theoretically reasonable and practically accessible in law and policy design as sustainability, and then a full description of this alternative paradigm and context model will be laid out.

1) Sustainability & the Ecosystem Approach

In the document that initiated the call for ecosystem management in the USFS, Dale Robertson argued, as its first principle, that a drastic departure had to be made from the traditional focus

ment core for environmental meta-policy.

14. Ecosystem management could represent a very important sea-change in the way we, in the United States, approach environmental policy. We want to commend the intentions of those who support an ecosystem approach, both inside and outside of government, but we also want to argue that if this new approach is to gain dominance of both resource policy and pollution and risk abatement policy, then sticking to a principle of sustainability as the core principle of ecosystem management will jeopardize the full and proper implementation of this paradigm shift in policy management.

on multiple-use management of the forests as resources first and ecosystems second.

> ***Principle 1: Sustain Healthy, Diverse And Productive Ecosystems In The Long Term:*** "... a narrow focus on uses obscures what these lands and resources really are: living dynamic, complex systems of plants, animals, water, soil, climate, topology, and people. In a word, they are ecosystems."[15]

This shift of focus requires a new emphasis on the ecological health and integrity of ecosystems, that is, on their "resiliency, resistance, stability, elasticity, constancy, and persistence."[16] These conditions of integrity are intrinsic functional concerns and are not part of the market-resource approach to environmental policy, which can only fully evaluate the use value of nature's resources. But here while the proponents of ecosystem management within the USFS break away from market approaches to the environment, they also simultaneously embrace the principle of sustainability as enough of a shift in core principle and fundamental assumptions to make the codification of Ecosystem Law possible.

> The need to define the concept of ecosystem health in practical terms arises because of the failure of current economic paradigms to protect the natural environment, which is, after all, the foundation for economic systems.... The goal of this dynamic process (ecosystem health paradigm) is to protect the autonomous, self-integrative processes of nature as an essential element in a new ethic of sustainability.[17]

There are therefore two distinct and related claims for those who promote ecosystem management. First, nature must be considered to have more than mere use value. As William Reilly states "... natural ecosystems have intrinsic values independent of human use that are worthy of protection."[18] Likewise, Bryan Norton argues that,

> ... there is an obligation to protect the health and integrity of ecological systems.... [to] recognize the crucial role

[handwritten margin note: Claims for Ecosystem Management Promotion: 1]

---

15. Winifred B. Kessler & Hal Salwasser, *Natural Resource Agencies: Transforming From Within* in A NEW CENTURY FOR NATURAL RESOURCES MANAGEMENT 179 (Richard L. Knight and Sarah F. Bates, eds. 1995).

16. BOYCE AND HANEY, *supra* note 1 at 3.

17. ROBERT COSTANZA ET AL., ECOSYSTEM HEALTH: NEW GOALS FOR ENVIRONMENTAL MANAGEMENT 4 (1992).

18. W. K. Reilly, *A Strategy To Save the Great Water Bodies*, 4 EPA JOURNAL 6 (1990).

of creative, self-organizing systems in supporting human economic, recreational, aesthetic and spiritual values....[19]

2.   Secondly, there is a continued reliance on a theory of instrumental value to generate a principle of sustainability as the normative core of ecosystem health.

> We think that a suitably comprehensive and long-term view of instrumental value—one that protects ecosystems' services by protecting the health and integrity of systems indefinitely—is sufficient to make the case [for the health of ecological systems] and will support aesthetic and moral values as well.[20]

> Sustainability is a relationship between dynamic human economic systems and larger, dynamic, but normally slower-changing ecological systems, such that human life can continue indefinitely, human individuals can flourish, and human cultures can develop—but also a relationship in which the effects of human activities remain within bounds so as not to destroy the health and integrity of self-organizing systems ...[21]

The common denominator for all those promoting sustainability and what separates sustainability from mere economic efficiency as a preferred principle for environmental policy design, is the imperative that 'present' use of the resource base "does not impoverish the future."[22] The concern of sustainable development as opposed to economic development is its encouragement of "development that meets the needs and aspirations of the present without compromising the ability of future generations to meet their own needs."[23] The focus is still on humanity, as in the Market Paradigm, and on our self-interested instrumental use of the environment, but now only in a way that can be continued indefinitely.

Sustainability still part of mkt paradigm b/c still related to development

> The question of sustainability is, therefore, one of enlightened self-interest. It requires finding a way in which the human species can live on this planet indefinitely ...[24]

The implementation of this combination of sustainability and ecosystem management by the USFS has not achieved the results

19.   Bryan Norton, *A New Paradigm For Environmental Management* in ECOSYSTEM HEALTH 24 (Costanza et al. eds. 1992).

20.   COSTANZA ET AL., *supra* note 17 at 5.

21.   NORTON, *supra* note 19 at 25.

22.   HERMAN E. DALY, BEYOND GROWTH: THE ECONOMICS OF SUSTAINABLE DEVELOPMENT 2 (1996).

23.   NORTON, *supra* note 19 at 27–32; FIKRET BERKES, COMMON PROPERTY RESOURCES: ECOLOGY AND COMMUNITY–BASED SUSTAINABLE DEVELOPMENT vii (1989).

24.   ANTHONY M. H. CLAYTON, SUSTAINABILITY: A SYSTEMS APPROACH 7 (1996).

that many expected. Even in the first decade of practice the reports of change were not good. For example, with respect to the issue of forest preservation, the Wilderness Society complained that ecosystem management is "doing very little to protect old-growth, riparian and roadless areas."[25] Likewise, even though ecosystem management is supposed to initiate a drastic paradigm shift in USFS affairs, the Columbia River Commission noted that there is still "a heavy reliance on logging to fix problems logging caused. It doesn't make any sense."[26] This remains the case four administrations and twenty years later.

From within the USFS itself, Winifred Kessler, the former head of the *New Perspectives Program* (which implemented ecosystem management), argues that ecosystem management in the strong sense is pushed aside by the power of convention and the failure to fundamentally change the administrative mission of the USFS. She argues that little change has been accomplished. "Ecosystem Management is a small, specialized substaff, combined with land management planning at the headquarters level, a small room in the basic multiple-use architecture."[27]

> ... the agency's transition to ecosystem management is severely impeded by an organizational structure that, while well suited to the previous era of multiple-use management, is obsolete ... The [institutional] architecture remains basically intact from the ... era.... when the identities of programs, budgets, and professional staff reflected the various "product lines" of multiple-use management ...[28]

Instead of a new era in environmental policy at the USFS, there seems to have been a failure to effectively implement ecosystem management as a replacement for traditional market-based multiple-use management. We do not have a new consciousness of ecosystems as wholes, but only as sectors in a more multi-layered multiple-use management paradigm. To use our terminology from chapter three, one might argue that the USFS has moved from an era of *maximum* timber supply, to an era of *optimal* multiple-use management, to a new era of optimal use management tempered by intergenerational or sustainability concerns.

These contentions are born out by the empirical facts. In the first comprehensive study of ecosystem management, Steven Yaffee[29] demonstrated that there was no significant shift in land management or restoration activity, which can be considered sound measures of the change from a narrow focus on use values to a

maximum use
→ *optimal use*

25. *Administration Unveils Sweeping New Plan* GREENWIRE, April 24, 1997 at 2.

26. *Id.* at 1.

27. KESSLER AND SALWASSER, *supra* note 15 at 184.

28. *Id.* at 184.

29. YAFFEE ET AL., *supra* note 1.

more holistic concern for ecosystem management. Within the USFS projects studied by Yaffee,[30] 0% showed any changes in management practices, and only 12.5% had achieved any restoration results. Meanwhile, only 37.5% had even initiated any restoration activities, while only 31.2% demonstrated any change in their approach to land management.[31] Considering that the ecosystem approach was by this time six years old, these are less than striking results for those interested in redirecting environmental law away from multiple-use toward a fuller concern for whole ecosystems. Why are these results so poor?

2) The Relationship Between Principle & Policy

If public policy design was entirely an empirical matter of positive rules, legal practice and management institutions, then adopting a new set of rules for an ecosystem management program ought to be enough to formulate new policy, make different choices among recommendations, and implement the new paradigm in place of old multiple-use management. However, the policy design process is more complex than superficial change can accommodate. In addition to management programs and administrative activity (in the periphery of the meta-policy), the formulation and implementation process relies on something deeper and more fundamental: a core normative principle and the logic that connects it to the law. In terms of law and policy design, a new context model requires a new paradigm.

Inherent in a meta-policy, and the most critical component of this concept, is the idea of the operating moral principle within each meta-policy. This core principle sets the policy design's internal standards of evaluation and justification, as well as the imperative for the law it renders. Thus whatever principle defines a meta-policy in Step A of the design process, it will limit the options for policy configuration, codification, and implementation in Steps B and C. By setting the standards by which persuasive argument and reasonable policy will be judged, principle creates practice. As long as this principle finds actualization in the institutional application of policy through law, and these results cause what *is* to measure up to what *ought* to be (as defined by the principle), then the dominant line of argument within the meta-policy holds its persuasiveness and law remains dynamic but consistent.[32] Overall, the law

[handwritten margin note: policy draws from core principle & is limited by it]

30. *Id.* studies 619 ecosystem management projects and provides both an assessment and catalog for each of them.

31. *Id.* at 73–75.

32. The concept of a dominant argument is related to the degree of persuasiveness one argument has in comparison with the others available in the policy design debate. Some arguments within a meta-policy may have short lives and some long, some may remain alternatives and as they become more persuasive, and the status-quo argument wanes in influence, they gain

is consistent in that the rules and expectations remain true to the central principle but dynamic in that the ongoing debate has established options and distinct competitive moral standards which can be brought to the meta-policy as time and need require.

The fundamental ***core principle*** that defines the meta-policy cannot be sacrificed without the wholesale change of the character of that meta-policy and the parent design process it creates to perpetuate itself. Although deliberation about a meta-policy may involve the consideration or balancing of many principles, public choice means the domination of one of these principles within the snapshot or synthesis solution that solves the dialectic of policy design in law. The core principle, when values conflict, will be decisive in the determination of this legal snapshot. As a *trump* principle it is therefore critical to decision-making and must be repeatedly applied over time in order to set expectations and establish consistency in the public law that administers the meta-policy. Dynamically, as a competitive argument gains in persuasiveness, its core principle will also gain more power in the deliberation process until it trumps the status quo principle and changes the conventional meta-policy. This process can be called the operationalization of a paradigm shift, which the USFS claimed would result in its shift to ecosystem management.[33]

But change in policy and law occurs only when we are no longer politically or legally persuaded that the dominant line of codified argument for the meta-policy and its inherent moral principle, setting the standards for practice, is the best basis on which to make decisions. Then we can examine the alternative lines of argument, produced by the law and policy design process, for a better definition of what is at stake, for how it should be handled, and for how the ends of the policy should be defined. This process of change can be gradual as one line of argument is found, over time, to be progressively more persuasive while the dominant standard fades, or it can be sudden as the dominant line of argument is abruptly replaced[34] by a competitor. One might define

---

dominance. Also, our focus on policy design as argument instead of policy as power comes from a concern for the study of the justification and advocacy of policy positions that marks the current debate about ecosystem management. What is going on within the legislative, judicial, and executive branch, as well as with NGOs and academic discussion internationally is built upon the power of argument to change administrative organization and policy practice.

33. JOHN MARTIN GILLROY, JUSTICE & NATURE: KANTIAN PHILOSOPHY, ENVIRONMENTAL POLICY AND THE LAW ch. 1 (2000).

34. Through election, violence, etc. One might argue that the "Republican Revolution" of 1994 is an attempt to cause the demise of a dominant line of argument as to the role of the state. It could also be argued to be an attempt to revive a long-time argument about states-rights that was waning.

the former pattern of change as evolutionary and the latter as revolutionary.[35]

Consider that the institutions and administrative structures that translate meta-policy into law are themselves the product of policy arguments. Institutions that we accept as authoritative[36] or legitimate[37] encapsulate those processes and practices that are persuasive to us. Lines of argument within a meta-policy, in this way, have an effect upon the evolution of the institutions and process that transform policy arguments into law. The development of meta-policy, as well as its ongoing dynamic quality, are therefore the result of an interactive dialectic process between competitive theories about what *ought* to be and the institutions and political processes that write and interpret these arguments as law: where *ought* becomes *is*. "The relationship between policy and its intellectual super-structure, or meta-policy, is a dialectic one."[38] The relationship creates transition through the engagement of dominant and competitive principle toward the replacement of one legal paradigm with another, the conventional argument with an alternative and one legal synthesis snapshot with a new one.

3) Sustainability as Efficiency

If the core determines the standards by which reasonable policy is judged in the periphery, as well as provides the norm by which institutions are organized or re-organized, then it is the core principle that must be different if a new meta-policy is to be created within the design process and overtake and replace a dominant policy argument as the more reasonable basis for the law. In our case, this would require ecosystem management, in the periphery, to have a distinct and ecologically compatible core principle as an alternative to optimal efficiency and its support of multiple-use management in the administrative superstructure that operationalizes it.

But USFS ecosystem management relies on the principle of sustainability which, we argue is no more than another definition of optimal use Kaldor efficiency, based upon the self-interested preferences of people and their willingness-to-pay. In other words, it is an instrumental value theory of nature, and different only in that *optimal* carries an inter-generational concern.[39]

---

35. MAJONE, *supra* note 6 at 147.

36. Through "rules of recognition," see H. L. A. HART, THE CONCEPT OF LAW 100 (1961).

37. JAMES S. FISHKIN, TYRANNY AND LEGITIMACY: A CRITIQUE OF POLITICAL THEORIES (1979).

38. MAJONE, *supra* note 6 at 166.

39. One might argue that all definitions of conservation carry a concern for future generations. See SAMUEL P. HAYS, CONSERVATION AND THE GOSPEL OF EFFICIENCY (1959).

Current natural resource statutes reflect this definition of sustainability as another form of Kaldor efficiency. For example, the **Multiple–Use, Sustained–Yield Act** (16 USCA §§ 528–31, 1960) defines its purpose as providing "resources to meet the needs of the American People ... to conform to changing needs and conditions ..." (§ 531 a) and in developing a sustainable "... high-level ... output ... of ... resources" (§ 531 b). The **National Forest Management Act** (16 USCA §§ 1600–14, 1976) sets its core principle in terms of efficient optimal output: "To serve the national interest, the renewable resources program must be based on a comprehensive assessment of present and anticipated uses, demand for, and supply of renewable resources from the Nation's ... forests" (§ 1600 3).

In the **Clean Air Act** (42 USCA §§ 7401–7671q, 1992), economic factors are considered in setting National Ambient Air Quality Standards (§ 7408 f2C), in writing State Implementation Plans (SIPS) (§ 7410), in regulations for Non–Attainment areas in the allowances for offsets and bubbles (ID–171 8) and even in the use of cost-benefit methods for setting technological standards in the control of air toxics (§ 7412). In fact, all of the technological standards options for controlling air pollution, Reasonably Achievable (REACT), Best Achievable (BACT), Maximum Achievable (MACT), are more considerate of economic efficiency and feasibility, than of ecosystem health and integrity.

The **National Environmental Policy Act** (42 USCA §§ 4321–4370d, 1969) has been interpreted by the Supreme Court to have only procedural significance in the face of economic use of nature (§ 4332).[40] In the Environmental Impact Study (EIS) provisions (C iii), environmental and preservation alternatives do not have to be considered, while (C v) makes consideration of "irreversible and irretrievable resources" necessary to any EIS.

Even in the **Endangered Species Act** (16 USCA §§ 1531–1544), economic considerations are present in the designation and definition of critical habitat (§ 1533 b2), in the establishment of the God Committee (§ 1536 e) which was added to the act to allow economic considerations to trump environmental considerations, and in the provision of economic hardship exemptions to species-taking (§ 1539 b2A).

The contention that sustainability is another species of optimal efficiency is also born out, unselfconsciously, by the practitioners of environmental sustainability who may view it as a new norm for policy and law, but who define it in terms of basic Kaldor efficiency.

---

40. Vermont Yankee v. NRDC 435 U.S. 519 (1978) and Robertson v. Me-   thow Valley 490 U.S. 332 (1989).

All these acts operate under mkt paradigm.

For example, they define it as the "maintenance of capital"[41] or the "... amount of consumption that can be continued indefinitely without degrading capital stocks ...".[42] Primarily, environmental sustainability ...

> ... seeks to improve human welfare by protecting the sources of raw materials used for human needs and ensuring that the sinks for human wastes are not exceeded, in order to prevent harm to humans ... [we must hold] ... waste emissions within the assimilative capacity of the environment ... hold depletion rates [of natural resources] equal to the rate at which renewable substitutes can be created ...[43]

These definitions are economic in origin and based upon a definition of optimal efficiency. This grounding limits the concept of sustainability to considering the natural world in terms of human-centered preference calculations for the most efficient environmental policy. Here, concern for ecosystems exists only to the extent that we maximize their use without destroying them altogether.

> ... environmental degradation should take place so long as the gains from the activities ... are greater than the benefits of preserving the areas in their original form. The idea that there is some **'optimum'** stock of natural assets based on this comparison of costs and benefits needs to be addressed ... to see why the conservation of existing stock should be elevated to a goal of sustainable development.[44]

Environmental policy therefore exhibits a consistent core Market Paradigm principle over time. We have evolved from a core concern for *maximum efficiency* (1776–1900) in the Pre–Progressive Era of land disposal policy, to a law of *optimal efficiency* (1900–1990) in the Progressive Era with the advent of a role for government in environmental regulation and then, within the contemporary era, to *sustainable efficiency* (1990–) as the contemporary Market Paradigm of legal practice. However, as our examination of the Market Paradigm demonstrates, as long as Kaldor efficiency is the dominant core principle for environmental meta-policy, we are restricted in our administrative structure and legal management schemes to policy that:

[handwritten margin note: max. efficiency -> optimal efficiency ≈ sustainable efficiency]

---

41. MICHAEL S. COMMON, SUSTAINABILITY AND POLICY: LIMITS TO ECONOMICS COMMON ch. 3 (1995).

42. COSTANZA ET AL. *supra* note 17 at 8.

43. *Taking Nature Into Account,* CLUB OF ROME 100 (Wouter van Dieren ed. 1995).

44. DAVID W. PEARCE & R. KERRY TURNER, ECONOMICS OF NATURAL RESOURCES AND THE ENVIRONMENT PEARCE, 20 *emphasis added* (1990).

▶ Is Human Centered or A Matter Of Self–Interested Preference, However Enlightened;

▶ Only Values The Instrumental Use Value Of Nature As A
Resource Base;

▶ Segregates Parts Of Natural Systems For Policy Decision-
Making, Not Wholes;

▶ Promotes The Subsistence Of Nature, Not Its Flourishing;

▶ Assumes Use And Places The Burden Of Proof On Those
Who Wish To Prevent Use And Promote Preservation;

▶ Focuses On The Maximum Use Threshold—Utilization Of
Nature Up To Just Below The Point Where Ecosystems
Breakdown;

▶ Defines Nature As A Private Fungible Good Best Allocated
By Efficiency–Driven Institutions Backed By Common Law.

These characteristics run directly counter to that part of the
ecosystem management approach that intends to design policy and
codify law to protect the health or integrity of whole ecosystems,
valued independently of human use. With the peripheral policy of
ecosystem management directly at odds with the core principle of
sustainability, and with the core principal setting codification and
implementation standards for administrative decision-making, the
USFS ecosystem approach is inadequate, by itself, to overcome the
strength of the core principle of sustainable efficiency. Its parameters will be bent to the needs of sustainable multiple-use management as core defines periphery and policy design defines the law.
The problem is a conflict between the need for comprehensive
consideration of human and nature's intrinsic values, as demanded
by ecosystem management, and the inability of sustainability as a
core policy principle to evaluate either comprehensively or in terms
of non-use value.

The Need for a New Core Principle:
Preservation of Ecosystem
Integrity

For ecosystem[45] management to effectively compete with multiple-use management within the USFS or anywhere else, it requires
a distinct core principle and paradigm that sets a different standard
for persuasive policy and represents the values of ecosystem management more accurately in its context model and administrative
institutions. If not sustainability, what is the core value?

---

45. Shortly, we will define "[E]co-
system" not just to include natural systems, but also as a more extensive interface including both humanity and
nature. This has been called the "Kantian" definition of Ecosystem, see
GILLROY supra note 33 at 130.

In practice, ecosystem management as environmental meta policy should concentrate on the flourishing of natural systems. Therefore, if we are to make the shift from multiple-use management to ecosystem management, we need a principle that can guide the legal system to evaluate:

▶ Policy For Ecosystems As Wholes Not As Resource Sectors;

▶ Ecosystems Independent Of Humanity And Therefore In Terms Of Intrinsic—Not Instrumental—Value;

▶ The Flourishing Of Natural Systems—Not Their Minimum Subsistence;

▶ Assuming The Non–Use Value Of Nature—Where The Burden Of Proof Is On Those Who Wish To Use The Environment;

▶ Nature As A Collective Not A Private Good.

Passmore[46] defines two distinct paths for environmental ethics and policy: conservation and preservation. Conservation seeks to protect nature's use value to humanity and is associated with goals of optimal efficiency and sustainability as defined here. Therefore, conservation is an inadequate principle to implement the ecosystem approach to management. This leaves us with preservation as an alternative core principle for ecosystem management.

> Notions of the "health" and "integrity" of natural communities would be useless to those who wish to design the factory farms, . . . and aquacultural feedlots of the future. Only those who consider nature an object for moral . . . attention need care about the integrity and health of ecosystems . . .[47]

Preservation is defined, by Passmore,[48] as the protection of those parts of the natural world yet untouched by humanity. But for the purposes of applying ecosystem management, we can extend this definition to focus on the preservation or reclamation of the functional integrity of any and all natural systems. Here, this preservation or reclamation would be conditional on the amount of active ecological characteristics retained by the ecosystem under scrutiny. An urban ecosystem, for example, would have a different level of integrity and therefore distinct preservation policy that would allow a great deal more human activity than a roadless wilderness.

46. JOHN PASSMORE, MAN'S RESPONSIBILITY FOR NATURE pt. 2 (1974).

47. Mark Sagoff, *Has Nature A Good Of Its Own?* in ECOSYSTEM HEALTH 62 (Robert Costanza et al. eds. 1992).

48. PASSMORE, *supra* note 46 at 101.

In this way, our expanded definition of natural integrity allows us to do more than just set aside wilderness in acts of preservation. Any act meant to retain or reestablish the functional health or integrity of any ecosystem can be seen as an act of preservation. Placing wolves back into Yellowstone, revitalizing an aquifer, reestablishing the Gettysburg Battlefield as it was in 1863, revitalizing an urban area with refurbished housing, or empowering a river by reconstructing its banks and current as they once were, all fit into this broader definition of preservation.

The main consideration of this expanded definition of preservation is the intrinsic needs of the natural system, independent of our use of it.[49] Nature's intrinsic value can then be defined in terms of the functional integrity or persistence of whole ecosystems.[50] We can then relate the moral preservation of ecosystems—their intrinsic value—to the ecological concepts of systemic "resiliency, resistance, stability, elasticity, constancy, and persistence,"[51] and so relate the moral imperative to preserve ecosystems to the practical scientific measures of their persistent flourishing. This gives us a principle which truly underlies and is compatible with an ecosystem management approach to environmental policy.

> Concepts of ecological health and integrity and their deployment in ecological science . . . make the most sense in relation to the intrinsic—the moral and aesthetic—value of ecological communities and systems. To suppose that natural communities may have intrinsic and not just instrumental value, after all, is to distinguish what may be healthy for nature from what may be healthful or beneficial for humanity.[52]

The core principle of preservation more naturally supports a peripheral reorientation to ecosystem management and sheds light

---

49. In Bryan Norton, *Conservation and Preservation: A Conceptual Rehabilitation*, 8 ENVIRONMENTAL ETHICS 195–220 (1986) he argues that conservation and preservation ought not be defined by their principles but by the policy they produce. He contends that "setting aside wilderness" can come from both conservationist and preservationist motives. However, his approach both neglects the critical role played by principle in defining policy while it also limits the act of preservation to setting aside wilderness. We argue that the principle of preservation, defined in terms of ecosystem integrity, allows for many more actions than just 'set aside.' Norton also moves in this direction because of his insistence that intrinsic value does not exist and therefore has no meaning.

50. See John Martin Gillroy, *Kantian Ethics & Environmental Policy Argument: Autonomy, Ecosystem Integrity, and Our Duties To Nature*, 3 ETHICS AND THE ENVIRONMENT 131–158 (1998) and GILLROY, *supra* note 33.

51. MARK S. BOYCE & ALAN HANEY, ECOSYSTEM MANAGEMENT: APPLICATIONS FOR SUSTAINABLE FOREST AND WILDLIFE RESOURCES 3 (1997).

52. SAGOFF, *supra* note 47 at 67.

on the direct conflict between the instrumental and intrinsic evaluation of nature.[53]

> To treasure an ecological community is to see it has a good of its own—and therefore a "health" or "integrity"—that we should protect even when to do so does not profit us ... if we do not value nature for ethical and aesthetic reasons, then we might well pollute and degrade it for instrumental ones.[54]

But what problems does a principle of preservation of integrity present to the lawyer in terms of the configuration, codification, and implementation stages of policy design? Is it not too theoretically extreme and metaphysical while being impractical to apply in an administrative context?

Let us consider the theoretical concerns: first, intrinsic value does not have to mean value independent of human evaluation, as its most extreme theoretical supporters might argue.[55] It can mean only that we value nature independent of our use of it, which is compatible with ecosystem management for the functional integrity of ecosystems. Second, applying intrinsic value to nature does not ignore human needs or wants, but is ideal rather than strictly want-regarding[56] and elevates nature from a strictly instrumental role in human life, to an equitable status that deserves evaluation on its own terms. We merely seek harmony between humanity and nature and consider the health and integrity of functioning ecosystems independently of our needs or wants.

Here *intrinsic* refers to the functional capacities of nature just as it refers to the moral capacities of human beings, and it seeks harmony between these distinct yet interdependent integrities. Our moral duty to nature is defined, not in terms of its subsistence for our use but, in terms of its flourishing as an interconnected system or functional whole.[57] Instead of treating nature as a 'slave' that we minimally nourish so it will subsist to supply our wants, we would evaluate nature as a whole with intrinsic functional value; its persistent flourishing becomes a pertinent consideration in any use of it as a resource. In moral terms, we would treat nature, as we treat ourselves, as an end-in-itself as well as a means to our ends.[58]

---

53. *Id.* at 70.

54. *Id.* at 67.

55. See note 64, Elizabeth M. Harlow, *The Human Face of Nature: Environmental Values and the Limits of Nonanthropocentrism*, 14 ENVIRONMENTAL ETHICS 27–42 (1992).

56. BRIAN BARRY, POLITICAL ARGUMENT 38 (1992).

57. GILLROY, *supra* note 33 at ch. 5: GILLROY, *supra* note 50.

58. *Id.* and two works by Kant, IMMANUEL KANT, GROUNDWORK OF THE METAPHYSICS OF MORALS (H. J. Paton trans. & ed. 1964 [1786]); CRITIQUE OF JUDGMENT (Werner S. Pluhar trans. & ed. 1987 [1790]).

Instead of assuming our right to use nature to the maximum that will not totally destroy the subsistence of ecosystems, we should support natural systems so that they thrive, while we also empower the functional capacities of ecosystems by restoring natural balance and correcting for past harm to functional interdependence. Nature would then have an independent status in our environmental meta-policy based on its functional capacity to achieve a balance of "resiliency, resistance, stability, elasticity, constancy, and persistence".[59] The responsibility of the USFS decision-maker should now include anticipating the effects of human activity on the functional integrity of our National Forests.

In terms of the practicality of preservation as functional integrity, it is both already present within environmental meta-policy/law and, as a public choice with essential priorities, is accessible as an alternative in administrative decision-making. First, references to ecosystems as wholes and to the preservation of human and natural capacities, exist as elements of a potentially competitive argument within environmental law.

For example, in the **Clean Air Act** (42 USCA §§ 7401–7671q, 1992), we see a competitive argument for the inclusion of ecosystem research (§ 7403 e) and ecosystem risk assessment (§ 7408 g) in the establishment of national air quality standards. In addition, there is a human intrinsic value/public health argument in setting air standards (§ 7409) that the Environmental Protection Agency recently used to tighten NAAQS for criteria pollutants.[60]

In the **Endangered Species Act** (16 USCA §§ 1531–1543, 1973) we have an argument for the designation of threatened and endangered species that can be made only on the basis of ecological data (§ 1533 b), as well as an argument for protecting critical habitat (§ 1533 b1B2) which states that "[t]he purposes of this chapter are to provide a means whereby the ecosystems upon which endangered species and threatened species depend may be conserved" (§ 1531 b). We also have a definition of conservation that supports "methods and procedures which are necessary to bring any endangered ... species ... to the point at which the measures provided ... are no longer necessary" (§ 1531 3). This definition is akin to our definition of preservation as reclamation.

The **National Environmental Policy Act** (42 USCA §§ 4321–4361, 1969) contains an argument for the harmony of humanity and nature in policy: "The purposes of this chapter are: To declare a national policy which will encourage productive and enjoyable harmony between man and his environment; to promote efforts which prevent or eliminate damage to the environment and

59. BOYCE AND HANEY, *supra* note 51 at 3.

60. *Whitman v. American Trucking Ass'ns*, 531 U.S. 457 (2001).

The Acts also contain some principles based on preservation, but these principles are not dominant.

biosphere and stimulate the health and welfare of man; to enrich the understanding of the ecological systems and natural resources important to the Nation . . ." (§ 4321).

More specifically, in the land and resource statutes, a competitive argument exists for considering the needs of ecosystems. The **Multiple–Use and Sustained–Yield Act** (hereafter MUSY) (16 USCA §§ 528–531, 1960) states that it is the "policy of the Congress that the national forests are established and shall be administered for outdoor recreation, range, timber, watershed, and wildlife and fish purposes" (§ 528) making at least half of the purpose of the National Forests supportive of preservation and ecosystem management. Also MUSY (§ 529) states that "The establishment and maintenance of areas of wilderness are consistent with the purposes and provisions of §§ 528 to 531 of this title," allowing forest managers to promote the preservation of old growth and roadless areas.

Meanwhile, within the **National Forest Management Act** (16 USCA §§ 1600–14, 1976), the requirements for timber cutting include the restrictions that harvest can only occur where "soil, slope or other watershed conditions will not be irreversibly damaged" (§ 1604 g2E). Where cuts are carried out, they must be "in a manner consistent with protection of soil, watershed, fish, wildlife, recreation, and esthetic resources, and the regeneration of the timber resource" (§ 1604 Fv).

In these ways and others, current environmental law provides more than efficiency, multiple-use arguments, but makes preservation of ecosystem, by our definition, an alternative argument within environmental statutes. However, it is not dominant in the synthesis snapshot that is contemporary environmental law. The seeds for a parallel *preservation or ecosystem management* argument exist within these statutes and is accessible to administrators. But because it lacks status as a core principle in an Ecosystem Paradigm and context model, it is not dominant, and creation of ecosystem management without a foundational Ecosystem Paradigm to anchor it is no more than a superficial and unproductive change, an ecosystem veneer over a core of market assumptions.

In addition to the fact that provisions for preservation and ecosystem management already exist in the statutes, there is further support for the ascendance of the preservation or ecosystem management argument in Supreme Court jurisprudence.[61] Here

61. These cases concern the Clean Air Act (Chevron v. NRDC, 467 U.S. 837 (1984), which requires that an agency have merely a permissible construction of the statute; the Endangered Species Act (Palila v. Hawaii, 649 F.Supp. 1070 (1986) which argues that an agency can move before harm is encountered to prevent it; the National Environmental Policy Act (Vermont Yankee v. NRDC, 435 U.S. 519 (1978), which contends that the agency decides on what substance Environmental Impact Statement procedures will have; and both the Multiple Use–

preservation can be made accessible by legal decisions allowing agencies to change meta-policy at its core if that change is a "reasonable construction of the statute."[62] If ecosystem management can first be demonstrated to exist as a competitive argument paradigm within environmental meta-policy, then it can also be justified as an alternative but reasonable construction of any statute where it appears. In this respect, choosing between accessible parallel constructions of the statute is within the power of the agency to affectuate.[63]

> If this choice represents a reasonable accommodation of conflicting policies that were committed to the agency's care by the statute, we [the courts] should not disturb it . . . [64]

Therefore, a dialectic exists between the demands of an ecosystem approach to policy management which is based upon a principle that can properly evaluate comprehensive intrinsic values (in terms of health or integrity), and its present core principle of sustainability which, as a variant of efficiency, is limited to piecemeal evaluation of instrumental economic values.

Overall, preservation ethics are theoretically rigorous without being extreme. They exist as a potential competitive argument within the present statutes and a paradigm shift to a core principle of preservation and a periphery of ecosystem management is within the power of federal agencies to actualize. Preservation, as a core principle for ecosystem management, is both reasonable and practical for law, policy design and evaluation. However, the full development of a logically intact alternative paradigm that can be called an ecosystem approach to environmental law has not occurred. Kantian Philosophy can provide this paradigm.

An Ecosystem Paradigm & Context Model: Moving Beyond Market Assumptions

An essential notion of the Market Paradigm is that the state's purpose is to improve the material welfare of its citizens. Based on the ideal that the state and its ends are identical with, and ought to

---

Sustained Yield Act and the National Forest Management Act (Robertson v. Methow Valley, 490 U.S. 332 (1989) which establish that the agency decides what constitutes reasonable procedures. These discretion cases were upheld more recently by the Supreme Court in Babbitt v. Sweet Home, 515 U.S. 687 (1995).

62. Chevron U.S.A. v. NRDC 467 U.S. 837 (1984)

63. "When a challenge to an agency construction of a statutory provision, fairly conceptualized, really centers on the wisdom of the agency's policy, rather than whether it is a reasonable choice within a gap left by Congress, the challenge must fail" (Stevens in Chevron). See **Statute Pointers Box** in chapter 2.

64. Chevron Quoting Shimer.

mimic those of the market, this stricture has come to be interpreted in various ways, and through various institutions (e.g. market, government), most notably through the use of cost-benefit methods. Common to all interpretations however are two ideas. First, the *good* of the person is some function of personal preferences regarding present, past, and future physical or material conditions. Second, the market (or the state as its surrogate) has no higher goal than to realize a social condition where the greatest proportion of consumers have their preferences for personal welfare satisfied. This state-of-affairs is considered efficient and, therefore, just by economic principle.   *efficient = just under econ. principle*

We have designated this set of fundamental assumptions, principles, material conditions, maxims and methods, examined in the last chapter as the Market Paradigm, and argued it is the foundation of both multiple-use and sustainability as well as current resource policy in mining, grazing, and forest law. If this is so, and if there is dissatisfaction with any of these policies, then, within Step A of the policy design process, we need to examine the Market Paradigm and its component parts to see how a different set of assumptions might create a distinct paradigm and a foundational argument for legal change.

Specifically, let us create an Ecosystem Paradigm as a competitive argument for the market approach to resources and see how it changes natural resources law. From an Ecosystem perspective, the Market Paradigm, as used in the formulation of public choices in general, and natural resource choices in particular, lacks two critical ingredients: first, a concern for the moral integrity of the individual and for the intrinsic value this internal capacity grounds for each human being as a person; and second, a concern for the intrinsic (or non-use) value or functional integrity of the environment.[65] Critical to moral integrity, as well as the human responsi-

---

65. While economic theory is devoid of any attempt to consider anything but the instrumental value of nature, even philosophers and practitioners alike have struggled with the notion of "rights" or "integrity" for nature. See HENRY DAVID THOREAU, A WEEK ON THE CONCORD AND MERRIMACK RIVERS; WALDEN OR LIFE IN THE WOODS; THE MAIN WOODS; CAPE COD. 1985; ALDO LEOPOLD, A SAND COUNTY ALMANAC (1977) or RODERICK NASH, THE RIGHTS OF NATURE (1989). The most significant dilemma is the attempt to have but a single "moral" definition of the ethical terminology that applies to both humanity and nature. This is a dilemma as long as the locus of value for human beings is their individual integrity while nature's integrity is holistic. In addition, the application of moral terms and responsibilities to nature seems to lack logical sense. How can individual animals have rights without duties? How can they have rights without moral capacities? If it is not the individual animal, then how can natural systems have group integrity or rights while the term is only applicable to individuals? A good example of the trouble with this concept of ecosystem integrity can be seen in LAURA WESTRA, AN ENVIRONMENTAL PROPOSAL FOR ETHICS: THE PRINCIPLE OF INTEGRITY. Here she attempts to make nature's integrity a centerpiece of environmental ethics and generates many problems for policy applications in the process. First, her ecosystems do not include humanity (xiii),

bility toward the functional integrity of natural systems, is the promotion of what we might call *practical reason* in policy choice. Practical reason is more than the instrumental expression and prosecution of one's preferences, it assumes that there are intrinsic (non-use) as well as instrumental (use) value in both humanity and nature and that there is a systemic and accurate way dialectically to incorporate these values in policy and legal choice. Practical Reason requires that both individuals and ecosystems be treated interdependently in the policy design process.

Here, where the biological and physical integrity of ecosystems holds equal weight with the economic use value of a forest. The role a species of wildlife plays in the biodiversity of a region is treated as a basis for legal argument and regulation that is as sound as the economic or Kaldor efficiency of human activity or recreation on public lands. To establish an alternative approach to environmental and natural resource questions we should move beyond a reliance on self-interested preference, welfare, and instrumental rationality; we should concentrate on the ramifications of individual practical reason as this translates ideas into human choices and physical actions involving the natural environment and extraction choices.

To create an Ecosystem Paradigm we will utilize the generic paradigm template of policy design organizing the fundamental assumptions, principles, material conditions of choice, maxims, and methods of an Ecosystem Paradigm as we did for the Market Paradigm. However, we will introduce new content to reflect the requirements of taking an ecosystem perspective on the natural environment.

---

her focus is primarily on pristine wilderness (41; 59; 217–18), her concept of integrity is both too complex (separating structural from functional integrity—Chapter 2) and too simple (trying to apply a single moral definition of integrity designed for human individuals to whole natural systems (67; 156–57)), forcing her to float uncomfortably between bio- and eco-centric environmental ethics (122; passim). These problems make it very hard to understand the complexity of the human-natural system interface and can only recommend, in the end, a hands-off policy toward nature and "buffer" or "integrity" "zones" to separate humanity from nature (216–219). Her palpable struggle to come to terms with the concept of integrity as it bridges human and natural worlds begs further argument and also attention to how the concept might find greater use as an evaluative tool in making policy for whole systems that include humanity and nature, in "pristine" and not so pristine condition, and where duties might be derived that would guide human collective and individual choice in the wide cross-section of issues facing environmental politics. One way to create a new and more useful definition of integrity is to begin with established philosophical systems that have already done much of the work to integrate concepts and derive principles (e.g. Kant's Philosophical–Policy).

1) Template—Stage I: Fundamental Assumptions—Ecosystems, Individuals & Nature

a) *Individual*

For the Market Paradigm and its foundations in classical economics, the individual is a rational consumer with wealth preferences. Within an Ecosystem Paradigm,[66] the analyst needs to respond to a complex individual who is more than a collection of wants, or different levels of wants.[67] We may assume that this person is not just a rational maximizer but a practical reasoner, struggling between their predisposition toward moral self-awareness and their propensity to be a self-interested agent,[68] to form a moral character, able to act on his or her own behalf. This person can consider and weigh intrinsic as well as instrumental values and considers themselves, as a repository of rights and responsibilities, to be of inherent value to themselves and to others. This person does not consider themselves to be the property of others and considers it immoral to merely use anything of intrinsic value without full consideration of this dimension of value in their deliberations. Here one's humanity is the core of one's intrinsic value.

[handwritten margin note: individual = practical reasoner, autonomous]

In addition to a recognition of the moral integrity of the individual citizen (not part of the Market Paradigm), the ecosystem resource-analyst must also consider that nature may have more than instrumental economic use value. Ecosystems as wholes may have physical, biological, and functional value independent of their use by humanity, and this component of their value needs to be considered on an equal footing in the deliberation of proper environmental law. Here, the functional integrity and harmony of whole Ecosystems, made up of human and natural systems and their interactions, become the basis for law. As one's morally intrinsic value is based upon practical reason and one's capacity, ability, and purpose in becoming an autonomous person and a moral agent, the functional integrity or capacity, ability, and purpose of nature must also be a policy priority. This presents humanity both with obligations to use nature carefully and without waste as necessary to human moral agency (Ecosystem Conservationism), but also to respect the integrity of natural systems as functional ends-in-themselves and pre-existing causal components of greater Ecosystems (Ecosystem Preservationism).

66. See GILLROY, *supra* note 33 at ch. 5.

67. MANCUR OLSON, THE LOGIC OF COLLECTIVE ACTION (1971) and A. K. Sen, *Choice, Orderings and Moral-ity* in PRACTICAL REASON 54 (Stephen Korner, ed. 1974).

68. HENRY E. ALLISON, KANT'S THEORY OF FREEDOM 146–162 (1990).

b) Collective Action[69]

The Market Paradigm builds a collective level of organization that is no more than the aggregate sum of individual wants and preferences, while collective action is primarily concerned with establishing just enough cooperation to satisfy the material wants of the most people possible. An Ecosystem approach needs to examine the political community as a distinct entity where individuals (the moral building blocks of collective action) and the just state (which ratifies and enforces the collective terms of cooperation to insure the moral character of individuals) coordinate and reinforce one another. The problem with collective action is in encouraging each individual's predisposition to act morally. The strategic situation is therefore not a prisoner's dilemma, but an *assurance game*[70] in which each citizen is assumed willing to cooperate in the production of morally-cooperative outcomes which consider both instrumental and intrinsic values within a just state, charged with more than aggregating welfare or use preferences.

In terms of collective action, the ecosystem resource-analyst should assume that when faced with the fear and uncertainty of exploitation in a community where no public regulation exists, the individual's underlying propensity toward self-interested behavior will dominate the individual's predisposition to act cooperatively.[71] One needs to be aware that the externalities of others behavior and the subsequent fear of exploitation by these external market effects may cause the individual to ignore their predisposition toward cooperative action and move to protect their core of integrity in isolation, acting to exploit others before they are exploited themselves. The resulting "mania for domination"[72] illustrates the government's failure to provide the conditions necessary to coordinate the assurance game and provides the decision-maker with the priority to protect individual integrity by regulating that behavior that would exploit essential moral capacity in some for the instrumental benefit of others (treating intrinsically valuable human agents as of merely instrumental value). The collective action implications of the assurance game promote a distinct public space for collective action that transcends the private interests and actions of the prisoner's dilemma. This new definition of 'public interest' is the reservoir of the moral precepts and traditions that define the right and the good, and therefore justice itself in terms

69. GILLROY, *supra* note 33, at ch. 6.

70. John Martin Gillroy, *Moral Considerations and Public Choices: Individual Autonomy and the NIMBY Problem* 5 PUBLIC AFFAIRS QUARTERLY 319–332 (1991); JON ELSTER, ULYSSES AND THE SIRENS: STUDIES IN RA-TIONALITY AND IRRATIONALITY (1979).

71. ALLISON, *supra* note 67 at ch. 5.

72. IMMANUEL KANT, ANTHROPOLOGY FROM A PRAGMATIC POINT OF VIEW (Mary Gregor trans. & ed. 1974 [1800]).

of supporting the essential intrinsic value of both humanity and nature in the law.

The Assurance Game

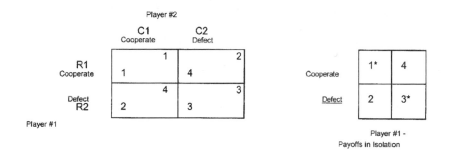

The ordinal preferences of each player are:

        (1) <u>B</u>est—<u>Universal Cooperation</u>

        (2) <u>S</u>econd—<u>Unilateral Defection</u>

        (3) <u>T</u>hird—<u>Universal Defection</u>

        (4) <u>W</u>orst—<u>Unilateral Cooperation</u>

The Preference and Rational Logic of an Assurance Game:

The logic here describes a rationality of intention to cooperate with an underlying capacity, and ability, to exploit. Unlike the prisoner's dilemma, where exploitation is the best alternative for the player, in the assurance game, the cooperative solution is preferred but the ability to exploit looms as a pertinent consideration of each player's strategic rationality. The worst reality for each player is still exploitation in unilateral cooperation, and even a failure to coordinate at all is a better option than being exploited. Without communication or central regulation to assure each player that they will not be exploited in the decision to cooperate (be a moral person) the game can degenerate into a fight for survival and a ruination of collective action as each player, fearing that they will be exploited, moves to exploit the other.

The precarious nature of the intention to cooperate, and the critical nature of outside signals to the individual playing the game, means that the assurance game has no dominant strategy (see Player #1 payoffs in isolation). If one is assured that the other player will cooperate, then one prefers to cooperate oneself, however, if no such assurance is understood, then one prefers to defect and protect oneself. Unlike a prisoner's dilemma, where each player prefers to defect whatever the other players do, the lack of a dominant strategy makes one player's payoffs contingent on the decisions of others. The uncertainty of this game, without a dominant strategy, makes the role of central coordination very important and the specter of the "mania for domination" even more real than in the prisoner's dilemma.

J.M. Gillroy—1995

c) The Role of the State[73]

From the standpoint of the Market Paradigm the state, or any allocation institution, has only two functions: to police and adjudicate contracts and to provide a surrogate exchange system that can step-in when markets fail and allocations cannot be made without the involvement of the state as a collective third party. For while many institutional forms other than markets can express economic efficiency, it is the allocation rules of markets that provide the standard by which all non-market allocations are judged for their efficiency. Markets, if they fail, are to be mimiced by the state. However, for an Ecosystem approach, we may want to envision the state as a distinct entity, functioning independently and prior to economic markets, and existing to anticipate and regulate them in a way that solves the assurance game and contributes to the "harmony of integrity" between humanity and nature. The Ecosystem approach recognizes both essential and elective goods as well as both private and public choice and takes on these dialectics as part of synthesizing a legal practice snapshot that defines harmony within this complexity.

Justice within the Ecosystem Paradigm is rooted in the characterization of the individual and the collective action problem just covered. Each individual is assumed to have the capacity to recognize themselves as a moral being. The just state is therefore defined as that set of institutions and regulations providing the material conditions for the protection and empowerment of the moral capacities of its citizens. This responsibility requires that the state support the public interest in that level of mutual assurance necessary to encourage cooperation and harmony of integrity. Harmony, in turn, is necessary to solve the long term assurance game and maintain social cooperation and persistence of the environment. Here, the *just state* empowers the individual's predisposition to act cooperatively or morally and defuses, or prevents, the 'mania for domination.'

From this viewpoint, the state is more than the sum of individual willingness-to-pay preferences and is established to maintain an independent and duty-based *sense of justice* that insures its long-term existence and justifies its legal choices. The institutions in a just state are responsible to the integrity of humanity and nature;

---

73. GILLROY *supra* note 33, at ch. 7.

they support those laws that simultaneously protect the essential intrinsic values of both humanity and nature while they encourage the flourishing of whole ecosystems as a critical basis for resource policy.

2) Template—Stage II: Principles & Material Conditions

a) *Operating Principles*[74]

Our next concern is with the entailments of these foundational assumptions, once chosen. Defining a rational or practically reasonable policy requires core operating principles to form the basis of the policy imperative for the decision-maker, and the creation of techniques or methods that the policy-maker can easily use to apply these principles to practical decisions.

For the Market Paradigm, the protection and facilitation of each person's voluntary economic trade is of prime concern. The principle of Kaldor efficiency does this by supporting the maximization of aggregate social welfare. For the Ecosystem analyst, the principle is **INTEGRITY**, given a dialectic between the moral integrity of humanity and the functional integrity of nature. Duty, individual rights, and community interests are balanced with the health of ecosystems by an active state attempting to protect and empower individuals and ecosystems as ends-in-themselves with intrinsic moral value.

b) *Material Conditions*[75]

Operating principles require material conditions that the decision-maker can manipulate to make normative value practical in the lives of citizens. In the Market Paradigm, the sole material condition of the principle of Kaldor efficiency is tangible property or *wealth*. Considering Ecosystems, we might argue that human and natural integrity are protected and empowered by concern for such considerations as, (1) the *Protection of Freedom* of whole Ecosystems (which is the consideration of both natural and human intrinsic value in policy design); (2) *equality* within the political community as guaranteed through the distribution and re-distribution of the physical property necessary to the widespread expression of human freedom through moral agency, and by (3) *civic independence* based upon the public space created by the assurance game that empowers the public provision of those opportunities necessary in order for anyone to apply their practical reason to both personal and political choice. The Ecosystem decision-maker is therefore

---

74. *Id.*   **75.** *Id.*

concerned with human and environmental integrity, collective and private property and social opportunity, to provide for the full citizenship of their constituents and in this way, a harmony of human (moral) and natural (functional) intrinsic values.

3) Template—Stage III: Maxims & Methods

a) Maxims[76]

The operating principle of integrity, and the material conditions it defines, can help the decision-maker distinguish which policy alternatives are acceptable to the CPA (promoting the principle) and which are not acceptable (rejecting the principle) by defining the maxims of decision-making that will inform this choice.

The Market Paradigm has but one maxim for the decision-maker: *Maximize Wealth!* The Ecosystem decision-maker will also have but one distinct maxim: **Protect Ecosystem Integrity!** The imperative is to protect and secure those environmental background conditions that are a prerequisite to the harmony of human and natural systems integrity and to inform human use of nature in terms of our trusteeship and responsibility to inherent value.

For resource law, this means viewing nature as ecosystems first and resources second, operationalizing the ecosystem approach to management we have already analyzed, and creating a new paradigm and context model for extraction law and policy independent of market considerations.

b) Methods[77]

With the principle of efficiency, the Market Paradigm renders the methodology of cost-benefit analysis so that the ends and means of public issues must submit to the Kaldor efficiency test in order to become policy. From the Ecosystem point of view, the decision-maker must seek to enforce the maxim to protect integrity by creating a **baseline function** representing the minimum requirements for the provision of human moral integrity and nature's physical or functional integrity and the harmony of each with the other. The baseline function is made up of those public environmental goods (E), private goods (p_i), and opportunity set (o) that each person needs to have their intrinsic value appreciated in public decision-making. The baseline function also represents the minimal set of conditions that provide for the functional integrity of nature, as the environmental public goods are not just resources

76. *Id. at ch. 8.*   **77.** *Id.*

but the consideration of the requirements of whole ecosystems as ends in themselves and not just means to human ends. The goal is for an equal consideration of those laws that protect and empower the essential capacities of humanity and nature so that the threshold below which the integrity of the whole interdependent system would fail is not crossed. Justice in collective policy choice requires government to consider, not an equal measure to each but, the basic protections that will solve the assurance situation and establish collective cooperation for the full expression of each person's practical reason and each ecosystem's natural flourishing in the world. The charge of the decision-maker is to create those circumstances in which each citizen's predisposition toward acting morally is empowered, supporting integrity in each and a harmony of moral agency for all within a sound and flourishing environment.

A Kantian Ecosystem Paradigm

	Individual	Collective Action	Role of the State	
Stage I Q=Why? A= F.A.	Moral Agent	Assurance Game	Active State: Anticipating Requirements of Justice	F.A.= Fundamental Assumptions
Stage II Q=What? A= O.P.	Moral Integrity — Freedom Equality Independence			O.P.= Operating Principle(s)
And M.C.	Ecosystem Integrity	Property	Opportunity	M.C.= Material Conditions of Principle(s)
Stage III Q= Whether A=Maxims	Protect	(Re) Distribute	Provide	
And Methods	(E, p_i, o_i)			

ANALYSIS → ← SYNTHESIS

J.M. Gillroy 1995

This argument is one that is suggested by the analysis of the USFS case and its failings, but the focus on integrity and its ideal-regarding role in the human relationship to nature is not new. In order to give a firmer foundation to the argument for an Ecosystem Paradigm, let us take a moment to see the similarities between the requirements of Ecosystem Law and the philosophical argument of Immanuel Kant.

Our Kantian Duties to Nature

In examining Kant's philosophical system[78] as a whole,[79] we begin by addressing the issue that Kantian moral and political philosophy is strictly anthropocentric and has no environmental ethic at all, especially one that considers nature for itself. We will then contend that there are arguments for two sources of human duties to nature that exist within Kantian exegesis: one based upon our responsibility to **conserve** nature as humanity's duty to itself (individually and collectively), and another focused on our obligation to **preserve** natural functioning for its own sake, as humanity's duty to the highest good[80] and the harmony between the realm of nature and the realm of ends considered as a whole biosphere made up of ecosystems.[81]

78. Most "modern" ethical philosophies (e.g. Locke, Rousseau, Hegel) were written when human relations with the environment were marked by perceived plenty rather than scarcity, and when the idea that humanity could seriously affect nature was eclipsed by human fear of natural systems and their power over individual life. They, therefore, did not consider the environment a subject of ethical or policy deliberation.

79. The reader should be aware that our argument is predicated upon a nonstandard definition of intrinsic or inherent value that is not identical to current usage and which makes no distinction between these two terms. We assume that "inherent" and "intrinsic" are interchangeable terms for the same concept of non-instrumental value which is different only in its application to humanity (where it has an individual moral foundation) as distinguished from nature (where it has a systemic functional foundation). Therefore, the core distinction is between instrumental and intrinsic value. Moral status in human deliberation is a function of classification by type of value (see RAYMOND PLANT, MODERN POLITICAL THOUGHT (1991); MARK SAGOFF, THE ECONOMY OF THE EARTH (1988)). The individual (or collective) will orient itself toward everything it encounters in the world and grant it a status as either something that can be used to one's benefit having only instrumental value, or something that has a status independent of its human use, which grants it

an intrinsic value. The basic dialectic between instrumental and intrinsic value is the foundation upon which all moral philosophies and personal ethical calculations are made and it is the starting point for anyone interested in the moral status of any entity in the human lexicon of ethical evaluation (ROBERT AUDI, THE CAMBRIDGE DICTIONARY OF PHILOSOPHY 829–30 (1995)).

80. KANT, CRITIQUE OF JUDGMENT *supra* note 58 at 450. *Please note that all page references to the work of Immanuel Kant at to 'Academy' page numbers that are available in most translations of his work.*

81. In her essay Harlow (*supra* note 55) defines four senses in which the value of nature might be considered "humanly independent" (at 28). To quote her "(1) we might want to say that the value of natural objects and processes is not reducible to human interests and preferences; (2) we might want to say that the value of natural objects and processes is not reducible to the value of human experiences or form of consciousness excited by them; (3) we might want to say that the value of natural objects and processes is independent of human good; or (4) we might want to claim that the value of nature and its processes is independent of human consciousness altogether" (*Id.*). Our argument is that rather than being a classically anthropocentric ethics, Kant's moral and political thought sup-

Although the first of these justifications for our duty to nature values the environment as instrumental to humanity, Kant's definition of instrumental, and what ends justify the instrumental use of nature, is unique and unconventional. For Kant, our instrumental duty to nature is brought about by our intrinsic duty to ourselves and is neither consequentialist nor want-regarding. Rather, it is concerned with the moral ideal of human integrity, which requires a sound environment and regulated use of resources, as it requires justice that serves the essential needs of all generations of human beings.

The second justification attributes a human duty to nature as a distinct component (with humanity) of Ecosystems[82] as wholes. Kant defines Ecosystems as the dialectical interface between human and natural systems making-up the whole biosphere or world system.[83] Our duty is to the intrinsic value of nature as a functional entity that has a capacity, ability, and purpose of its own, which has created us and of which we are the highest expression.[84]

From within Kantian Philosophy, humanity, being the most prominent moral and strategically rational species on the planet, has duties to nature not only because the environment affects human moral agency but also because of nature's existence as a functional end-in-itself. Thus, human consideration of integrity and its moral demands on how a person conducts individual and collective—political life will generate environmental policy which not only conserves nature as it essentially affects humanity but also preserves evolving natural systems, functioning independently of human concern.

1) Kantian Conservationism

A superficial reading of Kantian philosophy, as it regards nature and natural systems, begins with the contention that Kant is an anthropocentric or human-centered "rationalist" with an ethics that grants intrinsic moral value only to humanity.[85] Only

ports the independence of nature on all of these counts. Even the last, which, while it does not make sense in terms of the moral value of nature, which is impossible without human consciousness, makes sense for Kant in terms of the prior independence of time, space, and organic organization in a scientific or theoretical sense. See IMMANUEL KANT, CRITIQUE OF PURE REASON (Norman Kemp Smith trans. & ed. 1929).

82. Here "Ecosystem" is not understood as a synonym for nature but is the combination of human systems and natural systems. Our use of biosphere is also non-traditional in this same way.

83. For a look at world systems see ERICH JANTSCH, AND CONRAD H. WADDINGTON, EVOLUTION AND CONSCIOUSNESS (1976).

84. LEWIS WHITE BECK, A COMMENTARY ON KANT'S CRITIQUE OF PRACTICAL REASON 161 (1960).

85. ROBIN ATTFIELD, THE ETHICS OF ENVIRONMENTAL CONCERN 20–33 (1983).

humans are moral ends-in-themselves,[86] therefore we are the only intrinsically valuable life form. All other living systems exist to instrumentally support humanity in its search for moral perfection.

> Our duties toward animals are indirect duties toward humanity.[87]

> If a man has his dog shot because the animal is no longer capable of service, he is not in breach of duty to the dog, for the dog cannot judge, but his act is inhuman and damages in himself that which he ought to exercise in virtue of his duties to humanity.[88]

These assumptions about Kantian environmental—resource ethics are essentially true, but it does not follow that an environmental ethic therefore does not exist, or that it grants no intrinsic value to nature. Kant does ascribe ethics to humanity alone. This is logical, for mankind is the only species whose capacity, ability, and purpose has moral content which allows him to judge and act ethically. Kant, as all moralists are, is anthropogenic in taking a human, that is, an *ethical* point of view. Only humans are ethical ends-in-themselves with the capacity to recognize their duty, and the ability to take on obligations and perform them purposively, to create a just world.

Kant's concern is the distinction between the realm of ends and the realm of nature. The former is the world of human systems where individuals count because they are the focus of intrinsic value. The latter is the world of natural systems where intrinsic value is concerned with functional wholes which are the units of evolution and the focus of human duty. The individual animal or plant has functional value only as part of a greater system and not in-and-of-itself. This is why Kant states that our duties to individual animals can only be a duty to oneself. By discounting individual creatures, however, Kant does not simultaneously discount nature and its functional systems as having intrinsic value.

The human moral purpose in perfecting one's freedom or integrity is to take a higher-level control over one's life. The definition of human intrinsic value can attach concepts like duty, right, and justice to human conduct.[89] The second point however,

---

86. IMMANUEL KANT, GROUNDWORK *supra* note 58 at 427–29.

87. IMMANUEL KANT, LECTURES ON ETHICS 559 (Peter Heath, ed., J.B. Schneewind trans., 1997 [1755]).

88. *Id.* at 459.

89. Logicians call it a category mistake when one uses a term to connote a quality that a particular class of actors does not have. In this way to say that an animal has rights is like saying snow has a consciousness. Although it can be a logical and moral possibility that a human acted unjustly in killing another living entity, it may make neither logical nor moral sense to say that a wolf acted unjustly when it killed its prey, or should be held responsible for murder.

that is incorrectly drawn from the first, is that due to this moral distinction, all other species and natural systems are outside the pale of moral duty for humanity and can be used by mankind, at will, as instrumental values to supply his wants.[90] The important distinction here is between being inherently moral and being the subject of moral duty for those who are. While nature can never be the former, this does not disqualify it from being the latter.

As the instrumental value argument goes, with "personhood,"[91] which is the dominant force in ethics, "[e]verything other than a person can only have value for a person ... if x is valuable and not a person, then x will have value for some individual other than itself."[92] Therefore any moral argument (including Kant's) that is based on the "dignity" or "intrinsic value of man"[93] is antithetical to any environmental ethic which attributes a distinct and intrinsic value to the natural ecology and its component parts.[94]

Kant, although he grants no inherent moral status to nature, never recommends waste, exploitation, or cruelty to the natural world considered as a system.[95] These are all immoral acts against our ethical duties to ourselves and others.[96] Within this reading of Kant, one can argue that nature is still only 'instrumental' to human ends, but Kant's use of instrumental is unconventional because it is concerned with more that the mere *use* of nature to increase human utility.

For Kant, even if natural systems do not have intrinsic value (which we will shortly argue that they do) but only instrumental value, this still does not allow humanity to treat nature and its components merely as means to any and all of their subjective preferences. Kant's individual is required to function within the categorical imperative and has ethical duties to themselves that concern both their animal nature and their character as a moral

---

90. PETER SINGER, ANIMAL LIBERATION 231–32 (2nd. ed. 1990), TOM REGAN, MATTERS OF LIFE AND DEATH (1980).

91. H. J. McCLOSKEY, ECOLOGICAL ETHICS AND POLITICS 59 (1983).

92. Gregory Vlastos, *Justice and Equality* in SOCIAL JUSTICE 48–9 (Richard B. Brandt, ed. 1962).

93. William K. Frankena, *The Concept of Social Justice* in SOCIAL JUSTICE 23 (Richard B. Brandt, ed. 1962).

94. K. E. Goodpaster, *From Egoism to Environmentalism* in ETHICS AND THE 21ST CENTURY 26–28 (K. E. Goodpaster and K. M. Sayre, eds. 1979).

95. IMMANUEL KANT, THE METAPHYSICS OF MORALS 442–444 (Mary Gregor trans. & ed. 1996 [1797]).

96. The only specific reference he makes to the mere use of nature is in human use of those natural products that they grow themselves with the help of civil society (*Id.* at 344–46). These "natural products" which are considered "artifacts" of human social production are reduced to the status of things only by their existence as artifacts. However, in general, the components of natural systems, especially in the wild, are not classified as artifacts.

being.[97] Within one's duties to these dimensions of human character, permissible and non-permissible uses of nature can be defined within Kantian Conservationism.

Immanuel Kant's Categorical Imperative

Kant's assumption is that the ***categorical imperative***, otherwise known as the ***moral law*** is universal and necessary to the full development of practical reason in each person.
It has three component parts, each building and strengthening the last.

➤ The Form of the Moral Law: (Universalization Clause or Universal Law Formulation) "Act only according to that maxim by which you can at the same time will that it should become a universal law."

The Law of Nature clause of the categorical imperative is a standard insuring that one's maxims adhere to the moral law by not violating it. It is negative in that it tells one what is immoral without being able to distinguish between a moral and non-moral act. **THE QUESTION REMAINS:** Now that one can distinguish what is immoral, what standard allows one to tell the difference between a moral act (required by the categorical imperative) and an non-moral act (not so required)?

➤ The Material of the Moral Law: (Necessity Clause #1—Humanity or End in Itself Formulation) "Act in such a way that you always treat humanity, whether in your own person or in the person of any other, never simply as a means, but always at the same time as an end."

To supplement the universalization test and provide a thicker standard by which to make finer distinctions within the decision process, the concept of the individual rational human being as a non-producible end-in-himself is introduced. The concept of the end in itself provides an independent and necessary grounding for the maxims of the will and adds enough strength to make the distinction between a moral act that promotes the persistence and perfection of ends in themselves, and the non-moral act that does not involve humans as nonproducible ends. The material of the moral law—the end in itself clause—however, provides a necessary strengthening standard but two distinct incentives, both of which are necessary to the proper application of the categorical imperative in the real world: a) to refrain from interference with others as ends; b) to promote one's self and others as ends. **THE QUESTION REMAINS:** How can the negative and positive incentives of the materials clause of the moral law be harmonized and made real in one's decisions? How can one be sure one promotes the moral law?

➤ The Determination Clause: (Necessity Clause #2—Kingdom of Ends Formulation) "All maxims as proceeding from our own making of law ought to harmonize with a possible kingdom of ends."

This clause provides the individual with the moral law's thickest version of its requirements and a full manifestation of the individual's duties toward himself and others. If the maxim of an act of will (or the resulting choice), is not in harmony with one's ends and the ends of others (what is subjectively necessary to their full realization of objective capacity) so that the act of will respects and promotes the ends of all in a harmony of freedom, as in a kingdom of ends, then it is not a moral act of will. Consequently, we cannot expect the act to be respected as one that comes from the moral law. While the realm of ends is a moral realm and is inaccessible to political institutions, it provides the moral ideal for justice and the legitimate state, which are themselves necessary to the full development of the categorical imperative as a moral ideal.

©J.M. Gillroy 2008

---

97. *Id.* at 420.

When nature is 'instrumental' to one's perfection and preservation as an autonomous moral agent, then one's relationship with nature is not want-regarding but ideal-regarding and predicated on the role resources play in empowering one's integrity. The reinforcing and "transformative value" of nature is critical here.[98]

Nature plays a role in reinforcing humanity's value through empowering one's capacity to see beauty, show kindness and consideration, and act justly. When one acts so as to treat nature with respect, the use of practical reason in its application to the person is honed. In addition, nature empowers the integrity of the individual by transforming his preferences to those more compatible with the moral law. If we believe ...

> ... that experience of nature is a necessary condition for developing a consistent and rational world view, one that fully recognizes man's place as a highly evolved animal whose existence depends upon other species and functioning ecosystems ... such experiences have transformative value. Experience of nature can promote questioning and rejection of overly materialistic and consumptive felt preferences.[99]

Instrumental use of nature, from a Kantian point of view, is not consequentialist but non-consequentialist and finds its moral value in the maxims which recognize one's joint duty to seek excellence in oneself and justice for society.

> ... unresponsiveness to what is beautiful, awesome, dainty, dumpy, and otherwise aesthetically interesting in nature probably reflects a lack of the openness of mind and spirit necessary to appreciate the best in human beings.[100]

The standard is duty to one's basic capacity, ability, and purpose and the role that nature plays in preserving and perfecting the human being.

---

98. BRYAN NORTON, WHY PRESERVE NATURAL VARIETY? 188–191 (1987).

99. *Id.* at 189.

100. THOMAS E. HILL JR., AUTONOMY AND SELF–RESPECT 116 (1991).

From the standpoint of one's physical or animal being and its perfection, the use of resources must fall within the moral law. We are not concerned with human preference, economic efficiency, or one's utility but with the empowerment of moral integrity. In addition, the use of resources must be planned from a timeless and non-relative standpoint as all generations of humanity, all over the world, will require a similar resource base to preserve themselves and their opportunity to perfect their integrity.[101] Therefore, the imperative is to conserve resources with one's duty to justice as integrity in mind. Waste and abuse are immoral and the long-term empowerment of present and future moral agents must regulate humanity's designation and use of nature as a resource.[102]

Within a legal or policy design framework, the role of nature in fulfilling human private and public right requires humanity to treat nature in accordance with the demands of justice. A just state is a necessary, but not sufficient, condition for the realization of the Realm of Ends (the third formula of Kant's categorical imperative) and these conditions include a sound and evolving natural world that provides the physical setting for human moral and political advancement. As justice provides the basic distribution of freedom, nature provides a sound and thriving environment to bring out the best in humanity.[103] With the human consciousness of our role in nature evolves a further appreciation of the independent value of nature as an equal component in the "system of the whole earth," and with this realization, we have the essential conditions for the creation of Kant's Kingdom of Ends.

> . . . as we become more and more aware that we are parts
> of the larger whole we come to value the whole indepen-
> dently of its effects on ourselves.[104]

In the creation of a just political world and its reconciliation with the natural world, we find the roots for more than an evaluation of nature as it is instrumental to humanity. Kant did not write of the Kingdom of Ends as the sole consideration of

---

101. TALBOT PAGE, CONSERVATION AND ECONOMIC EFFICIENCY: AN APPROACH TO MATERIALS POLICY 7 (1977).

102. This might be defined as Kantian Sustainability.

103. Kant's treatment of property and human use of it (*supra* note 100 at 258–71) may hold lessons for the application of the moral law to environmental policy. Specifically the idea that property is a necessary prerequisite to human freedom is a powerful argument for Kantian Conservationism.

104. HILL, *supra* note 99 at 111.

human moral choice; he also writes of a preexisting Kingdom of Nature and the harmony of the Realm of Freedom with the Realm of Nature as necessary to effectuate the "highest good" of the human condition. Here, the unconventional argument for humanity's instrumental use of nature evolves into an argument for human duty to the intrinsic value of nature as an independent element in the greater whole of human experience and moral ends.

> Yet the opposition between nature and culture is to be finally overcome in the creation of "the perfect civil constitution" that would mark the end of political history, creating a new harmony between reason and nature by reshaping the latter in view of the former.[105]

2) Kantian Preservationism

When we posit that human integrity requires the environment to sustain and perfect our moral agency, we must also remember that, for Kant, the realm of nature lives independently of us and is our progenitor.[106] Nature produced humanity, but now that humanity has morally transcended nature we have separated ourselves from the complete control of nature. We are agent causes within a functionally causal world. But what about our duties to nature after human transcendence?

Inherent or intrinsic value can have more than one definition. The intrinsic value of nature is different from the intrinsic value of humanity. Humanity is of inherent value for its unique moral capacity, while nature is of inherent value in terms of its causality and systemic functioning. We can argue about whether nature has rights, but not with the assertion that it is a self-generating, functional system with the capacity for independent evolution. In its function, nature is an end-in-itself. Within the teleology of natural systems causality, evolutionary nature has value, not only to humanity but independent of us.[107]

105. YIRMIYAHU YOVEL, KANT AND THE PHILOSOPHY OF HISTORY 193 (1980).

106. KANT, *supra* note 79 at 427; JOHN H. ZAMMITO, THE GENESIS OF KANT'S CRITIQUE OF JUDGMENT 342 (1992).

107. Two points: First, it is controversial to attribute a "teleology" to nature. This is because one is transferring

Darwin explained the teleological character of the living world non-teleologically. The evolution process is not itself teleological, but it gives rise to functionally organized [natural] systems and intentional agents.[108]

Where humans have a particular capacity, ability, and purpose that grants them moral integrity and intrinsic value, natural systems exhibit a distinct capacity, ability, and purpose that grants them *functional* autonomy[109] or integrity.[110] For this reason, nature has an intrinsic value of its own, and can have an independent ethical standing in human policy decision-making.

A unique element of this Kantian argument is that valuing nature as a functional system not only grants it intrinsic value status, but defines intrinsic value not in human terms (rights, interests, etc.), but uniquely in terms of the specific physical,

what is a moral, goal-directed, agency-based attribute of a person to natural systems. However, as Kant has two definitions of intrinsic value, one for humanity and one for nature, he also argues for two concepts of teleology, the human variant having moral content, while the one used to describe nature is functional. For our purposes, "teleology" applied to nature simply means that natural systems have dynamic and systemic functional properties that change over time, sometimes to more complexity, sometimes to less. We assume with Frank Golly (A HISTORY OF THE ECOSYSTEM CONCEPT IN ECOLOGY (1993)) that the concept of natural systems evolution does not need to be strictly deterministic, and with George C. Williams (ADAPTATION AND NATURAL SELECTION ch. 5 (1966)) that natural systems behavior can be assumed to have a stochastic element that can be compensated for by the model used to explain it. This is not unlike the inclusion of stochastic components in statistical models that predict human behavior (see ERIC A. HANUSHEK & JOHN JACKSON, STATISTICAL METHODS FOR SOCIAL SCIENTISTS (1977)). Stuart L. Pimm (THE BALANCE OF NATURE? 131 (1991)) covers the bases when he argues that "[e]ven the most simple models of population change show a variety of behaviors that include a simple return to equilibrium,

cycles, cycles on cycles, and chaos ...". Overall, from our perspective, teleology or purpose applied to nature is a causal-functional teleology of nature's non-human sub-systems that finds changes of complexity in natural selection where evolution is progressive while it shows elements of entropy. Second, for years there have been efforts (See PATRICK RILEY, KANT'S POLITICAL PHILOSOPHY (1983)) to describe Kant's politics as dependent on his teleology as put forth in his Critique of Judgment. Elsewhere (GILLROY, *supra* note 33) we have argued that Kant's politics does not require his teleology but is a direct outgrowth of his moral theory applied juridically, that is, in terms of a justification of the rule of law. Kant's teleology has its role in building a bridge between the realm of nature and the realm of ends. In this way, consciousness of Kant's two definitions of teleology might be necessary for environmental law and policy design in particular.

108. AUDI, *supra* note 78 at 791.

109. We will avoid the use of the concept of functional autonomy, as with humanity as an agent-cause nature is no longer autonomous, though it does have an independent definition of "functional" resilience and persistence or integrity.

110. KANT, CRITIQUE OF JUDGMENT *supra* note 58 at 373–75.

chemical, and biological characteristics of nature, making the Kantian approach neither anthropocentric nor even anthropomorphic.[111]

Human beings are moral creatures. Kant suggested that humans have one foot in the material world and one in the spiritual.[112] Such placement gives human beings a moral quality; this moral dimension places requirements upon individual will and choice in our dealings with the material world.[113] The substance of the human moral quality is evaluation: the predisposition to place value on entities and make this evaluation the basis of our relationship with that entity. All valuing (produced through maxims) is human and all moral worth is a product of human deliberation and argument. Morality is measured in terms of duty; only humans can have or be responsible to moral duties. Therefore only those persons and things that invoke moral duty will count in human deliberation and ethical choice. The moral realm is a human realm, but that does not mean that humans are the only subjects of moral duty, or that valuation must transmit human ethical characteristics to non-human life (e.g. rights).

Pushing past the surface of Kant's remarks about the duties to non-human forms of life,[114] and examining the essential logic of his structural argument about intrinsic value, one finds a Kantian justification for humanity's relationship to natural systems, based on the intrinsic value of those systems, not as moral, but as functional ends-in-themselves in the greater world system.

The Realm of Nature and the Realm of Ends exist as parallel and interconnected systems of life, each dependent upon the other

---

111. Some ethical approaches to the environment, like Conservationism, places the value of humanity at the center of one's calculations and describes all non-human entities as having value only to the extent they can be used by humanity (e.g. a tree is only board-feet of lumber and a rain forest ecosystem only present and future drugs for human health). It is therefore classified as both anthropomorphic and anthropocentric. Other approaches are only anthropomorphic in that they attribute human characteristics to ecosystems (e.g. rights, duties) but not anthropocentric in that they value humanity and natural systems equally as one natural and interdependent system.

112. IMMANUEL KANT, RELIGION WITHIN THE LIMITS OF HUMAN REASON bk. II § 1 (Theodore M. Greene and Hoyt H. Hudson trans. & eds. 1960 [1793]).

113. Gideon Yaffe, *Freedom, Natural Necessity and the Categorical Imperative* 86 KANT STUDIES 446–458 (1995).

114. KANT, *supra* note 94 at 239–41, 443–44.

for persistence.[115] The duty of humanity is to establish harmony between these realms and to find coordination and perfection in their common evolution.[116] In effect, as the *ultimate* expression of nature, humanity is charged with reshaping both itself and nature in terms of the moral law. Humanity's obligation is to produce the "highest good as the *overall* harmony of experience and morality, or as moral nature ... created by human action (by man's reshaping of the sensuous world in light of a supersensuous idea, and by his creating new social and ecological systems) ...".[117]

Man protects his humanity through an active and just state. We are also responsible to protect and empower the environment as a functional end through an active policy of government regulation by the rule of law. This duty to nature comes from three practical realizations:

1. The moral integrity of humanity and the functional integrity of nature are dialectically interdependent in the greater "whole" or Ecosystem.

2. Human agency and technology presents the greatest challenge to the persistence of this scheme of interdependence.

3. Humanity alone has both the moral capacity and the strategic rationality to express freedom responsibly and innovate or adapt itself so that interdependence with the environment can persist over time and establish the harmony of human and natural realms.

Although humanity remains critical in its role as moral agent, in the realization of harmony, the duty one has is not only to nature in view of the end of man's integrity but to nature as a separate and independent causal component of greater Ecosystems where the interface between humanity and nature requires regulation and where the responsibility to establish harmony is humanity's alone. It becomes immoral for humanity to use a natural system as a means to its ends without simultaneously treating it as a living, functioning, end-in-itself. Respecting nature does not mean that we never use resources or place the environment at risk or

---

115. It is true that, for eons, nature persisted without humanity. Our point is that now, as Ecosystems are made up of the interaction of human and natural systems, each has a dialectic effect on the evolution and persistence of the other.

116. KANT, CRITIQUE OF JUDGMENT, *supra* note 58.

117. This has been characterized as Darstellung or "the externalization of morality in the natural world." See, YOVEL, *supra* note 104 at 70–71.

pollute it. Respect is the recognition that nature exists as a total system with capacity, ability, and purpose for perfection within itself, and by its own biological and chemical standards and processes, which command respect independent of us.

Within Kant's categorical imperative, an individual can morally "use" another person as long as they, simultaneously, respect that person's humanity as an end-in-itself.[118] Through the test of the moral law, humanity can also use a natural system if this use is responsible to the intrinsic value of that system and leaves its functional processes intact and/or enhanced or positively reshaped by the application of the moral law through environmental law.[119]

> Man is no longer a member among other members in nature. Rather, by virtue of his rational consciousness, he now becomes the focal point of nature itself . . . reason . . . makes nature itself possible by imparting a logical structure to it. Human reason thus becomes a world-shaping power.[120]

However, if humanity abuses the functional integrity of the environment so that natural cycles are permanently interrupted, species are lost forever, and natural energy and material cycles fail, natural systems will not persist as natural selection and, therefore, evolution is disrupted. This would be the result of immoral action on the part of humanity, independent of the fact that mankind will eventually cause its own demise by these perturbations.[121]

Therefore, humanity should be responsible and coordinate choices to establish harmony between natural and artificial worlds. As mankind is charged, through politics, to protect and empower the dignity of the individual, we must also, by the same means, endeavor to protect and empower the functional integrity of natural systems for their own sake as well as our own.

But the imperative to *reshape* nature has an active as well as protective meaning. In order to reshape, we must first protect and preserve that functionality that allows natural systems persistence in the first place. But the duty to reshape is one to enhance the

---

118. KANT, GROUNDWORK *supra* note 58 at 428.

119. See YOVEL, *supra* note 104 at 50. Treating natural systems as having intrinsic functional value involves not only a "negative" policy of non-interference but also a "positive" restoration and enhancement policy that empowers natural capacity, ability, and purpose. Without the support of humanity, with its scientific efforts to save species, and reinvigorate natural systems processes, one could argue that nature can look forward to a continued diminution of its component subsystems as entropy overcomes ecosystem organization, homeostasis fails, and evolutionary patterns cease. This may be the true basis of a dialectic of mutualism between humanity and the environment.

120. *Id.* at 136.

121. ROBERT E. GOODIN, THE POLITICS OF RATIONAL MAN 176–77 (1976).

natural capacity, ability, and purpose of nature as we empower our own moral integrity.

Humanity's destiny is dialectically tied to nature as nature's is to humanity's. With the governing of the moral law, in both our consideration of human and natural systems, we have a unique definition of environmental ethics that provides for human action, not only to conserve resources and preserve natural function, but also to empower natural evolution through the restoration and enhancement of natural systems' processes.

The imperative to protect and preserve the functional integrity of nature in resource policy and law might involve any or all of the following: restoring "native" species (e.g. wolves in Yellowstone) and extracting "exotic" ones (e.g. purple loosestrife) from natural systems; not sacrificing nature merely for man's utility maximization; not inflicting synthetic compounds on the environment or technologies that cannot be processed by a systems' natural cleaning mechanisms; keeping all pollution to the minimum necessary for supporting human moral integrity and always within the capacity of the natural system to process waste and cleanse itself; recycling or reusing as much of what we need as possible so that the cost of our technological requirements rests on humanity and not on the productive capacity of natural systems; domesticating species necessary to our survival so that the biodiversity of wild species can pursue their functional end within nature; replacing what we take from the environment as compensation in kind for each ecological sub-system (land reclamation, reforestation, purification of the water cycle, etc.); placing the burden of proof on those who would use nature and not on those who would preserve it from use; "allocating natural resources to peaceful uses and to the real needs of man"[122]; and, most generally, never imposing a risk on a natural system through a resource decision that has a high probability of irreversible or irrevocable damage to its functional integrity when the elective wants or efficiencies of humans are the only issue.[123]

Although nature can destroy itself and has the capacity to allow one species to die and another to continue to evolve, this internal natural selection is part of the unique capacity and potential of nature, therefore part of its functional properties, and a mark of its intrinsic value that man has a duty to protect and empower. Humanity, on the other hand, because it has both tech-

---

122. YOVEL, *supra* note 104 at 196.

123. From a Kantian point of view, respect for the functional integrity of a natural system is a respect for the whole, for the connections between organisms and levels of organization and unlike respect for moral integrity, does not concern each individual organism within a said ecosystem. That is, ecocentric not biocentric.

nologically and morally transcended nature, must innovate with minimal disturbance of the greater Ecosystem. The human capacity for freedom, and not nature's capacity for causal functioning, puts mutualism and the interdependence of human and natural integrity at greatest risk through human perturbation for resource production. This is where our duty lies.

To show proper respect for nature is a subject of justice. Individuals can anticipate the irresponsible expression of freedom through the construction of political institutions within just states, that not only protect and empower humanity, but the intrinsic value of nature. The mandate of the just state working for respect of natural systems can be characterized as the imperative to harmonize the freedom of humanity with the structure and function of nature so that the intrinsic value of each is appreciated and one complements the other harmoniously. In this way, the respect humanity shows itself and nature will be rewarded by the persistence of an environment that provides an evolutionary home, equally, for all human beings, and the life support system in which every person's practical reason is nurtured and perfected. Here, with a consciousness of nature, humanity can use resources without harming essential natural integrity.

Kant's Imperative for Policy Design & Environmental Law

For the policy-maker attempting to be just to both humanity and nature, the two duties can be simultaneously fulfilled by the same environmental and natural resource law. In the process of properly conserving those natural resources that we need for our moral integrity, humanity is ethically required, as a prerequisite, to respect nature as a duty to its unique causal capacity, evolutionary ability, and teleological purpose or potential, that is, its functional integrity. The functional integrity of nature is thus a necessary and primary component of the moral integrity of humanity.

When we make public choices that protect the environment and place the burden of proof on those who would use it to justify use as essential to human ends, we will coincidentally produce the best conditions in which the process of natural selection in nature and the quest for personal moral integrity by humanity both find their highest expression.

The harmony of integrity gives the imperative to humans to regulate their behavior in such a way that we harm neither ourselves nor nature in any essential, that is intrinsic, way. In this consideration however, nature has priority because it is vulnerable in the face of humanity's capacity to technologically innovate.[124]

Kant argues that in "creating man nature has transcended itself";[125] that, in its "ultimate purpose,"[126] nature has put itself at a disadvantage to its human progeny. But because only humanity has a moral dimension, natural systems have a strong call on humanity's moral sensibilities as nature has few options in its ongoing evolutionary gradient climb but to adapt to what humanity imposes upon it.

The overall moral imperative, the duty of man to nature through law and policy design, is to solve the dialectic and harmonize both types of life on earth: functional and moral. Only with proper self-regulation through law will humanity, nature, and the interdependent intrinsic values these represent, persist into the future, where each enhances the other's quality of life. "It may be the persistence of life itself, of which the forms of life (including man) are multiple investments, which provides the environmental imperative."[127]

The only species that can be moral, that can assign value to anything, is humanity. Mankind, under the moral law, assigns an intrinsic value to humanity through the moral capacity to be autonomous and perfect the self as a moral agent. Humanity is also part of the biota, evolved from within the process of natural selection. Placing Kant's theory in an ecological context, humanity is the most complex and perfect product of natural evolution; the highest or ultimate teleological purpose of nature is in humanity.[128] But without human self-regulation, nature can look forward to a continued diminution of its component subsystems until its evolutionary patterns begin to fail.

Overall, the integrity of nature is protected, both as an instrumental resource to humanity and as a functional end-in-itself, through the application of Kant's moral law to individual maxims and to collective juridical law.[129] In considering our freedom and the imperatives of morality and justice, we will not only understand how we ought to relate to one another but how we should best

124. The Kantian approach is more conscious of the unique capabilities of humanity than, for example, deep ecology, where humanity is equal to nature and just another class of organism with no special capacities or abilities. See BILL DEVALL AND GEORGE SESSIONS, DEEP ECOLOGY: LIVING AS IF NATURE MATTERED (1985).

125. JON ELSTER, ULYSSES AND THE SIRENS: STUDIES IN RATIONALITY AND IRRATIONALITY 16 (1979).

126. KANT, CRITIQUE OF JUDGMENT *supra* note 58 at § 82.

127. K. E. Goodpaster, *From Egoism to Environmentalism* in ETHICS AND THE 21ST CENTURY 35/fn (K. E. Goodpaster and K. M. Sayre, eds. 1979).

128. KANT, CRITIQUE OF JUDGMENT *supra* note 58 at § 82.

129. ZAMMITO, *supra* note 105 at 332.

handle the Ecosystem interfaces between humanity and the natural world.

Kant states that "... without man ... the whole of creation would be a mere wilderness, a thing in vain, and have no final end."[130] However, humanity's private and public responsibility is also to insure that *with* humanity the world does not become "a thing in vain," but is enhanced by the ethical conduct of its most versatile species.

> This dictum does not mean that the appearance of man as a *natural* being supplies the rest of nature with a teleological center to which all others are subservient. On the contrary, if man were just another link in nature, creation would still be "a thing in vain and have no final end." The universe needs man so that he, as a free and conscious creature, can *confer* its final end on the world and change himself and nature in such a way as to realize it.[131]

A Kantian argument for the Ecosystem Approach to Management is holistic because it grants morally relevant value to nature in terms of both the conservation of resources for human perfection and the preservation of nature's intrinsic functional value as a vital component of the dialectic of greater Ecosystems. Kant supports an ideal-regarding concern for both human and natural perfection and steers environmental law toward increasing harmony between humanity and nature while considering nature as both a necessary element to human freedom and to the "highest good" of biospheric evolution. Kantian philosophy provides just public policy for humanity and nature simultaneously. Beginning with two concepts of intrinsic value he prescribes a policy that considers the environment as an entity unto itself and worthy of equal representation in the public definition of justice and ethical perfection. For Kant, environmental law concerns something that is both essential and public, something best allocated through the expertise of administrative law.

> Nominally, Kant belongs with those for whom man is the center of creation. Yet for Kant man's preeminence is not given and automatically guaranteed; ... man enjoys a central position not by virtue of what he is, but by virtue of what he *ought* to do and to become. He must *make* himself the center of creation by using his practical reason to determine its end and by consciously acting to realize it.[132]

130. KANT, CRITIQUE OF JUDGMENT *supra* note 58 at 442.

131. YOVEL, *supra* note 104 at 180.

132. *Id.*

Kant's universal and necessary, or categorical imperative, requires humanity to overcome fear with morality and utilize intellectually approved principle to navigate in a world of uncertainty. In this search for moral integrity, humanity not only finds itself, and social justice, but also a respect for, and harmony with, the natural world. Our application of practical reason to environmental questions requires the equal and conscious consideration of nature as the prior functional component of a greater dialectic, an ongoing evolutionary process.[133]

With a definition of the Kantian world system and its component Ecosystems, containing human and natural systems as these interface and create a biosphere compatible with the demands of the moral law, we now have a justified base upon which our alternative law and policy design argument for ecosystem management can be built. This standard and its resulting paradigm and context model can now define a just resource policy as one that equally considers the intrinsic requirements of both humanity and nature; that is, one that considers what autonomous choice demands of the moral agent dealing with environmental media, resources, and species as well as with one another.

We have defined what it means to be a practical reasoner within an Ecosystem and have used Kant's argument to present a philosophical justification for the ecosystem model on the basis of its definitions and logic. We have argued that intrinsic value based on capacity, ability, and purpose is the source of respect for both nature and the practical reasoner. We have derived Kantian duties to nature as well as humanity, in the person that can be the basis for policy design and legal practice. If practical reason informing human agency and choice in the world is the duty of humanity, while evolutionary persistence is the purpose of natural systems integrity, then justice must consider both in its conceptualization, formulation, and implementation of environmental law. Only with this prerequisite will the eventual harmony of a Realm of Ends with a Realm of Nature (Kant's definition of Ecosystem) become a reality.

Using what is now our 'Kantian' Ecosystem Paradigm, we can adopt the methodology of the baseline to affect resource choices and outcomes. For environmental law, protecting integrity moves the burden of proof from the regulators to the resource developers and supports the use of standards to protect basic human agency and the physical integrity of nature in the face of collective assaults from market extraction, production, and disposal.

Differences will exist between the characteristics of the standards which, in this case, would be national or international and

133. KANT, CRITIQUE OF JUDG-
MENT *supra* note 58 at 449fn.

consider Ecosystems as wholes, and the degree to which the market should be regulated to provide for flourishing human and natural systems, rather than their minimal existence (which is the sole concern of Kaldor efficiency). Using the baseline function, the intrinsic value of functional natural systems is what is at stake in policy design. Preference or the superficial freedom of consumer choice are consequently not as important as empowering those essential components of the baseline function that assure each and every person's freedom as expressed in their essential capacity to choose. All policy choices are subject to an ideal-regarding test: is this alternative a means to the end of protecting the intrinsic value of humanity, or nature, or the harmony of both?

When resource use and environmental contamination are a collective threat to the intrinsic value of integrity, they should be considered a public phenomenon that can inhibit moral agency. When consideration of the intrinsic value of humanity and nature is essential in the resource decision, it should be protected and empowered by public choice. In light of such threats, the policy priority is to regulate extraction, especially on public lands, limiting the use of nature before it enters the economy or becomes waste. This can be done only by controlling what is used and how it is extracted *ex ante*. In this way, law can anticipate the negative externalities of the market and protect ecosystems. Such an imperative also produces duties and rights that take precedence over maximization of wealth and the processes that produce this wealth. These imperatives promote the needs of the *public* citizen as practical reasoner over the wants of the *private* consumer as rational maximizer.

No longer driven by market assumptions and principles, the state becomes independent and active in the provision and maintenance of collective action, and in the protection and empowerment of individual moral agency to which ecosystem integrity contributes. Resource choices become public as opposed to private concerns, not relegated solely to individual calculation. It is incumbent on the state to define which resource decisions are collectively acceptable and which are not, based upon the requirements of the baseline function, to inform each citizen what the risks of any particular choice are, and to provide for the regulation of those risks that would inhibit moral agency and therefore the individual struggle for integrity.

This Ecosystem Approach elevates the intrinsic value of humanity and nature over the instrumental value of things and gives paramount importance to the creation of that public reality which empowers the expression of moral agency and the flourishing of natural systems integrity. The environment of the political community, its capacity to persist and stop the exploitation of some of its citizens by others, may require that all risk-producing activity that causes collective damage to environmental security be justified as supporting moral-baseline needs before it can continue. This is a prescription for a *resource-conscious* society, where each environmental decision is analyzed by experts for its capacity to empower individual integrity and natural systems functioning before it is allowed to consider profit or willingness-to-pay. These priorities elevate administrative law over common law as proper sources for policy implementation.

We protect our humanity through an active and just state. We are also responsible to protect and empower the environment as a functional end through an active policy of government regulation. This duty is a Kantian duty which comes from the practical realization that the moral integrity of humanity and the functional integrity of nature are interdependent. Also, within this dialectic, human technology presents the greatest challenge to the persistence of the scheme of interdependence and that humanity alone has both the moral capacity and the strategic rationality to express freedom responsibly and innovate or adapt itself so that the environment can persist and law can establish the harmony of human and natural systems.

Although humanity remains critical in its role as moral agent in the realization of a harmony of integrity, the duty one has is not only to nature in view of the end of man's moral integrity, but to nature as a separate but dialectically engaged causal component of a global Ecosystem. Here, the interface between humanity and nature requires regulation where the responsibility to establish harmony is humanity's alone. It becomes immoral for mankind to use a natural system as a means to their own ends without simultaneously treating it as a living, functioning, end-in-itself. Respecting nature does not mean that we never use resources or place the environment at risk or pollute it. Respect means recognizing that nature exists as a total system with capacity, ability, and purpose for evolution within itself, and according to its own biological and chemical standards and processes. Law and policy design should respect the idea of this total system, independent of humans or our wants and before these are added to the mix.

The overall moral imperative, and therefore humanity's duty to nature through legal regulation, is to harmonize both types of life on earth: functional and moral. Only with proper self-regulation will humanity, nature, and the interdependent intrinsic values these represent persist into the future, sure that each enhances the other's quality of life. "It may be the persistence of life itself, of which the forms of life (including man) are multiple investments, which provides the environmental imperative.''[134] The Ecosystem Approach to Management based on Kant's Philosophy grants morally-relevant value to both humanity and nature and considers each, and both together, holistically, as complex dialectic components necessary to the perfection of the global Ecosystem.

The Resources–to–Recovery Context Model

As with the market, a context model built from the Ecosystem Paradigm provides a map of the policy design space that the theoretical paradigm entails. This map also defines an alternative approach to legal reasoning by providing a worldview that sets the priorities, relationships, and parameters of acceptable policy tactics and practical choice. A model of the worldview created by an Ecosystem Paradigm will examine the policy space and the design approach entailed by the new paradigm and replace the Traditional Sector Approach with a new conceptualization of the human—natural systems relationship.

1) Toward an Ecosystem Context Model

When applied to natural resources, the Ecosystem paradigm requires that the intrinsic value of humanity and nature have pride of place when law and policy design is used to assess the ends of public choice. Specifically, the maxims and methods of analysis prescribed for empowering the harmony of human and ecosystem integrity require supplanting concern for the instrumental value of human or environmental welfare with a universal and necessary concern for the intrinsic value of humanity and nature. In empowering integrity, a resource policy-maker should consider both the moral integrity of human systems and the functional integrity of natural systems. We can construct our context model from this new core concern.

Defining government as a market surrogate supporting and empowering market forces, while facilitating the immediate (TSA–I) or long-term (TSA–II) economic use of nature, is no longer supportable as a worldview for the Ecosystem Paradigm. The context model for Kant's Ecosystem Paradigm treats nature as a systemic and whole entity. Under this priority, its components are valuable first, because they support functioning natural systems, and second, because they can be resources or media for human use. On this basis, the legal relationship between humanity and nature requires a holistic approach to law that respects the inherent dialectic (human-nature). *Ecosystems* require more than dichotomous natural resources and pollution abatement law. They should

---

134. GOODPASTER, *supra* note 126 at 35, fn.26.

have an integrated and systemic *Ecosystem Law* that takes the dialectic between freedom and nature as a point of departure and is aware of the range of human—environmental interfaces that make for a comprehensive regulatory milieu.

Toward this end, our conception of human systems must also change. No longer will human contact with the environment be measured solely by extraction for use. Nor will human actions and artifacts receive automatic priority over natural systems functioning. Within human affairs, a focus on instrumental value will be replaced by an imperative to protect and empower integrity and therefore the burden of proof will be placed upon those who would risk it. Before public choices are made, legal arguments must be persuasively made as to what values (instrumental or intrinsic) are involved, and to whom or what (humanity or nature) these values apply. These arguments are necessary for determining what is the best policy for simultaneously protecting the essential value of humanity and the natural world.

The Ecosystem Paradigm requires us to define a responsible state, not as one that responds to consumer wants as expressed in markets, but as one with the capacity to anticipate harm to intrinsic value and prevent it. The state is the facilitator of integrity and all human systems (including the economy) should be considered artifacts created to enhance the quest for a harmony of human and natural systems. We have replaced isolated environmental sectors and human institutions with integrated human and natural systems and the generation of wealth with the empowerment of integrity, which should now motivate law and policy design.

With integrity as the core principle, the Ecosystem Paradigm's context model will be composed of two major entities, each with a distinct intrinsic value: human moral systems and natural functional systems. The intrinsic value of each of these components and how they can be enhanced without the major diminution of the other becomes the occupation and concern of lawyers. Because our duties to nature become tied to our moral duties to humanity, the priority of this context model is the protection and empowerment of nature's functional integrity as a prerequisite to an ecosystemic harmony of ends.

We have redefined 'Ecosystem' to include the interaction of human and natural systems, where human moral evolution beyond the confines of nature charges us with a responsibility to natural systems defined both as duties to ourselves and to nature as a functional end-in-itself. These duties produce a context model in which human and natural systems are dialectic and co-equal components characterized by both biotic (organic) and abiotic (inorganic or constructed) elements.

Human systems are now defined in terms of community, state, and economy, where the state is the major regulator of markets, individual action, and collective ends. We assume that in seeking integrity, individuals form built communities, synthesize technology, and create economies and political frameworks to achieve collective action. These artificial constructions form the **abiota** of human systems, allowing us to generate energy, transmit energy, and define ourselves and our systemic relations as people.

The moral agency of people is the primary **biotic** value in the consideration of human systems and their evolution. Integrity defines both the intrinsic value of the person and the political value of law and institutions as they protect and empower humanity in the person. Human beings and their political, social, architectural, and economic constructions define both the biological and artificial substance of human systems.

However, humans are 'of nature' and their freedom begins with, and is perfected through, their basic duties to nature. The other major component of the Ecosystem Paradigm's context model is nature, from which we came and to which we owe the genesis of our moral capacities, abilities, and purposes. Natural systems can be described in terms of their *biota* and *abiota*; integrating individual natural systems into interconnected sets of Ecosystems as they are confronted with the individual and collective actions of humanity.

Here we have a full manifestation of the ***Ecosystem Approach*** that the USFS and other land agencies seek to apply. Now the principle of efficiency matched with multiple-use management can be fairly challenged by the principle of integrity preservation and ecosystem management. If the interaction of human and natural systems creates the Ecosystems in which we live and interact with nature, then the condition of these Ecosystems ought to define human responsibility and, therefore, determine public policy and natural resource extraction.

Within this reordered context model, all tactical considerations of constraints, feasibility, or pitfalls, in policy arguments, must consider how human wants and needs bear on a world shared with nature, a world in which we bear moral responsibility to the environment as a functional end-in-itself. Those who use the environment will now bear the burden of proof to show that their use is moral and permissible, considering our collective responsibility to create a legal harmony between humanity and nature.

Our new model, with its redefinition of components, reorganizes the context of law and public choice. Specifically, the model treats human and natural systems as worthy of protection and empowerment by government. Furthermore, the priority between these components, as well as concerns for constraints and feasibility, have both been reconstituted by the shift of the burden of proof to those who would use the environment for private gain. For all the reasons so far stated, this new context model can no longer sectorize nature and consider its market uses, but should sectorize our own abiotic interfaces with the environment and harmonize these with nature's integrity and, in this way, with our own integrity.

2) A Resources–to–Recovery Framework for Ecosystem Argument

With human and natural systems that form Ecosystems, we have the major components of our practical context model. The model is built on the notion that the contact between human and natural systems, and the condition of these Ecosystems, ought to determine policy. The interface between human and natural systems can be represented by the **Resources–To–Recovery Model** first suggested by Campbell–Mohn.[135]

In taking a natural systems perspective, the **Resources–To–Recovery** approach examines human contact with nature by focusing on those human processes that change or modify nature's functional integrity. Instead of dissecting the environment into species, minerals, and media for use, human contact with the environment is configured into interfaces defined by our choices regarding extraction, production, and disposal. Each of these points of human contact with natural systems (that create Ecosystems) are of concern because they pertain to decisions about how, why, and whether we should use the environment for our own purposes. These points of interface represent ethically-critical decision situations; our duties to ourselves and to nature come into play such that our collective policy respects the intrinsic value of the human and natural systems involved and how they create resilient Ecosystems.

The Resources–To–Recovery context model reflects this new perspective because it integrates resources and pollution law, considers all the effects of human action on the functioning of nature as a whole, and replaces the piecemeal and media-by-media approach to environmental law with an integrated and systemic approach. Now all law that pertains to extraction decisions must be considered comprehensively, not on a species-by-species or a mineral-by-mineral basis. All law related to manufacturing or construc-

---

135. CELIA CAMPBELL–MOHN ET AL., ENVIRONMENTAL LAW: FROM RESOURCE TO RECOVERY 51–71 (1993).

tion and its pollution, and to the use of nature, becomes one concern. Disposal, along with reuse and recycling, becomes an integrated subject because these activities impact nature as a functional whole, and therefore bear on the way we regulate ourselves through the law.

We now assume that human systems interface natural systems through three pathways or steps. Each has its own effect on functioning natural systems and each requires comprehensive regulatory decision-making in the areas of preservation or conservation.[136]

> Each of these steps is divided into several parts. The laws that govern extraction are divided into laws defining areas that are off-limits to extraction, laws allocating resources for extraction, and laws governing the extraction process. Laws that govern the manufacturing process are divided into laws governing the process itself, laws governing the products manufactured, and laws governing information. The laws that govern disposal of the product include the laws governing recycling and waste disposal.[137]

In other words, in those decisions that may change the make-up, disposition, or condition of a pre-existing natural system (or group of ecological systems), human and natural systems interface, and our duties to nature and ourselves must be considered.[138]

Each of these interface pathways connects to the other in a hierarchy that originates with the decision to use nature as a resource, continues through the decision of how to use resources while minimizing the technological effects of our manufacturing and construction techniques, and concludes with the decision to reintegrate waste back into the environment.

For extraction decisions, we must define what parts of nature to consider a resource and what to consider part of the environmental commons that "preserve[s] the functioning of natural systems."[139] We should also decide who will extract these resources, and how. Finally, we must decide how to keep the process of

---

136. Conservation assumes use but spread over time in a sustainable way.

137. CAMPBELL–MOHN, *supra* note 134 at 53.

138. We are not responsible, nor do we owe a duty to ourselves or nature, when it is not our agency that is effecting nature. If a hurricane destroys a wetland, we are not morally responsible to restore the wetland. Under these non-agency conditions, restoration or protection is not a matter of justice but a matter of benevolence or beneficence, a good act, but not one carrying a moral or juridical imperative. Dysfunction caused by the interaction of natural systems, as when a lightening storm ignites a forest, is also outside of our moral obligation. Fighting the fire would require considering other than our moral duties to nature.

139. CAMPBELL–MOHN, *supra* note 134 at 54.

extraction from becoming too destructive to nature and/or humanity.

For manufacturing, we need to decide the best way to use extracted resources. What technology will have the fewest effects on nature and what standards will regulate the pollution generated from the processes of fabrication? We need also to decide what products human moral integrity requires, under what conditions these should be used, and which have the least potential risk. In addition, we must address what information should be provided to citizens about these products, their use, and the available substitutes.[140]

For disposal, we as citizens, through the just state, are responsible for monitoring disposal and regulating what is disposed, when, where, and how. In order to minimize our effect upon nature, it is our responsibility to reuse and recycle as much as we can, and to fabricate long-lasting and non-disposable products whenever possible. We must also be able to regulate risk within a system of law that does not discriminate by size of risk or ease of regulation, but only by the moral need to impose the risk. Is generating the risk essential? Currently, environmental law (specifically RCRA and CERCLA), places a severe regulatory burden on big business and industry, a less rigorous series of rules on small business, and appears indifferent to individual use and disposal of hazardous products. This variation in regulatory concern is unacceptable within an Ecosystem Paradigm, as it is not the source of the hazard but its potential harm to intrinsic value that should be the focus of law and regulation.

If we build the Resources–To–Recovery Interface from our Ecosystem Paradigm as its context model, then we supply the moral prerequisites of a core concern for intrinsic value, a focus on the moral integrity of humanity and the functional integrity of nature, a definition of duty to these values, and we place the duty with the only party that can bear it: humanity. The combination of Ecosystem Paradigm and the Resources–To–Recovery context model creates a new view of the world within which a policy design can be legislated and law codified.

---

140. Information is of special significance within the strategic context of an assurance game, as one's choice of whether or not to cooperate is based upon what you think the other players will chose.

The Resources To Recovery Context Model

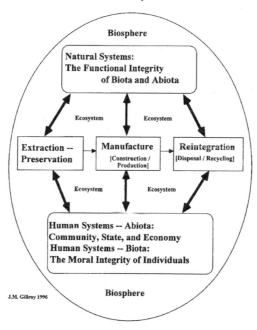

J.M. Gillroy 1996

In constructing this fully-integrated paradigm and context model, we have defined our Ecosystem Approach and provided decision-makers with a new strategic orientation for comprehensive policy argument about the environment. We have also redefined the terms of the debate about the environment in some important ways.

The Ecosystem Paradigm suggests a new truth about human use of the environment. Instrumental use ought to be made conditional on the demands of intrinsic value and the moral law as represented by the harmony of integrity. Whether we use one another or the environment, and although humans may use both in their expression of freedom, any use must also maintain respect for humans as moral ends and nature as a functional end-in-itself. Exploitative use is the premier preference for the individual deciding within a prisoner's dilemma context. But it is neither the predisposition of humanity approaching the environment within the context of an assurance game and with our duties to nature foremost in our mind, nor does use of any type, remain the core reason for human interactions with nature. Protection and enhancement of intrinsic value, in a harmony of moral and functional ends, now drive ethics, politics, law, and policy design.

Use is best viewed from the perspective of natural systems rather than from the perspective of human economy or market efficiency. If the policy-maker is predisposed to protect and enhance intrinsic value, then the instrumental value of nature has less priority than the requirements of its continued persistence. Use decisions are not one-dimensional. Making decisions about morally acceptable use of nature involves prior non-use choices and consideration of the future (both human, natural, and in terms of the evolution of Ecosystems). Primary questions exist about *a priori* preservation,[141] and the right to use nature only as regulated by public and private responsibilities to justice and the Ecosystem Paradigm. Use is no longer assumed to be normal, while regulation requires justification. The assignment of rights and therefore the burden of proof within a policy argument is now based upon concern for the protection and empowerment of intrinsic value, which places greater weight with natural systems, and requires a persuasive argument and justification in terms of human and/or natural systems intrinsic value, to segregate any sector of nature for use.[142]

The presumption of nature as a functioning whole worthy of our respect also requires us to anticipate our effects upon nature and plan to supply the needs of our intrinsic moral agency only when that does not significantly harm natural systems and therefore the Ecosystems we share. What we use, how we use it, and what alternatives exist to natural materials, must all be considered necessary questions in making environmental policy choices. Any other assumption would allow humanity to use nature as a means only, which would violate our duties to ourselves, to other humans, and to nature.[143] In effect, the distinct characteristics of an ecosystem management approach now have a complete logic and underlying structure to support them. With an Ecosystem Design Argument (paradigm and context model), where the principle replacing sustainability is preservation of integrity, and where a concern for Resources–To–Recovery replaces TSA, we can truly say that an alternative to the market has been created which makes . . .

---

141. Preservation can mean both non-use and the restoration of components of non-flourishing systems.

142. The distinction between intrinsic and instrumental value requires specific assignment of rights to the intrinsic side of the equation, as this is the only way to protect the priority status of human moral integrity and the functional integrity of the environment. Here we would disagree with Ronald Coase (*The Problem of Social Cost* 3 J. L. & Econ. 1–44 (1960)), who describes a world of symmetric instrumental value and suggests that who has rights, or is assigned the burden of proof, is irrelevant to the proper realization of an "efficient" policy outcome.

143. Use decisions are efficiency decisions and do not require any other standards or norms, as when cost-benefit methods uses Kaldor norms to judge both the means and the ends of a policy. However, an argument for non-use does require a standard(s) that are ideal-regarding and focus on either the more than economic instrumental values of humanity and nature, or their intrinsic values. This is necessarily outside the valuation capacity of the Market Paradigm.

▶ Policy For Ecosystems As Wholes Not As Resource Sectors;

▶ Considers Ecosystems As Interdependent Human—Nature Dialectics;

▶ Considers Ecosystems In Terms Of Intrinsic, Not Instrumental Value;

▶ Policy For The Flourishing Of Natural Systems—Not Their Minimum Subsistence;

▶ Law That Assumes The Non–Use Value Of Nature—Where The Burden Of Proof Is On Those Who Would Use The Natural World;

▶ Law And Policy Design That Considers Nature As A Collective And Essential, Not A Private And Elective, Good.

The economic logic that humanity has the moral imperative to use nature to the threshold past which nature breaks down[144] should cease to dominate policy debate and environmental law. Instead, the legal and moral imperative of an Ecosystem Paradigm interferes in the functioning of nature as little as possible, while providing for our essential needs, for the requirements of natural functioning, and therefore for a balanced and intrinsically valuable Ecosystem.[145] If one were to recommend pushing nature to its limits, the only acceptable policy argument would have to identify this alternative as the only way to protect essential integrity, and we would have to take special care to identify the threshold and not exceed it. To see how this would work, let us examine two applications of the Ecosystem Paradigm to environmental policy design and legal practice.

Ecosystem Integrity and the Extraction Decision: The Applied Cases of Wilderness & Wildlife

Applying the concepts of policy design to our case study at the beginning of this chapter, we might conclude that the dominant core of USFS meta-policy is characterized by a core principle of optimal efficiency and a periphery of multiple-use policy with its administrative and management organization functioning according to a TSA view of the world. Now the ecosystem approach is a competitive policy or management model, in the periphery, which is vying with the policy argument of multiple-use but which has not yet succeeded to replace it.

---

144. ROBERT E. GOODIN, THE POLITICS OF RATIONAL MAN 165 (1976).

145. This may require us to reconstruct nature to encourage its regeneration, as it requires us to substitute natural means for artificial ones (wolves to control deer populations instead of hunting).

However, even though the primary resource interface between human and natural systems remains the policy decision to use the attributes of nature to satisfy human needs and wants, let us explore two further case studies in order to see how the legal argument and policy design recommendations might be different employing an Ecosystem Model. If establishing and maintaining our integrity requires us, principally, to do no harm and to protect the integrity of nature for itself and as a component of our own status as moral agents, then how we regulate *Wilderness* and *Wildlife* may provide examples of the status of Ecosystem integrity in the law.

1) Integrity, Efficiency and the National Wildlife Refuge

Human use of refuge areas and the impact of these uses on wildlife management is our focus. In addition to this exposition of law, we are also interested in why a wildlife refuge would allow any human use given its mandate to protect and preserve species and habitat. Surely it is not counter-intuitive to expect that if the intrinsic value or integrity of nature can be accommodated in resources policy, it would be through the designation of wildlife refuges. In fact, one might argue that Ecosystem Law is best expressed in the wildlife refuge, as the extraction decision is absent, while the baseline imperative to preserve system integrity is persuasive.

However, the principle of efficiency, and its TSA context model, are alive and well in wildlife law. The history of wildlife law reveals a struggle for jurisdiction between state and federal governments with a single policy end; the primary concern on both levels is the persistence of species as they have *instrumental* value to humanity. If a concern for other than economic ends arises to affect wildlife law, Congress reacts to reaffirm the principle of efficiency as the core of wildlife policy argument.

The National Wildlife Refuge System is regulated by three statutes: The Refuge Recreation Act of 1962 (16 U.S.C.A. §§ 460k to k4); The Refuge Revenue Sharing Act[146] of 1964 (16 U.S.C.A. § 715s); and the National Wildlife Refuge Administration Act of 1966 (16 U.S.C.A. §§ 668dd–668ee). The three statutes[147] have but one purpose: to provide wildlife (primarily birds) with safe havens

---

146. The significance of this act is that it creates a state-based revenue sharing formula for National Wildlife Refuges.

147. The primary statute affecting wildlife is the Endangered Species Act (16 U.S.C.A. §§ 1531–43). However, other statute law is at the foundation of the refuge system. This law includes the Migratory Bird Treaty Act (16 U.S.C.A. §§ 703–711); the Migratory Bird Conser-

vation Act (16 U.S.C.A. §§ 715–715d, 715e, 715f–715k, 715n–715r); and the Migratory Bird Hunting Stamp Act (16 U.S.C.A. § 718). One can also consider the impact of specific pieces of legislation aimed at particular refuges like the Alaska National Interest Lands Conservation Act (PL 96–487). As in most cases the National Environmental Policy Act (42 U.S.C.A. §§ 4321–61) also applies.

for protection and breeding. The protection of species is, however, not protection for the sake of species integrity, but for the purpose of human recreation, study, and/or other anthropocentric instrumental value.

Some assert that with the enactment of the Endangered Species Act in 1973, species gained rights as part of the moral community in which humans live. Without doubt, the core element of federal wildlife law is the Endangered Species Act (16 U.S.C.A. §§ 1531 [ESA § 2]–1544 [ESA § 18]). However, it is less clear that this statute attributes any rights or intrinsic value to species. The mandate to "preserve" listed species and to designate and protect their habitat[148] may be misleading.[149] For, although only scientific criteria can be used in the designation of a threatened or endangered species (ESA § 3), economic criteria becomes a prominent consideration in designating habitat (ESA § 4), in writing recovery plans (ESA § 4), and in the consideration of exemption from the law under the "economic hardship clause," which appears toward the end of the act (ESA § 10). In addition, since the *Hill Case* (*TVA v. Hill* 437 U.S. 153 (1978)), Congress has established the "Endangered Species Committee" (ESA § 7) which can, for economic reasons, deny a species the protection of the act.

But if intrinsic value is not protected by the ESA, perhaps the refuge system itself empowers integrity. The specific legislation intended to consolidate and administer a National Wildlife Refuge System also contains a set of mandates that support a concern for economy over Ecosystem integrity and betrays the dominance of the Market Paradigm for wildlife policy-makers. In addition to designating these lands for "the conservation of fish and wildlife" (16 U.S.C.A. § 668dd (a1)), the Secretary of the Interior is authorized to "permit the use of any area within the System for any purpose, including but not limited to hunting, fishing, public recreation and accommodation, and access ..." (16 U.S.C.A. § 668dd (d1A)). The only restriction is that these secondary uses "... are compatible with the major purposes for which such areas were established" (16 U.S.C.A. § 668dd (d1A)).

The validity of the "secondary uses" of the Federal Refuge System is first described in The Refuge Recreation Act of 1962 (16 U.S.C.A. § 460k to k4). Here, the "mounting public demand" for

---

148. The Endangered Species Act (16 U.S.C.A. §§ 1531–1544) has distinct sections for designation of species (1533 a and b) and designation of vital habitat (1533 b6C) and the history of the application of the act shows that animals are listed more often than habitat is designated for them. If one assumes that without properly designated habitat the species will have a hard time surviving, the lack of success in designating habitat under the Endangered Species Act makes the refuge system even more vital for biodiversity purposes.

149. JACQUELINE VAUGHN SWITZER, ENVIRONMENTAL POLITICS 298–318 (1994).

the use of Wildlife Refuges is acknowledged (16 U.S.C.A. § 460k), while the act also directs that:

> ... any present or future recreational use will be compatible with, and will not prevent accomplishment of, the primary purpose for which the said conservation areas were acquired or established, the Secretary of the Interior is authorized, as an appropriate incidental or secondary use, to administer such areas ... for public recreation ... to the extent practicable ...[150]

In the written regulations of the Fish and Wildlife Service (50 C.F.R. Ch. I), the "secondary" and "incidental" uses of the Refuge System take up most of the more than two-hundred-and-fifty pages of regulations. In addition to allowing hunting (50 C.F.R. § 32) and fishing (50 C.F.R. § 33), provisions for other land uses such as "feral animal management" (50 C.F.R. § 30) and even mineral and oil exploration (50 C.F.R. § 29C) are established.

Throughout the regulations, this "balance" of secondary uses with the dominant mandate of species protection appears repeatedly. In dozens of individual regulations for individual Wildlife refuges,[151] different species and types of hunting and fishing are specified where the sportsman is constrained primarily by the need for a state license (50 C.F.R. § 32.2—hunting/§ 33.2—fishing). These acts, as regulated, are assumed to be eminently "compatible" with species preservation.

The most interesting and least logical argument for compatibility involves the specific federal regulations concerning the exploration for oil in the coastal plain of the Alaskan National Wildlife Refuge.

> ... It is the objective of this program to ascertain the best possible data and information concerning the probable existence, location, volume, and potential for further exploration, development, and production of oil and gas within the coastal plain without significantly adversely affecting the wildlife, its habitat, or the environment.[152]

Consequently, with the proper special permit (50 C.F.R. §§ 37.11 & 37.23), and the submission and approval of an exploration plan (50 C.F.R. §§ 37.21–.22), and a plan of operation (50

---

150. (16 U.S.C.A. §§ 460k).

151. The characteristics of the process of designating a Wildlife Refuge requires that a separate piece of legislation be written for each one. This is a unique practice and perhaps another hurdle for preservation values. However, this practice does make sense, from within the Market Paradigm, as the land is primarily for extraction and use and you would want as many safeguards as possible to prevent it from being "set aside" from economic use and therefore 'wasted'.

152. (50 C.F.R. § 37.1).

C.F.R. § 37.24), one can search for oil and gas as a "secondary" and "incidental" use of the Arctic National Wildlife refuge.[153]

Why does the federal government allow any human use of wildlife refuges? Is it not sufficient that they exist as in-tact natural systems in order to protect and preserve wildlife? Isn't it counterintuitive to allow hunting and fishing in a wildlife 'refuge' where the natural predatory cycles of nature ought to limit numbers and maintain balance, or, at least where species can find protection from human contact and perturbations? How can land development uses such as oil and gas exploration and extraction be considered "compatible" or "incidental" to the designation of a wildlife refuge?

Common sense suggests that the argument that other "secondary" uses are compatible with wildlife preservation is counterintuitive. In *Webster's New World Dictionary*[154] a refuge is "a place of safety; shelter; protection from danger." To allow hunting and fishing or oil exploration is to allow the opposite consequence, making these refuges dangerous and uncertain places for wildlife.

153. The case of the Arctic National Wildlife Refuge (ANWR) is a good example of the conflict between state desires and federal intentions to protect wildlife sanctuaries. Created in 1960 and divided into a combination of wilderness and refuge in 1980 with the passage of the Alaska National Interest Lands Conservation Act (PL 96–487), it is located in Alaska's extreme Northwest corner. The refuge includes the Brooks Range and what have been called vital habitats for caribou, grizzly, and polar bear, musk ox, Dall sheep, wolf, wolverine, peregrine falcon, and gyrfalcon (173 CONGRESSIONAL QUARTERLY YEARBOOK 1988). The Conservation Act created the regulations that govern oil and gas exploration in the Refuge (50 C.F.R. 37) and banned oil drilling on the designated wilderness within the Refuge but also required the Secretary of the Interior to study the quantity and quality of the oil and gas reserves in the coastal plane (108 CONGRESSIONAL QUARTERLY YEARBOOK 1991). Since then studies have shown that there is an extremely large reserve of oil and gas in this area, "a 95% probability that it contains at least 615 million bbl of oil and a 5% probability that it contains at least 8.8 billion bbl of oil." Lynn Garner, *GAO Confirms Interior Study's Findings on Potential of Alaska's Arctic Refuge*, 43 THE OIL DAILY at 1 (1993). This has set up a contest between the Alaska delegations in the House and Senate and environmental interests in Congress as to whether the entire refuge ought to be designated wilderness and made free from oil exploration or the entire refuge ought to be opened up. This debate has been attached to legislation many times, most recently when drilling in the ANWR became a core part of George W. Bush's National Energy Plan in 2001. The critical dimension of this debate, for our argument about states rights and preservation, is that it is the local Alaskan forces that have pushed the hardest for opening oil exploration, while the federal Congressional Committees have maintained the preservationist paradigm. However, by dividing up the territory between refuge and wilderness the Federal approach has been to allow exploration and state interests to have some "secondary" role in the determination of policy, while the preservation of species and habitat maintains primary value. Here, we have a classic example of federal primary use and state secondary use. In terms of Bush's Energy Policy, this particular component of the policy turned out to be very controversial and, even after the pressures of a post September 11th world were added to the mix, continually rejected by the U.S. Senate.

154. 2d ed., s.v. refuge.

The rhetoric of "secondary use" only becomes reasonable if one assumes the primacy of the Market Paradigm in wildlife policy argument. After all, the history of refuge law and the jurisdictional tension between state and federal government over wildlife conservation has not evolved within a paradigm and context model that supports natural systems integrity and the primacy of preservation, but rather has developed from the core principle of efficiency and instrumental resource use. The optimal functioning of the materials balance motivates the policy-maker; the sector here contains species for use.

Regulation of wildlife in the United States originated in English Wildlife Law which was primarily designed around the conservation of wildlife for the purpose of human utilization.[155] In English Law, wildlife was regulated in a highly centralized manner and by an elite few who controlled real property. These dimensions of English tradition were rejected in America.

American wildlife regulation is decentralized and delegated to the states in what is known as the State Ownership Doctrine.[156] In addition to this Doctrine, which gave states almost total control of all wildlife regulation, wildlife conservation by and for the elite was replaced by a democratic ideal that a wider cross-section of citizens should be able to hunt, fish, and, in other ways, use, extract or "take" wildlife.[157]

The democratization of hunting was so successful that by the end of the Nineteenth Century, many species were nearly hunted out.[158] Again, the materials balance was not maintained by the unregulated market under TSA–I, so government regulators entered the scene. The definition of efficiency changed so that, instead of maximum use of a species (e.g. bison), it became *efficient* only to pursue the *optimal* taking of wildlife over time. The state set the number and type of species for taking so that their numbers persisted. Here again, the regulation does not replace economic values with environmental values, but corrects the materials balance for long-term optimal efficiency. The view of nature seems constant, the motivating principle has not moved away from giving primacy to extraction. Only the terms of efficiency and the inclusion of government in the regulation of the materials balance were new. The original operating paradigm remained with a modified TSA context model.

---

155. THOMAS A. LUND, AMERICAN WILDLIFE LAW (1980).

156. MICHAEL J. BEAN, THE EVOLUTION OF NATIONAL WILDLIFE LAW 12–17 (1983).

157. LUND, *supra* note 154 at 23–25.

158. *Id.* at 58.

The specter of widespread extinction included wildlife species from the white-tailed deer on the East Coast to the bison out West.[159] In response to the propensity of our ancestors to discount the future and over-consume, many state governments and sportsmen's organizations began to regulate taking of wildlife with the establishment of seasons and fees for hunting. Using a *conservationist* rhetoric, policy argument adopted a principle of sustainability, searching for the optimal yield of animals for present and future generations of sports enthusiasts. This *sportsman's* version of the Market Paradigm dominated American Wildlife Law and became the conventional status quo; it laid the ethical foundation and fundamental assumptions of wildlife policy, even when the federal government entered the picture at the turn of the last Century.

Initially, the state's absolute discretion in wildlife law seemed to preclude any involvement of the federal government in animal regulation. The only means the federal government had to establish its jurisdiction was the Constitution of the United States. So federal wildlife law established federal jurisdiction through the treaty, property, and commerce clauses of our Constitution.[160]

Over the years, starting with the Lacy Act[161] of 1900 (16 U.S.C.A. § 701, §§ 3371–3378), and the *Geer* decision of 1896 in the Supreme Court, and ending with the Endangered Species Act (16 U.S.C.A. §§ 1531–1544) and the 1979 *Palila*[162] decision, the federal government has promoted a more protectionist policy regarding wildlife. However, a preservation argument to underlie this effort has not been successfully introduced and a new core principle to motivate wildlife meta-policy has not supplanted the core principle of efficiency. Current policy argument does not yet promote and protect the integrity of species and their habitat as functional ends in themselves, let alone a greater sense of ecosystem biodiversity.

---

159. *Id.* at 60.

160. BEAN, *supra* note 155 at 12.

161. This act took one of the initial steps in the preservation paradigm by utilizing the commerce clause of the Constitution to prohibit the interstate transport of any wild animal or bird that was killed contrary to state law. Notice here that state law still plays a significant role as the point of origin for federal concerns. The power of the federal government in bird conservation comes from their propensity to fly across state lines and invoke the commerce clause of the Constitution. See, for example, Geer v. Connecticut 161 U.S. 519 (1896). The Geer decision recognized that state jurisdiction went only so far and that it could

not conflict with the Constitutional powers of the federal government.

162. See Palila v. Hawaii Department of Land and Natural Resources 471 F.Supp. 985 (D.Ha. 1979) aff'd on other grounds, 639 F.2d 495 (9th Cir. 1981). This decision spread the effects of the Endangered Species Act to its widest venue and defined harm in a most general way that includes harassment and does not require killing or physically impairing the animal. This can be understood as the most significant and widest application of the preservationist paradigm in United States environmental and resource law. However, this approach has not yet been given the blessing of the Supreme Court.

Even in federal wildlife policy, the instrumental value of nature continues to shape the interface of law and extraction.

Efficient human taking remains the key to understanding both the primary and secondary uses of refuges.[163] Thus, although wildlife, as an economic or recreational resource has been supplemented with the proposition that wildlife served other ecological and scientific ends,[164] the reliance on instrumental economic value has remained at the meta-policy's core. Concern for science or concern for ecology are really concerns for data to drive efficient use. Here scientific method is used to discover nature's potential contribution to the economy, as that justification gives the imperative for Market Paradigm law.

The power of the Market Paradigm can also be seen in the state's control of wildlife use. If we consider species and their habitat to have a functional intrinsic value, then our universal duties to them cannot be satisfied by allowing sub-national governments to protect some species, in some places, while others have no moral status as ends. The focus on state dominance is an outgrowth of dependence on individual preference for welfare or willingness-to-pay as the ultimate standard for policy choice. It is only reasonable to allow decentralized regulation if wildlife taking is understood as something that ought to be controlled by contextual market value or state responsiveness to 'local' human preferences. If all natural systems as well as their components are considered to have intrinsic value, then policy design at the federal or even global level is necessary in order to respect what the imperative of integrity demands of a rule of law.

The status of Wildlife refuges represents a conflict between state concerns for the short-term efficient use of wildlife and their habitat and a federal interest in the longer-term protection of both. A federal sustainability ethic, stressing optimal efficiency over time, seems to dominate the Refuge system. This ethic, however, is still coping with the concerns of the states for ample and immediate sporting and other use opportunities. Although we may, as a nation, have decided that long-term sustainability is the central requirement of the refuge system, and although we have been able to somewhat override state concerns for ample recreational uses of wildlife, especially considering endangered species, we also continue to believe that long-term efficiency should . . .

> . . . not be construed as affecting the authority, jurisdiction, or responsibility of the several States to manage,

---

163.   BEAN, *supra* note 155 at 17.

164.   See the Endangered Species Act 16 U.S.C.A. 1531 (a3). Although all of these reasons for preservation are anthropomorphic, they exceed what the Market Paradigm would consider necessary for conservation.

control, or regulate fish and resident wildlife under State law or regulation in any area within the system."[165]

2) Preservation, Conservation, and Legal Wilderness

Within the context of natural resource extraction, the best opportunity for the intrinsic value of nature to determine policy is through the designation of wilderness areas, which is as close as American law comes to recognizing the integrity of whole natural systems. However, here again the concern for efficiency dominates policy. Although a preservationist ethic that includes environmental values is accessible through the idea of wilderness, the American conception of wilderness as foreboding and antithetical to economic prosperity has infused wilderness law and policy with ample veneration for the core value of efficiency and a perception of wilderness as wasted economic resources.

The United States is a settlement colony, founded by people who saw wilderness as frightening and foreboding.[166] The frontier ethic is to maximize economic growth and prosperity and to clear and civilize the wilderness. Security was only to be found in open, organized, and human-dominated spaces.[167] Given the ethical starting point of the association of security with order, and wilderness with disorder and fear, it is curious Americans have any legislation that sets aside wilderness areas at all. Have we converted to an ethic that considers the intrinsic value of wilderness as a central concern, or have we just utilized the designation of wilderness as a means for sustaining the materials balance when it otherwise would have failed?

Consideration of the resource uses of designated wilderness areas on public lands may help answer this question. However, the real subject is not resource use, but whether this use is at all limited, let alone trumped, by a concern for the intrinsic value or functional integrity and preservation of natural areas in a primitive condition. To fully comprehend the roots and constraints of wilderness law and policy, one must understand the moral dimensions of

165. (16 U.S.C.A. § 668dd (c)). A policy debate that reflects this tension is the Clinton Administration's efforts to get Congressional support for a national biological survey. Here the forces for states-rights and private property are allied against the preservationists and, although there is support in the relevant committees for this effort, it was eventually tabled, dying with the advent of the Bush Administration in 2001. See Bruce Babbitt, *Details: Biological Survey* 54 BUREAU OF NATIONAL AFFAIRS.

166. See, for example, RODERICK FRAZIER NASH, WILDERNESS AND THE AMERICAN MIND (1967) and CAROLYN MERCHANT, ECOLOGICAL REVOLUTIONS: NATURE, GENDER, AND SCIENCE IN NEW ENGLAND (1989).

167. GEORGE CAMERON COGGINS ET AL., FEDERAL PUBLIC LAND AND RESOURCE LAW ch. 2 (1993).

wilderness as myth and the negative connotation of wilderness preservation for Americans.

Americans are known in the world for having legally established wilderness areas.[168] However, our statutes and regulations specifically allow many other resource uses that seem antithetical to wilderness preservation. Cognitive dissonance in our wilderness law pits an ethic of preserving nature against a utilitarian ethic that considers a tree protected as a resource wasted and wilderness without human perturbation as a dark and uncivilized place without light.

Wilderness designation has only been formalized in the last thirty-five years. All wilderness areas on public lands in the United States, like wildlife refuges, are now designated by specific Congressional legislation[169] and managed by whatever public lands agency (Forest Service; Bureau of Land Management; Park Service; Fish and Wildlife Service) that supervised its pre-wilderness existence.[170] Although the specific management directives and uses for each wilderness area are contained in its enabling legislation, the wilderness preservation system was integrated and codified by a single statute.

The primary[171] piece of legislation to define wilderness in the U.S. is the Wilderness Act of 1964 (16 U.S.C.A. §§ 1131–36). Among other things, this statute establishes a National Wilderness Preservation System (§ 1131(a)), defines wilderness (§ 1131(b)), specifies how wilderness is designated (§ 1132), and describes allowable uses of wilderness areas (§ 1133).

168. Here we should say "North Americans," as Canada has also set aside wilderness areas. See WILLIAM R. LOWRY, THE CAPACITY FOR WONDER: PRESERVING NATIONAL PARKS (1994).

169. Since the passage of the Wilderness Act of 1964 there have been specific wilderness bills for many states and specific areas including, for example, North Carolina (PL. 98–323, 98 Stat. 259); Virginia (PL. 98–322, 98 Stat. 253); New Hampshire (PL. 98–425, 98 Stat. 1619); the Arizona Desert (PL. 101–628, 104 Stat. 4469) the Mississippi National Forest (PL. 98–515, 98 Stat. 2420) and the Vermont Wilderness Act of 1984 (PL. 98–322, 98 Stat. 253).

170. Larry Anderson & Patricia Byrnes, *The View From Breadloaf: Fostering A Spirit Of Wilderness In The Heart Of The Green Mountains* 56 WILDERNESS 10 (1993).

171. In addition to the Wilderness Act and the specific designation legislation for particular areas, Wilderness designation is also part of the Multiple–Use, Sustained Yield Act of 1960 (16 U.S.C.A. §§ 528–31), the National Forest Management Act of 1976 (16 U.S.C.A. §§ 1600–14) and falls under the Environmental Impact Requirements of the National Environmental Policy Act of 1969 (42 U.S.C.A. §§ 4321–61). In addition the Wilderness Act of 1964 has spawned both second generation general preservation statutes such as the Endangered American Wilderness Act of 1978 (16 U.S.C.A. § 1132) and specific preservation statutes such as the National Wild and Scenic Rivers Act of 1968 (16 U.S.C.A. §§ 1271–87). For an excellent treatment of the passage of the Wilderness Act, as well as what has happened since, see MICHAEL FROME, BATTLE FOR THE WILDERNESS (rev. ed. 1997).

The dominant goal of the Wilderness Act however is the promotion and preservation of nature in its primitive state. Like most resource law, it reflects the understanding that overtaxing the environment through an unregulated market under TSA–I caused scarcity and a resultant need for the conservation of nature so that its efficient use could be *optimized* over time. But, given this realization, should we not have replaced reliance on the Market Paradigm with other standards and policy design assumptions?

The statute originates in the concern that "increasing population, accompanied by expanding settlement and growing mechanization, [should] not occupy and modify all areas within the United States . . . leaving no lands designated for preservation and protection in their natural condition . . ." (16 U.S.C.A. § 1131(a)). Wilderness itself is defined as that "area where the earth and its community of life are untrammeled by man, where man himself is a visitor" (16 U.S.C.A. § 1131(c)).

This preservationist imperative is also evident in the specific regulations that govern the administration of wilderness areas. For example, both the rules governing the Bureau of Land Management (43 C.F.R. §§ 8500 & 8590, here specifically § 8560.0–6) and the Forest Service (36 C.F.R. § 293, here specifically § 293.2) state that management of wilderness should have three primary directives:

U.S. Gov. Wilderness Management Primary Directives

1. Natural ecological succession will be allowed to operate freely to the extent feasible;

2. Wilderness will be made available for human use to the optimum extent consistent with the maintenance of primitive conditions;

3. In resolving conflicts in resource use, wilderness values will be dominant . . .[172]

The primacy of "wilderness values," however, does not mean that the law will not allow or even encourage other instrumental uses.

The Act has specific provisions for the regulation of aircraft and motorboats as well as action to handle fire, insects, and diseases (§ 1133 (d1)). "Mineral Activities, surveys for mineral value" (d2) as well as "mining and mineral leasing laws" (d3) are regulated uses of wilderness, as is water utilization (d4), recreation (d5), limited commercial services (d6) and hunting/fishing activity (d8).[173] Therefore, recreation, hunting, fishing, and even mining are allowed in wilderness areas (16 U.S.C.A. § 1133). Wilderness itself is not set aside for its own sake, but for its "future use and

---

172. (36 C.F.R. § 283.2).

173. The regulations that define and restrict use are found in several places within the Code of Federal Regulations;

For example, see 36 C.F.R. §§ 227, 228; 36 C.F.R. 293; 43 C.F.R. § 19; 43 C.F.R. 8560; 43 C.F.R. 3802 and 43 C.F.R. 1600.

enjoyment as wilderness, and [to] allow for recreation, scenic, scientific, educational, conservation, and historic use" (43 C.F.R. §§ 8560.0–2).

All of these designated uses and the human-centered, instrumental arguments for wilderness have only two restrictions. First, almost all use is limited to that which existed when the land was designated as wilderness.[174] For example, wilderness status does not stop mining outright. The limitation here is that new mining claims will be more severely regulated than any pre-existing operations.[175] Second, each use is immediately made conditional on the primary concern for the "wilderness character" of the land.

> ... each agency administering any area designated as wilderness shall be responsible for preserving the wilderness character of the area and shall so administer such area for such other purposes for which it may have been established as also to preserve its wilderness character.[176]

However, even in regulations for a wilderness study area (a pre-wilderness designation), exploration and mining can be carried out "in a manner that will not impair the suitability of an area for inclusion in the wilderness system ..." (43 C.F.R. § 3802,0–2 (a)). Any mineral leases allowed on wilderness land "will contain reasonable stipulations for the protection of the wilderness character of the land" (36 C.F.R. § 293.14 (b)) and all actual mining operations conducted will include, by statute, "reclamation measures." This re-establishment of wilderness character "shall be commenced, conducted and completed as soon after disturbance as feasible ... and will include ... (1) Reshaping of the lands ... to approximate original contours; (2) Restoring such reshaped lands by replacement of top soil; and (3) Revegetating the lands." (43 C.F.R. §§ 3802.0–5 (a)). Even general access to a wilderness area must be "consistent with the preservation of such wilderness" (43 C.F.R. §§ 8560.4–3 (b)).[177]

174. Mark Pearson, *The Private Parts Of Paradise: Inholdings And The Integrity Of Wilderness* 56 WILDERNESS 20 (1992); Harold K. Steen, *Americans And Their Forests* 98 AMERICAN FORESTS 18 (1992).

175. Compare the statute language of the Wilderness Act at 16 U.S.C.A. § 1133 d2–3 with the stringent regulations for pre-wilderness study areas as outlined in 43 C.F.R. Subpart 3802. Here the specific requirements for a "plan of operations" (§ 3802.1–4) is especially revealing of the greater restrictions on exploration and mining compared with non-wilderness land (compare with 43 C.F.R. Part 3800).

176. (16 U.S.C.A. § 1133 (b)).

177. The most interesting thing about the case law is the general concern of the judges to maintain wilderness values and make their judgments of agency action dependent on the argument made for 'reasonableness' given the preservation standard. See, for example, NAPO v. U.S., 499 F.Supp. 1223 which involves handicapped access to wilderness; Pacific Legal Foundation v. Watt 529 F.Supp. 982 which involves mineral leasing and the actions of the Secretary of the Interior; Minnesota Public Interest Research Group v. Butz 401 F.Supp. 1276 involving logging and

Therefore, other than uses such as mining or grazing (36 C.F.R § 293.7) established before wilderness designation, and some hunting and fishing regulated by state law, any future non-preservation use is strictly regulated. The list of prohibited 'new' acts on wilderness is lengthy and comprehensive. These prohibitions include "commercial enterprises," "temporary or permanent roads," "aircraft landing strips," "use of motorized vehicles and equipment," "landing of aircraft," "dropping of materials, supplies, or persons from aircraft," structures or installations," and "cutting of trees" (43 C.F.R. § 8560.1–2).[178]

It is after wilderness designation that the strictest limitations on economic use go into effect. But how much economic use has already been made of wilderness lands before their designation? Can we truthfully define such lands as "untrammeled"? Are we serious about protecting natural systems in a primitive state or are we simply designating as "wilderness" those lands that have no further resource uses?

Wilderness legislation allows exploration and assessment of resource value, even in designated areas, and the resource status of any proposed wilderness is a major part of the Congressional debate over its designation.[179] This should be expected if economic efficiency is the primary motivation of wilderness designation. One might then assume that only lands found to have no economic value would receive this distinction. In this way, the stricture that resource use must be very closely regulated to be "compatible" with the primary "wilderness character" of the land has few repercussions in the application of the Market Paradigm or the maintenance of the materials balance.[180] The ongoing effort of the Congress to pass wilderness legislation is marked by a consistent and recurring battle between the forces of economic use and the forces of environmental preservation.[181] Many in Congress believe that if public land has any present or future economic value, it

---

Voyageurs Regional National Park Association v. Lujan (1991 WL 3423370 (D. Minn.)) which address the use of snowmobiles.

178. Exceptions are made for those restricted uses allowed in § 1133.

179. LOWRY, *supra* note 167.

180. FROME, *supra* note 170. The only exceptions to this rule are those Refuges which were designated before vast oil or resource reserves were found under them. For example, ANWR has come to be controversial because, since its designation, vast oil reserves have been found which change this barren, frozen, and therefore 'worthless' land,

into "valuable" land. The effort ever since has been to reclassify the ANWR so the oil can be fully exploited.

181. For specific examination of particularly cogent examples of this dialectic, see the Colorado Wilderness Bill (HR 631) see CQ WEEKLY REPORTS, June 19, 1993, at 1564; CQ WEEKLY REPORTS July 3, 1993, at 1732 and in the CQ ALMANAC 1992 at 292. For the Montana Wilderness Bill (HR 2473) see CQ WEEKLY REPORTS, March 19, 1994, at 667; CQ WEEKLY REPORTS, March 26, 1994 at 732 and the CQ ALMANAC 1992 at 289.

should not be designated as wilderness. The focus on optimal extraction persists.

Throughout the legislative record, arguments of those opposed to the designation of wilderness are replete with **fear** about leaving natural systems unused.[182] Resources, it is feared, will go unexploited; decay and depravation will overtake nature; wilderness as chaos will spread unchecked causing devolution of the natural world back toward its original status as a "wasteland" or "dark forbidding place."[183] Like many of our ancestors, wilderness skeptics see disorganization, decay, and terror in those areas "untrammeled by man" and they seek to limit the spread of "waste" and "darkness" by limiting the amount and degree of outright preservation on public lands.[184]

Even though regulations allow prospecting and mining in wilderness, and even though nowhere are these activities unconditionally prohibited by statute, mining journals argue that once a wilderness is defined "no resource exploration will ever again be allowed."[185] A myth exists that wilderness designation will curtail all resource use, forever.[186] Arguments for this point of view are replete with economic regrets, but also offer a polemic that wilderness preservation will forever preclude any prospects for social "order" and "good" will.[187]

With such a primeval ethical position and definition of wilderness, it is not just the economic resources in any tract of land that are of concern, but the idea that property should not be segregated "for all time" as an "untrammeled" natural system. Not surprisingly, legislators opposing preservation saw the 1964 Wilderness Act as particularly "disturbing" because designation of wilderness would mean a victory for disorganization and decay.[188]

182. L.W. Lane, *Wilderness: We're Losing Ground* 172 SUNSET 296 (1984). This point of view was best set out by James Watt in his efforts to open wilderness to oil and gas exploration rather than let them be "abandoned" to decay and destitution. Although he was unsuccessful the argument had its origin in the mythology of wilderness as "horrible" waste and became the central policy argument of Gail Norton, a colleague of Watt's under Reagan and Secretary of the Interior under George W. Bush.

183. *Watt's Reasonable Choice*, BUSINESS WEEK, March 8, 1982.

184. This is the opinion of long-term Congressman Young from Alaska. See for example, CQ WEEKLY REPORTS July 3, 1993.

185. See, *Wilderness Bill "Compromise" A Blow To Area Exploration*, OIL AND GAS, May 21, 1984 at 59.

186. ZACHARY A. SMITH, THE ENVIRONMENTAL POLICY PARADOX 202 (1992). This can be seen in the debate over the Forest Service RARE reports. For those invested in the Market Paradigm, these surveys of roadless public land for consideration of wilderness designation provide a forum for minimizing that land permanently set aside.

187. CQ WEEKLY REPORTS, June 19, 1993; CQ WEEKLY REPORTS, July 3, 1993.

188. CQ ALMANAC 1992.

Overall, the mythology of wilderness has produced statute and regulatory law with many exceptions, conditions, and authorized uses within wilderness areas, and has assured that little potentially productive land will be so designated. Nowhere in the law is there any mention of preserving nature for its own sake. This, combined with a powerful mythology and the conventional fear of profit loss that "wilderness" suggests, has led to setting-aside comparatively little wilderness. Only if future extraction is impossible, or future use inconceivable, is an area obviously fit for Congressional designation as a wilderness.[189]

3) Integrity, Ecosystem Argument, and Preservation

By applying the Ecosystem Paradigm Model I to these case studies, the core argument and practical recommendations for wilderness and wildlife law change noticeably. To preserve and protect the environment as a functional end-in-itself is now a duty of human integrity. Law and policy is now formulated on a predisposition to withhold natural systems from human use unless it can be persuasively argued that the use is necessary for Ecosystem integrity, affirming the intrinsic values of humanity and nature. Justice requires that the intrinsic value of humanity and nature be the primary consideration. Ecosystem Law places the burden of proof on those who would use a natural system to justify that use in the name of the 'will of all.' Law would require them to demonstrate one of two things in order to use nature at the extraction interface:

Human Use of Nature, Ecosystem Paradigm

1. That Human Intrinsic Value Is At Stake And That It Is Imperative That Natural Systems Integrity Be Put At Risk For Our Own (Integrity–Based) Needs ... or ...

2. That Natural Systems Functional Integrity Is Not At Stake In The Extraction And Use Decision.

At this point, economists usually remind us that without use of the environment modern society would not exist, while to establish priorities like those just articulated would all but force us out of our houses and into caves. A switch of paradigms need not produce such drastic consequences.

First, while the comprehensive functional integrity of natural systems is the primary duty of legal regulation within an ecosystem approach to management, this is considered within a context of the human use of nature as an end-in-itself. Second, wilderness and

189. Even the Clinton Administration, which had the most pro-preservationist definition of wilderness in the past forty years, was unable to significantly alter this fact. Clinton ended up using the American Antiquities Act of 1906 (16 USC §§ 431–433) which allows Presidents to create National Monuments, without Congressional approval, to set aside almost as much preservation area on public lands as the father of this legislation, Theodore Roosevelt.

wildlife are legal issues that strategically sort the sources of environmental law to correspond to their character as *public* choices over *essential* goods. This means that integrity and use will be judged by administrative law and expert-driven institutions in the codification and implementation of law and policy design. Such an imperative suggests that separate wildlife and wilderness distinctions are not suitable law. Each natural system as it constitutes an interconnected web of species, minerals, and media cycles ought to be the focus of systematic public policy. Therefore, the priority of the policy-maker is to classify and categorize these natural systems in a kind of biological zoning regime that would separate unique from common systems and "untrammeled" systems from those in which humans already play a major reconstructive role.

Third, most use, if moderate, conscious, and well-planned will not result in significant deterioration of natural systems functioning and may even enhance their resilience and flourishing. Using natural systems as a human resource must be justified, but by defining use in terms of Ecosystem integrity, both our own moral agency and nature's functional wholeness will require us to satisfy our needs in ways that harmonize nature's ends and our own. This approach calls for clean energy, concentration of human use in areas already reconstructed by humanity (e.g. cities), and production processes that create safe results in safe ways with minimal pollution.

Within Ecosystem Law, we can designate use that provides what we need, and takes from nature where it causes the least harm to the intrinsic values involved, perhaps even allowing us to enhance or re-establish the environmental functioning of a used or abused natural system (e.g. wolves in Yellowstone). Our policy and law will strive for use that affects natural functioning the least, and which is constructive toward our own moral agency as it is compatible with the continued wholeness of the environment.

From the standpoint of the Ecosystem Paradigm, a single law is needed that designates **wild areas** and **priority natural systems** and prohibits human use within these designated areas. Such legislation would require administrative law to use its expertise in creating a national biological survey and a new natural systems zoning plan that provides the biological, hydrological, geological, and chemical status for each defined system. With this information as a foundation, all prospective uses would have to be justified by the prospective extractor with concern for human integrity and how it would affect the functioning of pertinent natural systems. Government could, through such a performance zoning scheme,[190] in-

---

190. This is a call not for traditional 'bulk and density' zoning but for performance zoning that plots use in terms of environmental and ecological factors

form prospective extractors of what plots of land, what natural systems, and what components of natural systems are available for use as resources. Each potential user would then be obliged to provide a plan in which extraction techniques as well as quantities and other specifics were detailed. At this point, a government agency would authorize the use or not.

Any proposed extraction plan ought to be comprehensive and focus on both how the use would enhance our moral integrity and what total species and media effects would be forthcoming. It should demonstrate how specific extraction levels and procedures would limit harm to the integrity of a natural system. In addition, such plans would have to specify if the area would be environmentally revitalized *ex post* and how. The more drastic the proposed use the more complicated and costly the planning should be, but in all cases the costs of extraction must account for both the moral integrity of humanity and the functional integrity of natural systems.

Presumably, wild areas and preserved natural systems would only be one designation in the greater national zoning plan, but it would be the most important designation and should allow no use or only emergency use (if no other alternatives were available and humanity was in drastic straits). From this perspective, natural systems are but one component of Ecosystems, protected and empowered through the baseline integrity function. Here, the demands of integrity create both our duties to ourselves and to nature, and, together they require the zoning system to provide evidence for all use and extraction decisions.

Humanity should recognize that in protecting wild areas we are fulfilling our duties not only to nature but to ourselves. The set-aside systems therefore must not be abandoned and economically valueless tracts of land, but natural systems designated for their ecological qualities: systems that are intrinsically (biologically) unique and/or critical to biodiversity (e.g. old growth forest). In addition, because the larger Ecosystem picture is critical, all natural systems, both urban and rural, must be part of a comprehensive zoning inventory. We should never use nature's functional integrity merely as an elective means to our own ends. We must consider the overall health of functioning Ecosystems as we use any particular environmental component of them. Therefore, we ought to concentrate land use in areas that are already utilized for human habitation and set aside areas that to-date have been left relatively undisturbed. The constant human expansion into forests and farm lands for redundant housing is a violation of this duty.

as well as the geography and geology of a place. See DANIEL R. MANDELKER & ROGER A. CUNNINGHAM, PLAN- NING AND CONTROL OF LAND DE- VELOPMENT: CASES AND MATERI- ALS 328–30 (3rd ed. 1990).

Intrinsic value has priority within this paradigm, and the comprehensive health and dignity of the Ecosystem depends on the harmony of human existence with natural systems. Our use should cause minimal harm to the intrinsic qualities of functioning Ecosystems as we find them, and require us to respect their present state, as well as protect them from potential harm to essential functioning, that may be created by any of our extraction plans.

In addition to causing the least harm, the imperative to preserve and empower natural systems functioning places us as trustees of the Ecosystem and its human and natural components. Here, using our Ecosystem Paradigm, property at the baseline is presumed public and can be transferred into private hands only for the expression of essential freedom. To express integrity means not violating our duties to ourselves or others (including nature); this requires that we use private property only for the greater good of Ecosystems. The regulation of private property should fit within the guidelines of providing, protecting, and/or empowering Ecosystem integrity.

We need to adopt a timeless predisposition to the idea that natural systems and their tangible assets are primarily for the ends of environmental functioning and a harmony of integrity. Our national zoning system therefore, would focus on classification of wild areas as a public trust making them unavailable for subjective use based on above baseline wealth (i.e. recreational as opposed to subsistence hunting) or individual profit (e.g. mining, clear-cutting) that systematically exploits either human or natural integrity for elective ends. Although any use of nature that harms its integrity must be justified through the needs of active moral agents, making policy choice by the 'will of all' requires the distribution of any such use profits to those who suffer by the use. This includes nature and its reclamation *ex post*. In wild areas these use strictures must be the tightest. Trusteeship can mean nothing less.

In terms of the baseline function, the imperative is to protect integrity. The just state gains an active role in providing both humanity and nature with the opportunity for independent functioning as component parts of Ecosystems. This means that in addition to concern for harmonious cooperation between human freedom and natural systems evolution, respect for the specific capacity, ability, and purpose of nature, on its own, is paramount in the choices of human moral agents. This will require anticipatory institutions that set-aside places where natural systems progress without human perturbation as part of our moral use of, and planning of, the extraction interface with nature.

In our assessment of nature, we should designate the "untrammeled" systems as wilderness and preserve the functioning and evolution of these spaces with the help of technology. Technology needs to be redefined so that its effects on both humanity and nature become important in the decision process. We should make policy distinctions between what we *can* accomplish with technology, and what we *ought* to accomplish so that invention provides for ourselves and the integrity of nature simultaneously.

We should seek renewable energy, minimal packaging, maximum reuse and recycling, and minimal land use so as to limit extraction itself. As trustees we should be conscious of our true needs and conserve nature so that its integrity is as intact as possible. This does not mean we move back into caves, but may mean that we drive less, hunt less, have fewer and lighter cars, and fewer one-use disposable goods.

If use is secondary to integrity and must be conditioned by it, then our institutions, to provide for moral independence, must also provide for the development of technology that imposes the least risk for the most harmless use of the environment. Here, the shift in the burden of proof, necessitated by our focus on intrinsic value, requires those who justify and plan for extraction to consider and force the development of technology that is risk neutral and compatible with natural and human capacities. In some natural systems our duty may be to extract resources so as to cause the least disturbance of systemic integrity or to provide compensation for use in the form of resource replacement or enhancement of nature for its own sake (e.g. rebuilding spawning grounds).

Conclusion

Overall, the Ecosystem as supported by a principle of integrity as preservation demands that practical reason be applied to the environment and its uses. If a natural system is old-growth or supports a unique biodiversity and is relatively untrammeled, it ought to be preserved by our zoning system as a wild area, free from use (e.g. Tongass Forest in Alaska). If the natural system has sustained extensive human use, then empowering it requires us to either concentrate human use in these areas or replenish and restore its ecology to the best of our abilities. In all cases, having a market for use of a component or sector of the natural world is no longer enough to justify that use. The extraction interface requires that we treat nature with respect as a functional end-in-itself and as a component of Ecosystems that require both our active citizenship and our consciousness of moral duty.

Now, in addition to the Market Paradigm, we have an Ecosystem Paradigm and Context Model based upon Kantian Philosophy and the Resource–To–Recovery worldview. However, the question remains whether one has to buy into the idea of the intrinsic value of nature in order to have an ecosystem model for the law. Although the ecosystem model in this chapter is built from a concern for integrity as an ideal-regarding intrinsic value, as the next chapter will demonstrate, one can also build an ecosystem model on the foundation of the instrumental value of nature to the capabilities of each person.

Chapter 5

AN ECOSYSTEM APPROACH TO ENVIRONMENTAL & RESOURCE LAW: ALTERNATIVE II

The model of law and policy design introduced in the previous chapter shows how law might appeal to a Kantian ideal of justice that protects the environment's *intrinsic value*. In this chapter, we introduce a model of policy design for legal analysis that appeals to a different ideal of justice, one that protects the environment's *instrumental value*. Unlike current policy tools that define the environment's instrumental value in economic terms, the model of law and policy design introduced in this chapter—Ecosystem Approach II—assesses the environment's non-economic instrumental value. In particular, this ecosystem model seeks to capture the environment's instrumental value to people's *capabilities* to pursue ideals of human functioning, such as physical health and personally meaningful relationships with plants, animals, and broader nature. We will demonstrate how these ideals can provide a richer normative basis for evaluating and designing environmental policies. Water quality will be the substantive policy area we use to demonstrate the importance of incorporating non-economic instrumental values into the forms of law, policy design, and evaluation that environmental regulation requires. Specifically, this chapter will introduce a new paradigm for designing and evaluating environmental policies and then use that paradigm to suggest improvements in the current analysis of the legal rules regulating one important area of water pollution.

Conventional Law & Policy Analysis for the Environment

In the United States, conventional 'policy analysis' shapes much of the information that is brought to bear on political and governmental decisions about the environment. William Dunn defines policy analysis as a field that "uses multiple methods of inquiry and argument to produce and transform policy relevant information that may be utilized in political settings to resolve public problems."[1] Following Dunn, 'policy analysis' or 'policy evaluation' refers to a field of research and analysis that evaluates public policies in order to inform political decisions shaping those policies. In this context, 'public policies' are political agreements through which governmental institutions pursue courses of action (or inaction) that address problems on the political or legal agenda.[2] These agreements solve collective action problems by getting individuals to cooperate and coordinate their actions in a way that (ideally) serves various and conflicting dialectic interests.[3] 'Policy analysts,' who usually work for government agencies, are the practitioners that locate, create, analyze, and organize the administrative law used to operationalize public policies.

As providers of knowledge and advice to legislators and agency officials who participate in public decision-making, policy analysts play an important information-giving role. Sometimes legislators and agency officials use policy analyses instrumentally to directly affect a political decision about a policy.[4] Perhaps more commonly, policy analysis has an 'enlightenment' function that is more diffuse. Over time, information from policy analyses can filter through agencies, where bureaucrats use it to solve very specific problems and to formulate broader policy ideas that eventually influence future policy choices.[5]

Because law and policy analysis can have both immediate and long-term influence on political decisions, the kind of information

---

1. WILLIAM DUNN, PUBLIC POLICY ANALYSIS 35 (1981).

2. FRANK FISCHER, EVALUATING PUBLIC POLICY 3–6 (1995) (provides a concise history of policy analysis).

3. JOHN MARTIN GILLROY AND MAURICE WADE, THE MORAL DIMENSIONS OF PUBLIC POLICY CHOICE: BEYOND THE MARKET PARADIGM vii (1992).

4. For example, DAVID WHITEMAN, COMMUNICATION IN CON-GRESS: MEMBERS, STAFF, AND THE SEARCH FOR INFORMATION 181 (1995) studies how policy analyses flow through congressional communication networks, concluding that the information in policy analysis plays "a significant role in congressional deliberations."

5. See ROBERT HEINEMAN ET AL., THE WORLD OF THE POLICY ANALYST: RATIONALITY, VALUES, AND POLITICS 37–38 (2002).

that analysts gather and organize has important normative implications. While analysts seek to inform political decisions with an understanding of a given policy's relationship to important social goals, how an analyst conceives of these social goals determines whose individual interests matter and what values have the opportunity to become the focus of public attention and the content of codified law. For example, if analysts equate a policy's social goal with its Kaldor efficiency, then the written evaluation of a public choice will require information about consumer preferences, prices, externalities, the production of goods, etc. Other social goals, such as a law's contribution to culture, history, or the non-economic dimensions of individual liberty and social justice, will be overlooked, requiring distinct kinds of information.[6] Law and policy analysis has normative implications because it shapes (1) the information about individuals and society that legislators and public officials understand as politically relevant, and (2) how people participating in political decision-making understand these legally relevant values.

1) The Cost–Benefit Method & Market–Based Valuation Techniques

In contemporary law and policy, cost-benefit analysis (CBA) is the dominant framework used to organize and evaluate policy relevant information.[7] In its simplest form, we can understand CBA as a weighing mechanism that balances the costs a policy imposes against the benefits it creates. Its primary objective is to assess whether the aggregate gains to people made better off by a policy are greater than the aggregate losses to people made worse off by the policy.[8] The underlying logic of CBA is straightforward: the best law will be the one that maximizes the net benefits affecting individuals that the law affects.[9] To calculate these benefits, CBA defines gains and losses in terms of the amount of money individual people pay (or would be willing to pay) in order to receive benefits

---

6. FRANK FISCHER, CONFRONTING VALUES IN POLICY ANALYSIS: THE POLITICS OF CRITERIA (1987).

7. In order to manage and oversee federal spending, several environmental laws and executive orders require or authorize agencies to complete these analyses. For example, CBA is currently authorized by the Toxic Control Act of 1976, the Federal Insecticide, Fungicide, and Rodenticide Act of 1972, and the 1996 Safe Drinking Water Act. Several executive orders dating back to Jimmy Carter's presidency also require CBA as part of the "Regulatory Impact Assessments" that the president's Office of Management and Budget requires agen-

cies to complete when they plan to promulgate new and expensive environmental rules.

8. A. Myrick Freeman, III., *The Ethical Basis of the Economic View of the Environment* in THE ENVIRONMENTAL ETHICS AND POLICY BOOK 269 (Donald VanDeVeer and Christine Pierce eds., 2nd ed. 1998).

9. The idea is to put a value on goods so that the policy analysts can select the policy that yields the greatest net gain. See KERRY TURNER, DAVID PEARCE AND IAN BATEMAN, ENVIRONMENTAL ECONOMICS 93 (1993).

or avoid losses that a law will bring about. Then, by aggregating these individual benefits and costs, and subtracting the benefits from the costs, CBA produces a numerical figure that represents the public policy's overall value to society.

Within this cost-benefit framework, analysts rely on markets and hypothetical market analogies to put monetary values on environmental resources that a policy affects.[10] Valuation techniques that provide a 'true' measure of individual welfare attempt to capture individuals' expressed or revealed preferences as a way of gauging how citizens themselves view the worth of a resource. In some techniques, policy analysts look at an individual's *actual market behavior* to determine their 'willingness-to-pay' for an environmental resource. For example, an analyst might determine the value of clean air by considering differences in the prices people pay for property in areas subject to different levels of air pollution.[11] Policy analysts can also make this kind of *indirect estimate* by considering the expenditures households save on services such as laundry, cleaning, building upkeep, health care, etc. in neighborhoods with cleaner air. Similarly, since people do not pay for national parks, analysts can indirectly estimate the value of the recreational benefit of parks by looking at how much people pay in travel costs to get to park locations.[12] In each of these instances of 'market-based' valuation, legal and policy analysts base the value of a resource on the actual choices people make.

In contrast, other kinds of valuation techniques rely on a person's *hypothetical market choices* to determine a person's willingness-to-pay for a resource. For example, a questionnaire might present the value of clean air in terms of different hypothetical prices from which a person can select the one that best represents its worth to her. In addition to these ways of measuring environmental resources that people use, legal and policy analysts also rely on hypothetical market analogies to determine "option" and "existence" values. The option value of a resource is the maximum amount (above use value) a person would be willing to pay to ensure his own access to an environmental amenity at some date in the future. In contrast, the existence value of a resource is the amount a person is willing to pay to preserve a resource that she

---

10. See ELIZABETH ANDERSON, VALUE IN ETHICS AND ECONOMICS 193 (1993).

11. Here analysts must try to hold all other influences on the price of property constant, such that the only way in which the homes differ is in the quality of air that surrounds them. Since the houses typically differ in many ways, it can be difficult to isolate the effect of air quality on property prices. See KEVIN WARD AND JOHN DUFFIELD, NATURAL RESOURCE DAMAGES: LAW AND ECONOMICS 247–256 (1992).

12. See Kerry Smith and Yoshiaki Kaoru, *Signals or Noise? Explaining the Variation in Recreation Benefit Estimates*, 72 AMERICAN JOURNAL OF AGRICULTURAL ECONOMICS 419–33 (1990).

has no intent or wish to ever use. For example, existence value might reflect the value non-users put on a resource because they benefit from the pleasure of another person or future generation's access to it. Thus, while some market valuation techniques attempt to calculate the amount individual people do pay or would pay to *use* a resource, other techniques (i.e. those assessing option and existence values) attempt to determine the monetary worth of a resource's *non-use* value to people living today, perhaps because they wish to preserve a resource for people living in the future.[13]

The conventional approach to law and policy evaluation directly translates this information about people's willingness-to-pay for the environmental resources into an estimate of the law's overall social value. Determining a policy's social value simply involves adding-up (or aggregating) what each individual is willing to pay, and then situating these benefits within the organizing framework of CBA by comparing them to a policy's aggregate costs, which usually indicate the amount of money it will cost the regulated industries to comply with the policy.[14] To complete the calculation of a policy's 'net social value,' the costs are subtracted from the benefits or the benefits are subtracted from costs (depending on which is lesser). This estimate of a policy's net social value provides the basis for comparing one law to alternative policy options or to the option of pursuing no public intervention.

2) The Justification & Treatment of Environmental Value

To understand this economic approach to policy evaluation, it is important to emphasize that the combination of CBA and market valuation techniques permits judging policies in terms of the extent to which they demonstrate that government decisions are mimicking the 'Pareto efficiency' of the free market through Kaldor improvements.[15] From an economic point of view, many environmental resources are 'public goods,' open to use by all members of society and not priced by normal mechanisms of private ownership. Because the market does not price and allocate these resources, the normal free interplay of supply and demand for goods does not fend

---

13. See PETER MENELL AND RICHARD STEWART, ENVIRONMENTAL LAW AND POLICY 83 1192 (1994).

14. In theory, the costs that analysts include in a policy analysis can range widely. Adam Jaffe, Steven Peterson, Paul Portney, and Robert Stavins, *Environmental Regulation and the Competitiveness of U.S. Manufacturing: What Does the Evidence Tell Us?* 33 *JOURNAL OF ECONOMIC LITERATURE* 132 (1995), provides a taxonomy, but

explains that "most analysts ... would identify the capital and operating expenditures associated with regulatory compliance as the fundamental part of the overall costs of the regulation." U.S. CONGRESSIONAL BUDGET OFFICE (CBO), ENVIRONMENTAL REGULATION AND ECONOMIC EFFICIENCY (1985), explains problems that challenge measurement of compliance costs for environmental regulations.

15. See GILLROY & WADE, *supra* note 3, at 7 and the Appendix of this volume for more detail on the relation-

off threats of under-production or non-sustainability. Under such 'non-ideal' conditions, governments must intervene in the market to prevent what economists refer to as market failure (i.e. a failure of the market to allocate goods in a way that achieves the highest social welfare). The point of imputing a price by estimating what people *do pay* in real or surrogate markets, or what they *will pay* in hypothetical markets, is to arrive at an understanding of how these resources would be priced if people were (in fact) voluntarily exchanging them as private goods.[16] Thus, by treating environmental resources as a set of economically priced goods and services, it is possible to price them and then identify which governmental intervention best mimics the market in producing and satisfying the consumer demand for these public goods at the least cost (i.e. efficiently).

In this way, the economic approach to policy evaluation provides a criterion for public policy choice that replicates market choice, but with the externalities (resulting from market failure) internalized.[17] In an idealized market, an allocation of resources meeting this criterion is Pareto efficient in the technical sense that no person can be made better off without making some other person worse off. By pricing and aggregating a policy's costs and benefits, CBA makes it possible to assess whether the policy will allocate resources efficiently. However, as we discuss in previous parts of this book and in the Appendix, although the idealized market achieves the condition of Pareto efficiency, in practice, CBA relies on the narrower condition of Kaldor efficiency; which only requires that total benefits outweigh total costs.[18] Therefore, by conducting CBA, legal and policy analysts can identify which of the alternative policy options is efficient, or which is 'most economically efficient' in terms of having the largest benefit-to-cost ratio. When analysts provide this information to political and legal decision-makers, they ensure that decision-makers can give routine consideration to a policy's Kaldor efficiency.

3) Values, Reasons, & Principles in Law & Policy Choice

Critics of this current approach to policy analysis argue that the condition of Kaldor efficiency too frequently operates as a decision criterion for policy choice.[19] Rather than merely "helping policy makers avoid the most egregious of the available errors,"

ship between Pareto efficiency and Kaldor efficiency.

16. See argument about voluntary exchange in Herman B. Leonard and Richard J. Zeckhauser, *Cost–Benefit Analysis Applied to Risk: Its Philosophy and Legitimacy* in VALUES AT RISK 31–48 (Douglas MacLean ed. 1986).

17. See E. J. MISHAN, WHAT POLITICAL ECONOMY IS ALL ABOUT: AN EXPOSITION AND CRITIQUE (1982).

18. See Appendix of this volume.

19. GILLROY & WADE, *supra* note 3, provide a collection of articles on this topic.

Kaldor efficiency provides the choice criteria by which policy-makers determine whether a proposal for public action is desirable or undesirable.[20]

When Kaldor efficiency determines both the means and ends of public policy, there are important reasons to question its normative legitimacy. Most simply put, the problem is that public decisions are made in the context of political interactions, not in the context of markets. While Kaldor efficiency may be a sufficient standard for judging the ends of a competitive market, public decisions require additional justification.[21]

Critics argue that Kaldor efficiency is inadequate as the sole justification for policy action in many different ways. Some challenge the underlying normative assumptions that justify the use of CBA in political settings. For example, J. M. Gillroy argues that while advocates of CBA may claim they merely seek to introduce rational economic arguments into politics, the methodology of CBA appeals to *values* that efficient policies do not necessarily ensure. In particular, Gillroy argues that advocates of Kaldor efficiency assume that policies achieving this standard will protect individual freedom; however, protection of these values will in fact require policies that are inefficient from a narrow economic point of view.[22]

Others argue that policy choice is a matter of public rationality that requires certain *reasons* for action that CBA cannot supply.[23] CBA arrives at the measurement of Kaldor efficiency by aggregating information about individual preferences. Once revealed in market choices, this information about preferences serves as a "proxy for individuals' ends or aims," which individuals cannot reformulate in light of new information and collective reasoning.[24] Thus, to arrive at an account of a policy's Kaldor efficiency, CBA leaves no room for the kind of "intelligent instrumental reasoning" that resolves conflicts by reformulating individual and collective

20. IRWIN M. STELZER AND PAUL R. PORTNEY, MAKING ENVIRONMENTAL POLICY: TWO VIEWS 18 (1998), typify advocates of CBA who claim that it should not aim at determining policy goals, but should merely ensure that policies achieve those goals efficiently.

21. GILLROY & WADE, *supra* note 3 at Part I.

22. See JOHN MARTIN GILLROY, JUSTICE & NATURE: KANTIAN PHILOSOPHY, ENVIRONMENTAL POLICY & THE LAW, ch. 5 (2000).

23. For example, see HENRY S. RICHARDSON, DEMOCRATIC AUTONOMY: PUBLIC REASONING ABOUT THE ENDS OF POLICY 119–129 (2002) and CASS SUNSTEIN, THE PARTIAL CONSTITUTION 17–27 (1993). Here, as Sunstein explains, the fundamental idea is that "[t]he American constitutional system is a deliberative democracy, not a maximization machine, and many social judgments should be made by citizens engaged in deliberative discussion with one another rather than by aggregating the individual choices of consumers," Cass Sunstein, *Cost–Benefit Analysis and the Environment*, 115 ETHICS 14 (2005). See also WILLIAM BESSETTE, THE MILD VOICE OF REASON (1992).

24. RICHARDSON, *supra* note 23 at 121.

ends based on new reasons that emerge from deliberation and debate.[25]

Additionally, some argue that policy choice is a political decision that requires the application of *principles* such as fairness or justice, which are distinct from Kaldor efficiency.[26] For example, Joe Bowersox argues that because democratic society is in principle committed to minimizing coercion, when policies require people to give up something previously permitted or subsidized, these people must at least perceive that society is treating them fairly.[27] In reference to John Rawls's statement that "justice is the first virtue of social institutions,"[28] Charles Anderson makes the similar point that "[j]ustice might be taken as the paramount criterion for policy evaluation."[29] While there is significant debate over what standard of justice legal analysis ought to employ, and what entities it ought to cover, the general point raised by Bowersox and Anderson is that public choices require justification for differential treatment. The Kaldor efficiency standard—which aims to produce law that maximizes net benefits defined by people's willingness-to-pay—tends to underplay the importance of how a given policy distributes the benefits it maximizes among different people. For this reason, although a policy's economic Kaldor efficiency might be a key component of its overall social value, Kaldor efficiency cannot be the exclusive consideration relevant to the evaluation of public law.

4) The Distributional Consequences of Kaldor Efficiency

Foremost among the challenges confronting CBA are the distributional consequences that result from policies favored because they maximize Kaldor efficiency.[30] As a criterion for policy evalua-

---

25. *Id.* (the use of "intelligent" in describing adequate public reasoning refers to a "flexible willingness to remake one's aims in light of new information, especially information about costs").

26. From a practical point of view, in order to evaluate a policy in terms of whether it will make society just, we have to make comparisons of how the policy will impact different people, whereas economic efficiency requires that we use aggregate measures.

27. See Joe Bowersox, *Environmental Justice: Private Preference or Public Necessity*, in THE MORAL AUSTERITY OF ENVIRONMENTAL DECISION–MAKING: SUSTAINABILITY, DEMOCRACY, AND NORMATIVE ARGUMENT IN POLICY AND LAW 45 (John Martin Gillroy and Joe Bowersox eds., 2002).

28. JOHN RAWLS, A THEORY OF JUSTICE 3 (1971). Rawls's statement involves three claims: Justice applies to social institutions, such as courts, agencies, and the marketplace. Justice is a virtue of social institutions (in contrast to its more historical association with individual character and conduct). Justice is the first virtue of social institution, which means it has priority over other institutional virtues, such as economic efficiency.

29. See Charles W. Anderson, *The Place of Principles in Policy Analysis*, in GILLROY & WADE *supra* note 3 at 387–409.

30. We argue that the distributional consequences are foremost among social concerns because distributional inequities are widely recognized as matters of legal and political concern in contempo-

tion, the Kaldor standard advises that a policy should be adopted if and only if those who gain from the policy *could* fully compensate those who lose and still be better off.[31] In other words, the Kaldor efficiency criterion asserts that a policy is efficient if those who benefit as a consequence of the policy could *hypothetically* compensate those who experience losses as a consequence of the policy, such that the winners are still better off after compensating the losers. There are obvious benefits of such a criterion—not least, the adoption of policies that maximize aggregate wealth. However, the problem with the criterion is that the standard is indifferent to wealth distribution within society. As Laurence Tribe notes, the Kaldor criterion "does not require that compensation actually takes place; it posits a change to be unambiguously desirable whenever it generates enough 'net gain' to make compensation possible."[32]

Hence, on its own, the Kaldor efficiency criterion does not ensure legal outcomes that prevent major distributional inequities.[33] In some cases, public policies may disproportionately benefit the same groups that they disproportionately burden.[34] In other cases, public policy may disproportionately benefit one group and disproportionately burden another. The latter case may be a particularly bad democratic outcome for at least two reasons. First, as advocates of 'environmental justice' commonly claim, such outcomes are undemocratic if the procedures that produce them do not permit equal consideration of the interests of those who benefit from a law and those who bear the burdens.[35] Second, the problem of disproportionate burden can conflict with important constitutional ideals. For example, if disproportionate burdens for some groups produce large accumulations of private wealth for other groups, significant inequality of political opportunity can result.

rary society. We consider other issues relevant to environmental valuation, such as the moral status of animals, to be less widely recognized as an important "social" concern that is relevant to politics.

31. See Nicholas Kaldor, Welfare Propositions of Economics and Interpersonal Comparisons of Utility 49/195 ECONOMIC JOURNAL 549 (1939) and John Hicks, The Valuation of the Social Income 7/26 ECONOMICA 105 (1940). Another name for this type of efficiency is Kaldor–Hicks.

32. See Laurence Tribe, *Policy Science: Analysis or Ideology?* 2 PHILOSOPHY & PUBLIC AFFAIRS 71 (1972) also reprinted in GILLROY & WADE *supra* note 3; see also AMARTYA SEN, *COLLECTIVE CHOICE AND SOCIAL WELFARE* 56–57 (1970).

33. For example, Kenneth Arrow et al., *Is There a Role for Cost–Benefit Analysis in Environmental, Health, and Safety Regulation,* 272/5259 SCIENCE 5259 221–22 (1996).

34. See CASS SUNSTEIN, RISK AND REASON: SAFETY, LAW, AND THE ENVIRONMENT 156 (2002).

35. This is a central claim that the "Environmental Justice Movement" asserts. See, for example, ROBERT BULLARD, UNEQUAL PROTECTION: ENVIRONMENTAL JUSTICE AND COMMUNITIES OF COLOR (1993) or RICHARD HOFRICHTER, TOXIC STRUGGLES: THE THEORY AND PRACTICE OF ENVIRONMENTAL JUSTICE (1993).

Fear of such inequality underlies both libertarian and republican traditions of American constitutionalism, which view the concentration of power (in both public and private spheres of society) as the greatest threat to individual freedom. It is for this reason that even those who favor minimal governmental intervention must support some accumulation of power in the hands of the state; without this public power, "private power-wielders would terrorize ordinary people and engross collective resources."[36]

In focusing on a policy's Kaldor efficiency, policy analysis therefore fails to account for how the resulting distribution of resources can concentrate private power in a way that too easily translates into concentrations and misuse of political influence and authority.[37] Further, environmental law, like many other kinds of policy choices, are not merely valuable to the extent that they are compatible with the Kaldor efficiency of the market. They are also relevant to other social values, such as justice or preventing injurious private actions that result from private accumulations of power. Regardless of whether policy analysis is addressing these values as a matter of principle or as a matter of public reasoning, the design and evaluation of environmental law requires information about its impact on particular people that is different from what CBA currently provides.

5) Ecological Value & Uninformed Preferences

In addition to ignoring a policy's distributional impacts, there is another problem that challenges market-based approaches to valuing resources based on people's subjective preferences. In theory, subjective preferences define a person's welfare or utility, and hence, how much a policy contributes or takes away from it. In this sense, current policy analysis provides a *subjective* account of individual well-being: it identifies what is good for a person with what the person herself wants or values, given what the person knows and believes about her own welfare or interests. As this section will discuss, a primary problem with this subjective account of well-being is that people often lack important information about the environmental implications of the market choices they make. Thus, there is an additional reason why subjective preferences provide an inadequate basis for determining the value of environmental resources: people's preferences are often uninformed.

36. STEPHEN HOLMES, PASSIONS AND CONSTRAINT: ON THE THEORY OF LIBERAL DEMOCRACY 11 (1995).

37. See KRISTIN SHRADER–FRECHETTE, ENVIRONMENTAL JUSTICE: CREATING EQUALITY, RECLAIMING DEMOCRACY 49–69 for a discussion of how government funded agricultural policy can produce private power that leads to inequality of political power.

Defining individual welfare or utility as a function of individual preferences is a key feature of modern neo-classical economic theory.[38] The theory makes two important assumptions that bear on the role and definition of preferences in policy analysis. First, it assumes that individuals know what is best for them and have sovereignty over all judgments regarding their self-interest.[39] In the context of this assumption, a person's preferences explain her choices; they are like desires that combine with a person's beliefs to provide an explanation for her action.[40] It follows that information about the preferences people reveal in choices can inform us about the values that emerge from people's own thoughts and judgments, telling us about the ends that people value given how they conceive of their own interests, well-being, goals, etc. Second, the theory assumes that people act rationally and that their preferences are consistent. Specifically, if a person prefers option a over option b, and option b over option c, then the person prefers option a to option c.[41] In the context of this assumption, a person's preferences do not explain her choices but are simply revealed through them. Preferences therefore allow us to study patterns of behavior but they do not convey a psychological reality explaining what a person thinks is best.[42]

Critics of neo-classical economic theory charge that this second view of preferences is particularly unconvincing. It conceives of one's preferences as conceptually indistinguishable from one's actions, which gives us no means for understanding whether patterns of behavior that appear irrational and inconsistent—thus contradicting the theory—really are so.[43] More precisely, the problem is that in order to make sense of the patterns of behavior people exhibit, we have to refer to something besides what they choose, such as the "objectives or values" that people pursue in the choices that define their actions.[44] Although this problem with the second view of preferences suggests that the first view would provide a stronger grounding for policy analysis, additional barriers remain.

---

38. See JOHN O'NEILL, THE MARKET: ETHICS, KNOWLEDGE AND POLITICS 35 (1998).

39. E. J. MISHAN, *supra* note 17, at 33.

40. See MARTHA NUSSBAUM, WOMEN AND HUMAN DEVELOPMENT: THE CAPABILITIES APPROACH 120 (2000), who links this conception of what a preference is to the writings of Gary Becker and Amartya Sen.

41. O'NEILL, *supra* note 38, at 35.

42. See NUSSBAUM, *supra* note 40, at 119, who links this conception of what a preference is to the writings of Paul Samuelson, John Hicks, and more generally, to the behaviorist movement in psychology.

43. See Amartya Sen, *Choice Functions and Revealed Preference and Behaviour and the Concept of Preference*, in CHOICE, WELFARE, AND MEASUREMENT (Amartya Sen ed., 1982).

44. See NUSSBAUM, *supra* note 40, at 120.

Specifically, the first view understands preferences as providing information about what people themselves take to be relevant and valuable to their own well-being. However, the problem with reading an individual's welfare from an individual's preferences is that people often make mistakes about what is good for them. Sometimes people will make errors of judgment due to cognitive limitations, and sometimes they make mistakes due to a lack of information.[45] Consider, for example, how a lack of information can pose problems for law and policy analysis. When asked to put a price on a given tree, people may value it because it provides timber for logging, or shade from the sun, but they may not be aware that it also contributes to the earth's oxygen cycle and therefore to the conditions that sustain the possibility of human life.[46] If having this information would make people value the tree differently, then assessing people's uninformed preferences will not accurately account for the value of the tree with respect to its role in generating oxygen.

In this example, the problem with basing value on preferences is not merely that the technique of valuation does not ask people to value the tree in light of its role in generating oxygen; the problem is also that even if people are asked this question, they still lack knowledge of the tree's capacity in this role. The individual valuing the tree can neither answer the question if asked it, nor integrate this value into her monetary assessment with respect to a different and more specific purpose, such as logging.[47] Some scholars explain

45. See Clive Splash, and Nick Hanley, *Preferences, Information, and Biodiversity Preservation*, 12 ECOLOGICAL ECONOMICS (1995). Sophisticated defenses of preference-based accounts of individual welfare therefore link individual welfare to what people would in fact value if they were competent to make the required judgments and be fully informed. For example, see RICHARD BRANDT, A THEORY OF THE GOOD AND THE RIGHT (1979) or JAMES GRIFFIN, WELL–BEING: ITS MEANING, MEASUREMENT, AND MORAL IMPORTANCE (1986) while O'NEILL, *supra* note 38 at 47–49, and Olof Johansson–Stenman, *What Should We Do with Inconsistent, Nonwelfaristic, and Undeveloped Preferences?* in ECONOMICS, ETHICS, AND ENVIRONMENTAL POLICY: CONTESTED CHOICES 112–115 (Daniel Bromley and Jouni Paavola eds., 2002), provide brief arguments opposing this response.

46. In Kenneth Arrow and Robert Costanza, *Economic Growth, Carrying Capacity, and the Environment* 268 SCIENCE 520–521 (1995) the authors explain, on average, that people do not understand the importance of scientific matters such as the resilience of entire ecological systems.

47. Particular conceptual difficulties challenge efforts to integrate the ecological value of a tree into monetary valuations. Even if people attain information about the significance of ecological processes, it is still difficult to conceive of particular environmental resources within those processes. This is because unlike commodities that people buy and sell in markets, ecological processes do not conform to discrete units. It is difficult for people to imagine drawing boundaries around them. In, A. Vatn and D.W. Bromley, *Choices Without Prices Without Apologies* 26 JOURNAL OF ENVIRONMENTAL ECONOMICS AND MANAGEMENT 137 (1994) the authors argue that ecological systems involve webs of "functional relations between different entities." Because they

the problem by analogy to market relationships: just as one cannot solve for the price of a good in a market interaction without knowing the prices of all other interdependent goods, one cannot determine the price of one element of an ecological system without determining the prices of all the interdependent elements of an ecological system.[48] Therefore, when legal and policy analysts measure the market value of easily bounded environmental resources (e.g., trees) without accounting for their ecological contribution at this second level of life support, they can end up with *partial* valuations—valuations that do not account for a particular resource's value as part of a larger life support system. This system also contributes to human welfare, even if limited human knowledge prevents accurate reflection of its value in people's expressed preferences.

While introducing people to new information may induce stronger preferences for protection of environmental resources (it is well-known that it often does), lawmakers may still lack information they need for making judgments about the extent to which environmental policies contribute to people's welfare. Here it is important to distinguish two ways in which new information can increase people's welfare. First, information can increase individual welfare because it enables individuals to make better decisions about whether pursuit of their *current* preferences will produce outcomes that increase their welfare in the ways that matter most to them. Second, information can also lead individuals to form *new* preferences, so that they start to value the environment in ways that do in fact contribute to their welfare.

This second role of information is particularly important. In forming people's preferences, information makes people desire new things that are more compatible with their welfare. For example, people may learn about features or properties of environmental resources that lead them to attach greater value to those resources.[49] Notice, however, that in such instances the actual properties of resources drive determination of what contributes to people's welfare.[50] In other words, it is the features or properties of resources that matter in understanding their relationship to individu-

---

are not "precisely demarcated" objects, they defy "precise valuation." Meanwhile, John O'Neill and Clive Splash, in *Appendix: Policy Research Brief: Conceptions of Value in Environmental Decisionmaking,* 9 ENVIRONMENTAL VALUES 527 (2000) also discuss the difficulty of separating resources (as distinct units) from functional ecological relations.

48. Jeroen Van den Bergh, C.J.M. and Jan van der Straaten, *Historical*

and Future Models of Economic Development and Natural Environment in TOWARD SUSTAINABLE DEVELOPMENT: CONCEPTS, METHODS, AND POLICY 224 (Jeroen van den Bergh and Jan van der Straaten eds., 1994).

49. See JOHN O'NEILL, ECOLOGY, POLITICS AND POLICY: HUMAN WELL BEING AND THE NATURAL WORLD 78–80 (1993).

50. See O'NEILL, *supra* note 38, at 47–48.

als. The fact that people have preferences for those resources would seem to be relatively unimportant. James Griffin succinctly illuminates the problem this raises for policy analysis. "If what really matters are certain sorts of reasons for action, to be found outside desires in the qualities of their objects, why not explain well-being directly in terms of them [i.e. the reasons]?"[51]

Thus, given (1) the potential for error in translating complicated information about the relationships of particular resources to ecological conditions into monetized values, and (2) that the features and properties of these resources determine the preferences people form for them, policy analysis should at least supplement information about people's preferences for individual resources with additional information about their value in relation to the ecological conditions that directly contribute to human welfare. This would move law and policy analysis toward providing information about the value of resources that is independent of what people happen to know about those resources. It would move analysis toward providing an account of a law's impact on ecological conditions that are central to human life and welfare, which people may not know about, and therefore may not value as a matter of subjective preference.

Toward Ideal–Regarding Environmental Evaluation

To evaluate environmental law in terms of something besides the extent to which they satisfy people's subjective preferences or wants is to move toward an ideal-regarding approach to policy evaluation. Whereas want-regarding policy analysis considers the extent to which a policy produces outcomes that satisfy wants or preferences, ideal-regarding valuation suggests that want satisfaction is not the only criterion for judging policies. Specifically, to treat the environment as having instrumental value in the context of an ideal-regarding approach to policy evaluation is to treat it as something that is instrumental to intrinsically valuable human purposes, or ends. These ends or purposes are understood as valuable in themselves, regardless of whether they satisfy individual wants. For example, an ideal-regarding approach to evaluating policies might assign greater value to public outcomes that contribute to beliefs about the kind of things it is good or right for a society to protect, or to valuable social goals like prevention of exposure to risk in the workplace or protection of the health and resilience of earth's ecological systems.

In order to assess the environment's instrumental value to intrinsically valuable ends or purposes, the analyst must have some

51. GRIFFIN, *supra* note 45, at 17; also see O'NEILL, *supra* note 49, at 79.

account of the ends or purposes that a society ought to make available to citizens. For this reason, an ideal-regarding approach to evaluation requires some account of basic protections and entitlements that are justifiable in a liberal-democratic society such as ours. Once analysts have an account of these ends or purposes, they can proceed to evaluate policies based on the extent to which they protect the environmental conditions that are instrumental to them. In practice, existing environmental laws tend to assert vague and lofty aims, such as acting "to protect and enhance the quality of the Nation's air resources so as to promote the public health and welfare"[52] and conserving "ecosystems upon which endangered species and threatened species depend."[53] These goals are important, not least because they have survived a process of political justification, but they lack an analytic breadth and specificity that can provide a basis for an ideal-regarding approach to legal evaluation. Thus, in order to develop substantive analytic tools for ideal-regarding evaluation, we must first have an account or theory of what government ought to provide citizens in a good or just liberal-democratic society.

A) Nussbaum's Capabilities Approach as a Basis for Ideal–Regarding Evaluation

One promising account of what a government ought to provide its citizen's comes from Martha Nussbaum's theory of justice. Nussbaum refers to this theory as the "capabilities approach" because it defines the responsibilities that governments have to citizens in terms of "central human functional capabilities."[54] By "capabilities" Nussbaum means the conditions or states of enablement that make it possible for people to achieve different things. Specifically, capabilities are people's real opportunities to do and achieve things, such as being able to "hold property," "have adequate shelter," "live to the end of a human life of normal length," and "enjoy recreational activities."[55] Nussbaum argues that without these capabilities, people are especially subject to common forms of oppression and deprivation, and they will therefore often remain unable to live a life that is "worthy of the dignity of a human being."[56]

---

52. See 42 USC 7401[b].

53. See 16 USC 1531[b].

54. See NUSSBAUM *supra* note 40, and MARTHA NUSSBAUM, FRONTIERS OF JUSTICE: DISABILITY, NATIONALITY, SPECIES MEMBERSHIP (2006).

55. See NUSSBAUM, *supra* note 40, at 78–80 and NUSSBAUM *supra* note 54, at 76–78. In this chapter, we will use the term "central human functional ca-

pabilities" interchangeably with the terms "central human capabilities" and "central capabilities."

56. The idea of human dignity, and a life that is worthy of it, appears throughout Nussbaum's work on the capabilities approach. Her reference to the idea of human dignity, or human worth, provides the basis for arguing that there is a threshold level at which "a person's capability becomes what Marx call 'truly human,' that is, *worthy* of the

Central to Nussbaum's capabilities approach is the idea that it is not necessarily enough for government to protect people against incursions on basic liberties (such as free speech and private property), or to provide each person with some pre-specified set of material goods (such as income and wealth).[57] What matters is what people are actually able to do, given the protections or goods available to them. Some people will be able to translate their liberties and material goods into actual achievements. Other people will face circumstances that prevent similar achievements, even if they have the same liberties and material goods.

For instance, a disabled person who uses a wheelchair to get around cannot use a given amount of income as effectively as people who are not disabled. The disabled person will have to divert her income to the added costs of maintaining her wheelchair, to making various modifications in her home, and to her special needs for exercise and bodily care.[58] Due to these variations in individual circumstance, Nussbaum defines a government's responsibilities to its citizens in terms of capabilities because she is concerned with whether people are able to translate the protections and goods they have into actual achievements that characterize a minimally decent and dignified life. In this respect, what matters is what people are actually about to do, given their particular situations.

The specific list of central human functional capabilities that Nussbaum believes a just society ought to protect as fundamental entitlements is as follows:[59]

1. **Life.** Being able to live to the end of a human life of normal length; not dying prematurely, or before one's life is so reduced as to be not worth living.

2. **Bodily Health.** Being able to have good health, including reproductive health; to be adequately nourished, to have adequate shelter.

3. **Bodily Integrity.** Being able to move freely from place to place; having one's bodily boundaries treated as sovereign, i.e. being able to be secure against assault, including sexual assault, child sexual abuse, and domestic violence; having

human being." Marx's thought is particularly important to Nussbaum because he followed Aristotle (and on Nussbaum's account, departed from Kant) in emphasizing that the major human powers require material support. See NUSSBAUM, *supra* note 40 at 72–73; and NUSSBAUM, *supra* note 54, at 70–78. For a detailed discussion of why a life without the capabilities for "affiliation" and "practical reason" do not meet this standard of human digni-

ty see Martha Nussbaum, *Human Functioning and Social Justice: In Defense of Aristotelian Essentialism* 20 POLITICAL THEORY (1992).

57. See NUSSBAUM, *supra* note 54, at 283–284.

58. See Amartya Sen, *Equality of What* in SEN, *supra* note 43, at 357–358.

59. See NUSSBAUM, *supra* note 40, at 78–80 and NUSSBAUM, *supra* note 54, at 76–78.

opportunities for sexual satisfaction and for choice in matters of reproduction.

4. **Senses, Imagination, and Thought.** Being able to use the senses, to imagine, think, and reason—and to do these things in a "truly human" way, a way informed and cultivated by an adequate education, including, but by no means limited to, literacy and basic mathematical and scientific training. Being able to use imagination and thought in connection with experiencing and producing self-expressive works and events of one's own choice, religious, literary, musical, and so forth. Being able to use one's mind in ways protected by guarantees of freedom of expression with respect to both political and artistic speech, and freedom of religious exercise. Being able to search for the ultimate meaning of life in one's own way. Being able to have pleasurable experiences, and to avoid non-necessary pain.

5. **Emotions.** Being able to have attachments to things and people outside ourselves; to love those who love and care for us, to grieve at their absence; in general, to love, to grieve, to experience longing, gratitude, and justified anger. Not having one's emotional development blighted by overwhelming fear and anxiety, or by traumatic events of abuse or neglect. (Supporting this capability means supporting forms of human association that can be shown to be crucial in their development.)

6. **Practical Reason.** Being able to form a conception of the good and to engage in critical reflection about the planning of one's life. (This entails protection for the liberty of conscience.)

7. **Affiliation.** (A) Being able to live with and toward others, to recognize and show concern for other human beings, to engage in various forms of social interaction; to be able to imagine the situation of another and to have compassion for that situation; to have the capability for both justice and friendship. (Protecting this capability means protecting institutions that constitute and nourish such forms of affiliation, and also protecting the freedom of assembly and political speech.) (B) Having the social bases of self-respect and non-humiliation; being able to be treated as a dignified being whose worth is equal to that of others. This entails at a minimum, protections against discrimination on the basis of race, sex, sexual orientation, religion, caste, ethnicity, or national origin. In work, being able to work as a human being, exercising practical reason and entering into meaningful relationships of mutual recognition with other workers.

8. **Other Species.** Being able to live with concern for and in relation to animals, plants, and the world of nature.

9. **Play.** Being able to laugh, to play, to enjoy recreational activities.

10. **Control Over One's Environment. (A) Political.** Being able to participate effectively in political choices that govern one's life; having the right of political participation, protections of free speech and association. **(B) Material.** Being able to hold property (both land and moveable goods), not just formally but in terms of real opportunity; and having property rights on an equal basis with others; having the right to seek employment on an equal basis with others; having the freedom from unwarranted search and seizure.

In Nussbaum's theory of justice, a threshold level of each of these capabilities must be protected for each person, treated as an end in their own right.[60] This means that if people fall below the threshold on any one of these capabilities, there is a failure of basic justice that government must address.[61] Furthermore, because having more of one capability cannot be made up for by having less of another, there is no reason to assume that environmental resources and conditions enabling these capabilities are substitutable.[62] For example, if a person's relationship to a river embodies an emotional attachment to the past and future of her community, then destruction of that river cannot be made up for by agricultural advances that contribute to the person's bodily health capability. In short, the resources and conditions that enable one capability cannot be eliminated for the purpose of enabling another.

This account of what a liberal democratic society ought to provide its citizens has features that make it instructive as a basis for an ideal-regarding approach to environmental valuation. First, the capabilities approach recognizes that commonly protected civil and political liberties (such as the right to vote and free speech) may have material prerequisites such that a broader range of social and economic protections are necessary preconditions for realizing these liberties.[63] For example, in order to take advantage of one's right to vote, one may need the time and resources necessary for attaining basic skills of reading and critical thinking; likewise, one's

---

60. See NUSSBAUM, *supra* note 40, at 5–6, 74 and NUSSBAUM, *supra* note 54, at 71, 78, 166–67.

61. NUSSBAUM, *supra* note 54, at 167.

62. See John O'Neill, MARKETS, DELIBERATION AND ENVIRONMENT 34 (2007); Breena Holland, *Jus-*

tice and the Environment in Nussbaum's "Capabilities Approach": Why Sustainable Ecological Capacity is a Meta–Capability, POLITICAL RESEARCH QUARTERLY, Volume 61, Number 2 (2008), pages 319–332.

63. NUSSBAUM, *supra* note 54, at 289.

bodily integrity capability must allow for the freedom of movement necessary for getting to the polling booth. In this way the capabilities approach treats certain material and social circumstances as preconditions of individual choice—these conditions are necessary for enabling a person to choose to realize various liberties, such as voting and speaking freely about one's political beliefs.

Nussbaum does not fully theorize the connection between people's capabilities and the environment. However, because the environment is an important dimension of one's material well-being, we can understand it as a precondition of individual choice in a decent and just society. Most immediately, the environment provides basic life support functions, such as generating oxygen, recharging groundwater, and maintaining the chemical composition of the atmosphere. These life support functions must be operative for people to have any and all of the central capabilities that Nussbaum advances as fundamental entitlements.[64] Additionally, the environment creates particular resources and natural places that are instrumental to material, personal, and social well-being. For example, natural resources are the basis for current energy supplies, and certain natural places are bound up with individual and community identities in ways that make interaction with them both personally and socially meaningful.[65] In these roles, the environment contributes to important capabilities such as "life," "bodily health," "senses, imagination, and thought," "affiliation," and "other species." Thus, just as Nussbaum's list of central human functional capabilities are the preconditions of individual choice, so too are the environmental conditions and resources that are instrumental to human capabilities.

An approach that accounts for the instrumental value of environment to individual capabilities would recognize the environment's value as an independent *meta-capability* that is necessary for achieving all of the requirements on Nussbaum's list. Here, adequate threshold amounts of environmental quality establish the difference between justice and injustice for the individual.

64. For example, the basic life support functions that ecological systems include (1) control and maintenance of the chemical composition of the atmosphere, (2) water catchment and groundwater recharge, (3) formation of topsoil and maintenance of soil fertility, (4) fixation of solar energy and biomass production, and (5) storage and recycling of nutrients. See Rudolf de Groot, *Environmental Functions and the Economic Value of Natural Systems*, in INVESTING IN NATURAL CAPITAL: THE ECO-LOGICAL ECONOMICS APPROACH TO SUSTAINABILITY 152 (Ann Mari Jansson, et al. eds.).

65. See WILLIAM VITEK AND WES JACKSON, ROOTED IN THE LAND: ESSAYS ON COMMUNITY AND PLACE (1996), for a compelling set of essays on the importance of relationships between people and place. Also see PETER CANNAVO, THE WORKING LANDSCAPE: FOUNDING, PRESERVATION, AND THE POLITICS OF PLACE (2007).

Nussbaum's Justice Threshold Box

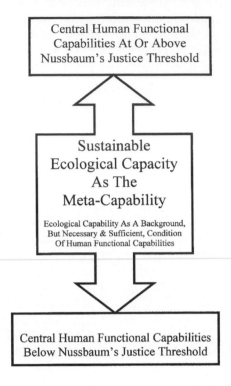

This instrumental relationship between the environment and human capabilities can provide a basic conceptual structure for an approach to law and policy analysis that overcomes the problem of uninformed preferences, challenging the current cost-benefit approach to law, policy design and evaluation. Specifically, if analysts are going to treat the environment as a precondition or basis of choice, then they will have reason to value it independent of the monetary valuations people express when they treat the environment as an object of choice in their consumer purchasing. In this respect, law and policy analysis has to go beyond measuring the value of environmental law in terms of people's willingness-to-pay for the resulting benefits. A capabilities approach to law and policy analysis can provide a framework for capturing additional dimensions of the environment's value because it recognizes that things have value prior to, and independent of, what people know and therefore express as individual wants. *Assessing this prior and independent value requires a scientific account of how a policy will impact the environmental conditions and resources that are instrumental to individual capabilities.* Furthermore, information about the environment's instrumental contributions to capabilities are important regardless of whether people make use of them in the different activities and states of being they choose to pursue.

A second reason why the capabilities approach is instructive as an ideal-regarding approach to environmental valuation has to do with the basic ends or goals it claims ought to be available to citizens. The list of central human functional capabilities provides an ideal of the basic conditions or opportunities one ought to have in order to live a good human life in a just and liberal democratic society. If treated as the normative basis for policy, governmental responsibilities would not seek to satisfy the greatest quantity of individual wants, and they would involve more than protecting people from interference with their existing civil and political rights. In particular, government would need to make it possible for people to take advantage of a broad array of opportunities for leading a dignified life, such as developing attachments to people, places, and settings outside ourselves, and attaining adequate nourishment, shelter, and play activities.

In providing this richer and more nuanced view of the conditions of a good human life, Nussbaum's list of central human capabilities offers multiple points for assessing the extent to which a policy will impact the relationship between the environment and various dimensions of individual well-being. However, rather than aggregating the quantity of satisfied preferences across individuals to determine the net benefits of an environmental policy, *a capabilities approach to policy evaluation would require an assessment of the extent to which a policy will impact the environmental conditions and resources that are instrumental to the central human functional capabilities of each person.* Public outcomes that protect some people's capabilities while changing ecological conditions in ways that push other people's capabilities below the threshold level of protection that justice requires produce a failure of basic justice.[66] Likewise, laws that protect or enhance one capability for a given person while impacting ecological conditions in ways that undermine other capabilities of that person, will also fail to meet the standards of justice. By assessing the impact of policies on the central capabilities of each person, this approach to law and policy analysis can overcome the distributional problem that challenges the normative legitimacy of economic policy analysis.

Overall, the informational and distributional features of Nussbaum's capabilities approach call for analysis that considers the ways and the extent to which a policy impacts the ecological conditions and environmental resources instrumental to the central human functional capabilities of each person the law affects. First, by making it possible to treat the environment as a basis of choice,

66. See HOLLAND *supra* note 62.

the capabilities approach provides justification for going beyond people's subjective preferences in defining the environment's value. Rather than asking people how much they are willing to pay for use of some particular resource, natural place, or level of environmental quality, a capabilities approach to policy evaluation requires an independent scientific assessment of how a policy's impact on resources, a place, or a level of environmental quality will in turn impact central human capabilities. Second, in providing a nuanced account of what government ought to provide people, the capabilities approach advances an ideal of social justice that requires assessing the distributional impact of a policy on each person's central human capabilities. Rather then aggregating preferences across individuals in order to determine the overall social value of a policy, a capabilities approach to policy evaluation requires a disaggregated analysis that considers a policy's impact on the various capabilities of particular people. Here, it is the nature and extent of a policy's impact on different people, and on the different capabilities of each particular person, that determines its social value. If a policy undermines some people's capabilities and improves others, or if it pushes some of a person's individual capabilities below a threshold while increasing other capabilities of that person, then we have good reason to question whether it meets standards of social justice.

Given this understanding of the instrumental relationship between the environment and human capabilities, we can now construct a paradigm template for an environmentally-informed capabilities approach to designing and evaluating environmental law. Like the Ecosystem Paradigm and context model that the previous chapter advances, this capabilities-based paradigm and context model will also move beyond the Market Paradigm that underlies cost-benefit analysis. We will use this template to propose changes in the design and evaluation of existing water pollution control policy. These changes will help to identify how water pollution control policy can meet the demands of social justice, defined by capabilities, rather than by the goal of Kaldor efficiency.

B) A Capabilities Paradigm and Context Model

Like the Ecosystem Paradigm presented in Chapter Four, the content of the 'Capabilities Paradigm' will reflect an ideal-regarding perspective that values whole ecosystems in addition to particular natural resources. However, the Capabilities Paradigm will focus on the environment's instrumental value to the individual rather than its intrinsic value.

1) Template—Stage I: Fundamental Assumptions

A paradigm for law and policy design is built upon a set of fundamental assumptions that justify the policy outcomes it recommends. These assumptions are about the purposes that individuals and collectives ought to pursue, and about the role of the state and the natural environment in supporting these purposes. It is important to understand these fundamental assumptions because different conceptions of individual and collective interests will produce different arguments for what the state ought to do to further these interests, and, therefore, for what kind of environmental policies the state ought to adopt.

a) The Individual and Nature

In contrast to the Market Paradigm, which views the individual as a rational and self-interested utility maximizer seeking satisfaction of his or her individual preferences, the Capabilities Paradigm is grounded in Aristotelian ideals of human flourishing. The individual is conceptualized as a political animal with a deep interest in individual choice. However, individual choice concerns a much broader range of activities than rational consumption; what matters to people is "the choice of a way of life and of political principles that will govern it."[67] On this Aristotelian view, people are characterized by a fundamental sociability, and their own ends may include the shared ends of the community of which they are part. Thus, individuals have moral inclinations that lead them to judge the good of others as an important part of their own individual ends and goals. As Nussbaum explains, "[c]ompassion for others is felt as part of one's own good."[68]

The Capabilities Paradigm also incorporates a Marxian understanding of the material dimension of human life and freedom. While recognizing that people of all types can be free, the capabilities perspective admits that due to the constraints that material circumstances create, people are not equal in their powers and abilities. Consequently, people will have different needs for resources and care. Likewise, a single individual will have varying needs for material support depending on her time in life (e.g. people that are both young and old tend to require the care-giving and material support of others).[69] Thus, unlike the Market Paradigm, which assumes that in all normatively relevant respects people are equally able to serve their individual goals and purposes through consumer choice, the Capabilities Paradigm recognizes that what individuals can achieve through the choices they make in political and market processes is deeply constrained and influenced by the material conditions they face when they enter those processes.

In these ways, a capabilities-based approach to law, policy design, and evaluation requires that analysts respond to a complex

---

67. NUSSBAUM, *supra* note 54, at 88.

68. *Id.* at 91.

69. *Id.* at 88.

individual, an individual struggling to balance individual and shared ends; an individual facing material circumstances that may unjustly determine his or her ability to choose to pursue the most valued ends. This attentiveness to the material underpinnings of individual life and well-being predisposes the Capabilities Paradigm to protect that which provides for individuals' material needs. Like the Kantian individual, the capabilities approach conceives of the individual as more of a practical 'reasoner' than a rational 'maximizer.' However, from the Capabilities perspective, the process of reasoning is constrained by the material reality that shapes one's choices, including one's choice to reason about the value of one's own ends. In the lives of real people this means that under conditions of oppression and duress, one may adapt one's preferences for the purpose of coping with these unjust circumstances.[70] For example, a person may find reasons to believe that she does not want what she cannot have, accepting her lot in life and finding pleasure in whatever "small mercies" she can.[71]

To reiterate these two points, with respect to the individual, the Capabilities Paradigm balances an understanding and appreciation for the reasoning capacity of individuals with an understanding and appreciation for the material dimensions of individual freedom and choice. As we will now discuss, this multifaceted view of the individual predisposes the Capabilities Paradigm to account for the instrumental value of the various environmental conditions that can both constrain and enable individuals to pursue ends they value.

From the capabilities perspective, an individual's ends may involve having meaningful relationships to plants, animals, and the world of nature, as Nussbaum's eighth capability emphasizes the importance of, or they may involve particular religious or affiliative experiences made possible by natural places and the plant and animal species for which these places provide habitat. It is important to note that either of these capabilities require the existence and health of whole ecosystems that enable the conditions of organic life, on which the lives of all humans depend. For example, one's capability for life—Nussbaum's first capability—and therefore for all the other capabilities, requires that ecosystems as well as large ecological cycles and processes carry out activities such as soil stabilization, groundwater recharge, and the production of oxygen. Likewise, having adequate shelter, a component of Nussbaum's second capability, partly depends on the extent to which ecological systems are able to maintain the chemical composition of the

70. See NUSSBAUM, *supra* note 40, at 111–66.

71. See Amartya Sen, *Well–Being, Agency and Freedom: The Dewey Lec-* *tures 1984*, 82/4 THE JOURNAL OF PHILOSOPHY 169–221 (1985).

atmosphere, so that temperature change and the consequent environmental change occurs on time scales to which humans can adapt.

In recognizing that human life is deeply constrained by its material underpinnings, the Capabilities Paradigm admits that the ecological conditions determining the possibility and quality of these underpinnings are central to individual enablement, and therefore to one's freedom to pursue a way of life one values. Furthermore, the importance of these material underpinnings is treated as relevant to public decisions regardless of whether individuals can or would pay for this or that particular resource. In other words, the environment, or nature, cannot be a mere bundle of separable parts (or commodities) to be bought and sold based on individual preferences. The creation and supply of these individual parts depends on the functioning of whole ecological systems, and the functioning of these whole systems has independent value in providing the pre-conditions for all life, both human and non-human. For this reason, the Capabilities Paradigm seeks to regulate the natural environment in a way that ensures its supply of the resources and conditions necessary for protecting a threshold level of central human functional capabilities.

b) Collective Interests and Action

The Capabilities Paradigm also differs from the Market Paradigm in how it reflects the collective interests of the political community and how those interests ought to influence law, policy design, and evaluation. The Market Paradigm defines the good of the collective as that which satisfies the largest aggregated sum of individual wants without force or fraud in market exchange. Policies that maximize the satisfaction of individual wants are therefore understood as good for the political community, that is, as meeting the demands of the collective level of political or social organization. In contrast, the Capabilities Paradigm provides for the good of the collective as something that is served by justice, not the maximization of want satisfaction. Because the ends of individuals include shared ends, justice for each person is understood as good for everyone, for justice "is one thing that human beings love and pursue."[72] This does not mean that cooperation toward this end of justice is inevitable. The Capabilities Paradigm recognizes that people often seek to dominate others, treating others as instruments to their own ends. But this tendency is not so central to human nature that it will inevitably resist revision by activities that provoke the benevolent sentiments of citizens aimed at the collective good.

72. NUSSBAUM, *supra* note 54, at 89.

Given these competing inclinations, the collective action problem for the Capabilities Paradigm is to develop benevolent sentiments (such as compassion for others) in the lives of real people.[73] Although individual choices that involve acts of domination can short circuit these sentiments, people are nonetheless understood as having a predisposition toward benevolence. According to Nussbaum, "[s]uch benevolent sentiments are ubiquitous in the lives of real people; the problem is that we simply do not extend them consistently or wisely. But an appropriate scheme of public moral education could support their appropriate extension."[74] For example, such an education would provide citizens with a view into the plights of other people, and through our imaginative identification, help us to picture their sufferings vividly and go to their aid.[75] Thus, one solution to the collective action problem is state support for the kind of moral education that encourages citizens to attend to what other people need in order to live decent and dignified lives.[76] By cultivating citizens predisposition toward benevolence, citizens will be less inclined to engage in individual actions that violate the capabilities of others. They will be more likely to support state action aimed at protecting a threshold level of the central human capabilities, which includes protection of the environmental conditions on which those capabilities depend.

c) The Role of the State

Although the cultivation of benevolent behavior though moral education does in this way support and complement the capability protections that justice requires, sustaining these sentiments over time requires a great deal from human beings. This is in part because "people's conceptions of what they owe to self and others are actually very fluid, responding to social teaching." For example, a public culture such as ours teaches many things that work against benevolence, such as "the poor cause their poverty, [and] that a 'real man' is self-sufficient and not needy."[77] Because the Capabilities Paradigm admits of this potential for variability in the individual commitment to benevolence, it also relies on the state to make benevolence stable, even during times when people fail to act in accordance with what benevolence requires. Thus, in the Capabilities Paradigm, the state's role is twofold: it must foster public moral education that will cultivate development of benevolent sentiments, and it must uphold the conditions of justice, even when people's predisposition toward benevolence is disrupted such that they do not demand the conditions of justice that benevolent sentiments would require. In short, the state must act as a primary

73. *Id.* at 91.
74. *Id.*
75. *Id.* at 412.

76. *Id.* at 156–157.
77. *Id.* at 413.

agent in fostering a moral education and in establishing protections of capabilities and the environmental conditions on which they depend.

This role of the state as moral educator and capability protector in the Capabilities Paradigm is distinctly different from the state's role as understood in the Market Paradigm. The legitimate state in the Market Paradigm is one that enforces contracts and provides a surrogate decision process when markets fail. As we previously discuss, this involves maintaining existing markets, as well as the property rights of individuals, and mimicking market allocations where markets break down. To fulfill these demands, the state requires information about the natural environment as a marketable good; the cost-benefit approach to policy analysis supplies this information. However, in order to foster a moral education and protect central capabilities, the state must pursue different kinds of activity, and that activity must be informed by different kinds of information about the relationship between people and the natural environment.

Specifically, as a starting point, a moral education that fosters benevolent sentiments among citizens requires an understanding of the plights of others, so that citizens are able to imaginatively picture these sufferings, becoming aware of their own vulnerability.[78] Given the significance of human relationships to the natural environment, such a moral education would also involve understanding the natural environment as a dimension of human vulnerability. Rather than understanding the environment as a mere commodity to be bought and sold in market exchange, a moral education will include activities that involve imagining the situations of those whose material vulnerability has been exacerbated by environmental degradation, both now and in the future. For example, citizens might learn about the health impairments of children who live near polluting facilities that produce goods for the kind of large-scale consumption that thrives in contemporary democratic and capitalist societies. Information about what people are willing to pay for access to or use of the environment as a marketable good is insufficient for this kind of moral education because it does not provide insight into the range of ways in which the environment is a key component of our material vulnerability.

Additionally, in order to protect a threshold level of capabilities, the state must also protect the environmental preconditions of these capabilities. This will require information about how various activities impact the environment, and through those impacts, the human capabilities that the environment enables.

78. *Id.* at 412.

Overall, the state is not a set of institutions that merely enforces existing market interactions and policies for which citizens would be otherwise willing to pay. It is responsible for providing a moral education for its citizens and for protecting the central human capabilities and the environmental preconditions on which they depend through law. In order to meet these responsibilities, the state must gather information about the relationship between the natural environment and human capabilities. Current cost-benefit analyses of environmental policies do not provide this information, and therefore they do not help bring this information to bear on environmental policy decisions. However, as we now discuss, the Capabilities Paradigm relies on principles and conditions that can guide the state toward fulfilling this broader and more nuanced role.

2) Template—Stage II: Principles and Material Conditions

Principles and material conditions play an important part in defining an alternative paradigm and context model for law, policy design, and evaluation. Specifically, the operating principle sets the standard for policy choice by defining the criterion according to which analysts assess the quality of an existing or planned public policy. The material conditions characterize what is necessary for manifesting a principle, such that it can be empowered, protected, or otherwise made to manifest in society.

a) *Operating Principle*

In the Market Paradigm, Kaldor efficiency is the operative principle. In embodying the Market Paradigm, CBA is an approach to law, policy design, and evaluation that seeks to maximize the 'net benefits' or 'aggregate social welfare' a policy will produce—a condition referred to as Kaldor efficiency. While this condition characterizes a policy outcome that hypothetically allows for those who gain to compensate those who lose such that no person is worse off than they were prior to the policy, it does not in fact require that such compensation take place.[79] In this respect, the operative principle of the Market Paradigm is one that disregards how the benefits and costs of an existing or proposed policy are distributed. In short, the principle of Kaldor efficiency is concerned with maximization, not with distribution.

Advocates of the Market Paradigm claim that because CBA measures the benefits through identifying the amount people are willing to pay for different policy outcomes, the goal of Kaldor efficiency can claim to have the consent of the citizenry. For

---

79. Such compensation would impose additional costs, produces perverse incentives, and is otherwise unrealistic. See LEONARD AND ZECKHAUSER, *supra* note 16, at 32–33.

example, Leonard and Zeckhauser argue "voluntary consent of both parties to an [economic] exchange is sufficient to ensure that the arrangement is productive for the parties involved and for the society."[80] It follows that a centralized decision process should try to achieve an outcome like those generated by full private consent in private markets because this comes closest to ensuring that "the outcome generated for each agent is, in his judgment, preferable to what he could obtain without participating."[81] Thus, although the principle of Kaldor efficiency cannot claim to produce outcomes that are fair from a distributional perspective, advocates claim that it will produce outcomes justified by the "voluntary consent" of citizens and thus will respect ideals of individual freedom.

In contrast, the Capabilities Paradigm recognizes that people often do not have the full information necessary for making informed judgments, and that even if they have this information they may be living in especially deprived or oppressive conditions; that is, conditions that make them unable to pursue the goals toward which their informed judgments would otherwise guide them. For these reasons, rather than appealing to the consent of citizens that are potentially uninformed, deprived and/or oppressed, the Capabilities Paradigm appeals to the basic dignity of each person: it demands that policy protect the capabilities that allow each person to live a dignified human life. This is a life in which each citizen is guaranteed a threshold level of protection for the central human capabilities. These protections have value that resonates with people the world over,[82] and they are also "particularly central in human life, in the sense that their presence or absence is typically understood to be the mark of the presence or absence of human life."[83]

Thus, whereas the Market Paradigm draws on ideals of individual consent to justify basing policy on the principle of Kaldor

---

80. *Id.* at 35.

81. *Id.*

82. Nussbaum believes her list would gather broad cross-cultural support; in fact, the list has emerged from years of cross-cultural discussion, which has shaped its content. In this sense, it already represents an "overlapping consensus," which refers to the Rawlsian idea that people with diverse conceptions of the good may support the list, without accepting any particular metaphysical view of the world (see NUSSBAUM, *supra* note 40, at 76). She also follows Rawls in introducing the list of capabilities as a basis for political judgments only. In this respect she defends it as free from any metaphysical grounding that might divide people along lines of culture and religion (see NUSSBAUM, *supra* note 54, at 79).

More abstractly, it might be said that Nussbaum differs from Rawls in her approach to arriving at the content of *what* is to be justified through the method of reasoning toward reflective equilibrium. She relies on a "freestanding moral idea" that "certain human capabilities exert a moral claim that they should be developed," NUSSBAUM, *supra* note 40, at 83.

83. NUSSBAUM, *supra* note 40, at 71–72; NUSSBAUM, *supra* note 54, at 215–216.

efficiency, the Capabilities Paradigm draws on the ideal of living a dignified human life to justify basing policy on protecting a threshold level of central human functional capabilities for each person. Rather than maximize the net amount of preference or want satisfaction, the legal goal is to provide and distribute to each person a minimum threshold of what concern and respect for human dignity requires. In practice, to provide each person with the basis for living a dignified life, an active state must balance individual interests and community interests in a way that enables ecosystems to function well enough to sustain the environmental preconditions necessary for maintaining this minimum threshold level of capability protection.

b) Material Conditions

Nussbaum's list of central human functional capabilities suggests a basic set of *material conditions* that are necessary to enable people to live dignified lives. Already included in her basic list of capabilities are private goods necessary for bodily health, such as shelter and nourishment, and public goods necessary for using one's senses, imagination, and thought, such as an education in basic mathematical and scientific training and creative activities that allow for exposure to religious, literary, and musical works. In developing a Capabilities Paradigm to guide environmental law, policy design, and evaluation, it is necessary to include the particular environmental resources essential for central human functional capabilities. One should also expand the list of central capabilities so that it includes the functioning ecological systems necessary for sustaining a supply of these resources, and for absorbing waste produced by various human activities that the capabilities enable. Thus, in the Capabilities Paradigm, in addition to the public and private goods that Nussbaum's list of capabilities already requires, material conditions must also include ecological systems that provide various environmental goods, conditions, and services instrumental to protecting a threshold level of capabilities for each person.

These material conditions are different from the Market Paradigm's material conditions in two important ways. First, in pursuit of maximizing Kaldor efficiency defined in terms of the greatest aggregate amount of preference satisfaction, the Market Paradigm seeks to manifest material conditions that maximize economic production, and thus the goals of consumption, trade, and economic wealth that flow from a productive economy. In contrast, the Capabilities Paradigm seeks to manifest material conditions necessary as preconditions for participating in these economic activities; it also seeks to manifest material conditions that contribute to a range of human activities outside of economic interactions. Specifically, in bringing attention to these material preconditions for participating in various economic activities (e.g. employment, property ownership and exchange, attainment of shelter), the Capabilities Paradigm offers a more nuanced account of what is necessary for enabling people to get some of their capability thresholds met through market exchange. However, it also offers a broad account of the non-economic activities that material conditions should enable, such as "being able to search for the ultimate meaning of life in one's own way," and "being able to be treated as a dignified being whose worth is equal to that of others."[84]

Second and consequently, the Market Paradigm's demand for Kaldor efficiency and economic wealth requires ecological conditions distinct from those that the Capabilities Paradigm requires. Primarily this is because the ecological conditions necessary for sustaining economic productivity will be different from the ecological conditions necessary for sustaining a threshold level of the central human capabilities for each person. To put this point differently, the level of ecosystem functioning necessary for sustaining the economy may be much lower than the level of ecosystem functioning necessary for sustaining the various non-economic activities that make it possible for each person to live a dignified life. For example, an ecosystem that can provide the natural resource inputs for consumer goods may at any given time allow for the elimination of species to which people have the kind of personally meaningful attachments that the eighth capability (i.e. Other Species) requires. Likewise, ecosystems necessary for providing natural resource inputs for consumer goods can operate at a lower level of ecological functioning or "resilience"[85] than may be necessary for ecosystems to effectively absorb pollutants that interfere with people's life and bodily health capabilities.[86] Finally, because these non-economic activities are not priced as market goods, and because they have value that is often not expressible in monetary terms, the market's pricing mechanism—whether real or hypothetical—is not able to adequately account for their value. These points suggest that the material conditions that the Capabilities Paradigm demands can or will require ecological systems that function at a higher or healthier level than what is required for merely sustaining the conditions of economic production and consumption.

---

84. These are components of Nussbaum's fourth and seventh capabilities, respectively.

85. By "resilience" we refer to the "ability of a system to return to its original state after a perturbation." See MILLENNIUM ASSESSMENT PANEL, ECOSYSTEMS AND HUMAN WELL-BEING: A FRAMEWORK FOR ASSESSMENT 68 (2003).

86. HOLLAND, *supra* note 62, at 5–7 identifies many additional ways in which the conditions of a dignified life are dependent on functioning ecological systems. The idea of resilience is discussed below in the section titled "An Ecosystem Health Context Model."

Thus, because the Market Paradigm identifies a narrow set of human activities (i.e. consumption and the pursuit of wealth accumulation) as worthy of protection, it will allow for levels of environmental degradation that surpass what is permissible in a society that seeks to protect the material conditions that enable people to live diverse and fully dignified lives. To reiterate, ecological systems that function at a level necessary for maintaining the material conditions that enable the central capabilities for each person, will demand environmental protections that differ from those necessary for merely maintaining the values and ways of life people pursue through market exchanges.

3) Template—Stage III: Maxims and Methods

Having established the Capabilities Paradigm's operating principle and the material conditions necessary for producing law and policy in accordance with it, we can now identify the basic tools and methods that policy-makers can use to apply this paradigm. For the purpose of this application, *maxims* are imperatives that help to create and identify policies that are compatible with a paradigm's operating principle and material conditions. The *method* is the decision-making tool necessary for implementing the maxim.

a) Maxims

As we have previously discussed, the maxim that the Market Paradigm offers the decision-maker is to maximize wealth! Specifically, this maxim implores the decision-maker to design and evaluate policies for the purpose of maximizing the total amount of preference or want satisfaction across the population, with as little government intervention as possible. Because price is the basis for quantifying the extent of this total satisfaction, the aggregated price people are willing to pay for environmental protection is what determines whether an existing or proposed policy will achieve the maximizing goal. Thus, the imperative to maximize wealth will produce and favorably evaluate policies that protect those aspects of the environment for which aggregate willingness-to-pay is highest.

In contrast to the Market Paradigm, the Capabilities Paradigm requires decision-makers to **protect and distribute a threshold level of capabilities!** This maxim includes provision of the environmental preconditions of human capabilities for each person. Here the imperative is to protect ecological systems that sustain the resource provision and waste absorption processes that enable each person to live a dignified life. This maxim will produce and favorably evaluate laws that protect ecological systems at the level necessary for sustaining those resources and waste absorption capacities that enable the entire range of central human capabilities, not just the capabilities to which economic productivity directly contributes. Thus, rather than try to aggregate the benefits of a policy across the population, when guided by the Capabilities Paradigm, decision-makers will have to determine the impacts or outcomes of an existing or proposed law on the full range of capabilities for the full range of people in society. The distribution of those impacts, as well as whether they violate the capability thresholds, will determine whether a given or proposed law meets the demands of the maxim.

b) Methods

In the Market Paradigm, CBA is the decision-making tool necessary for implementing the maxim to maximize wealth, which is derived from the principle of Kaldor efficiency. This involves assigning monetary values to the various costs and benefits associated with an existing or proposed policy, and calculating the difference between the aggregate costs and aggregate benefits so that a law that maximizes the net monetized benefits can be selected or designed.

The cost-benefit method is essential for understanding a policy's economic impact. By measuring the aggregate costs to industry involved in complying with the policy, and the aggregate of individual citizens' willingness-to-pay for the benefits a policy will produce, the cost-benefit analyst can calculate the difference between these costs and benefits to arrive at an account of what a policy's overall impact would be on producer and consumer activity. As we have discussed in Chapter Three, this tool allows the decision-maker to apply the Market Paradigm without retracing the steps of the logical schema that underlies it and with little intellectual effort.

Although there is no decision-making method for the Capabilities Paradigm that has been operationalized for application to environmental policy, it is clear that applying the Capabilities Paradigm will involve more than the kind of economic analysis that CBA provides. In particular, a method that will implement the Capabilities Paradigm's maxim to protect and distribute the environmental preconditions of human capabilities for each person at a threshold level will involve an account of the following: (1) how a policy will impact the ecological conditions that enable each person's capabilities, (2) how a proposed policy will impact each capability independent of the environmental impact, and (3) whose capabilities are enhanced and whose are diminished by a specific legal alternative. In other words, a method for applying the Capabilities Paradigm will involve, respectively, an ecological analysis, a capabilities analysis, and a distributional analysis.

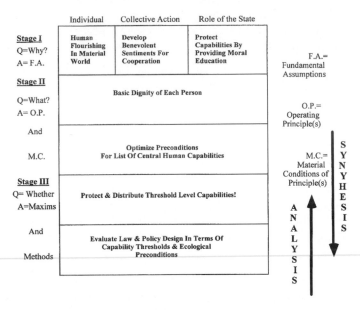

CPA Box For Ecosystem Model II: Capabilities Approach

Although some of the information about the extent to which people's capabilities are enhanced or diminished will be hard to gather, the ecological analysis is the most important component for the purpose of moving beyond the limitations of CBA in environmental law, policy design, and evaluation. The purpose of the ecological analysis is to determine the extent to which an existing or proposed environmental policy will provide a level of protection for ecological systems that supports the broad conception of human well-being that the list of capabilities captures. To protect these capabilities at a threshold level, environmental policies must provide a level of protection to ecological systems that maintains their functioning within some margin of safety above the threshold. This will require some speculation as to where the threshold is or should be. But an ecological analysis can at least provide information about whether a given law or policy is strong enough to maintain the level of environmental quality necessary for a given threshold level of capability protection. Toward this end, the concept of *ecosystem health* can serve as an initial context model.

C) An Ecosystem Health Context Model

A context model acts as an intermediary between a given theoretical paradigm and that paradigm's policy instruments which create the law. For the purpose of law, policy design, and evaluation, the context model should provide a worldview that identifies the information and relationships relevant to assessing an existing or proposed policy. Specifically, the worldview defines and arranges the policy space around the core principle and components of the policy paradigm, which can then compete with the core principle and components of the dominant paradigm as providing the most reasonable arguments for policy decisions.[87] Given the Capabilities Paradigm's focus on the non-economic instrumental value of the environment, the concept of ecosystem health will provide its context model.

As we refer to it here, ecosystem health is a measurement of the stability and sustainability of an ecological system. A healthy ecological system "is active and maintains its organization and autonomy over time and is resilient to stress."[88] An unhealthy ecosystem is one in which characteristics such as primary productivity, biodiversity, habitat suitability for endemic species, fragility, and vulnerability are reduced. For example, in terrestrial ecosystems, the recurrent features of stress include impairments in primary productivity and nutrient cycling, reduced resilience, altered community dominance favoring species with shorter reproductive cycles and of smaller size, increases in non-native species, increased prevalence of disease, and reduced biodiversity.[89] While specific indicators (e.g. biodiversity, community dominance, sediment loads, and the nutrient status of receiving waters) can therefore provide an assessment of ecosystem health, those who study ecosystems seek to systematically integrate these measurements of 'health' with indicators of the quality of human life.[90] For example, changes in socio-economic conditions and the availability of environmental amenities in a given geographical area can be used as proxies for measuring changes in human quality of life.[91] In this respect, ecosystem health can also be used in a broader sense, to characterize the relationship between natural systems and human well-being in a way that also corresponds to how the Capabilities Paradigm characterizes the environment, people, and their relationships.

87. See GIANDOMENICO MAJONE, EVIDENCE, ARGUMENT, & PERSUASION IN THE POLICY PROCESS 158–159 (1989).

88. ROBERT COSTANZA, BRYAN NORTON AND BENJAMIN HASKELL, ECOSYSTEM HEALTH: NEW GOALS FOR ENVIRONMENTAL MANAGEMENT 9 (1992) and DAVID RAPPORT et al., ECOSYSTEM HEALTH (1998).

89. See RAPPORT et al., *supra* note 88.

90. See I. Conforth, *Selecting Indicators for Assessing Sustainable Land* *Management* 56 JOURNAL OF ENVIRONMENTAL MANAGEMENT 153–179 (1997), and A. Michalos, *Combining Social, Economic and Environmental Indicators to Measure Sustainable Well-Being* 40 SOCIAL INDICATORS RESEARCH 221–258 (1997).

91. For example, see Tsai Deller, D. Marcouiller and D. English, *The Role of Amenities In Rural Economic Growth* 83 AMERICAN JOURNAL OF AGRICULTURAL ECONOMICS 352–365 (2001).

As part of a comprehensive and integrated understanding of the relationship between the quality of ecological systems and the quality of human life, an Ecosystem Health Context Model for law, policy design, and evaluation requires an analysis that relates changes in the health of ecosystems to changes in various benefits to particular individuals that those systems provide. However, the Capabilities Paradigm conceives of people as engaged in a variety of life activities and states of being besides consumption and the preference satisfaction consumption provides. Thus an adequate policy analysis will define benefits as contributions to people's basic capabilities to achieve these various different activities and states. Willingness-to-pay for specific environmental goods and experiences (e.g. timber, or access to parks) may provide some information about how these goods and experiences contribute to some capabilities (e.g. shelter or recreational activities), but this monetized assessment of the environment's value will not account for the range of capabilities to which the environment is instrumentally valuable. For this reason, the Ecosystem Health Context Model demands an account of the impact of a given policy on the health of whole ecosystems, not just the particular environmental goods (e.g. timber and parks) that people subjectively value as objects of consumer choice. Specifically, it demands an account of how the health of ecosystems contributes to subjectively valued goods and experiences that are not marketed or monetized. In addition, one must account for unrecognized and unknown contributions those systems make to the full list of central human capabilities which people may not recognize or understand due to their lack of information and/or education. In this respect, the Ecosystem Health Context Model directs policy analysts to gather information for identifying whether an existing or proposed environmental policy protects the level of ecosystem functioning to support the various dimensions of human well-being that Nussbaum's list of central capabilities protects at a threshold level.

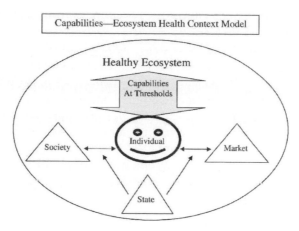

Built from the Capabilities Paradigm, the Ecosystem Health Context Model requires that policy analysis provide this information, because without it the state cannot carry out its responsibility to protect a threshold level of human capabilities and the ecological systems on which they depend. Current policy analysis only provides information about whether and to what extent a policy will meet the conditions of Kaldor efficiency. In the Capabilities Paradigm, the state's purpose is not to merely solve market failures by pricing and allocating environmental goods according to market ideals. Rather, the state must foster the development of benevolent sentiments and protect and distribute a threshold level of capability protection for each person. This may require constraining market outcomes that interfere with these goals, and, therefore, it may involve supporting policies that fail to meet the condition of Kaldor efficiency. In other words, the Ecosystem Health Context Model serves a state that prioritizes laws and policies fostering the protection of a threshold level of the central human capabilities for each person. A Kaldor efficient policy is only valuable to the extent that it serves this goal. Thus, if the goal of Kaldor efficiency is to bear on policy decisions, then policy analysis must establish the contribution of a Kaldor efficient policy outcome to protecting threshold levels of human capabilities.

In this way, the Ecosystem Health Context Model subsumes economic activity within the broader goal of capability protection, requiring that economic activity be justified based on its contribution to people's capabilities. Here the state mediates the impact of market activity on the environment so that both can continue to operate in ways that sustain a threshold level of capability protection. This may require that the state mediate interactions between individuals and markets, just as the state mediates interactions between individuals and other institutions in society that threaten to undermine basic capabilities, such as hate groups or those that promote child pornography.

Having outlined the basic features of a Capabilities Paradigm, as well as how an Ecosystem Health Context Model might guide the tactical operation of methods evolving from that paradigm, we can consider how this paradigm and context model bears on an existing analysis of the legal rules regulating water pollution. The remainder of this chapter will draw on this paradigm and context model to critique and suggest improvements in the Environmental Protection Agency's evaluation of effluent guidelines drafted for controlling pollution released in one particular industry.

Valuation of Water Pollution Control Policy: The Legal and Administrative Context

The Clean Water Act of 1977 amends the Federal Water Pollution Control Act Amendments of 1972 and sets out a national goal to "restore and maintain the chemical, physical and biological integrity of the nation's waters" for the purpose of protecting and propagating fish, shellfish, wildlife, and recreation in and on surface waters in the United States.[92] In order to assess and justify specific clean water standards and guidelines that will achieve this goal, the Environmental Protection Agency (EPA) conducts policy analyses that document the benefits of proposed improvements in water quality. If promulgated, these standards operate as major administrative rules necessary for implementing the Clean Water Act, and they therefore have the status of law. For present purposes, we will explore EPA's benefits analysis of standards for one particular area of water pollution control policy—the effluent emissions guidelines established for the organic chemicals, plastics, and synthetic fibers (OCPSF) industry.

In regulating this industry as required by the Clean Water Act, EPA relies on both regulatory and non-regulatory tools to control discharges of pollutants from point and nonpoint sources into U.S. waters. The benefits analysis we discuss here addresses water pollution coming from "point sources" of pollution, which include any "discernible, confined and discrete conveyance" that discharges (or that might discharge) pollutants. Technology based effluent standards control these sources of pollution by regulating dischargers according to a "best practicable technology" (BPT) or a "best available technology" (BAT) standard.[93] In determining effluent

---

92. See 33 USC 1251[a].

93. The BPT standard regulates conventional pollutants while the BAT standard regulates toxic and non-conventional pollutants. EPA writes these standards as performance standards rather than design standards. While they do not require the installation of

reduction requirements, EPA separates industrial sources into different categories (such as iron and steel manufacturing, organic chemical manufacturing, petroleum refining, etc.) so that it can define industry-specific standards that approximate the average amount of control achievable by existing industry specific technologies. The legal mandate establishing these standards directs EPA to consider the total cost (in relation to benefits) resulting from the effluent reductions requirements it proposes; however, in practice the technological capabilities of the control technology tend to have a large influence on the reduction requirements.[94]

It is important to situate the effluent emission standards for the OCPSF industry in an historical context, which will help to further contexualize our discussion of the benefits studies used in EPA's cost-benefit analysis (CBA). After the initial establishment of effluent emission guidelines in the early 1970s, groups representing the affected industries launched a series of legal challenges against EPA.[95] At the direction of court remand, EPA responded to industry complaints by withdrawing some of the regulations. However, EPA consequently failed to meet deadlines specified in the original Federal Pollution Control Act of 1972, and environmental groups subsequently sued.[96] EPA reached a settlement agreement with environmental groups that proceeded in two stages. In the first stage, EPA developed a program and met a court-ordered schedule for controlling sixty-five "priority" toxic pollutants through BAT standards and "pretreatment standards for existing and new sources" in 21 major industries. After incorporating these standards into the 1977 Clean Water Act, EPA pursued the second stage, developing a court-ordered timetable for tighter standards for toxic and conventional pollutants.

It was in this second round of activity that EPA promulgated codified law in the form of effluent guideline regulations for the OCPSF industry. In discussing EPA's benefits analysis for these guidelines, we will focus on the valuation of (or the benefits arising from) improvements in water quality resulting from the effluent guidelines. As previously stated, our primary goal is to illustrate why the want-regarding approach of the exiting cost-benefit analysis is inadequate, and to consider the ways in which the more ideal-regarding Capabilities Paradigm and context model would change evaluation of the effluent emissions guidelines.

specific control technologies, the effluent limitations are set at a level that EPA believes can be achieved by technologies it selects.

94. In regulating conventional pollutants (as opposed to toxic pollutants) EPA uses "best conventional technology standards" (BCT) and considers whether the benefits of reduction are worth the costs.

95. See Union Carbide Corp. v. Train, 73 F.R.D. 620 (S.D.N.Y 1977), and FMC v. Train, 539 F.2d 973 (4th Cir. 1976).

96. See NRDC v. Train, 545 F.2d 320 (2d Cir. 1976).

1) EPA's Benefits Analysis of Effluent Emissions Guidelines

EPA generally assesses benefits for many industry-specific effluent guidelines by predicting expected changes in the number of violations of established water quality criteria. However, Executive Order 12291 requires a more detailed account of costs and benefits for regulations projected to require compliance costs of over $100 million.[97] Because EPA expected the costs of compliance for the OCPSF industry effluent guidelines to exceed this $100 million benchmark, it conducted a detailed CBA.

In particular, to assess water quality benefits resulting from the effluent emission guidelines for the OCPSF industry, EPA's benefits analysis relies on three different studies: (1) three site-specific case studies, (2) a National Water Quality Benefit Assessment, and (3) a National Assessment of Predicted Health and Ozone–Related Benefits.[98] While these analyses reflect EPA's effort to account for *all* relevant beneficial outcomes, they primarily rely on benefits that practitioners can quantify and monetize. These consist of the following: water quality benefits for recreational boating, fishing, and swimming; for commercial fishing and non-use values (which include "option" and "existence" values for nonuser benefits); and air quality benefits arising from reductions in cancer and smog levels.[99] Unfortunately, much of the technical discussion explaining these different analyses focuses on the rationale involved in quantifying and aggregating information about individual values associated with water quality.[100] For our purposes, discussing these

97. Typically this document comparing costs to benefits is referred to as a Regulatory Impact Analysis (RIA). Originally, RIAs were intended to provide a mechanism for the President's Office of Management and Budget (OMB) to halt the implementing of environmental rules and regulations involving compliance costs that vastly outweigh their benefits.

98. In this discussion, we will focus on the national assessments, rather than the case studies. While there were notable problems with all three investigations, the national assessments and the case studies for the most part look at the same relationships. However, the case studies appear less thorough and there was insufficient information to determine whether the location-specific results they provided were at all typical for the nation. See RICHARD MORGENSTERN, ECONOMIC ANALYSES AT EPA: ASSESSING REGULATORY IMPACT 112 (1997).

99. Although it is not possible to monetize many benefits (due to data and method deficiencies), EPA's analysis does admit the importance of benefits not accounted for in its analysis, particularly those resulting from (a) a reduction in health risks from air emission of non-carcinogenic pollutants, (b) reduction in health risks associated with non-priority pollutants from direct and indirect dischargers, (c) reductions in health risks from consumption of fish and drinking water contaminated by the regulated pollutants, and (d) reductions of health risks from dermal exposure to pollutants in water-recreation.

100. For the analyst, quantification and aggregation are important parts of the analysis. In fact, in the "National Water Quality Benefits Estimate" these aspects of the analysis are the primary reason given by MORGENSTERN, *supra* note 98, at 113, for questioning the validity of the results. In this chapter, we focus on other reasons for questioning the results.

technical aspects of monetization and aggregation in the benefits assessment is less important than exploring how the assessor conceives of the relevant individual values and relates them to the relevant water resources. Therefore, we will focus on what occurs in the analyses prior to quantifying and aggregating values.

2) Valuation of Water Quality

To evaluate environmental policies from a want-regarding per-spective is to treat want-satisfaction as the only criterion for judging the benefits of public policies. This want-regarding perspec-tive is most evident in the report EPA uses to account for the recreational and non-use value benefits, which is a component of its "National Water Quality Benefit Assessment" study referred to above. Specifically, to measure the "recreational and intrinsic"[101] benefits of water quality improvements resulting from the effluent emissions guidelines, EPA uses the benefit estimates from a "Will-ingness to Pay for National Freshwater Quality Improvements" report conducted by *Resources for the Future,* an independent research organization.[102] Authored by Mitchell and Carson (1984), the report follows a straightforward survey format, drawing on detailed interviews with people in geographically diverse locations across the country. The survey's primary goal is to determine how much individuals (or households) are willing to pay for different levels of water quality, which it categorizes as "boatable," "fisha-ble," and "swimmable," where boatable characterizes the worst water quality and swimmable characterizes the best.

In order to establish a connection between these different levels of water quality and individual values, the survey asks respondents a variety of questions about recreational and intrinsic-value benefits they associate with water resources. The survey defines "Recreational" benefits to include many different activities, such as boating, fishing, swimming, waterskiing, wading, picnick-ing, camping, bird watching, duck hunting, and living in a vacation cottage.[103] The survey defines "Intrinsic" benefits in terms of the satisfaction people derive from "knowing other people may use and enjoy freshwater" and from "knowing that the nation's water is cleaner."[104] To quantify these (recreational) "use" and (intrinsic)

---

101. The word "intrinsic" as used here does not mean inherent or morally essential but a non-use benefit.

102. The benefits of the OCPSF in-dustry improvements are calculated on the basis of the industry's percentage contribution to the total national pollu-tant loadings. See MORGENSTERN, *su-pra* note 98, at 112. For the original report, prepared for the EPA, see *Will-*

ingness to Pay for National Freshwater Improvements (Robert C. Mitchell and Richard T. Carson eds., 1984).

103. For example, see survey ques-tion numbers 12 and 20 in MITCHELL AND CARSON, *supra* note 102 at A–5 and A–7.

104. For example, see survey ques-tion number 23 in *Id.* at A–9.

"non-use" values for water quality, the survey asks questions that we can group into three different types. One type of question addresses *how much* people use water resources for recreational purposes. For example, the survey asks respondents, "About how many days did you/household member go freshwater fishing in this state?"[105] A second type of question concerns a person or household's *willingness to spend money* for an improvement in water quality. For example, the survey asks respondents, "How much [is] you/your household willing to pay each year, if anything, to reach each of three goals [i.e. boatable, fishable, and swimmable water quality]?" A third type of question concerns the *absolute level of importance* of recreational and intrinsic water-related values to the respondent. For example, to understand the importance of freshwater fishing as a recreational activity, the survey gives respondents the following options from which they can select an answer: "very important," "somewhat important," and "not at all important."[106]

These questions demonstrate a want-regarding approach to policy evaluation because in each instance the analyst is gathering information about a respondent's existing wants and desires for access to water resources. The number of days people go freshwater fishing indicates some minimum number of days that people want to enjoy the recreational fishing benefits that clean water provides. The amount that people are willing to pay for the different levels of water quality that recreation requires provides information about how much they want to pursue these recreational activities in comparison to other things for which they might pay money. The level of importance people attach to freshwater fishing indicates some extent to which people want this activity to be prioritized. If a policy analysis were to rely solely on this kind of information about

---

105. See survey question number 17 in *Id.* at A–5.

106. Although less important to the present discussion, the survey also asks two additional questions that do not fall within these categories. One survey question asks respondents to compare the benefits of pollution control to the costs of pollution control by selecting one of the following statements as the most agreeable:

  1) Protecting the environment is so important that pollution control requirements and standards cannot be too strict and continuing improvement must be made regardless of cost.

  2) We have made enough progress on cleaning up the environment that we should now concentrate on holding down costs rather than requiring stricter controls.

  3) Pollution control requirements and standards have gone too far and they already cost more than they are worth. See survey question number 4 in *Id.* at A–3.

Another question asks the respondent to select which source of water pollution they think probably causes the most pollution in freshwater lakes, rivers, and streams. Here the survey provides respondents with an option to select from the following sources of pollution: (1) Runoff from agriculture, (2) Sewage from cities and towns, (3) Drainage from mines, (4) Runoff from roads and highways, (5) Seepage from garbage dumps, and (6) Dumping of factory waste into water bodies. See survey question number 7 in *Id.* at A–4.

individual wants for environmental experiences, then it would exemplify an unambiguously want-regarding approach to evaluation.

We have discussed two primary problems with such a want-regarding approach to evaluating policies: one distributional, and one informational. Not surprisingly, these problems are evident in the Mitchell and Carson study[107] of recreational and intrinsic value benefits of water pollution control policy. First, the study does not consider who bears the benefits and burdens of the effluent emissions guidelines for the OCPSF industry. Recreational fishing and appreciation of nature's intrinsic values may be of great importance to some people in society and of little importance to others. Likewise, taking advantage of these activities may require financial and social resources that are available to some, and not available to others who are equally or more interested in pursuing them. In this respect, the recreational and intrinsic value component of National Water Quality Benefit Assessment fails to account for how the effluent emissions guidelines will distribute the benefits of water pollution control.

Second, in assessing the extent to which people want these recreational and intrinsic value benefits, the Mitchell and Carson study relies entirely on respondents existing basis of knowledge about the importance of water resources. If people are not aware of the ways in which water quality relates to ecological systems, and through those systems to other environmental resources that are instrumental to individual health and well-being (as well as to broader social purposes), then the benefits analysis will fail to incorporate and account for this additional instrumental value of policies controlling water pollution. In other words, the recreational and intrinsic value component of the National Water Quality Benefit Assessment fails to account for the various ecological dimensions of water quality's instrumental value; therefore the valuation of water quality it incorporates into the analysis is partial.

The second report EPA uses, the "National Water Quality Benefits Estimate," is less want-regarding than the Mitchell and Carson report, but it nonetheless falls short of providing the kind of information necessary for a systematic and justifiable ideal-regarding approach to policy evaluation. Authored by A. Myrick Freeman, the second report focuses on the value of water for "commercial fishing" and "withdrawal uses."[108] Freeman's estimates come from his critical review of many different valuation studies, which each present monetary estimates for the benefits of water pollution

107. See MITCHELL AND CARSON, *supra* note 102.

108. See A. MYRICK FREEMAN, III., AIR AND WATER POLLUTION

CONTROL: A BENEFIT–COST ASSESSMENT 132 (1982).

abatement resulting from the Federal Water Control Act Amendments of 1972.[109]

Specifically, to assess the *commercial fishing* benefits of reducing water pollution, Freeman looks at producer and consumer benefits resulting from increases in the biological productivity of fisheries or from improvements in other fishery resources (such as shellfish beds). Freeman considers two different valuation approaches.[110] One approach defines benefits as the prevention of losses in fish catches that normally result from excessive pollution. Here Freeman uses a *National Academy of Science* report to get the upper bound benefit estimate. This report looks at how changes in the allowable content of polychlorinated biphenyls (PCBs) influence the chemical contamination of fish, and therefore, the landed value of both marine and freshwater fisheries.[111] A second approach looks at the relationship between water quality and biological productivity. This approach defines benefits in two ways: as a decrease in consumer price of fish, and, as an income increase for fishermen (i.e. resulting from increases in fish harvests due to pollution reductions that improve the biological productivity of marine life).[112]

To account for *withdrawal use* benefits, Freeman relates the positive impact of water quality improvements to four diversionary uses: drinking water, treatment costs for municipal water suppliers, appliance and upkeep costs for households, and treatment and cooling costs for industry. Freeman relies on two studies to estimate reductions in health risks resulting from a decrease in polluted drinking water. The first study identifies the number of cases of disease traceable to polluted drinking water in a given time-period; in each case, the costs of medical treatment and lost earnings determine the dollar value of benefits (i.e. costs avoided).[113] To calculate a total value this report assumes that the proposed water quality improvements will eliminate all such cases of waterborne disease. A second study assesses the number of diseases and deaths judged to result from cases of gastroenteritis, hepatitis, and salmo-

---

109. In the benefits analysis for the OCPSF effluent guideline both the estimates of MITCHELL AND CARSON, *supra* note 102, and FREEMAN *supra* note 108 were then adjusted downward to account for improvements in water quality conditions that occurred after these original estimates were developed. See MORGENSTERN, *supra* note 98, at 112.

110. FREEMAN, *supra* note 108, at 165–166.

111. See NATIONAL ACADEMY OF SCIENCES, POLYCHLORINATED BIPHENYLS (1979).

112. This approach drew on research by Frederick W. Bell and E. Ray Canterbery, *An Assessment of the Economic Benefits Which Will Accrue to Commercial and Recreational Fisheries from Incremental Improvements in the Quality of Coastal Water* (University of Florida, 1976).

113. Samual G. Unger, *National Benefits of Achieving the 1977, 1983, and 1985 Water Quality Goals.* (Environmental Protection Agency, 1975).

nellosis resulting from contaminated drinking water. This study arrives at a quantified assessment of benefits by pricing each avoided death between $100,000 and $250,000.[114]

To account for *municipal water supplier* benefits, Freeman assesses decreases in treatment costs that improved water quality creates. Here, two studies investigate the percentage of municipal water supply treatment costs attributable to point source pollutants. Freeman estimates that the water quality objectives of the effluent emission standards will reduce municipal water suppliers' treatment costs by this same percentage.[115]

To assess the *household benefits* of water pollution control, Freeman looks at how water pollution control will decrease the amount of money households spend to address problems such as stains on water fixtures, mineral deposits, and appliance damages. Here he reasons that point source discharges at least partly cause water hardness and the presence of dissolved solids in municipal water supplies. Therefore, decreases in point source pollution will also reduce the cost of fixing these household damages.[116]

Finally, to account for the benefit of reductions in *industry treatment costs* resulting from water pollution control, Freeman relies on studies assessing the costs of process water, boiler feed water, and cooling water. He defines the industry treatment cost benefits of point source pollution control as a yearly estimate of these costs.[117]

The Freeman study's contribution to the benefits analysis of water pollution control policy for the OCPSF industry is important in gathering information about the instrumental value of water quality to dimensions of human well-being besides the recreational and intrinsic value estimates assessed in the Mitchell and Carson study. Additionally, Freeman's estimates incorporate the impact of water quality on ecological conditions such as the biological productivity of aquatic environments and on important dimensions of human health, such as the impact of water quality on the risk of disease. These aspects of Freeman's report help to address the unknown ecological value of water quality that makes important instrumental contributions to individual well-being. Because people may lack information and knowledge about the relationship be-

114. H. T. Heintz, A. Hershaft, and G. C. Horak, *National Damages of Air and Water Pollution* (Environmental Protection Agency, 1976).

115. See *Id.* and UNGER, *supra* note 113.

116. Freeman relies on studies by Dennis P. Tihansky, *Economic Damages to Household Items for Water Supply* *Use* (Environmental Protection Agency, 1973) as well as values given in UNGER, *supra* note 113, and HEINTZ, HERSHAFT, AND HORAK, *supra* note 114.

117. Freeman again relied on UNGER, *supra* note 113 and HEINTZ, HERSHAFT, AND HORAK, *supra* note 114, for these estimates.

tween water quality and the biological productivity of marine environments, or about the relationship between water quality and the incidence of waterborne diseases, the Freeman study is helpful in bringing this important information into the analysis of water pollution control.

However, the Freeman study fails to provide a systematic account of the water quality's ideal-regarding instrumental value. This is because the study reduces important information about the ecological and human health value of water quality to a very limited set of individual and social benefits. Although the Freeman study assesses these benefits independent of an explicit expression of individual wants for them, the benefits nonetheless account for a limited range of individual and social ends or purposes to which water quality is treated as instrumental. Specifically, water quality's ecological value is relevant to more than the commercial fishing industry, and the impact of water quality on people's lives includes more than the benefits of disease reduction and the various cost-savings to municipal water suppliers, households, and industry.

Like the Mitchell and Carson report, the Freeman study also is limited on distributional grounds, for it does not provide information on how the effluent emissions guidelines will distribute the benefits and burdens they create. For consumers that entirely avoid fish because it costs more than they can afford to spend, a drop in the price of fish might be especially good. Likewise commercial fisheries may have more to gain from increases in biological productivity than other individual, commercial, and public interests impacted by changes in aquatic ecosystems. More generally, water quality has ecological impacts that span over long distances to sometimes shape the lives of people in distant places, and these people may not have had anything to do with the waste that pollutes water. As Marla Cone recounts "biotransport" of pollutants is slowly poisoning people living in the Artic because fish pick up PCBs in polluted water and transport those chemicals when they migrate home to Alaskan lakes. When they spawn and die, those chemicals are passed to other fish that eat their carcasses, all the way up to large predators that make up the diet of Artic people.[118] This has important human health consequences. For example, regular consumption of PCB-contaminated fish has been shown to cause lower IQs and reduced memory skills, as well as immune system repression, among other dangerous health effects.[119]

118. MARLA CONE, SILENT SNOW: THE SLOW POISONING OF THE ARCTIC 167 (2005).

119. See *Id.* at 139, 153–155.

In these ways, the Freeman study, while moving EPA's benefits analysis toward a more ideal-regarding account of environmental value, still fails to account for water quality's full ecological value to human well-being, and for how changes in water quality will impact differently situated people. The ecological value of water quality is instrumental to more than the commercial and withdrawal uses the Freeman study analyses. Additionally, the benefits of water quality differ for people in different places, which create distributional impacts that are quite relevant to basic protection of human life and health.

The third study EPA uses in its benefits assessment of the effluent emissions guidelines of the OCPSF industry makes some progress in providing a more thorough account of human health benefits. The "National Assessment of Predicted Health and Ozone–Related Benefits" study assesses the benefits from the reduction in volatile organic compound (VOC) air emissions resulting from improvements in water quality. Due to the limitations of biological treatment systems, significant health and environmental damages result from the OCPSF industry's release of volatile and semivolatile pollutants into water, which later travel into the air. In conducting the benefits analysis of the effluent emission guidelines for the OCPSF industry, EPA sought to account for how much the guidelines would decrease the amount of VOC emissions transferred from water to air.[120]

The logic of EPA's assessment in this study is straightforward. EPA predicts the OCPSF industry guidelines will reduce VOC emissions from OCPSF dischargers by 84 percent. This substantially reduces the magnitude of VOC emissions contributing to the formation of tropospheric ozone (i.e. smog), which EPA defines as an "environmental" benefit. With regard to "health" benefits, EPA estimates that the resulting decrease in exposure to smog will avert 1.1 excess cases of cancer per year. Finally, EPA also calculates health benefits resulting from a decrease in human exposure to levels of benzene and chlorobenzene that exceed existing health-based thresholds.

This study takes an important step toward accounting for specific ecological and human health benefits of water pollution control policy. Information about the impact of water quality on tropospheric ozone levels (i.e. smog levels), on cancer, and on non-cancer health benefits (i.e. reducing exposure to unhealthy levels of benzene and chlorobenzene) does provide some scientific account of non-economic instrumental benefits of water quality about which people may generally lack information. However, these instrumental benefits are still narrowly focused on human health benefits,

---

120. MORGENSTERN, *supra* note 98, at 113–115.

and even so, on a narrow range of human health benefits. Perhaps most importantly, there may be synergistic effects of exposure resulting from the release of benzene and chlorobenze into an airshed already contaminated with a variety of other regulated and unregulated pollutants. Although existing health-based standards often fail to take these synergistic effects into account, if policy analysis does not provide an account of their real or potential impact on human well-being, then it will fail to provide important information about the benefits of pollution control.

There are also significant distributional implications of a reduction in VOCs emissions that the VOC study does not take into account. For example, a reduction in tropospheric ozone will have important benefits for people who already face long-term exposure to smog, especially those with asthma or other respiratory conditions. African Americans, for instance, often live in areas with severe air pollution. For this reason, the prevalence rate of asthma attacks is 32 percent higher in African Americans than is for Whites. Similarly, African American children are four times more likely to die from asthma than White children and three times more likely to be hospitalized for asthma.[121] Because asthma can also have significant negative affects on work and school attendance, as well as on one's social life and emotional well-being, there may be additional but less severe consequences of a reduction in VOC emissions. Thus, not only does the VOC study fail to account for the full range of benefits resulting from the effluent emissions guidelines, it also fails to account for how those benefits are distributed among different people. In this case, people already facing exposure from excessively high levels of smog might experience important gains from reductions in VOCs that the effluent emissions guidelines require.

Given the limitations in each of the studies EPA uses to draft its benefits analysis of the effluent emissions guidelines for the OCPSF industry, we can now identify how an approach to law and policy evaluation emerging from the Capabilities Paradigm and Ecosystem Health Context Model would help to overcome these limitations.

3) Toward a More Adequate Ideal–Regarding Valuation of Water Quality

The Capabilities Paradigm requires an assessment of the extent to which a law will impact the environmental conditions and resources instrumental to the central human functional capabilities of each person. An evaluation of water quality based on this

121. J. SZE, NOXIOUS NEW YORK: THE RACIAL POLITICS OF URBAN HEALTH AND ENVIRONMENTAL JUSTICE 95 (2007).

paradigm provides information about a policy's contribution to goals of social justice, defined as a threshold level protection for each person's central human functional capabilities. Legal outcomes that protect the capability threshold for some people while damaging the ecological conditions necessary for protecting a threshold level of other people's capabilities are policies that fail to meet standards of justice. Similarly, policies that protect one capability while undermining environmental conditions necessary for a person's other capabilities, also fail to meet standards of justice.

To account for this relationship between water quality and social justice, EPA's analysis of the effluent emissions guidelines will require different information about water quality and different information about people. First, in order to account for the impact of changes in water quality on the central human capabilities, the Capabilities Paradigm requires an analysis of how the effluent guidelines will impact the ecological systems that enable the central human capabilities. Second, in addition to looking at how the proposed policy will impact ecological conditions that are instrumental to capabilities, the analysis will also need to account for how the proposed effluent guidelines will impact the central capabilities, independent of the environmental impact. For example, in complying with more stringent guidelines, polluting industries may be less profitable, and thus wages in certain fields may fall, ultimately reducing some people's capabilities to do things like engage in various forms of social interaction (Nussbaum's seventh capability) or to be able to play and enjoy recreational activities (Nussbaum's ninth capability). Third, evaluation of the effluent guidelines will also require a distributional analysis that identifies whose capabilities the guidelines enhance and whose capabilities the guidelines diminish.

Our focus has been on the first (and to some extent the third) of these three types of analysis that the Capabilities Paradigm requires—the ecological analysis and the distributional analysis. This ecological component and the distributional component of the three part analysis seeks to determine whether a proposed policy will provide a level of protection for ecological systems that supports the broad conception of human well-being that the list of capabilities is intended to promote for each person. Given our context model, EPA's existing analysis must account for the following: how changes in water quality bear on the health of broader ecological systems; how changes in water quality relate to dimensions of human well-being that expand beyond a narrowly defined set of recreational and human health benefits; and how changes in water quality impact a broader range of people.

To begin with the latter, in accounting for the conditions that enable people to live good lives, the ecosystem health context model directs the policy analyst to conceive of water quality as having ecological worth beyond its instrumental value to producers and consumers of fish. In particular, because people are conceived of as engaged in a variety of important activities, besides production and consumption, policy analysis must account for benefits to dimensions of human well-being that are furthered outside of market interactions. The Freeman study that EPA incorporates into its benefits analysis accounts for producer and consumer benefits. We can understand these benefits as relevant to producers and consumers' "life" and "bodily health" capabilities. Specifically, biological productivity promises producers a viable livelihood—one that will create the financial resources necessary for attaining their basic needs for life and bodily health. Likewise, to the extent that the biological productivity resulting from improved water quality produces a decrease in the price of fish, it also benefits the life and bodily health capabilities of consumers (e.g. consumers will be more able to afford fish and this will also free up monetary resource they might need to attain other basic needs). But water quality is also valuable to people who do not fit into these categories of producers and consumers. For example, some people rely on fish as their primary source of protein (such as native Alaskan Indians or poor people living near major wetland areas) precisely because it is available to them for free, as a public good that can be drawn from publicly-owned water resources. These people will experience enormous health gains from less polluted aquatic ecosystems, but not because the price of fish decreases due to changes in biological productivity of fisheries. Specifically, because these people do not purchase fish like ordinary consumers, its value to them will therefore not be reflected in the market price of fish. Likewise, because subsistence fishing is a way of life and survival for some, it is unlikely that the value of these benefits will be reflected in people's willingness-to-pay estimates for recreational fishing opportunities, for the value of a way of life cannot be quantified in terms of willingness-to-pay.

In looking at how changes in water quality bear on the multiple dimensions of human well-being that the central human capabilities characterize, the Ecosystem Health Context Model will also guide analysts to account for how these changes relate to the full list of central human capabilities. In particular, the overall health and stability of aquatic ecosystems plays an important role in fending off significant threats to human capabilities, such as disease and the social instability disease can create. For example, degraded aquatic ecosystems can undergo a loss of plant life that normally filters out pollutants on which certain disease-harboring forms of algae thrive. If diseases that thrive in these algae manage to jump into drinking water resources—like they did during a cholera outbreak that struck India and Bangladesh in 1993—then they can create problems that reverberate through the communities in which people live, undermining people's sense of social stability, and their emotional and affiliative capabilities (among others).[122] Likewise, the loss of plant life in degraded aquatic ecosystems might have important implications for one's sentimental experience with a freshwater resource, such as a river or a stream; that is, it may be a significant component of one's "other species" or "emotions" capability. For these reasons, although improving water quality may benefit the life and bodily health capabilities of people who produce and consume marketed fish, water quality can also be an important part of protecting a broader range of capabilities, and thus bear on the wider variety of people to whom those capabilities are important.

Finally, the ecosystem health context model also requires that policy analysis relate the changes in water quality that produce these impacts on people's capabilities to the broader health and resilience of ecological systems. For this purpose, EPA could use the multimetric Index of Biological Integrity (IBI) to evaluate how changes in water quality impact broader ecological systems. The IBI attempts to account for the impact of human actions on multiple ecological dimensions of complex water-resource systems, such as sedimentation, organic enrichment, toxic chemicals, and flow alteration.[123] More specifically,[124] the IBI can:

1. Tell us whether we are maintaining water bodies, water supply, and flow through the water cycle, along with the vital resources the water cycle supports.

2. Allow us to compare the effects of single acts with the cumulative effects of many activities on water systems.

3. Permit comparisons across time and space, of the effects of different human activities through time at the same site or of landscape conditions in different geographic regions.

4. Allow us to measure and compare the relative impacts of different human land uses, including recreation, farming, logging, and urbanization, and to compare such impacts

122. See P. Epstein, *Emerging Diseases and Ecosystem Instability: New Threats to Public Health*, 85 AMERICAN JOURNAL OF PUBLIC HEALTH 168–172 (2005).

123. See James Karr, *Assessment of Biotic Integrity Using Fish Communities*, 6/6 FISHERIES 21–27 (1986) and James Karr, *Biological Integrity: A Long-Neglected Aspect of Water Resource Management*, 1 ECOLOGICAL APPLICATIONS 66–84 (1991).

124. See James Karr, *Health, Integrity, and Biological Assessment: The Importance of Measuring Whole Things* in ECOLOGICAL INTEGRITY: INTEGRATING ENVIRONMENT, CONSERVATION, AND HEALTH 220 (David Pimentel, Laura Westra, and Reed F. Noss eds. 2000); see also, James Karr and Ellen Chu, *Sustaining Living Rivers*, 422 *HYDROBIOLOGIA* 1–14 (2000).

with those affecting water bodies directly, such as pollution, channelization, or dam building.

To accomplish these tasks, the IBI models human influence on water bodies against biological response conveyed through simple dose-response curves that incorporate a broad range of biological features. In particular, ecologists can track four key features of aquatic systems: species richness, species composition, individual health, and tropic (food web) structure. Further, these features allow ecologists to detect changes in (1) species, including the identity and number of species present in the regional biota; (2) ecological processes such as nutrient dynamics and energy flow through food webs; and (3) the health of individuals, which is likely to influence demographic processes. Thus, some of these changes concern local ecosystems (e.g., changes in the identity and number of species), and some of these changes concern cycles and processes expanding beyond particular ecosystems (e.g. energy flow through food webs and demographic processes of particular species). While such modeling is a relatively new area of research, it has the potential to illuminate important dimensions of ecosystem health.[125]

Using measures such as the IBI to incorporate an understanding of how changes in water quality will impact broader ecological systems can move EPA's benefits analysis a good distance toward a more systematic ecological assessment of the benefits of the OCPSF effluent emission guidelines.[126] In other words, to assess how changes in water quality will impact the health of ecological systems on which humans are dependent, policy analysts can use the IBI to expand common understandings of water quality beyond standards that meet "swimmable," "fishable," or "boatable" conditions.[127] A body of water that is "swimmable" may have a different impact on ecological conditions than a body of water that is "boatable." For example, the swimmable water will be less contaminated by human-created pollutants that can damage particular

---

125. See James Karr, *Ecological Integrity and Ecological Health Are Not the Same* in ENGINEERING WITHIN ECOLOGICAL CONSTRAINTS 104–5 (Peter Schulze ed. 1996).

126. For other purposes, federal agencies (among others) have already adopted the IBI. See OHIO EPA, BIOLOGICAL CRITERIA FOR THE PROTECTION OF AQUATIC LIFE, VOLUMES 1–3 (1988). Also see James Plafkin et al., RAPID BIOASSESSMENT PROTOCALS FOR USE IN STREAMS AND RIVERS: BENTHIC MACROINVERTIBRATES, EPA/440/4–89–001 (1989), and Richard Thorne and Peter Williams, *The Response of Benthic Invertebrates to Pollution in*

Developing Countries: A Multimetric System of Bioassessment, 37 FRESHWATER BIOLOGY 671–86 (1997).

127. When analysts define water quality with respect to "swimmable" or "fishable" conditions, they focus solely on chemical contamination of water. A more comprehensive account of the value of water quality must also consider issues such as ecological risk, the effects of numerous contaminants, and the effects of water resource problems caused by other human influences, such as degradation of physical habitat or alternation of water flow. See Karr (1991) *supra* note 123.

species within an ecosystem. Furthermore, a level of water quality that protects higher levels of an ecosystem's natural diversity and complexity provides the best possible insurance against unavoidable calamities, and keeps the gene pool of species diverse and flexible.[128] This is because each species in an ecosystem makes an important contribution to the structure of that system, creating tightly packed and highly integrated relationships that are more able to respond to stress without collapse.[129]

Conclusion

Taken together, the Capabilities Paradigm and Ecosystem Health Context Model provide a logic and justification for an approach to law, policy design and evaluation that can create and identify policies that support the ecological conditions necessary for protecting a threshold level of the central human capabilities. By treating the water quality as part of a complex ecological system that supports a range of capabilities necessary for living a dignified human life, it is possible to better evaluate policies in terms of their contribution to goals of justice, not just to goals of Kaldor efficiency. By bringing these arguments about the justness of environmental policies into public discussion and debate, they can play an important role in reshaping the policy space in which the current Market Paradigm dominates and in redefining what makes one policy more reasonable than another, one law more affective than another.

This alternative Capabilities Paradigm for law, policy design, and evaluation overcomes problems that challenge the Market Paradigm and the cost-benefit method of analysis through which it is applied. First, by requiring a scientific account of the consequences of policy actions on the ecological systems necessary for maintaining threshold levels of central human functional capabilities, the Capabilities Paradigm and Ecosystem Health Context Model overcomes the informational problem challenging the narrowly want-regarding approach to policy evaluation. In the Capabilities Paradigm, it is not just the subjective wants and preferences of

---

128. See Bryan Norton, *On the Inherent Danger of Undervaluing Species* in THE PRESERVATION OF SPECIES: THE INHERENT VALUE OF BIODIVERSITY 110–137 (1986). Norton argues that each species in an ecosystem has prima facie utilitarian value that does not depend on discovering some economic or industrial use for it. He advances five arguments for why "natural diversity" in ecosystems has utilitarian value, in and of itself.

129. See *Id.* at 118. James Karr and Daniel R. Dudley, *Ecological Perspective on Water Quality Goals* 5/1 ENVIRONMENTAL MANAGEMENT 56 (1981) refer to a similar "integrity objective." An ecosystem with this integrity "can withstand, and recover from, most perturbations imposed by natural environmental processes, as well as many major disruptions induced by man."

individuals that matter, but the real impacts environmental change has on the ecological systems that enable people to do and be different things. Regardless of whether people know about or understand these impacts, and therefore reflect the value of environmental changes in their subjective accounts of a policy's value, this approach to policy analysis requires an account of the impacts.

Second, by requiring that legal and policy analysis assess the consequences of collective action on the full range of central capabilities of each person, the Capabilities Paradigm and Ecosystem Health Context Model addresses the distributional problem that challenges the current aggregative approach to assessing the overall social benefits of a policy. Rather than quantifying and summing up a narrow set of benefits, this alternative approach to law, policy design, and evaluation requires assessing the range of capability impacts a policy has on the range of people it actually impacts. With this information, a policy's distributional implications can be brought to bear on public decisions so that the policy's contribution to social justice, and not just economic efficiency, is part of the criteria for making reasonable political and legal choices.

Conclusion

A LOGIC OF ARGUMENT FOR LAW & POLICY DESIGN

Now that we have organized and explained distinct paradigms, or sets of principles and assumptions, from both the market and two ecosystem approaches to environmental law and policy design, we offer the reader a template for developing the logic of legal arguments that can be used to shape the process of policy design. The dialectic process that is law and policy design is based upon the competition of policy arguments in the shaping of a persuasive policy snapshot or synthesis solution to the law and policy design process. It falls to us, as citizens, scholars, and legal practitioners to create persuasive legal arguments about how humans should approach the use of nature that can effect change in natural resource policy and environmental law.

Although there are many ways to approach the formation of arguments in law and policy design, we will set out a logic that has proven, over the last twenty years, to work in our teaching, for law students, undergraduates and graduate students alike. Anyone can learn this basic model and then, with practice, expand its parameters to fit their needs.

Our logic divides the process of developing legal argument into six component parts with rules for each part. These component parts each have a distinct job within the argument and each plays a role in the argument's overall logic. This helps to produce an integrated argument that is concise and powerful. We recommend that an individual learning this framework begin by trying to write each of the components, thesis first, as proscribed in this conclusion, and then focus on editing their components into an integrated two-page single-spaced result. We also recommend that you begin a new paragraph with each of the six logical components and re-sort the information used in your argument according to its function, until each unit of the argument only contains that information proper to its logical role in the law and policy design argument. As in all things, it is actual practice that makes perfect. We recommend patience and many edits until the way one thinks about law and policy mimics the order and role of the components of this argument framework.

§§

The purpose of legal argument is to present the principle and meta-policy in a short concise and logical way so that it can be persuasive in the policy design process. This means that a specific logical form is necessary to the successful prosecution of an argument. Writing argument is not like writing narrative. In narrative we save the punch-line for the end, while a good argument packs the entire itinerary of the argument up front and uses the rest of the argument to demonstrate the initial thesis. As you will see from the logical form suggested in this conclusion, the dialectic, its core principle and the position taken by the writer are all set out at the beginning of the argument in the question, the point of departure and, most importantly, the thesis. Then, the remainder of the argument is used to demonstrate that thesis through elaboration and the presentation of counterargument and evidence toward the end of a persuasive policy design argument. For policy design argument, we do not wait until the end to find out that the "Butler Did It." We know this proposition from the beginning and use the argument to develop the justification of this premise and convince the reader that no other conclusion is more reasonable.

In argument it is also important not to use emotive words because they turn argument into polemic. Neither is it good to just state opinion, for the purpose of this argument framework is to critically review your opinions in the process of turning them into logical and well-justified arguments. Because critical reason is the key to argument, it is also necessary that in the process of writing an argument you remain open to the possibility that you will find your original thesis wanting and change your position on the issue under scrutiny. Given these rules of thumb, the components of a legal argument can be used to create your own paradigm and defend it by making short, concise, and persuasive arguments about current environment and resource law or the path it ought to take in the future.

Toward this end, legal argument should be comprised of the following six components, and written for presentation in this order. You may want to think and construct the argument by starting with the question, then going to the thesis, and then the point of departure (POD), entailments, and evidence, but always present the argument in the following order:

1) Core Question

The core questions should be 'Single–Barreled,' that is, it should ask only one question and not two or more at the same time, and this question should be either empirical [e.g. 'is,' 'does,' 'has'] or normative [e.g. 'should,' 'ought']. Take care not to ask either/or questions, but always use a question that suggests a dialectic or point of tension or opposition that characterizes the core dialectic of the argument. **For Example:** *Does the Market Paradigm adequately support the transition to "Ecosystem" management within the USFS?*

This is a good question, as it asks for only one answer involving ecosystem management and the Market Paradigm, while it implies the core dialectic between multiple-use management as the conventional approach within the USFS and ecosystem management as the alternative. It is also important to frame the question in terms of a norm or standard by which the argument will be judged. In this question it is the idea of 'adequate' that provides this norm. It could have been 'efficient' or 'effective' or 'fair' or any other normative concept, but the question needs to establish both the dialectic and the standard by which the dialectic will be judged. Once you have decided on the dialectic and standard, and put them into the question, they should remain intact, and in the same language, for the rest of the argument. If you find that the nature of the dialectic or the norm changes as you write, then go back and reedit the question to reflect these changes.

2) Point of Departure From the Reading

After stating the question, next the writer needs to address the background history necessary for the reader to understand the dialectic and the norm involved, and the definition of the terms that have been used in the question and thesis. In the point of departure, one needs to state the current status of the dialectic. A good way to do this is by using a text or existing argument about the law or policy in question as a 'point of departure' from your research. A quote from a case, casebook, statute, or article is ideal for this task.

In addition, one should use this component of the argument to define all of the essential terms in the argument, that is, in the question and thesis. In addition, you will need to define the norm by which you will ultimately judge the dialectic. For this example (in reference to the question given in the previous section), one needs definitions for "Market Paradigm," "USFS", "ecosystem management," "multiple-use management," and the standard "adequate." In addition, you need to define the terms of the Y clauses in the thesis (next section) and so, before you write your point of departure, it is critical that you work out your thesis. In this example, the thesis adds a requirement for one to define "sustainability as optimal efficiency," "intrinsic value," and "old-growth forest." A good place to look for these definitions is in your research or texts that have been used to create the argument itself, but it does not matter here where the definitions come from, so long as the terms are defined here (nowhere else) and so long as one sticks to these definitions throughout the entire argument. It is also critical, for example, to use the same word (i.e. adequate) throughout the argument so that the reader is not confused about what norm is being used to judge the dialectic. Do not use "adequate" in one place and "sufficient" in another place unless you take time, here in the point of departure, to construct a 'bridge' between these two words. For example, "For the purposes of this argument I will assume that adequate and sufficient mean the same thing." This is especially important when using standards like 'efficient' and 'effective,' which have inherently different meanings but which are sometimes used interchangeably. Lastly, it is good to start the point of departure section with the words, "... **Based on existing research, some contend...**"

3) Thesis

The single most important component of an argument, and the one that dictates the parameters of the entire logic of policy design under consideration, is the thesis. With the thesis you establish or take a position on the dialectic set out in the question, that is, you agree with one side of the opposition that appears in the question. In this case you can agree with the Market Paradigm being 'adequate' or 'inadequate' for a transition to ecosystem management.

The thesis is made up of two sections, the X clause, which states the writer's position on the dialectic, and two or more Y clauses, which state the reasons why the writer thinks that their position on the core dialectic is the most reasonable one. The X clause is easily written by simply taking a side in the dialectic opposition set up in the question. Using the norm or standard within the question, state it in the same language used in the question. Do not get fancy here with new or additional wording. Simply restate the question, beginning with the words **"I will argue that..."** Using our example: **(X)** *I will argue that the Market Paradigm is inadequate to support the transition from "Multiple–Use" to "Ecosystem" management within the USFS.*

Once you have the X clause, then you need to state your reasons for this choice. The writer does not have to go into detail here or explain their choice at this point (that is for the next unit of the argument), but you do have to set out more than one reason for your choice in a short and concise way so the reader can simply see the point of the legal argument. This also protects the writer from having a policy design argument rise or fall on the persuasiveness of a single reason. A rule of thumb to remember here is that while the two Ys need to be independent of one another (i.e. distinct reasons for arguing X), the ***subject*** of the X clause and of the two Y clauses should be the same. If the X is about the inadequacy of the Market Paradigm for the transition to ecosystem management, then both Y clauses should also be about the inadequacy of the Market Paradigm to the transition to ecosystem management. This is better than, for example, making one of the Y clauses about the superiority of the ecosystem approach.

Although you can have any number of Y clauses, in order to learn the framework, we recommend that you start with only two. This will prevent the argument from spiraling out of control before you have a sense of its entire structure. Here it might be helpful to look at your research and see what two reasons for X are backed by the best outside authority. This will help to keep the two Y clauses separate, as distinct evidence usually means distinct Y clauses; it will also help you to write the evidence section, which comes later.

To pick reasons supporting *why* your position on the dialectic and the core standard are more reasonable than the alternative, you need to reflect on the research material you has studied on the issue. What does the law say on the issue that seems, in this case, to make the Market Paradigm inadequate? What other considerations are being neglected? What are two good and authoritatively backed-up reasons for one's position?

Once the two reasons (i.e. Ys) are selected, then each should be introduced by the word **"because"** and set out in the order in which one will consider them within the rest of the argument. Remember, you have two Ys because you do not want your position in the argument to rest on only one stilt, so make sure that the Ys are distinct and singular. Make sure that each is different. That is, make sure that each has a different root (i.e. one is a moral reason [intrinsic value]; one is an economic reason [(sustainability is not holistic)]). Additionally, do not use "and" or "or" to put lists of things into a single Y clause (e.g. don't say *'because the Market Paradigm fails to protect, secure, and empower nature'* as each of these 'failures' requires a separate Y clause).

Remember, each Y should have a single and distinct topic. For example: .... **(Y1){Reason #1 why X is more reasonable}** ...*because* the Market Paradigm cannot properly evaluate the intrinsic value of an old growth forest which is critical to ecosystem management and ... **(Y2) {Reason #2 why X is more reasonable}** ... <u>because</u> the Market Paradigm relies on the principle of *sustainability which is not holistic enough to foster ecosystem management.*

Therefore, the thesis should contain three clauses set out like this: *I will argue that the Market Paradigm is inadequate to support the transition from "Multiple–Use" to "Ecosystem" management within the USFS because the Market Paradigm cannot properly evaluate the intrinsic value of old growth forest which is critical to ecosystem management and because the Market Paradigm relies on the principle of sustainability which is not holistic enough to foster ecosystem management.*

4) Logical Entailments

After you have established a dialectical question with an inherent norm, a point of departure defining the terms of the argument, and a thesis stating the position of the writer on the dialectic and the reasons for this position, the argument has reached to the point where two types of elaboration must take place to demonstrate and justify what has been posited.

First, you need to explain the Y clauses to establish them as reasons for X and explain why they are important to the success of the position that the thesis takes on the dialectic. What do the Y clauses have to do with making the chosen side of the dialectic more logical and persuasive than its opposite? Second, one needs to bring in outside authority to support the position. The latter elaboration is the job of the next unit (i.e. the evidence), and the former is the function of the entailments, which we will now discuss.

In order to elaborate on the logic of the Y clauses as reasons for X and demonstrate their persuasiveness, the first thing one must do in the entailments is state a counterargument. The role of the counterargument is twofold: first, it demonstrates that the other side of the dialectic has logic and a viable point (i.e. that the other side is not a straw man nor is it being dismissed by the writer). Second, it provides a counterpoint from which you can demonstrate that your own entailments and evidence have greater value as persuasive argument.

For the purposes of a short argument, the counterargument does not need to be elaborate. One way of doing this is to write out the exact opposite of the thesis which contains the opposite of the X and Y clauses or the alternative side of the dialectic. You should begin the entailments with the words ... **Some may argue.** For our example an adequate counterargument might be: *Some may argue that the Market Paradigm is adequate to the transition from multiple-use to ecosystem management within the USFS because intrinsic value is not as critical to the law as the instrumental value of nature to Man which is adequately measured in multiple use*

*planning and because sustainability means more than optimal use
and is holistic enough to consider the scientific idea of ecosystem,
which is the definition critical to law and policy design.* Yes, this is
a long sentence, but work with the ideas now and edit later.

With the counterargument, or opposite of the thesis drafted, it
is now important, in part two of the entailments, to take each Y
clause, in the order in which they appear in the thesis, and
elaborate on how they make the thesis' X clause more reasonable
than the counter-argument. Here it is important not to quote
outside authority (that is for the next component of the argument)
and not to assume that the reader can make the logical connections
about why your argument is more reasonable than the counterargument. Specifically, the writer must carefully lay out why, in the
case of our example, intrinsic value (Y1) and holism (Y2) matter to
the contention that the Market Paradigm is inadequate.

Specifically, beginning with the words **I contend that**... and
continuing from the counterargument one might state: *I contend
that this is not the case. First (Y1) because ecosystems, like old
growth forests that are unique and contain a specific biodiversity
that pre-dates humanity, live independently of us, and should be
considered to have a functional intrinsic value that the market is
unable to adequately reflect. Specifically, the Market Paradigm is a
foundation for multiple-use management because it values nature
instrumentally or for human use alone. Since it cannot adequately
evaluate intrinsic value, it ignores a very important dimension of
ecosystems and their management. In addition, (Y2) the core principle of the Market Paradigm, sustainability, by all conventional
definitions, is not holistic or capable of considering ecosystems as
whole integrated entities like ecosystem management requires. Instead, it focuses on optimal use which requires the analyst to
consider nature only in terms of its distinct component parts and
their utility. Without adequate holism, one cannot say they are
analyzing an ecosystem. If one does not have a foundational principle or paradigm that supports intrinsic value and holism, then the
management institutions built upon these ideas cannot properly
evaluate ecosystems but only the multiple use of components of the
greater environment, which defeats the purpose of ecosystem management.*

The pertinent question here is "So what?" To answer this, you
need to get the reader to understand, in this case, **how** intrinsic
value and holism are critical to the adequate evaluation of nature
and the transition to ecosystem management and **why** the Market
Paradigm fails on these matters.

5) Evidence

The next section of the argument framework is the evidence.
Once the writer has stated the question, set up the thesis in the

point of departure by defining its terms, set out a counterargument and then elaborated why the Y clauses of the thesis make the X clause of the thesis more reasonable than the counterargument, it is time to demonstrate that there is empirical evidence to back up the point of view taken in the thesis. It is here where scientific data, case law, or quotes from one's research should be used to make the logic of the argument, set out in the entailments, stronger by its substantiation. In the evidence section you can take the data or words of others and show how they support or lend credibility to your position on the dialectic.

Although there may be many pieces of evidence available from your research, it is crucial that you pick the information and data that best support the points being made in your thesis. You need one piece of evidence for each Y clause that demonstrates X. In our example, we need one piece of evidence about 'intrinsic value' that demonstrates why the Market Paradigm is inadequate for the transition to ecosystem management. We also need one piece of evidence about 'sustainability and its lack of holism' that demonstrates why the Market Paradigm is inadequate to the transition to ecosystem management.

For example, to support Y1 as a reason for X we may find a quote from a conservation biologist stating that "old growth forests, like many parts of nature, are resources but also are marked by specific biodiversities and functional characteristics that make them unique ecosystems." Alternatively, you may also find a case where the Court argues that an agency cannot ignore the "non-use values" of a forest or a national park, or find an economist stating that "optional or Kaldor efficiency measures instrumental values only." These pieces of evidence supporting your Y clauses also contribute to the more general point that intrinsic values as well as instrumental values are critical to ecosystem management but not part of the Market Paradigm.

To support Y2 as a reason for X, you may find a statement defining sustainability as "use" or "resources for the future" in which each resource is understood as a distinct utilitarian component of nature rather than something that contributes to a whole ecosystem. Any statement that connects sustainability to instrumental value and use of specific species or media in isolation will allow the writer to imply the lack of a more critical holism and thus to demonstrate X. You may also find scientific data demonstrating that it is the synergistic or systemic relationships that make up an ecosystem and not just its isolated resource components. This implies that holism is critical to proper ecosystem management, something ignored by optimal efficiency within the Market Paradigm.

It is very important that you do not assume that a chosen piece of evidence is self-evidently connected to the X clause. It is the job of the writer to make this connection for the reader and demonstrate how the piece of evidence chosen for each Y, does, in both fact and logic, demonstrate X.

Overall, remember that the evidence unit is where one quotes outside authority to back up or substantiate one's position. In demonstrating your X clause, evidence makes the thesis persuasive. You need one piece of evidence e.g. data, quote, authority etc. for each Y that demonstrates X. It is here where case material, statutes, examples, scientific material, and other forms of verification for your argument come into play.

EXERCISE I: Can you find a quote in this book or elsewhere to demonstrate that intrinsic value is critical for the transition to ecosystem management? Can you find one that shows sustainability fails to have the holistic perspective necessary for a transition to ecosystem management?

6) Conclusion

The final integration of your argument is its conclusion. The conclusion confirms your thesis by restating it. However, now the entailments and evidence have made the core of your synthesis or snapshot answer to the dialectic complete (i.e. fully argued). Begin the conclusion with the word *Therefore* and restate your thesis now that you have presented the argument for it and, in this way, made it more persuasive. There is no need to fully reprise the entire argument, just the thesis will do.

EXERCISE II: Taking the question above and the thesis and entailments as written, can you find two pieces of evidence within this chapter to support X in terms of each Y? Now take all the parts and put them together in a short two-page maximum (single-spaced) argument. Indent a new paragraph for each component part. It should be clear that the restatement of the thesis in the conclusion of your argument is more convincing than its original statement before the entailments and evidence were explained. If it is not, edit the argument until it is.

EXERCISE III: Now take the opposite position on the original question. Write your thesis first. What are two good reasons for supporting the Market Paradigm in the transition to ecosystem management? These are your Y clauses. Identify what terms need to be defined in the pod. What is the counter argument (i.e. the opposite of the thesis)? What are the logical entailments of each Y that demonstrate X? In your own words, explain why the Y clauses are necessary to X; that is, why do the Y clauses make X more reasonable than the counterargument? What evidence is there to complete your argument?

PRACTICE! The only way to write good concise argument is to edit the same argument over and over until every word counts.

POLICY DESIGN ARGUMENT: POINTERS

➤ Argument: General Considerations
  ❖ Non-Emotive Language
  ❖ Not A Narrative, Critical Information Up-Front
  ❖ Let The Reader Conclude – Do Not Use Words Like "Obvious"
  ❖ Key Is Not Writing But Editing
  ❖ Don't Confuse The Reader, Use Common Terms Through-Out
  ❖ Be As Specific And Concise As Possible
  ❖ Each Component In Its Place
  ❖ Don't Use "Unrealistic" As A Reason For X, Unpack Your Ideas

➤ Question: {Purpose: State Dialectic & Norm}
  ❖ Single-Barreled {One Question, Not Two!}
  ❖ Suggest Both Sides Of The Dialectic, Focus On One
  ❖ State The Norm or Standard

➤ POD: {Purpose: Definitions & Background For Thesis}
  ❖ All Definitions Needed For The Thesis Ought To Be Here
  ❖ Try Not To List But Have Flowing Prose
  ❖ Explain & Set Evaluative Term In Context
  ❖ Any Background History (But Just Enough)
  ❖ All Normative/Evaluative Terms: Definitions & Bridges To Other Terms

➤ Thesis: {Purpose: Position On Dialectic And Reasons For The Choice}
  ❖ X Clause = A Position On The Question's Dialectic In The Same Words
  ❖ Y Clause(S) = Why X Is Reasonable "because"
  ❖ Nothing But These, In Order, Un-Separated

➤ Entailments: {Purpose: Analysis Of Counter-Argument And Elaborate Y Clauses}
  ❖ Start With Counter-Argument: The Other Side Of The Same Dialectic
  ❖ Elaborate & Justify Each Y Clause, In Order To Explain And Analyze Your Ys So That
    They Are More Reasonable To The Reader Than The Counter-Argument.

➤ Evidence: {Purpose: Outside Substantiation Or Demonstration Of Thesis}
  ❖ Support X Clause
  ❖ Outside Authority {Quote, Facts, Cases, Statistics, Examples (Make The Hypothetical
    More Plausible With Connection To X)
  ❖ Have A Distinct Piece Of Evidence For Each Y In Terms Of X

➤ Conclusion: {Purpose: Restatement Of Thesis To A Now Persuaded Reader}
  ❖ Re-State Your Thesis
  ❖ Should Match? If Not You Need More Editing!

Lastly, let's consider a completely new subject and set out a two-page argument using the logic, order and form we have just introduced. Later we provide a form for case briefs, using the same environmental issue, which will aid in your study of law and policy design.

(1) Question: Does American Environmental Law effectively protect the population from lead poisoning?

(2) Point of Departure From the Reading: The research contends that lead contamination is a serious problem for children's health largely because of their exposure to lead-based paint. To respond to this threat, in 1971 Congress passed the *Lead–Based Paint Poisoning Act*, which became part of the *Toxic Substances Control Act of 1976* (15 U.S.C.A. §§ 2681 et seq.). This legislation generated regulations written by the Department of Housing and Urban Development (42 C.F.R. § 750.1 et seq.) and a series of court cases that refined the regulations. The central concern of this law is the definition of hazardous exposure to lead paint and the remediation of such risks to children in public housing. Under § 302 of the original statute (now in TSCA—15 U.S.C.A. § 2681), HUD was required to write specific regulations to protect children from the "immediate hazard" of lead paint "as far as practicable" which is the working legal definition of effective protection.

(3) Thesis: (X) I will argue that the law does effectively regulate lead contamination (Y1) because the statute and intent of Congress focuses upon prevention of child exposure, which is the most serious protection problem, and (Y2) because the common law has extended the definition of "immediate hazard" to include not just un-intact paint but also intact paint, which together account for all the critical exposure pathways between lead-paint and children.

(4) Logical Entailments: Some may argue that lead contamination is still a great problem in this country, because children are not the only constituency that requires protection and because the common law is not the proper venue for the reformulation of Congressional intent. I contend, however, that this is not the case. Lead poisoning is most harmful to the developing brains and organs of children, who are the most vulnerable constituency and who are the subject the original statute and regulations, as well as the courts attention. In addition, while HUD originally interpreted its mandate under the definition of "immediate hazard," to include only paint that was not intact but cracking, chipping, and peeling off walls of their apartments and houses, more recent studies have argued that intact lead paint was also dangerous to children and needs to be abated. This revelation caused those living in public housing to seek remediation from HUD, of both intact and un-intact lead paint. In order to include intact paint however, HUD needed to redefine "immediate hazard" under the statute and re-write its administrative regulations which it has now done under court mandate.

(5) Evidence: My argument is that with the addition of common law to clarify the Congressional statute and the administrative regulations written from it, protection from lead contamination is effective within American Environmental Law. The peer-reviewed science on the subject states that more than 75% of lead injuries are from child exposure to lead paint (NSF 1969, 3, 23, 34). These studies were the proper basis upon which the intent of Congress has been built. Specifically, the assumption is that "children are most at risk" (HUD 1970, 56). However, the 1971 *Lead–Based Paint Poisoning Act* only protected children from un-intact lead paint, because Congress was told at the time that this was the biggest problem. Since then the science has improved and the intent of Congress has been further expanded by the courts through common law adjudication, so that exposure to lead paint in both intact and un-intact conditions is considered under the law (Litcraft, 1992, 455). This reinterpretation of the intent of Congress by the courts made the law more effective. Specifically, in two legal cases, those living in public housing were able to persuade the federal courts that HUD's definition of "immediate hazard" erred, as it included only non-intact paint. This denied the wider intent of Congress under the statute to create effective protection from lead contamination under the *Toxic Substances Control Act*. First, in *City–Wide Coalition Against Childhood Lead Paint Poisoning v. Philadelphia Housing Authority* 356 F.Supp. 123 (E.D.Pa. 1973), the tenants were able to convince the court that intact paint was as serious a health risk to children as cracking, chipping and peeling paint. Then, in *Ashton v. Pierce* 716 F.2d 56 (D.C.Cir. 1983), the tenants of another public housing complex were able to obtain a summary judgment from the federal district court (affirmed on appeal) that required HUD to extend its definition of "immediate hazard" under § 302 of the statute to include intact paint, and perform remediation in all of its housing. Now the *Toxic Substances Control Act* (15 U.S.C.A. § 2681) provides for abatement (§ 2681(1)) of both "accessible surfaces" (§ 2681(2)) and "deteriorated surfaces" (§ 2681(3)), making the law adequate to protect children from lead based paint contamination.

(6) **Conclusion:** Therefore, the law does effectively regulate lead contamination because the statute and intent of Congress focuses upon prevention of child exposure, which is the most serious protection problem, and because the common law has extended the definition of "immediate hazard" to include not just un-intact paint but also intact paint, which together account for all the critical exposure pathways between lead paint and children.

In order to study cases, it is important to isolate the essentials of the arguments, majority, concurring and dissent, and understand how these are related to the law under scrutiny and other such cases. There are many ways to do this, but considering a case within the context of law and policy design, we suggest the following outline:

Ashton v. Pierce
716 F.2d. 56 (D.C.Cir. 1983)

The Facts & Policy Design Issue: Assuming Lead to be a serious health problem Congress passed the Lead-Based Paint Poisoning Prevention Act (ACT) in 1971. In 1973 the ACT was strengthened by adding section 302 to protect children from the "immediate hazard" of lead in paint. Section 302 of the ACT required HUD to write regulations based on this statute for public housing which would "as far as practicable" remove lead paint hazard to children. HUD interpreted the statute to be limited to paint which is not intact but cracking, chipping and peeling, and wrote regulations to remove such defective paint. Tenants claim that HUD has misinterpreted the intent of Congress in section 302 of the ACT by not including intact paint under the definition of "immediate hazard."

Question: Is the intent of Congress within section 302 of the ACT to require HUD to write regulations to remove only paint that is cracking, chipping and peeling or ought the definition of "immediate hazard" pertain also to intact paint as the tenants claim?

Decision: District Court granted summary judgment to the tenants who also won the appeal which required HUD to write new regulations requiring intact paint to be covered by section 302 of the ACT.

Majority Reasoning: Immediate hazard ought to include intact paint while (1) Congress, which debated the ACT over two sessions, removed language specific to cracking and peeling paint in the final consideration of section 302 of the ACT and (2) Congress had to have considered other data made public through the decision in *City-Wide Coalition Against Childhood Lead Paint Poisoning v. Philadelphia Housing Authority*, 356 F.Supp. 123 (E.D.Pa.1973) which showed the hazard for children in intact lead paint. (3) Therefore, although "intact paint" is not specifically mentioned, section 302 reveals a shift in Congressional intent from concern for the condition of the paint to the children's exposure which is as hazardous whether paint is intact or defective as long as the child ingests lead.

[This is a minimal case brief. A more extensive model would also look at any concurrences, dissents, and their reasoning.]

Case Chains: Are there other cases that deal with the same question? How are the circumstances the same?... different? Do these cases, taken together proceed logically from one-another or are there inherent contradictions in the separate decisions?

facts?
main legal issues?
arguments?
policy change recommended?

Appendix

LAW, EFFICIENCY & COST–
BENEFIT METHODS

A common assumption of those who analyze law and public policy is that a good standard for public choice is *economic efficiency* or the condition of obtaining the most economic benefit for the least economic and other costs. This idea finds its natural home in the economic ideal of the exchange or consumer market which, as a competitive allocation mechanism for the free exchange of goods between individuals, allows each person to satisfy his or her preferences in such a way as to give that person the greatest personal freedom of choice and utility of outcome.[1] The principle of efficiency is the core principle for market decision-making.

Although we acknowledge that efficiency has utility in certain contexts, as a basis for some types of public decision-making, we contend that:

1. Outside the market context, efficiency can be discussed either as cost-effectiveness analysis, which judges only the most efficient means to policy ends, or as cost-benefit methods, which use efficiency to judge both the means and the ends of policy choice.

2. Although efficiency is a sufficient "economic" primary decision standard to judge the ends of a competitive market, it may require additional 'moral weight' to judge ends outside

---

1. JOHN MARTIN GILLROY & MAURICE WADE, THE MORAL DIMENSIONS OF PUBLIC POLICY CHOICE: BEYOND THE MARKET PARADIGM, 5–6 (1992) for the account of the necessity that cost-benefit methods involve the efficiency of both means and ends of policy, the contribution by Sagoff, pp. 165–194 for a critique of efficiency as providing utility and the contribution from Gillroy, pp.195–216 for a critique of the connection between efficiency and a "thin" sense of autonomy. Also, for a complete argument that efficiency claims to represent both human utility and autonomy, but does not do so, see JOHN MARTIN GILLROY, JUSTICE & NATURE: KANTIAN PHILOSOPHY, ENVIRONMENTAL POLICY & THE LAW (2000).

of markets that affect health, well-being, and environmental or human integrity.

3. The use of cost-benefit methods rather than cost-effectiveness analysis implies that its use not only produces the most efficient outcome but simultaneously satisfies the additional moral requirement of providing for the utility and/or integrity of the individuals involved.

To understand the conventional use of the principle of economic efficiency in law and policy analysis, one should begin with the basic concepts that define efficiency in a market and determine how the demands (for a standard of choice) from the public sector and the market differ, making a principle other than efficiency necessary in environmental decision-making. If the principle that motivates and defines welfare in a market context is efficiency, and efficiency is about preference satisfaction through material goods, then the means to efficient allocation is trade in material goods to satisfy those preferences. The market is the framework of trade and it defines the terms of exchange, considering only the desires or wants of each individual within the context of a free interplay of supply and demand for material goods.[2]

In markets, trade proceeds between individuals until each person is satisfied to the extent that no further trade will make one party better off without making the other one worse off. This efficiency condition, called ***Pareto*** optimal efficiency, is the rational standard by which different possible allocations of goods are judged within markets. It is a non-interpersonal standard in that satisfaction is an individual subjective judgment. It is an outgrowth of the ordinal preferences of *each* person who ranks states of affairs in isolation and in terms of the initial endowment of goods with which each person begins to trade.

One allocation outcome is said to be Pareto superior to another when an exchange can be made so that everyone is indifferent between the status quo and the new outcome ($p^0 \, I \, p^1$), while at least one person [i] strictly prefers the new allocation to the status quo ($p^1 \, P_i \, p^0$). The allocation is said to be Pareto optimal or rational, and therefore efficient, if no further trades can be made without someone being made worse off.

> ***Pareto Superiority:*** For all an indifference relation holds ($p^0 \, I \, p^1$), while for at least one individual a preference for the new state-of-affairs making them better off ($p^1 \, P_i \, p^0$) is established.

2. The market also assumes a set of legal background institutions including courts, dispute settlement structures, and the law of contracts and property, among others.

Pareto Optimality: No allocation p* exists that makes anyone in p¹ better off without making someone else in p¹ worse off.

[p0 = status quo; p1 = new allocation; and p* = a third alternative]

The problem with Pareto optimality is that more than one point of optimality can exist at a time, depending on the initial endowments that the traders had before transactions started. One can assume that distributions of the amount of a good between traders can vary and that each redistribution gives the traders a different status quo point (bundle of goods in certain quantities) from which to begin trade (w_i). Each of these status quo points will find a distinct Pareto-optimal point at which trade will be stopped (w^*). One can be faced, therefore, with a series of Pareto-optimal allocations that assemble along what an economist calls a contract curve or efficiency frontier, a series of points at which no Pareto-superior moves are possible and agreement to stop trade can be made. This Pareto frontier will correspond to the range of possible distributions between the traders of initial endowments, where each original distribution of the total quantity of goods will render a single Pareto-optimal point on the frontier. Pareto efficiency will therefore reflect and maintain any initial asymmetries in the allocation of entitlements as initial endowments.

Cost-benefit analysis, as a technique by which government can design and evaluate law and policy while remaining faithful to market norms, is justified first and foremost as a set of criteria that allows the economic efficiency of the free market to be *mimiced* in centralized decision making. However, cost-benefit analysis concerns a choice problem with a difference. Traditionally, the Paretian efficiency standard has rendered a series of Pareto-optimal points (w^*) on an efficiency frontier, and the social-choice dilemma involves finding a normatively acceptable means of choosing between these points.[3]

Cost-benefit evaluation, however, is an attempt to use economic technique, in place of formal market bargaining or price setting, to locate a Pareto-optimal policy alternative—that is, to find the frontier in the first place. In this case, the individual status quo points are off the frontier at the point of initial endowment for each player (w_i). The job of the policy-maker using cost-benefit technique is to find an alternative allocation for each individual (w^*) that is Pareto-superior to the individual's present position, or at least potentially so.

3. ALLEN M. FELDMAN, WELFARE ECONOMICS AND SOCIAL CHOICE THEORY 140–142 (1980).

In many ways, this is a more interesting and all-encompassing social-choice dilemma because it does not assume that the Paretian standard has already been decisive in presenting and defining the public-choice options to the political decision-maker. It leaves evaluation options open, so that cost-benefit methods can make a case for why the policy it recommends should be considered superior. This situation also shows the comprehensive nature of the cost-benefit test, for it assumes that it is sufficient both to locate the frontier and then either to recommend a specific 'efficient' allocation as the goal of law, policy design, and evaluation, or to deny its value as a collective-choice option. In this way, cost-benefit method makes the case for both efficiency (finding the frontier) and normatively optimal social choice (choosing between points on the frontier).

Within cost-benefit analysis, no single policy alternative will satisfy the demands of Paretian efficiency by making everyone it affects either indifferent to, or better off in, the new proposed allocation. The reality of policy-making is that there will be welfare winners and losers as a result of any collective decision. In addition, most choices will be irreversible, in that once a path is chosen it will be hard or impossible to switch back to an alternative that was passed over. In any case, after a law is made, a large, real and permanent opportunity cost is incurred by the welfare losers that makes the new *status-quo* more attractive to the winners than any other options that have already, for other reasons, been discounted.

Because of the existence of both winners and losers in legal and public policy choice, the definition of efficiency must be altered, for no clear Pareto solution (where no losers exist) is, by the definition of Pareto efficiency, possible. Therefore, the case for finding the efficiency frontier is supplied by a weaker set of requirements than Pareto superiority. The substitution that welfare economists supply is the **Kaldor** criterion, which is an effort to efficiently maximize wealth across a population through choosing the policy alternative that maximizes net economic benefit to those who win over the general costs incurred by those who lose.

The introduction of the Kaldor test as a Paretian substitute contends that, as long as the gains to the winners in a potential policy allocation outweigh (in welfare terms) the losses of those who incur the costs, a hypothetical situation is created where the winners can, through transfer of wealth, compensate the losers while still being better off in the new state-of-affairs. In other words, the maximization of total wealth creates a situation where everyone's welfare could be potentially improved to Paretian standards if the winners transfer some of their excess wealth to those who lost in legal choice. Kaldor efficiency is, in effect, a **potential** Pareto improvement with, consequentially, a much more substantial efficiency frontier than Pareto. However, the operative word here is potential, as the transfer need not be more than hypothetical for the new state-of-affairs to be judged Kaldor efficient and superior to the status-quo.

Pareto & Kaldor Efficiency

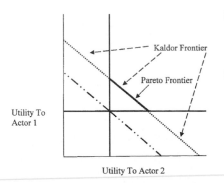

> Pareto Improvements Have A Short Efficiency Frontier As They Require That Both Actors Be As Well Or Better Off In Order For Any Move To Be Efficient.

> Kaldor Or Potential Pareto Improvements Have A Much Longer Efficiency Frontier As They Only Require A State Of Aggregate Wealth Maximization That Would Allow The Winners To Hypothetically Compensate The Losers.

Public decision-makers can use cost-benefit methods to find the Kaldor-efficient frontier that maximizes net social benefit over incurred cost. But since the wealth of the individual is subject only to the personal evaluation of their preferences, policy-makers need to translate them to judge the net social benefit of any policy. "The most important thing to bear in mind about the concept of value is that it is based on what people are willing to pay for something rather than on the happiness they would receive from having it."[4]

The translation of preference value into willingness-to-pay, and then into an aggregated quantity that can be read by a policy-maker, takes place in the following fashion. One begins by assuming that for each proposed policy alternative, each individual has a money valuation that corresponds to the individual's willingness-to-pay for, or to avoid, a certain outcome. This valuation can be represented as v_i. If an individual benefits from a policy alternative (the net benefits being more than incurred cost), then their v_i will be positive and will reflect the monetary amount they are is willing to pay to get that policy choice enacted. If the net effects indicate that, in terms of personal welfare, the policy will cost them more than the benefits it will bestow, then their v_i will reflect the amount they will suffer, and its value will be less than zero.

The task of the person evaluating the public choice is to collect and aggregate these subjective valuations, producing an aggregate **V**, so that the collective net benefit will be reflected in a sum greater than zero [$\Sigma v > 0$]. Correspondingly, the net aggregate cost

4. RICHARD POSNER, THE ECO-NOMICS OF JUSTICE 60 (1983).

is demonstrated in a sum that is less than zero $[\Sigma v < 0]$ which would be enough for rejection of the policy on Kaldor-efficiency grounds.

Therefore, to recommend policy (x) over policy (y), the efficiency-oriented lawyer or policy-maker needs access to tools for two processes. First, she must be concerned with the subjective valuations of all persons affected by the policy. Second, she must strive to calculate the price equivalent of these effects on the welfare of each and then all individuals affected by the choice. All measures of welfare need to be converted into the common currency of money, which attests to their fungibility and instrumental value to the end of an efficient economic allocation. Those commodities that do not have an obvious market price, like the biological integrity of an ecosystem, must be given a shadow price that reflects the opportunity costs of their use or protection and the individual's willingness-to-pay for each marginal unit of that use or protection.

Another distinction inherent in the Market Paradigm is that the production of wealth and the efficient allocation of the resulting benefits are of paramount importance, while all questions concerning the distribution of benefits and costs are much less critical. Economists justify this priority by treating efficiency as a "rational" and objective goal that can be mathematically calculated and judged, independent of any ethical considerations. But while this argument may be adequate for 'real' competitive markets for private goods being judged by the standard of Pareto superiority, it is our contention that it is less satisfying when applied in the context of decision-making about public goods that have more than quantifiable economic value.[5] In the law and public policy context, centralized decision-making by government replaces real individual choice generating supply and demand in the market. Expert definition of willingness-to-pay replaces any real aggregation of preference calculations by individual consumers with abstract individual valuations and the need for an aggregation rule to define societal preference based upon presumption rather than real exchange. Even if the goods under scrutiny were limited to fungible private goods, this would be troublesome. However, with environmental goods holding degrees of instrumental value and perhaps even intrinsic value, and requiring concern for equitable distribution as well as efficient allocation, Kaldor efficiency seems especially lacking. While both Kaldor and Pareto efficiency are "indifferent to questions of equity in distribution,"[6] Pareto, unlike Kaldor, has a stronger sense of allocation that is more sensitive to distributional concerns.

---

5. See, this book chapters 4 and 5 as well as Gillroy, supra note 1 at ch. 5 for arguments about the more than instrumental value of nature.

6. See BARRY in GILLROY & WADE, *supra* note 1 at 336.

The criterion of Pareto superiority as a necessary condition of something's counting as an improvement is, in one sense, strongly concerned with distribution. For it obviously has the implication that no gain, however large, to one person can counterbalance an uncompensated loss, however small, to another. But it is at the same time in another and more important sense sublimely unconcerned with distribution inasfar as it provides no basis on which to assess the status quo against which Pareto superiority is to be measured.[7]

Where Kaldor, like Pareto, is deficient in the second instance, Kaldor also loses the benefit of the stronger sense of uncompensated loss. For now under the Kaldor criterion, any large gain, even one that causes massive maldistribution of wealth, can be recommended as a legitimate legal goal if only the hypothetical possibility of compensation exists. In fact, if Kaldor efficiency depends on winners winning enough to hypothetically compensate the losers, then it is conditional on large maldistributions of wealth. Inherently, reliance upon Kaldor efficiency as a basis for public law has a bias toward producing wealth benefits to winners that are as large as possible. The purpose of Kaldor-driven cost-benefit methods is to substitute for a rational Pareto criterion by maximizing economic wealth allocations to some, no matter their affect on social distribution, who benefits, or who pays the costs.

In law and public policy, therefore, the work of the analyst and decision-maker trying to allocate efficiently is as abstract and general as an economist might say the effort to distribute in a market must be. At this point, a general question arises: Given these drawbacks, why would a market standard of efficiency be recommended as the primary basis on which to judge collective choices?

The answer lies in the argument for the normative primacy of efficient allocation, which eliminates any distinction between the **basic** standard that preferences are being satisfied efficiently and the **higher** standard that the proper ends of policy are being obtained. Essentially, monetary cost and benefit figures (these less than unambiguous efficiency results) are the outcomes of a market process (real or mimicked) that is assumed to be built upon a human "ethical consensus" that important social values are best promoted by markets. The ethical argument for Kaldor has the following steps.

First, it is contended that the prescriptive capability of market efficiency lies primarily in an 'ethical consensus' for markets that supports a society's value system.

7. *Id.* at 338.

Although we can agree that ethical beliefs change over time, . . . at any given time some ethical consensus is to be found in any viable society. And if there is to be a normative economics, from which prescriptive propositions and policies can be derived that are applicable to a particular society, then it cannot be raised on any presuppositions that do not accord with whatever ethical consensus remains in that society.[8]

Second, it is assumed that markets derive support from a more stable and timeless "ethical consensus" that recognizes and promotes basic moral principles that are universal and necessary to the flourishing of all individuals. Cost-benefit method, therefore, holds a position of priority in the evaluation of policy as both a morally sanctioned and formally rational technique.[9]

Within this argument, Kaldor efficiency is all that lawyers and policy-makers must pursue in their decisions to ensure that the basic moral principles of their society are simultaneously promoted. If a decision-maker using Kaldor can find a way onto the efficiency frontier, he or she will also have found a policy that maximizes personal welfare or utility and/or has the ethical ramifications of respecting individuals and their hypothetical choices to seek their own ends through wealth maximization. It is not surprising, then, to see that Kaldor efficiency and its tool, cost-benefit analysis, hold great influence in the contemporary evaluation of law and policy choice. The argument from "ethical consensus" adds power to the initial contention that allocation is a more rigorous process than distribution, while allocation can also be said to respond to an ethical foundation that makes markets best for the protection of both individual and collective well-being, independent of distributive concerns.[10]

The methodology of cost-benefit procedure involves a comprehensive process that attempts to judge both the means and ends of alternative public policies. Unlike cost-effectiveness analysis, which attempts to judge only the most efficient means to policy ends that have been arrived at on the basis of other than efficiency standards, cost-benefit analysis aspires to judge not only the most cost-conscious means to policy ends but also the Kaldor efficiency of the ends themselves.

The ethical consensus for maximizing allocative Kaldor efficiency, the primary test of public choice, is combined with the belief

---

8. E. J. MISHAN, INTRODUCTION TO NORMATIVE ECONOMICS 17 (1981).

9. HERMAN B. LEONARD & RICHARD J. ZECKHAUSER, *Cost–Benefit*

Analysis Applied To Risk: Its Philosophy and Legitimacy, in VALUES AT RISK, 31–48 (Douglas MacLean ed., 1986).

10. POSNER, *supra* note 4 at ch. 3.

that efficiency supports deeper moral ends so that cost-benefit methods can act as a comprehensive approach to policy judgment. What if Kaldor efficiency were competing against other policy principles such as equality[11] or integrity[12] and is not justified in terms of them, as it would have to be were its practitioners aware of its lack of *moral weight*? The power and popularity of cost-benefit procedures lies in its assumed comprehensive empirical and normative character. One's use of it is made imperative by its status as the primary shorthand for the consideration of both the economic and moral welfare of the citizen as consumer.

Without its comprehensive nature and its capacity to judge public ends, cost-benefit methodology is reduced to cost-effectiveness analysis, and the need for independent arguments for the selection and justification of policy or legal ends becomes less critical. Because of its comprehensive nature, cost-benefit methodology requires a stronger normative foundation than its purely economic counterpart (cost-effectiveness analysis) in order to claim the higher ground in the public-choice sphere and set the ends as well as the means of the policy agenda. Those who recommend cost-benefit methods as a basis for policy decision making either believe it carries moral weight from some kind of "ethical consensus" for markets or incorrectly apply it in the public sphere.[13]

11. ARTHUR M. OKUN, EQUALITY AND EFFICIENCY: THE BIG TRADEOFF (1975).

12. GILLROY, *supra* note 1.

13. Some will counter that cost-benefit analysis can be used merely as a simple tool for organizing and accounting for the positive and negative consequences of a law or policy, See CASS R. SUNSTEIN, RISK AND REASON: SAFETY, LAW AND THE ENVIRON-MENT (2002). But, in fact, this is not cost-benefit analysis but some form of cost-effectiveness analysis, as cost-benefit analysis requires a core principle of Kaldor efficiency and this principle, in turn, requires the comprehensive economic evaluation of both ends and means. See GILLROY, *supra* note 7 for a more rigorous evaluation of the role cost-benefit methodology plays in environmental risk.

Index

References are to Pages

355

†